THE ONE YEAR® BOOK OF HOPE DEVOTIONAL

THE ONE YEAR®

BOOK *of* HOPE

DEVOTIONAL

DAILY BIBLICAL COMFORT FOR WHEN LIFE HURTS

NANCY GUTHRIE

TYNDALE
MOMENTUM®

A Tyndale nonfiction imprint

Visit Tyndale online at tyndale.com.

Visit Tyndale Momentum online at tyndalemomentum.com.

Visit Nancy Guthrie's website at nancyguthrie.com.

Tyndale, Tyndale's quill logo, *Tyndale Momentum*, and the Tyndale Momentum logo are registered trademarks of Tyndale House Ministries. Tyndale Momentum is a nonfiction imprint of Tyndale House Publishers, Carol Stream, Illinois.

The One Year Book of Hope Devotional: Daily Biblical Comfort for When Life Hurts

Designed by Sarah Susan Richardson

For information about special discounts for bulk purchases, please contact Tyndale House Publishers at csresponse@tyndale.com, or call 1-855-277-9400.

Library of Congress Cataloging-in-Publication Data

Guthrie, Nancy.
The one year book of hope / Nancy Guthrie
p. cm.
ISBN 978-1-4143-0133-4 (sc)
1. Hope—Prayer-books and devotions—English. 2. Hope—Religious aspects—Christianity. 3. Devotional calendars. I. Title.
BV4638.G88 2005
242′.4—dc22 2005008045

ISBN 979-8-4005-1137-0 HC

Printed in China

31 30 29 28 27 26 25
7 6 5 4 3 2 1

Comfort is the one thing you cannot get by looking for it.
If you look for truth, you may find comfort in the end:
if you look for comfort you will not get either comfort or truth—
only soft soap and wishful thinking to begin with and, in the end, despair.

C. S. LEWIS, MERE CHRISTIANITY

DEDICATION

With profound gratitude, I dedicate this book to three of the people who have faithfully taught me the Scriptures. You planted the seeds that have blossomed into this book.

Dr. James Walters, my Bible professor at John Brown University, my guide and companion in the fellowship of tears—
You sent me on a search for the glory of God, a journey I'm still on, a destination I'm still longing for. You opened my eyes to the adventure of searching the Scriptures, the gain from wrestling with its implications, the joys and sorrows of an authentic life.

Sue Johnson, my Bible Study Fellowship teaching leader, mentor, friend, hero—
From the first day when you asked if anyone needed a miracle, your invitations and questions were always just for me and I could never get enough. The principles you gave are on every page of this book. My desire to be just like you when I grow up never fades.

Dr. Ray Ortlund Jr., my pastor—
You have fed my hungry soul with the truth of God's Word and altered my perspective from duty to delight. What a gift. I wish you had known Hope and Gabe. Someday you will.

TABLE OF CONTENTS

ACKNOWLEDGMENTS

With gratitude to my Saturday morning *One Year Book of Hope* support group, who met with me every month for a year, helping me to shape the concept, reading and giving input as I wrote, talking it through with me, encouraging me when I wanted to give up, praying for me, and believing with me for the manna. Oh, how you helped me! Bonita Benefield, Sue Johnson, Wendy Martin, Jani Ortlund, Melinda Perry, Terri Petway, Angela Robbins, Susan Shafer, and Julie White, you have honored me with your time and friendship and interest in this project, and I am forever grateful. Will you keep on coming over? I'll see you on the patio and we'll laugh together and listen to the birds. I love you.

I'm grateful to Dr. Jim Walters for being willing to grade one more paper for me and for offering keen insights, important corrections, and valued encouragement.

Friends who know I've worked in publishing for many years assume that I understand grammar, punctuation, sentence structure, and all those pesky details required for communicating well, and that I should therefore be of great help to Matt with his homework. My editors at Tyndale—Stephanie Voiland and Lisa Jackson—know better. Thanks for all the valuable input, careful editing, and gentle nudges to do better. And thank you to Jan Long Harris and Doug Knox for coming up with the idea for this book over lunch and asking me to do it. I am privileged to have you and the rest of the Tyndale team in my corner.

My special thanks to David and Matt for putting up with a whole year of constant conversation (and occasional whining) about "the book." Your belief that I could do it, your confidence that God will use it, and your willingness to lose me to it have kept me going. The joy of living this life with you will only be surpassed when we're all together as a family of five one day. Every once in a while I can almost feel it.

INTRODUCTION

My friend, I don't know what may be causing you pain—it might be a broken relationship, a difficult diagnosis, a devastating disappointment, a death. It may stem from a sudden loss that changed everything about your life in an instant, or an ongoing situation that is wearing on you like a steady drip. It may be something that happened long ago but is still leaving its achy fingerprints on your heart, or a steady series of lesser hurts that just don't seem to heal. I want you to know that I would never presume to say that I know how you feel. I don't. Nobody can. But I do know what it is like to hurt. And I know where to find comfort when there are no words for the pain. I know because I've been on that search too, looking for answers to my questions, hope for the future, and companionship for the journey. I can't say that I've found *all* the answers. But I can say that I've found some, and I've chosen to embrace the Source for the answers to all the questions that taunt us in the midst of tears and keep us awake in the night.

Would you join me in pursuing him throughout the coming year in the midst of our pain?

When Hurt Invaded My Life

While you'll find snippets of my story throughout the devotions in this book, I want to share a bit of it with you before we begin our journey together. But honestly, I'm a bit hesitant to do so. I recognize that my pain is not especially unique or noteworthy. I'm well aware that many people have suffered in more significant and ongoing ways than I have. I share my background with you only so you will know that while I may not completely understand your suffering, I've tasted some myself—hopefully enough that you will see me as a worthy companion for the weeks and months ahead as we look for truth to comfort our pain together.

On the day that we had anticipated would be one of our most joyful experiences, hurt invaded my otherwise happy existence. That day in November 1998, my husband, David, and I, along with our son, Matt, welcomed our daughter, Hope, into this world. David saw the obstetrician and nurse exchange knowing glances shortly after Hope was born, but I was too oblivious to notice, too relieved to have had a successful birth, too overjoyed in holding my beautiful daughter that I had wanted for so long.

"She has club feet, but that is easily fixable," the doctor said. "You're going to want to have the pediatrician look her over, but don't worry, it's not Down's or anything like that."

That night our pediatrician came to our room with a list in his hand of all the "little things" wrong with Hope. She had club feet; she was lethargic and unresponsive; she had a large soft spot, extra skin on her neck, and a flat chin. She wouldn't suck and wouldn't hold her temperature. "When we see a number of small problems, they often add up to something bigger," he said.

The next day a pediatric orthopedist put casts on both of Hope's feet, and a geneticist examined her. He entered our room with another doctor, and with a grim look on his face, he shut the door. He explained that he suspected Hope had a rare metabolic disorder called Zellweger Syndrome—something we had never heard of—which meant that she was missing subcellular particles called peroxisomes that do the work of removing long-chain fatty acids from the cells. He explained that without peroxisomes, the long-chain fatty acids build up and become toxic, that there is no treatment and no cure, and that most children with the syndrome live less than six months.

He handed us two pages copied from a medical textbook that detailed in very medical language everything that is wrong in the body of a child with Zellweger Syndrome—including severe brain damage, the inability to see or hear, internal bleeding, and seizures. It described what these children's lives and deaths are like and featured postmortem photos of babies with Zellweger. I couldn't read it for about five days. It was too much reality for me, too overwhelming to take in.

After a week of learning to feed Hope with a tube we inserted down her throat, and after a battery of tests that seemed to reinforce the diagnosis of Zellweger Syndrome, we took Hope home. It wasn't the homecoming I had anticipated. I knew I was bringing Hope home to die. And I was afraid of what it would be like for her—and for me.

Over the six months God gave us with Hope, we focused on keeping her comfortable and on enjoying her to the fullest. The reality was that her first day was her best and she was on a steady decline. She likely could not see or hear, and she developed seizures that were difficult to keep under control. But honestly, I tried not to despair as things got worse every day, because I didn't know how much worse they were going to get and I knew I couldn't afford to fall apart yet. And I didn't want to spend her life grieving her death.

Hope slept in our room throughout her life. One night, David got up in the middle of the night to check on her and she was cold to the touch. "She's gone," he whispered to me. Though we had shed our share of tears during her life, and while I was hopeful that those tears would lighten my load of grief after her death, it didn't seem to work that way. In the months that followed Hope's death, I felt empty and disappointed, lonely and sad.

It seems to me that most losses aren't just one loss, but a series of losses. For a while I grieved Hope's death. Then I grieved her limited life. Then I grieved our loss of potential.

You see, to have a child with Zellweger requires that both parents be carriers of the recessive gene trait for the syndrome. So after we had Hope, David and I knew that we are both carriers and that any child of ours would have a 25 percent chance of having the fatal syndrome. Matt had hit those 75 percent healthy odds, but Hope had not. So we faced a decision: Should we take the chance of having another child? We decided that we simply couldn't risk putting Matt and our family and friends through such a difficult ordeal again. So David had a vasectomy.

Evidently it didn't work.

A year and a half after Hope died, we discovered that I was pregnant. We were shocked, to put it mildly. But we weren't just shocked. We were afraid. We still felt battered by the last storm, and suddenly another one was headed in our direction.

We kept the news mostly to ourselves until we could get the results of prenatal testing. Then the day came when the doctor called with the test results—positive for Zellweger Syndrome. We then knew we would welcome a second child with Zellweger Syndrome into our family, that we would love and lose another child.

It was the same but different, if that makes sense. It was strange to spend nine months carrying a child we knew would have a short and difficult life, strange to figure out how to respond to the well-wishes and comments of people we didn't know, strange to plan for both life and death.

Gabriel was born on July 16, 2001. We thought he would be with us longer than Hope because he seemed a little bit stronger than Hope was. But in fact, he was with us a few days less. And once again, we were back to a family of three, feeling the loss.

In the days and weeks ahead, I'll share more of our experiences with Hope and Gabriel. It is only natural because it is the context in which so much of Scripture has come alive with meaning for me. And while I hope what I share helps you in your own journey, I want you to know that it is *your* pain I have had in the forefront of my mind as I have written these daily devotions. Of course, I can't know the specifics of every person who picks up this book, but in some sense, pain is pain—emotional, physical, or relational. And while my story takes up much of the ink in this book, it is your story that has prompted me to write, your loss that is heavy on my heart. My words here are wasted if your hurt does not find healing as you apply God's Word to your life.

Manna from Heaven

I'll never forget standing in my kitchen with my sister-in-law, Caroline, after Hope's memorial service. "How do you do this?" I asked her, wondering how I would get through that day and keep facing the days to come. Caroline knew what it was like to bury someone she loved. Before my brother came into her life, she had dealt with the devastating loss of her first husband when he was killed in a car accident two weeks after they got married. Her answer to my desperate question was simple: "Manna."

She explained that just as the children of Israel were dependent on God to provide manna to sustain them every day while they wandered in the wilderness, I had to depend on God to give me the manna I needed every day to sustain me as I grieved my loss. After she left, I found a note from her taped to my mirror that read, "Don't forget the manna." I kept it there a very long time. (I'm still grateful for those wise words, Caroline.)

She was right. Manna is what I needed. Every day. I needed the nourishment that comes from the hand of God, the words of truth that come from the mouth of God. In fact, I was desperate for it to soothe my emptiness and give me the strength to keep getting up in the morning. I discovered that nothing else really satisfies or soothes our suffering except the Word of God. Revenge, ritual, and retreat are all short-term solutions that bring no lasting comfort.

And the thing about the manna God provided to the Israelites was that they couldn't store it up. They needed a fresh supply every day—and so do we. Every day we need a fresh touch, a fresh word to nourish us and sustain us. Yesterday's manna, yesterday's insights may inform us, but every day we need something new to keep us moving forward toward healing.

HOW TO USE
THE ONE YEAR BOOK OF HOPE DEVOTIONAL

Processing pain and embracing its lessons are daily endeavors. Every day we need a little more light to illumine our darkness. That's what I want this book to be for you—a daily dose of truth and comfort.

Daily is a good thing. Just as you can't eat enough food in one meal to last all week, you need a spiritual meal each day if you want to walk through each day in a transforming awareness of God. This book is designed to feed your hurting soul a little bit every day and give you something to chew on throughout each day. I've picked fifty-two themes—one for each week of the coming year—that have been especially meaningful to me in my grief and questions. If you choose to use it this way, there are devotions for each day of the week, Monday through Friday, and a guide for reflection, meditation, and prayer for the weekend.

But you may decide you want to sit down with this book once a week or occasionally and read through a week's worth of devotions on a particular theme and then spend time in prayer and reflection about what you've read. That's fine too.

The goal is for you to use this book as a resource over the coming year for insight and healing. If you're like me, if you think you have to keep up with assignments, you are tempted to quit when you get behind rather than feel like a failure. That's why I haven't used days of the week or dates in the book. I don't want you to feel guilty when a day or a week goes by that you don't get to it. I just want to welcome you back when you can open it again and pick up where we left off.

Each day's devotion includes a "Digging Deeper" question that will take you into God's Word for yourself. I think you will find that the treasures hidden there are worth your extra effort and a few minutes of extra study.

At the end of each week, there are some questions for reflection as well as a guide to meditation and prayer. You may want to write out your answers to these questions in a journal or notebook, which will help you clarify your thoughts and determine your response to the truth you've read. The guide to meditation and prayer will help you focus on God's Word when it is hard to concentrate. It will help you pray when it's hard to find focus in prayer. You may have never developed a habit of private meditation and prayer before, and if so, spending the next year using this book as your guide will help you solidify this nourishing and restful practice in your life.

I've ordered the weeks in a way that I think makes sense for someone who is working through loss, but you may choose to go in a different order, following the themes that seem to meet your most urgent need. Feel free to skip around if that is your preference, working your way through all fifty-two weeks.

Just as no one can tell you exactly what path your grief will take you on or give you a timetable for feeling better, no one can determine the pace at which you are able to ingest the truth that will bring healing. But I encourage you to give it a try on a regular basis, even when you "don't feel like it"— perhaps especially when you don't feel like it.

I hope your hunger to hear from God in the midst of your pain will keep you coming back to him every day through the pages of *The One Year Book of Hope*. And while my prayer is that my words may add to your understanding of the Scriptures and provide companionship to you, I know it is only God's Word that satisfies and soothes. His Word is life. My words have nourishing power only as far as they capture and convey the truth of God's Word. I will be truly satisfied if they instill in you a hunger to search out more of God's Word for yourself.

I feel honored to be your companion during this tender time in your life, and I am eager to get started. There is so much I want to share with you in the days ahead that I believe will truly make a difference in your pain. There's hope and comfort to be found. What a privilege to discover it together.

WEEK 1

BROKENHEARTED

Brokenhearted. Crushed in spirit. Does that describe the state of your soul? Are you wondering if you will ever feel good again, ever feel hope again? Are you desperate to find a salve to sooth the searing emotional or physical pain that has invaded your existence?

Your feelings may tell you that God is very far away from you right now. But the reality is that he is drawn to you. If you have invited God into your life, he is especially near to you now because you need him so desperately.

You may feel that no one wants to be around you. Deep down we know that it is not a lot of fun to be with someone who is sad. But God loves brokenhearted people. He doesn't avoid them. He is closer to you now than ever, waiting to talk with you, comfort you, and offer you hope and healing as you face the future.

THIS WEEK'S PASSAGE FOR MEDITATION

The LORD is close to the brokenhearted; he rescues those who are crushed in spirit.
—PSALM 34:18

TELLING YOURSELF THE TRUTH

I WEEP WITH GRIEF; ENCOURAGE ME BY YOUR WORD. KEEP ME FROM LYING TO MYSELF; GIVE ME THE PRIVILEGE OF KNOWING YOUR LAW. I HAVE CHOSEN TO BE FAITHFUL; I HAVE DETERMINED TO LIVE BY YOUR LAWS. —PSALM 119:28-30

When we are hurting, it seems like everyone wants to fix us. And advice is often free-flowing. Well-meaning friends and family tell us what to do and how to feel, only adding to our confusion. And then there's the voice inside our own minds speaking to us too. Oh, the painful thoughts that go through our heads when the hurt is deep! *I will never be able to be happy again. My life is over. I will be alone forever. God must not love me. God must be punishing me. I am such a failure.*

The psalmist must have recognized this voice and realized it is a voice that cannot be trusted. "Keep me from lying to myself," he said. In the midst of personal pain, he was desperate to hear the truth and live by the truth. He knew that emotions lie to us and people mislead us, but God's Word speaks the truth we are desperate for, even as we weep with grief.

So how do we keep from lying to ourselves in the midst of pain? Instead of believing the voice inside us that says, "God must not care about me," we gaze upon the God we see throughout Scripture who lovingly cares for his own. Even when our feelings tell us, "I will never feel good again," we hold tightly to the truth that God "heals the broken-hearted, binding up their wounds" (Psalm 147:3).

Am I talking about denying real feelings by quoting quips and clichés? Not at all. Honestly, I resent it when someone seems to pat me on the head with a Bible verse in a way that seems to devalue my genuine hurt and dismiss my deep questions. I'm talking about confronting our very real fears, feelings, and thoughts with scriptural truth. I'm talking about digging deep in God's Word to figure out who he is and what his purposes are in the world and in our lives. Truth soothes our fears, changes our feelings, and shapes our thoughts. The truth is what we need most when the hurt is the deepest. Would you walk through the Scripture with me over the year ahead in search of truth to soothe your soul?

My Source for what is true, I desperately need the encouragement that I know can only come from your Word. Open my eyes to the truths that can dispel the doubt and discouragement I feel from the lies I have listened to.

DIGGING DEEPER

Read as much of Psalm 119 as you have time for, noting the benefits of studying and knowing God's Word when you're hurting. What does the psalmist ask God for that you also want to ask of God?

YOUR TEARS MATTER TO GOD

YOU KEEP TRACK OF ALL MY SORROWS. YOU HAVE COLLECTED ALL MY TEARS IN YOUR BOTTLE. YOU HAVE RECORDED EACH ONE IN YOUR BOOK. —PSALM 56:8

I remember going up to the cosmetics counter a few weeks after my daughter, Hope, died and asking if the mascara I was considering would run down my face when I cried. The salesperson assured me it wouldn't and then asked with a laugh in her voice, "Are you going to be crying?"

"Yes," I answered. "I am." And I have. I used to rarely cry, but now tears are always close to the surface, just waiting to be released. It is as if there is a broken place inside me where tears are stored. Letting them out has been the only way to release the pressure of the pain.

Along with relief, there is also the uncomfortable loss of control that is a companion to tears, isn't there? Some see tears not only as a loss of control but also as a lack of faith. It is as if the physical manifestation of tears gives evidence of a spiritual deficiency—that if our faith was big enough or deep enough or developed enough, we simply wouldn't be this sad. It is as if we think our grasp of spiritual realities can erase the hurts of being human. But when you've lost something or someone who is valuable to you, when you have been forced to let go of a dream or live within a nightmare—that is something to be sad about. So let yourself be sad.

And know that God does not discount or dismiss your tears. They are precious to him because you are precious to him. In fact, when God reveals glimpses of the culmination of human history—in a future that will fully reveal and be fully worthy of his glory—he includes, as a centerpiece, this promise in Isaiah 25:8: "The Sovereign LORD will wipe away all tears." Picture in your mind right now the Lord of the universe reaching down to gently and lovingly wipe away your tears. He doesn't ignore them or tell you that if you really had faith you wouldn't cry. He wipes them away. And Revelation 21:4 tells us that not only will he wipe away tears, he will remove all of the sorrow that caused them. God's plan for the future is to destroy forever the evil that has brought you so much pain and then to live forever with you in a place he has lovingly prepared where there will be no more tears.

My Tear Collector, sometimes you seem so far away, it's hard for me to grasp that you are sad with me. Give me the faith to see you now beside me and to see a future in which your hand will wipe away my tears forever.

DIGGING DEEPER

Read Psalm 56. Make a list of what David determined to do despite his tears.

GUARD YOUR HEART

DON'T WORRY ABOUT ANYTHING; INSTEAD, PRAY ABOUT EVERYTHING. TELL GOD WHAT YOU NEED, AND THANK HIM FOR ALL HE HAS DONE. IF YOU DO THIS, YOU WILL EXPERIENCE GOD'S PEACE, WHICH IS FAR MORE WONDERFUL THAN THE HUMAN MIND CAN UNDERSTAND. HIS PEACE WILL GUARD YOUR HEARTS AND MINDS AS YOU LIVE IN CHRIST JESUS. —PHILIPPIANS 4:6-7

Broken hearts are very vulnerable; they must be guarded carefully. When your heart has been broken, it can either become more soft and pliable to the work of God, or it can become hardened toward God and the things of God. And it is a strong temptation to harden our hearts toward God when he has disappointed us and when it feels like he has deserted us.

If your heart is broken, are you willing to allow this hurt to serve as a softening agent that makes you more aware of God, more alive to his purposes, more sensitive to his Spirit at work on you and in you? Or will you let your heart become hardened so that you no longer hear his word, accept his rebuke, experience his mercy?

In his letter to the Philippians, Paul explains how to keep our hearts from becoming hardened. "Tell God what you need, and thank him for all he has done. If you do this . . . his peace will guard your hearts and minds as you live in Christ Jesus." To nurture a soft heart, keep telling God what you need, even when you hardly know what to say or what to ask for or if he hears you. Thank him for who he is and what he has done, for all he has given you, and for the ways he is making himself known to you. Gratitude plows up the ground for God's peace to grow. This is the kind of peace in the midst of pain that is foreign and unintelligible to the world, and can only come supernaturally. Peace is a gift of God, but we prepare ourselves to receive this gift as we pray about everything, cultivate gratitude, and refuse to surrender to worry.

You can emerge from your days of sorrow with a heart that has been softened to the Spirit of God—what a beautiful and profitable experience that will be! Or you can allow your heart to be hardened by bitterness and resentment toward God, and rejection of his peace and grace—what a dark place that will take you to . . . a place far away from the loving embrace of God. "They are far away from the life of God because they have shut their minds and hardened their hearts against him" (Ephesians 4:18).

Heart Mender, take this broken heart of mine and make it soft and sensitive to your Spirit. I want to stay close to you and soft toward you.

DIGGING DEEPER

Read Hebrews 3. What led to the Israelites' hearts being hardened? What were the consequences? From verses 12-15, what do you need to do or refrain from doing to avoid hardness of heart?

BITTER BEYOND WORDS

He shot his arrows deep into my heart. The thought of my suffering and hopelessness is bitter beyond words. I will never forget this awful time, as I grieve over my loss. Yet I still dare to hope when I remember this: The unfailing love of the Lord never ends! By his mercies we have been kept from complete destruction. —Lamentations 3:13, 19-22

Sometimes I feel guilty about my grief. Not because I think there is something wrong or unspiritual about recognizing my loss and valuing my loss. I feel guilty because sometimes I think my grief is more about me than about Hope or Gabriel. I feel sad not just when I think about them and their difficult, limited lives, but when the mental snapshots remind me of the pain *I* felt, the fear *I* felt, the disappointment that swallowed *me*.

I remember when it first hit me. The depth of the cry bordering on a scream bubbled inside and then burst out of me. It scared me, and I know it scared David. I think that is when he first wondered if he'd ever get his wife back, or if she was gone forever, lost to sorrow.

I am well aware that so many have suffered in much more significant ways than I have, but there is no real comparison of pain. It all just hurts. And with the author of Lamentations, I would say, "the thought of my suffering is bitter beyond words." And I echo his words: "I will never forget this awful time."

But I would also echo the ray of light that peeks out of his next phrase: "Yet I still dare to hope." The memory of hope is as vivid as the memory of pain. What could have made him dare to hope? What could possibly give *you* the courage and confidence to have hope in the midst of your bitter suffering? Remembering the love of God. Rehearsing his past faithfulness to you. Choosing to think about the sufficiency and eternity of God's love. It may seem daring to make room in your mind for what you know is true about God, and honestly, it is difficult when it feels as if he has shot his arrows deep into your heart. But the truth of God's love transforms our thoughts and our feelings when we choose to remember and choose to believe.

Lord, how the hurt lingers, making it hard to remember that your love is unfailing and eternal. Remind me of your love—my only source of hope for the future. Make the reality of your faithfulness more vivid than my pain.

DIGGING DEEPER

Read Lamentations 3. What phrases can you relate to in verses 1-20? What does the writer choose to do and to believe in verses 21-66 that generates hope?

BUT I AM TRUSTING

I AM DYING FROM GRIEF; MY YEARS ARE SHORTENED BY SADNESS. MISERY HAS DRAINED MY STRENGTH; I AM WASTING AWAY FROM WITHIN. BUT I AM TRUSTING YOU, O LORD, SAYING, "YOU ARE MY GOD!" MY FUTURE IS IN YOUR HANDS. —PSALM 31:10, 14-15

We had known I was pregnant with Gabriel for almost eight weeks and it had been three weeks since the prenatal testing, and we were waiting for the call with the test results. I wrote about it in my journal, the morning of January 26, 2001:

> *I get a sinking feeling in my stomach when I think about knowing one way or the other, but today, I'm just ready to know, ready to know how to feel, how to plan. Mostly, I want to say yes to God in whatever he has for us. If someone had asked me when I was pregnant before if I wanted to experience what we did with Hope, I'm sure I would have said no. And yet it was the most profound experience of blessing we've ever had. She brought us so much joy. I would have been a fool to say no. So I find myself now wanting to say yes to whatever God has for us because I know his plans for me are better than I can plan for myself.*

That day the call came from the geneticist, who delivered the news that the child I was carrying was already suffering the fatal effects of Zellweger Syndrome. David and I stood in the kitchen and went over a list of Scripture verses to put on the letter we were preparing to send out to everyone we knew, looking for the verse that would best express the reality of our fear as well as our resolve. Then we found it: "But I am trusting you, O LORD, saying, 'You are my God!' My future is in your hands."

I would like to tell you that our desire to trust in God erased the fear we had about the future—but it wouldn't be true. What I will tell you is that we *determined* to trust God with the future of our family. And it wasn't a decision we made one day for forever. It is a decision we made again every day (or at least most days) and a decision we continue to make every day. It's the same for you. Will you trust God today even as your life feels shortened by sadness? Will you surrender your future into the loving hands of God?

You are my God, and I want to trust you with the hurts of my past and the pain that may be in my future. Today I choose to trust you and believe you'll give me the grace to trust you tomorrow, too.

DIGGING DEEPER

Read Psalm 40. On what did the psalmist base his choice to trust God? What kind of impact did it have on the people around him? What were his circumstances? What are the benefits of trusting God?

WEEK 1

BROKENHEARTED

REFLECTION

What are some of the untruths you hear from others and from your own mind that you need to confront with the truth?

Have you determined to trust God with your future? How is that evident in your life?

MEDITATION

The LORD is close to the brokenhearted; he rescues those who are crushed in spirit.
—PSALM 34:18

Quiet yourself in the presence of God, and meditate on the comforting promises of this verse.

Express your brokenheartedness and crushed spirit to God, laying it all before him.

Ask God to make the closeness of his presence known to you, and open yourself to his rescue.

PRAYER

Praise God that his hands are big enough and strong enough to hold you and your future, no matter what happens.

Thank God for loving you enough and caring deeply enough to keep track of your sorrows and treasure your tears.

Intercede for those you love, that God would use the hurt in their lives to soften them toward himself and keep their hearts from being hardened.

Confess your tendency to focus only on the bitterness of your suffering and to forget God's unfailing love and faithfulness.

Petition God to replace the lies you have told yourself with an ever-flowing fountain of his truth.

WEEK 2

JESUS, MAN OF SORROWS

I have a hard time accepting dramatic presentations of the story of Jesus. Not because I think they shouldn't be done—they usually expand my understanding of who he is and what he came to do. My problem is with the portrayal of Jesus in these productions. How can any actor capture the complex personality and passion of Jesus in an authentic way? Sometimes they seem too syrupy sweet, sometimes too casual or flippant, sometimes too serious-all-the-time. And when I look at the Gospels, I see so many different emotions and attitudes in the person of Jesus.

I see him teaching with authority, touching with compassion. I see righteous anger, courageous boldness, exhaustion, and determination.

But I suppose what we all want to see are the aspects of Jesus that meet our own unique needs and answer our deepest questions. And what *I* have needed to see is the sorrow of Jesus. Because in seeing his sorrow, I find comfort and companionship. I find guidance for dealing with my own sorrow and acceptance of my tears.

Perhaps the greatest comfort I find in seeing Jesus as a man of sorrows is the affirmation that tears do not reflect a lack of faith; indeed, they are a companion to authentic faith.

THIS WEEK'S PASSAGE FOR MEDITATION

While Jesus was here on earth, he offered prayers and pleadings, with a loud cry and tears, to the one who could deliver him out of death. And God heard his prayers because of his reverence for God. So even though Jesus was God's Son, he learned obedience from the things he suffered. —Hebrews 5:7-8

ACQUAINTED WITH GRIEF

He was despised and rejected—a man of sorrows, acquainted with bitterest grief. We turned our backs on him and looked the other way when he went by. He was despised, and we did not care. —Isaiah 53:3

It was Matt's last day of second grade, which was devoted to a big outdoor carnival. With Hope in the stroller, I was making the rounds, resisting the urge to tell everyone who stopped to greet us that their good-bye to her for the summer would likely be the last time they would see her.

One woman at Fun Day knew what that felt like. Several years before, Audrey had lost a son who lived only nine months due to a heart condition. As we discussed the realities of facing death and the awkwardness of discussing that reality with other people, she shared with me one of the most painful aspects of losing her son. It was when people didn't say anything to her after her son died. She said, "I wanted to tell them, 'How could you add to my pain by ignoring it?' " It was helpful for me to talk to someone who understood my fears and feelings, and helpful to know in advance that there would be those who would not—or at least appear not to—care.

The prophet Isaiah paints a picture of the coming Messiah as "a man of sorrows, acquainted with bitterest grief" (Isaiah 53:3). Maybe Isaiah included this aspect of Jesus' character in his description because he knew that you and I would need the kind of comfort and companionship on our road of sorrow that we can find only with someone who has "been there." Does it help you to know that Jesus can relate to your sorrow? It helps me.

Jesus can also relate to your feelings of loneliness and betrayal when you feel that those around you do not care deeply about the hurt in your life, when they turn their backs on you at the moment of your greatest need. Have you thought that no one really understands your feelings of rejection and pain? Have you felt that no one cares? Jesus understands. Jesus cares.

Man of Sorrows, I see you more clearly as this aspect of your character and experience comes into view. How I need your understanding companionship on this road of grief. Show me how to respond the way you did to those who seem not to care: with forgiveness.

DIGGING DEEPER

Read Isaiah 53, noting the numerous ways Jesus suffered, as well as how he responded to the suffering. Which of his sufferings can you relate to?

WHY DID JESUS WEEP?

When Jesus saw her weeping and saw the other people wailing with her, he was moved with indignation and was deeply troubled. "Where have you put him?" he asked them. They told him, "Lord, come and see." Then Jesus wept.
—John 11:33-35

Have you ever wondered why Jesus cried at the death of Lazarus? After all, he knew he was about to raise him from the dead. He is the one who had said, "Lazarus's sickness will not end in death. No, it is for the glory of God" (John 11:4). Then he is the one who said later, "Lazarus is dead. And for your sake, I am glad I wasn't there, because this will give you another opportunity to believe in me" (11:14-15). So why the tears? What was it that troubled him? In this story, I believe Jesus reveals how he feels about death and about our response to death, and both are important for us to understand.

It troubled Jesus deeply when he saw Mary's despair and the wailing mourners with her. Perhaps he could see in her weeping and hear in their wailing the unbelief that robbed them of being able to grieve with hope and left them with only despair. Perhaps his indignation was triggered by intense disappointment that they did not believe or value his words when he told them, "I am the resurrection and the life. Those who believe in me, even though they die like everyone else, will live again" (11:25). Grief is different for the believer than it is for those who do not know Christ—at least it should be. Actually, death is the great revealer of what we really believe and of how much we value resurrected life after physical death.

But beyond his frustration over their despairing grief, I think Jesus wept because he was personally pained by the hurt that death caused to people he loved. His were tears of compassion for Mary and Martha, and tears of determination, perhaps, to finish the work he came to do, to win a victory, once and for all, over the power of death. It breaks the heart of God that death has so much power to hurt those he loves. Look here and see tears on the face of God, because he feels the hurt and emptiness that death leaves in its wake, and he longs with us for the day when death is destroyed forever.

Brokenhearted Jesus, as I see the tears on your face in this story, I believe you weep with me, too. Help me to grieve with hope, believing that the eternal life you offer to those who are yours is far better than life on this earth.

DIGGING DEEPER

Read John 11:1-44. What statements does Jesus make? What instructions does he give? What questions does he ask?

CRUSHED WITH GRIEF

[JESUS] TOOK PETER AND ZEBEDEE'S TWO SONS, JAMES AND JOHN, AND HE BEGAN TO BE FILLED WITH ANGUISH AND DEEP DISTRESS. HE TOLD THEM, "MY SOUL IS CRUSHED WITH GRIEF TO THE POINT OF DEATH. STAY HERE AND WATCH WITH ME."
—MATTHEW 26:37-38

"My soul is crushed with grief to the point of death." It may sound strange to say this, but I remember feeling relieved when I read this verse. I know what it feels like to be crushed with grief. Flattened out by it. Feeling that it is pressing the life out of me and stealing the air around me. I know what it feels like to wonder if I will ever be out from underneath it.

Whenever I read that Jesus was "crushed with grief," tears come. I feel a sense of kinship with Jesus' pain and a sense of relief that he understands what mine feels like. I can't receive instruction on living with pain from someone who has never hurt. I can't receive encouragement to hold on to hope for the future from someone who has never wrangled with death. But I can listen to and receive from this Jesus who knows what it feels like to be filled with anguish and deep distress.

And from the rest of the story recorded in this passage, I see that he also understands the loneliness of grief that has at times overwhelmed me. Even those closest to him could not stay awake and pray with him in the most agonizing hours of his life.

But it was not only his disciples who abandoned him. As he prepared for the Cross, prepared to drink the cup of the wrath of God, he anticipated the ultimate loneliness and abandonment that was ahead: when God would turn his face away from his Son. This would be a desperate loneliness that would cause him to cry out, "My God, my God, why have you forsaken me?" (Matthew 27:46).

Do you know what it feels like for your soul to be crushed with grief to the point that you wonder if you can survive it? Have you felt forsaken and abandoned by those you hoped would be there in your most difficult hour? If so, Jesus understands. In your anguish and deep distress, find comfort in companionship with him.

Abandoned One, it is such a relief to know that you fully understand from experience the grief that has overcome my mind and emotions. Will you also show me what it looks like to emerge from this place of pain into peace?

DIGGING DEEPER

Examine Jesus' instructions, requests, and repetitions in Matthew 26:36-46. What can you learn about what to do when your soul is crushed with grief?

THE GREATEST TRAGEDY

As they came closer to Jerusalem and Jesus saw the city ahead, he began to cry. "I wish that even today you would find the way of peace. But now it is too late, and peace is hidden from you . . . because you have rejected the opportunity God offered you." —Luke 19:41-42, 44

"Tragedy" seems the only way to describe some of what we see around us, doesn't it? When we read about floods or earthquakes where masses of people die, we can't help but think of it as a tragedy. It's how I felt when recently a friend lost her husband just as he prepared to retire. Their dreams of traveling and growing old together came to an abrupt end. It felt tragic. *The American Heritage Dictionary* defines tragedy as "a dramatic, disastrous event, especially one with moral significance." But I wonder, *What would God label as a tragedy?*

As Jesus entered the city of Jerusalem, a crowd surrounded him shouting out, "Bless the King who comes in the name of the Lord!" (Luke 19:38). You might think he would be happy as they spread out their coats for him and welcomed him. But he began to cry.

Jesus saw beyond that day to the time quickly coming when the shouts of the people would become "Crucify him!" He could see beyond their words and into their hearts. And what he saw was hardness toward God, superficiality in their words of welcome, rejection of God's offer to replace their religiosity and ritual with a relationship that would be soul-satisfying and spirit-saving.

What is it that moves God to tears? It is not just physical death. It is eternal death. He looks over the people he created, and he weeps over their rejection of the opportunity to experience his love and to know him in a life-transforming, death-overcoming way. He weeps because it is not just a tragedy; it is the ultimate definition of tragedy. There is no tragedy in being ushered from this life to the next when that next life is spent in the presence of God. The only real tragedy is a life that ends without that hope. When a person rejects the free gift of eternal life God has offered through a relationship with his Son, *that* is a tragedy. That brings God to tears.

Weeping Father, while I often label losses in my life and in the lives of those around me and those around the world as tragic, help me to see the bigger picture—that the ultimate tragedy is a life that ends without hope in you.

DIGGING DEEPER

What was Jesus' response to two tragedies recorded in Luke 13:1-5?

WRESTLING WITH GOD'S PLAN

While Jesus was here on earth, he offered prayers and pleadings, with a loud cry and tears, to the one who could deliver him out of death. And God heard his prayers because of his reverence for God. So even though Jesus was God's Son, he learned obedience from the things he suffered.
—Hebrews 5:7-8

One of the hardest parts of trusting God with my own experience has been reckoning with the fact that God had the power to make my children healthy, and yet he chose not to. How can I love him and believe he sorrows with me if he had the power to change it but chose not to?

I suppose it was the same faith struggle Rabbi Harold Kushner faced when his son died of premature aging. In his popular book, *When Bad Things Happen to Good People*, which looks at the story of Job, he concludes that the following cannot all be true:

God is all-powerful and causes everything that happens.

God is just and fair, giving everyone what they deserve.

Job is a good person.

Kushner concludes that since it is clear that Job was righteous, God is not all-powerful. He suggests that God hates suffering but is limited in his power to eliminate it.

I understand his confusion, because it is hard to accept that our loving God has the power to eliminate suffering and yet chooses not to. It was Hebrews 5:7-8 that helped me in my wrestling with this. I have clung to these verses in the lowest days of grief. In it I see the fully human, fully God Jesus facing the Cross and crying out to his Father, who has the power to make another way, enact another plan . . . but chooses not to.

And I see his submission to that perfect plan of God, a plan that included suffering and death. It helps me to know that even as he submitted to it, Jesus wrestled with God's plan to redeem the world through his death on the cross. It helps because I, too, have wrestled with God's plan for my life even as I have sought to submit to it.

Have you cried out to God in frustration, with questions about how he could have the power to heal and yet choose *not* to heal the one you love? Have you agonized in an effort to reconcile your understanding of a loving God with One who allowed the accident, the atrocity, the abuse? I have. And we're not alone.

All-powerful God, I believe by faith that your plans for my life are perfect and flow out of your love for me, but parts of this life have caused me such pain! Show me how to submit, teach me obedience, and allow me to see your glory.

DIGGING DEEPER

Read Hebrews 4:14–5:10. What are the good things that result from God's plan? List the benefits you have experienced and will experience from this plan.

WEEK 2

JESUS, MAN OF SORROWS

REFLECTION

Remove distractions from your crowded mind, and ask Jesus to reveal himself to you as a Man of Sorrows.

Enjoy his companionship in the loneliness of your grief.

Experience the comfort of Jesus, a worthy companion in sorrow.

Let him love you, and love him in return.

See him struggle with and submit to God's perfect plan that includes suffering, and seek to follow his example.

MEDITATION

While Jesus was here on earth, he offered prayers and pleadings, with a loud cry and tears, to the one who could deliver him out of death. And God heard his prayers because of his reverence for God. So even though Jesus was God's Son, he learned obedience from the things he suffered. —Hebrews 5:7-8

As you read through these verses, picture Jesus praying and pleading with his Father. See his tears and hear his cries.

Allow yourself to feel the companionship of Jesus in your tears, in your submission to God's plan, and in your obedience to God's instructions.

PRAYER

Praise God for his perfect plan of redemption that included the suffering and death of his Son.

Thank God for his tears of compassion and shared sorrow for those he loves who grieve.

Intercede for those facing the ultimate tragedy over the rejection of God's love and the refusal to repent.

Confess your own struggle to accept God's plan that has caused you pain.

Petition God to fill you with his Spirit so that you can forgive those who have abandoned you in your time of sorrow and suffering.

WEEK 3

THE FATHER HEART OF GOD

The word *father* conjures up a unique set of mental images and emotions for each of us. For some of us it is warm and secure, strong and sensitive. For many others it is cold and unstable, distant, or even abusive. Most of us would have to admit that it is a mixture of these things, because our images of fatherhood are shaped by our imperfect earthly fathers.

As children, we learned early whether or not our daddies were safe places to go and soft places to land when our knees were skinned, our feelings were hurt, or our dreams had died. Their response to us in our pain revealed their heart toward us.

In the pain you face today, are you wondering if your heavenly Father's heart will be tender toward you? Does he care? Will you find love or just a lecture? Acceptance or rejection? Let's look closely at what Scripture reveals to us about the Father heart of God.

THIS WEEK'S PASSAGE FOR MEDITATION

The LORD is like a father to his children, tender and compassionate to those who fear him. For he understands how weak we are; he knows we are only dust. —PSALM 103:13-14

OUR FATHER IN HEAVEN

Your father knows exactly what you need even before you ask him! Pray like this: Our Father in heaven, may your name be honored. May your kingdom come soon. May your will be done here on earth, just as it is in heaven.
—Matthew 6:8-10

Jesus said that your Father knows exactly what you need even before you ask him. In one breath, Jesus, our brother, tells us that the Father already knows what we need, and then he tells us to pray and shows us how to pray. So praying to our heavenly Father must be about more than asking God to meet our needs. Because if he already knows what we need, why ask? Surely he does not want us to go through the motions if prayer is not meaningful.

Notice that when Jesus is modeling for us how to pray, asking God for what we want is not at the top of the list! Praying according to Jesus' model begins with the recognition of our family relationship to God. By calling him Father, we recall that we are his children, with all of the benefits and responsibilities that come with being in his family. Then Jesus continues with three affirmations that emphasize the desire for God's agenda to be our agenda. What is important to him should be important to us—more important than getting what we want. And God's agenda is that every creature and all of creation celebrate and honor who he is and what he has done. Jesus wants us to anticipate and welcome God's Kingdom on the earth. He wants us to long for a day and a world in which God is praised and obeyed, a world where God reigns.

If God's will were to be done here on earth, just as it is in heaven, how would it be done, and who would do it? Psalm 103:21 says that armies of angels serve him and do his will. In heaven, the angels joyfully and quickly obey. If we pray as Jesus taught us, we are offering ourselves as obedient servants in a Kingdom where the will of God is done with great joy and without hesitation, just as it is in heaven.

Why pray? Because placing yourself in God's family and under his authority, welcoming his work and his way, and giving yourself to serve him completely—these are not just meaningless phrases or preambles to our list of requests. When we pray in the way Jesus prescribes, they are at the top of our list! Getting God's priorities into proper perspective changes our own.

My Father, may my life bring honor to your name. May your Kingdom come even as I submit to your authority today. I want to obey quickly and joyfully.

DIGGING DEEPER

What does Matthew 6:1-18 reveal about what your Father knows, what he does, and what he will do?

A FATHER'S JOY

He returned home to his father. And while he was still a long distance away, his father saw him coming. Filled with love and compassion, he ran to his son, embraced him, and kissed him. "This son of mine was dead and has now returned to life. He was lost, but now he is found." So the party began.
—Luke 15:20, 24

There was a time in my life when I longed for the comfort of being close to God, but it seemed as if I had been on my own so long and had tried so many times to find my way back, I wasn't sure how God would receive me. I dreaded the rebuke I knew I deserved. My understanding of repentance was very limited, and my picture of God was very harsh.

Many of the people of Jesus' day had misconceptions of what God was like based on the distortions promoted by harsh religious leaders. So Jesus used parables to draw a picture of God for them. He used the story of a father and his prodigal son to show them—and you and me as well—how God feels about rebellious, mistake-ridden, broken people—people who want to come home.

By asking for his inheritance before his father's death, the son in the story basically expressed his utter disregard for his father, almost as if he said, "I wish you were dead." And yet the father gave him his full inheritance, which likely required that he sell off parts of his farm. And beginning on the day his son walked away, the father began waiting and longing for his return. No resentment for the rebuff. No sense of "good riddance" or indifference to the void his son left behind. Just looking, longing, loving.

Finally, when the son came to the end of his resources and the end of himself, he headed home, practicing his speech for his father, "Father, I have sinned against both heaven and you" (Luke 15:21). But he had no opportunity to give the speech because his father was so eager to forgive. With each gift the father presented to his repentant, returning son, he spoke acceptance, not judgment; restoration, not retribution.

This parable serves as an invitation to you if you have walked away from your Father's loving provision and want to come home. Our Father's heart is happy when he sees one of his own walking toward him. Won't you come home?

Forgiving Father, I've often been afraid of your rebuke because I know I deserve it, and yet you wait to offer me forgiveness and welcome me home. Show me your loving Father's heart so I will run toward your embrace.

DIGGING DEEPER

What do the parables in Luke 15 tell you about God? Note the choices and attitudes of the Prodigal Son, the older son, and the father. Which do you best relate to?

A FATHER GIVES GOOD GIFTS

YOU PARENTS—IF YOUR CHILDREN ASK FOR A LOAF OF BREAD, DO YOU GIVE THEM A STONE INSTEAD? OR IF THEY ASK FOR A FISH, DO YOU GIVE THEM A SNAKE? OF COURSE NOT! IF YOU SINFUL PEOPLE KNOW HOW TO GIVE GOOD GIFTS TO YOUR CHILDREN, HOW MUCH MORE WILL YOUR HEAVENLY FATHER GIVE GOOD GIFTS TO THOSE WHO ASK HIM.
—MATTHEW 7:9-11

Recently there was a prayer service for someone I know who is fighting a vicious cancer. How I would love to see God work a miracle and rid her body of the disease that is slowly robbing her of life! I love her and her family, and because I know firsthand how awful and painful it is to watch someone you love die, I don't want them to have to endure it.

Surely we can ask God for what we want. We can freely tell him that what we want is for those we love to be healed. We want a job. We want our marriages to be restored. We know he's our heavenly Father and desires to give good gifts to those who ask him. The problem is, because we are so limited in our understanding, we don't always know what is good.

I want to give my son, Matt, good things. But that is not always what he asks for. He wants chocolate Cocoa Pebbles, and I give him Shredded Wheat. I know, better than he, what he needs. He wants new basketball shoes and I want him to learn to be content with what he has. I have his long-term best interests in mind. I'm trying to shape his body and his mind and his character, so I don't always give him what he asks for.

And I recognize that as much as I might want God to give me what I ask for, I trust that my heavenly Father knows what is best. Sometimes his "good gifts" don't appear that way to my limited perspective. He gives me broccoli when I want ice cream. Sometimes he uses frustrating circumstances, unwarranted criticism, or disappointing delays to develop in me the good gifts of patience and humility. He calls me to trust him, to know that he is my wise and loving Father, and my ultimate good is his heart's greatest desire.

Would you be willing to stop pounding on heaven's door, to stop begging for God to give you what you believe is best, and to open your hands to receive the good gifts your heavenly Father wants to give to you?

Good Father, I know you are committed to making me holy, more than just happy or healthy. Open my eyes to my greatest need—more of you. Open my heart and hands to receive the good gifts you want to give me.

DIGGING DEEPER

Look for the good gift the Father wants to give in Luke 11:11-13. How does this definition of a good gift change how we should pray to our Father?

HEIRS OF THE FATHER

YOU SHOULD NOT BE LIKE COWERING, FEARFUL SLAVES. YOU SHOULD BEHAVE INSTEAD LIKE GOD'S VERY OWN CHILDREN, ADOPTED INTO HIS FAMILY—CALLING HIM "FATHER, DEAR FATHER." FOR HIS HOLY SPIRIT SPEAKS TO US DEEP IN OUR HEARTS AND TELLS US THAT WE ARE GOD'S CHILDREN. AND SINCE WE ARE HIS CHILDREN, WE WILL SHARE HIS TREASURES—FOR EVERYTHING GOD GIVES TO HIS SON, CHRIST, IS OURS TOO. BUT IF WE ARE TO SHARE HIS GLORY, WE MUST ALSO SHARE HIS SUFFERING. —ROMANS 8:15-17

My brother, Tom, was adopted when I was in the second grade, and he is one of the best things that ever happened to our family. I can't help but think about how much it has meant to have Tom in our family when I read Romans 8. I am reminded of how beautiful it is when a child is lovingly taken in by a family and bonds at a heart level. To think that God has seen our neediness and made us his very own children by adopting us into his family, with all of its rights and privileges! Now we can be at home with God, free from fear and insecurity, filled with tenderness toward our Father and dependent upon him so that it is only natural to call him "Daddy." The Holy Spirit enables us to talk to God this way, as he whispers assurances deep inside us that we are truly his child. One day by God's grace we, along with our brother, Jesus, will inherit everything God has for us.

Yesterday Tom called to tell me I owe him thirty dollars for my share of taking our dad out to eat for Father's Day. He lives near my parents and is always taking them out, helping them with projects, and doing all the other stuff the in-town kid is called on to do, so he likes to tell me and my sister that the eventual inheritance my parents leave is *not* going to be split evenly three ways! He's making his claim for the bigger share because he's done more than his share of parent care! (But you're really just kidding, right Tom?) I must admit that even though I haven't had the hassles or hardship, the inheritance sounds good. I suppose the truth is, I want the inheritance without the hardship.

Paul tells us that part of belonging to God's family is a willingness to share in both glory and suffering. You must be willing to suffer, not just as a victim of circumstances, but as one who chooses to endure persecution and hardship for the sake of the Kingdom. It is a result of obeying Christ in hard ways, ways that result in not just suffering, but sharing in his suffering by our identification with him. It is the painful privilege of being God's child, the hardship that comes with the inheritance.

Brother Jesus, I confess that I want the inheritance without the hardship. I look forward to sharing in your glory, but I'm slow to share in your suffering. Give me the family courage and commitment so I can suffer and reign with you.

DIGGING DEEPER

Compare Romans 8:15-17 with Galatians 4:1-7, looking for common truths.

A LOVING FATHER DISCIPLINES HIS CHILD

If God doesn't discipline you as he does all of his children, it means that you are illegitimate and are not really his children after all. Since we respect our earthly fathers who disciplined us, should we not all the more cheerfully submit to the discipline of our heavenly Father and live forever? —Hebrews 12:8-9

When we hear the word *discipline* we think about work and self-denial and maybe punishment. Many of us have experienced punishment that was delivered not out of love, but out of wrath, so we recoil from the very idea.

But God's discipline flows out of his love for us, not his anger. God is not out to get you. He does not want to hurt you. He does not lose his temper and lash out. God disciplines you as his own beloved child. The truth is, it is an uncaring and abusive parent who does *not* discipline his child.

Your Father is willing for you to hurt a little if it is needed to conform you more fully to his character or to equip you to carry out his calling on your life. And if you want to benefit from his discipline, you must submit to it.

My family loves to recall the time when my sister and I were in the back of the station wagon as toddlers. I don't know what my sister was doing, but my dad had threatened her a couple of times that if she did not stop, he was going to halt the car and give her a spanking. Sure enough, she didn't stop. He pulled the car over and opened the back of the car and grabbed for my sister to pull her out and spank her. But instead of grabbing her, he grabbed me by mistake! I was sound asleep in the back of the car and was awoken by an undeserved spanking!

God never makes those kinds of mistakes. His discipline is never too harsh or inappropriate, even when it doesn't seem right to us. Just as a child might think that going to bed with no supper is not fair or that a grounding would be better than a spanking, we do not always know what is the right discipline for us. But God does. He is the perfect parent who always does what is right with us. He does what is needed to shape our character and correct our course. And while his discipline is rarely pleasant at the time, when we learn from it, it makes us better.

Father, I recognize how often I resist your loving discipline as I seek to satisfy myself and determine my own direction. Thank you for loving me enough to discipline me. Give me the grace to submit to your loving hand.

DIGGING DEEPER

According to Hebrews 12:7-11, what are the benefits of submitting to God's discipline?

WEEK 3

THE FATHER HEART OF GOD

REFLECTION

How have your experiences with your earthly father influenced your perception of the Father heart of God?

How would you like to see your relationship with your Father God deepened and enhanced as you receive his forgiveness, trust his provision, and accept his discipline?

MEDITATION

The LORD is like a father to his children, tender and compassionate to those who fear him. For he understands how weak we are; he knows we are only dust. —PSALM 103:13-14

Meditate on the truth of this verse and the other verses we've looked at this week, and allow these truths to shape and reshape your view of your Father God.

Call upon your Abba for the help you need and the comfort you crave. Imagine what it would be like to crawl onto his lap and open your heart to him. Allow yourself to be soothed by his presence and acceptance.

PRAYER

Praise God for defining for us in his own character what a loving Father is like.

Thank God for giving us good gifts, disciplining us in love, and accepting us when we repent.

Intercede for those prodigals you know who have not come to the end of themselves and have disregarded and rejected the love of their Father.

Confess your slowness in doing God's will and your tendency to ask for your will rather than God's will in your prayers.

Petition God to reveal his heart to you so that you might love him more fully and accept his love more freely.

WEEK 4

HOLY SPIRIT, COMFORTER

Helpless. Powerless. Trapped. Have you ever felt this way? Perhaps it describes your circumstances even now, or at least your perspective about your circumstances. The Holy Spirit offers you the help you desperately need, the power only he can supply, and the freedom to enjoy God fully.

Whatever you've heard or believed about the Holy Spirit in the past, hear this: The Holy Spirit is God loving you up close, drawing near to you, living inside you. He is the gift of the Father whose purpose is to draw attention to the Son as he works in us to make us holy. He brings conviction of sin, but he also brings comfort in distress. He points us to the truth and prays for us when we can't pray. He is our source of power to overcome harmful addictions and to understand his holy Word. He offers freedom from the desires that would destroy us and guidance toward a life that will fulfill us. "When the Holy Spirit has come upon you, you will receive power" (Acts 1:8).

THIS WEEK'S PASSAGE FOR MEDITATION

I can never escape from your spirit!
I can never get away from your presence!
If I go up to heaven, you are there;
if I go down to the place of the dead, you are there.
If I ride the wings of the morning,
if I dwell by the farthest oceans,
even there your hand will guide me,
and your strength will support me. —Psalm 139:7-10

BORN OF THE SPIRIT

Jesus replied, "The truth is, no one can enter the Kingdom of God without being born of water and the Spirit. Humans can reproduce only human life, but the Holy Spirit gives new life from heaven. So don't be surprised at my statement that you must be born again." —John 3:5-7

In the late 1970s, the label "born again" became popular. I still occasionally hear people refer to a certain "type" of Christian as "born again." I'm not exactly sure, but I sense they mean a category of believers who are a little more radical about Jesus than those who simply want to go to church and follow Christ's moral teachings. To them, a "born-again" Christian is different from a "regular" Christian. Without saying it, they reveal their belief that something as radical as being born a second time by the power of the Holy Spirit is not only difficult to understand, it is unnecessary.

But Jesus said that being born again was not just an optional addition or a form of saving faith; it is the *only* form of saving faith. He said that "*no one* can enter the Kingdom of God" without it (John 3:5, emphasis added). Not your pastor. Not the Pope. Not your grandmother. Not your neighbor. Not you.

Before we go any further in this book, I must ask you: Have you been born again? Or are you like the religious person Jesus was speaking to, confident that your religious background is enough or that your sincere search for God is enough or that you've suffered enough? Maybe you are looking for ways to improve yourself so you'll be acceptable to God. But you can't generate new and eternal life through your own efforts. It requires a supernatural washing and rebirth that happens only when you ask the Holy Spirit to cleanse you and give you new life, in full recognition of your inability to generate life or goodness on your own.

When we hear that we must be born again, like Nicodemus we want to point out that it is impossible to become a baby and be born all over again. That would require a miracle. More than that, it would require that we surrender ourselves to a spiritual mystery, and that makes us incredibly uncomfortable. But at the same time, the suggestion that we could start all over again is such a relief. That is what Jesus offers. Being "born again" is more than a label. It is the Holy Spirit at work in you; it is a fresh start on a whole new way of life.

Life Giver, I cannot be religious enough or righteous enough to deserve to enter your Kingdom. I need a miracle of rebirth only you can provide.

DIGGING DEEPER

Read the story of Nicodemus in John 3:1-21. What did Jesus say about believing in him? about judgment? about why people reject him?

YOU'RE MINE

YOU ALSO HAVE HEARD THE TRUTH, THE GOOD NEWS THAT GOD SAVES YOU. AND WHEN YOU BELIEVED IN CHRIST, HE IDENTIFIED YOU AS HIS OWN BY GIVING YOU THE HOLY SPIRIT, WHOM HE PROMISED LONG AGO. THE SPIRIT IS GOD'S GUARANTEE THAT HE WILL GIVE US EVERYTHING HE PROMISED AND THAT HE HAS PURCHASED US TO BE HIS OWN PEOPLE. —EPHESIANS 1:13-14

My husband has given me many nice gifts, but one of the first gifts he gave me was also one of the best. It wasn't expensive or fancy, and I'm still not sure what made him think of it or how he did it. But to me it is precious.

Our marriage was the product of an office romance. I worked in book publishing, and he was just down the hall in print music publishing. One day we were both at the same restaurant having lunch with colleagues when Ken Barker said to David, "You need to meet that Nancy Jinks. She sings." Exactly one year after that day we were married.

And I'll never forget returning from our honeymoon and heading back to the office—together. On my desk was a sign with my new name, Nancy Guthrie, a gift from my new husband. To me, it was his way of saying, "Things have changed. You are mine. I want everyone to identify you with me." It was not only a reminder of who I belong to, but of his promises to me as my husband.

When you accepted God's offer of himself, he gave you a gift to serve as a seal of his promises, to identify you as his. He gave you the Holy Spirit. The Holy Spirit within you reveals not only his ownership but also your security as his child.

When troubles come, it's easy to wonder if something has happened to our secure place in God's family. But if we listen, we will hear God's Spirit within us whisper, "You are mine. I bought you with a price, and you are precious to me. No one and nothing can snatch you from my hand" (see Psalm 116:15; John 10:28; and 1 Corinthians 6:20). Rather than lingering far away, God comes near, even inside us, reminding us that we are his.

Holy Spirit, gift of God, what a beautiful sign and seal you are. You bind me forever to my Savior and Lord; you remind me of his promises, and you identify me as his own. May I never bring sorrow to you by the way I live.

DIGGING DEEPER

Read Ephesians 4:20-32. What are some of the ways of living that bring sorrow to the Holy Spirit and are incompatible with being identified with God?

SPIRIT-FILLED, SPIRIT-CONTROLLED

Let the Holy Spirit fill and control you. Then you will sing psalms and hymns and spiritual songs among yourselves, making music to the Lord in your hearts. And you will always give thanks for everything to God the Father in the name of our Lord Jesus Christ. —Ephesians 5:18-20

I sat in a meeting last week with a man who described himself as "Spirit-filled." I know what he meant. He was revealing his religious stripe. But the truth was, I didn't see the Spirit spilling out of him. Instead, I saw anger and bitterness and pettiness. And as I walked away, I couldn't help but think, *If that is what being Spirit-filled is all about, I'm not interested.* But I also wondered what others have seen spilling out of *me* in my less-than-the-best moments.

What does it mean to be Spirit-filled and Spirit-controlled? The Bible teaches that the Holy Spirit actually comes to live inside us as a gift from God when we become believers. But does the fact that he dwells with and in us mean that we are "Spirit-filled" and "Spirit-controlled"? No, because even within the believer, a battle for control is going on between the flesh and the Spirit. Before you were a believer, you had no power to fight the battle. Now, you have the Holy Spirit. And he will fill you up and control you as much as you allow him to. The truth is, many of us want God to save us, but we don't always want him to change us or control us.

The key question is not "How do I get more of the Holy Spirit?" If you have placed your faith in Christ to save you, you already have the fullness of the Holy Spirit inside of you. The question is, *Are you willing to give him more of you?* Perhaps he is inside you, but you've kept him confined, refusing to give him full room and reign to change your attitudes, alter your perspective, order your steps. Are you willing to move your demanding ego and consuming desires out so that he can become the central force and sweetest desire in your life? Are you willing to see your agenda and appetites diminish so he can accomplish his purposes?

If so, "Spirit-filled" will be more than a label; it will become an ever-increasing reality in your life. And when your life is bumped by difficulty, what will come spilling out will be what fills you—an abundance of the Holy Spirit. You will show the world what it truly means to be Spirit-filled and Spirit-controlled.

Spirit, I really do want you to fill me and control me, but as you move in I feel the squeeze. Help me surrender my plans and my agenda, recognizing that nothing is as satisfying as more of you in my being.

DIGGING DEEPER

Read Galatians 5:16-26. How do the desires the Holy Spirit gives differ from the sinful nature? What flows out when you are controlled by the Spirit?

NO WORDS

The Holy Spirit helps us in our distress. For we don't even know what we should pray for, nor how we should pray. But the Holy Spirit prays for us with groanings that cannot be expressed in words. And the Father who knows all hearts knows what the Spirit is saying, for the Spirit pleads for us believers in harmony with God's own will. —Romans 8:26-27

When the geneticist closed the door behind him after delivering the bitter news of a fatal diagnosis for Hope, we were left alone to feel the deep jolt of pain. Out of our fear and despair, David and I began to cry out to God. I'm not sure all of what we said. Eyes open and looking up, I know we said, "We need you . . . we need courage . . . we need wisdom . . . we trust you." I think we expressed trust more out of a desire to trust than a confession of the reality in our souls. We knew it was our only option.

In the weeks that followed, we found ourselves praying together often as we lay in bed in the dark. We were profoundly aware of our utter dependence upon God, our powerlessness to change our situation, and our desperation to see God work. But we also found, as time wore on, we prayed less often. And we felt guilty that so many people were praying for us so diligently when we were so prayerless—partly because it was difficult to know how to pray.

I want to pray. I want to pray in harmony with God's will. But sometimes I just don't seem to have the will to pray, nor do I know how to pray. What a relief to know that the Holy Spirit helps me in my weakness and confusion. When we are weak-willed and weak-minded, when distress has consumed our energy and emotions, the Holy Spirit helps us.

And his prayers are not passionless or impersonal. He prays for us with deep groanings that reflect his understanding and identification with our need. He prays for us with deep devotion and perfect articulation when we have no words—only tears and questions. When we wonder if heaven hears our cries, the Holy Spirit is pleading on our behalf in a language heaven hears and understands and responds to, because the Holy Spirit's prayers are in complete harmony with God's plans and purposes for us.

My Prayer Warrior, what a joy and comfort it is to know that you are praying for me when I have neither the will nor the words. Pray for me now.

DIGGING DEEPER

Read Ephesians 6:18 and Jude 1:20. How do these verses instruct us to pray? How does your understanding of how the Spirit prays from Romans 8:27 affect your understanding of prayer?

GOD'S DEEP SECRETS

His Spirit searches out everything and shows us even God's deep secrets. No one can know what anyone else is really thinking except that person alone, and no one can know God's thoughts except God's own Spirit. And God has actually given us his Spirit (not the world's spirit) so we can know the wonderful things God has freely given us. But people who aren't Christians can't understand these truths from God's Spirit. —1 Corinthians 2:10-12, 14

Significant suffering leaves us with significant questions. Before the hurt invaded our lives, perhaps we were content for our understanding of God's sovereignty and his way of working in the world to be fuzzy. But now the issues are not theoretical. They're very real, and we want real answers. We want the truth, not just clichés or religious-sounding pat answers. This is when we need the Holy Spirit like no other time, when we're facing an uncertain future and trying to make sense of it all.

This is where the disciples were when Jesus explained that he was leaving them. They still had so many questions, so much they didn't understand about who he was and why he came, and their questions created anxiety. Jesus assured them: "I will ask the Father, and he will give you another Counselor, who will never leave you. He is the Holy Spirit, who leads into all truth. The world at large cannot receive him, because it isn't looking for him and doesn't recognize him. But you do, because he lives with you now and later will be in you" (John 14:16-17).

Questions about the suffering in the world send so many on a search for truth. They study world religions, travel to sacred places, seek out secular saviors. But the truth—God's wisdom and an understanding of the big picture—is not something that can be discovered with our minds. It is something that can be revealed to us only by the Holy Spirit. And the Spirit does not reveal the truth to those who are on a mere intellectual exercise without their hearts or wills engaged. God reveals himself to those who earnestly seek him. As he dwells within us and as he illumines our understanding of his Word, he helps us understand the "wonderful things God has freely given us."

My Guide to truth, how I long to understand the big picture of what God is doing in the world and in my life. Will you share with me the deep secrets of God? Open my heart and mind to the truth that only you can reveal to me.

DIGGING DEEPER

Read Deuteronomy 29:29; Acts 2:22-24; Romans 11:33-34; and 1 Corinthians 2:9. What do these verses tell you about the secrets and plans of God?

WEEK 4

HOLY SPIRIT, COMFORTER

REFLECTION

When have you sensed that the Holy Spirit was praying for you? What does it mean to you that he does?

What activities, appetites, and affections are squeezing out the filling and control of the Holy Spirit in your life? Are you willing to make room for more of the Holy Spirit?

MEDITATION

I can never escape from your spirit!
I can never get away from your presence!
If I go up to heaven, you are there;
if I go down to the place of the dead, you are there.
If I ride the wings of the morning,
if I dwell by the farthest oceans,
even there your hand will guide me,
and your strength will support me. —Psalm 139:7-10

Read through this celebration of the Holy Spirit's abiding presence several times, allowing your spirit to enjoy its rich promises.

PRAYER

Praise God for the Holy Spirit, who intercedes for you when you are unable to pray.

Thank God for the gift of the Holy Spirit, who seals your inheritance and guarantees the fulfillment of God's promises.

Intercede for those who reject the truth that they must be born again to enter the Kingdom of God.

Confess your reliance on other sources for truth and understanding rather than the Spirit of truth.

Petition God to fill you and control you as you release new aspects of your heart and mind to him.

WEEK 5

SUFFERERS

Who wants to suffer? Not me. And in our modern culture with modern medicine and modern conveniences, somehow we're convinced we shouldn't have to. Rather than anticipating that living in this world will include some suffering, we're shocked and shaken when it comes our way. We say, "I don't deserve this!"

This is not how it is in most of the world today, nor has it been this way throughout history. For most of humanity, the question has not been *if* I will suffer, but *when*. Perhaps we need a perspective change about suffering and those who suffer.

First Peter 4:1-2 reads this way in *The Message*: "Since Jesus went through everything you're going through and more, learn to think like him. Think of your sufferings as a weaning from that old sinful habit of always expecting to get your own way. Then you'll be able to live out your days free to pursue what God wants instead of being tyrannized by what you want."

Would you like to live out your days free to pursue what God wants instead of being tyrannized by what you want? If so, you may need to change how you think about your suffering. We need to learn to think like Jesus does about suffering—to begin to see the hurts in our lives and respond to these hurts in a way that sets us free to pursue what God wants for us.

THIS WEEK'S PASSAGE FOR MEDITATION

Since Christ suffered physical pain, you must arm yourselves with the same attitude he had, and be ready to suffer, too. For if you are willing to suffer for Christ, you have decided to stop sinning. And you won't spend the rest of your life chasing after evil desires, but you will be anxious to do the will of God. —1 Peter 4:1-2

JOB, HISTORY'S MOST SIGNIFICANT SUFFERER

Job stood up and tore his robe in grief. Then he shaved his head and fell to the ground before God. —Job 1:20

I studied Job's story two weeks before Hope's birth. I'm sure I had read it before, but somehow that week it came alive to me. This man who lived during the time of Genesis became a real person, and his loss seemed real, as did his response to loss. I could hardly wait to get back together with my Bible study group that week to talk about what struck me in his story.

First, I noted that Job was chosen to suffer because of his great faith. God brought up Job's name in his conversation with Satan, saying that Job would be faithful to God, no matter what happened to him. I marveled that Job must have been so faithful to God leading up to that point for God to have that kind of confidence in him. And I wondered about my own life. Would it be possible to become so consistently faithful to God that he would have that kind of confidence in me? It seemed like a lofty but worthy goal.

But most amazing to me was Job's initial response to the loss that God allowed Satan to bring into his life. He had lost everything—his possessions, his family, his health—and what did he do? In the midst of the deepest kind of agony and pain from loss, he fell on the ground to worship God. It amazed me because I knew my first reaction would probably not be worship.

Is it realistic to think that you and I can worship God, not after we've figured it all out, but as our initial reaction to loss in our lives? Job shows us it is. Worshiping God does not require that we understand or approve of what God has allowed into our lives; it simply requires a heart that desires to trust God and a will that is bent toward obedience to God regardless of our feelings. We worship God because he is worthy, not because we necessarily feel like it. And as we worship in the midst of our pain, we are able to gain perspective on that pain. This is a costly worship—which makes it all the more worthwhile and precious to God.

Almighty God, sometimes I feel like a hypocrite as I sing and say things about you in worship that I am questioning here in my pain. But I worship you today because I know you are worthy, and I believe that as I focus on you rather than on my pain, you will give me a new perspective.

DIGGING DEEPER

Read Job 1:20–2:10, noting all of the ways Job initially responded to the suffering in his life.

GOD HEARS THE CRIES OF HIS PEOPLE

The Israelites still groaned beneath their burden of slavery. They cried out for help, and their pleas for deliverance rose up to God. God heard their cries and remembered his covenant promise to Abraham, Isaac, and Jacob. He looked down on the Israelites and felt deep concern for their welfare. —Exodus 2:23-25

"God, do you hear me? Do you even care?" Sound familiar? Sometimes we can't help but wonder if God hears our groanings and our calls for help. He doesn't seem to move. He doesn't seem moved. So we give up. Our groaning becomes complaining, and instead of looking up to God for deliverance, we look around for narcotic fixes to anesthetize the pain, or look down, focusing only on the despair of our situation.

Surely the Israelites grew weary of groaning and crying out to God for help. They must have wondered if God heard them. And if he did, did he even care? There was no way for them to comprehend that God's plan for deliverance was already in motion when Pharaoh's daughter pulled baby Moses out of the river. They couldn't see the burning bush hundreds of miles away as God called and began to prepare Moses to lead them out of Egypt. They wanted relief *right now*, just as we do.

Though they may have felt their prayers were going nowhere, these verses reveal that God *heard*, he *remembered* his promise, he *looked* at their need, and he *felt deep concern* for them. And his concern moved him to action.

And if you are his child, you can be confident that God hears your cries. Those around you may have stopped listening, or you may be good at hiding your tears from others, but God hears. And when he hears, he remembers his promises to you—to walk with you and guide you and to be a refuge for you in times of trouble. He sees what is happening and not happening in your life, in your family, inside your body, outside of your control, and he cares deeply. He will act in his own timing, which may be far different from yours. So keep crying out to him. He hears. He cares deeply.

My Deliverer, I'm determined to keep crying out to you in faith even when I don't sense that you hear me. By faith I believe that you not only hear me, but that you also care and will fulfill your promises to me in your perfect timing.

DIGGING DEEPER

Read Nehemiah 9:9-31; Matthew 20:29-34; and Mark 6:34. What caused God to respond to his people with compassion? What did he do out of that compassion?

THE GREATEST MAN

I ASSURE YOU, OF ALL WHO HAVE EVER LIVED, NONE IS GREATER THAN JOHN THE BAPTIST. —MATTHEW 11:11

What would it be like to have Jesus say that you are the greatest person ever born? That's how Jesus described John the Baptist, affirming that who he was and the work he had done in preparing people for the coming of the Messiah was significant because of his anointing by the Holy Spirit from the womb.

And yet when Jesus says this, John the Baptist is languishing in prison as a result of his prophetic ministry and bold calls for repentance. As he sat in prison, doubts began to set in. The truth is, Jesus had not delivered what John expected. He anticipated that Jesus would fulfill all the Old Testament prophecies at that time, little realizing that while Jesus had come the first time as the suffering Messiah, he would come again as the conquering Messiah and complete the fulfillment of the prophecies. Does it help you to know that even the person Jesus described as "the greatest man" had to deal with doubt about who Jesus is and what he is doing in the world? It helps me.

At the same time, John the Baptist's story is troubling to me, because I know how his story ends. John was beheaded in prison. You see, I want to think that if God himself says you are a "great" man or woman, surely you will not have to suffer, that he will bless you with a comfortable life. I want to think that if I strive to live a life that pleases God, then he will spare me from the intense losses of life. But the life and death of John the Baptist show us that goodness and godliness don't guarantee that we won't have to suffer.

If Jesus, who loved John the Baptist dearly and honored him above all others, would allow him to suffer in prison and then be beheaded, why do we think that if Jesus loves us, he won't allow us or someone we love to suffer or even die an early and unjustified death? Will you bring your doubts and disappointments to Jesus and ask him to reveal himself to you?

Jesus, I often find myself in a prison of doubt and disappointment because I've believed the lie that if you love me, you will make my life easy and pain-free. Like John, I bring my questions and doubts to you, and I find comfort in knowing that you are God and I can trust you with my life and death.

DIGGING DEEPER

What do you learn about John and his ministry from Luke 1:15-17? John died before Jesus returned to heaven and sent the Holy Spirit to live inside believers. How does this help to explain Matthew 11:11?

A SWORD WILL PIERCE YOUR SOUL

SIMEON BLESSED THEM, AND HE SAID TO MARY, "THIS CHILD WILL BE REJECTED BY MANY IN ISRAEL, AND IT WILL BE THEIR UNDOING. BUT HE WILL BE THE GREATEST JOY TO MANY OTHERS. THUS, THE DEEPEST THOUGHTS OF MANY HEARTS WILL BE REVEALED. AND A SWORD WILL PIERCE YOUR VERY SOUL." —LUKE 2:34-35

My husband, David, vividly remembers hearing a chapel speaker in Bible college say that he had come to the conclusion that God cannot use someone significantly until that person has been hurt deeply. David says he responded with very mixed emotions. While a part of him knew that this was likely the truth, it was a truth he resisted strongly. There was a part of him that couldn't help but say, "Well, then, I'm not sure I want to be used."

In Luke 1, we read Mary's beautiful and hopeful song of praise as it began to sink in that she was going to be the mother of the Messiah. "For he, the Mighty One, is holy, and he has done great things for me," she sang (verse 49). She was full of hope for the future and the joy of being chosen and used by God to bear his Son.

Then, after Jesus was born, she took Jesus to the Temple in Jerusalem. There Simeon explained to Mary that while Jesus would be accepted by many, more would reject him. He would cause their hardness of heart toward God to be exposed. And then perhaps Simeon looked deep into Mary's eyes and said with tears in his own, "A sword will pierce your very soul."

Could he see that day coming when Mary would stand at the foot of the cross and see her son die? Did Mary think of Simeon's words as she watched the soldier plunge his sword into Jesus' side to make sure he was dead?

Perhaps you know what it feels like for a sword to pierce your very soul, to experience deep pain that seems to cut ruthlessly and defy the senses. If so, you are in good company. And perhaps this soul pain is something that will make you uniquely usable to God to accomplish his purpose in the world and in your life. Do you want to be used?

Lord, I've been pierced to my very soul, and I really didn't know I could hurt this deeply. And so at this point, if I have to go through this, please don't let this pain be wasted in my life. Use it. Use me.

DIGGING DEEPER

Read Mark 3:20-21, 31-35; and Acts 1:14. What does this reveal about Jesus' relationship with his earthly family, including his mother, and how their faith developed through hardship?

MY GRACE IS ALL YOU NEED

To keep me from getting puffed up, I was given a thorn in my flesh, a messenger from Satan to torment me and keep me from getting proud. Three different times I begged the Lord to take it away. Each time he said, "My gracious favor is all you need. My power works best in your weakness."
—2 Corinthians 12:7-9

There was a time in my life when I read God's response to Paul in this passage as a dismissive pat on the head. Perhaps because I'd so cheapened the significance of God's grace. Perhaps because I'd heard similar words spoken in a tone that seemed to dismiss the suffering this promise is applied to. Or perhaps I had not believed that God's grace is up to the task of addressing some of the suffering I see around me.

Why does the sentiment, "God is enough" or "Jesus is the answer" ring so hollow to my modern ears? I said it a couple of weeks ago to a woman whose body is being ravaged by ALS (Lou Gehrig's disease) even as she endures the taunts of a cruel husband and the despair of a daughter who has begun cutting herself. I apologized as I said it, knowing it might sound simplistic in the face of such suffering. But deep in my soul I know it is true, and it is not at all simplistic.

Because I choose to believe God's Word and because I have experienced it in my own life, I thoroughly believe that the grace God provides is all you need—it is enough—for whatever you face. It will be delivered to you in the form and quantity and timing your circumstances require. It is enough to enable you to endure rejection and betrayal without becoming bitter. It is enough to generate joy in the midst of great sorrow. It is enough to help you endure the loneliness of your bed and the reminders of loss everywhere you turn. It is enough to enable you to continue believing that God is good and he loves you.

The grace God provides to you is enough for whatever suffering he allows into your life, not just enough to survive but enough to equip you to emerge from your suffering with faith intact and hope for the future. What God said to Paul he also says to you: "My gracious favor is all you need" today and for everything you will face in the days to come (2 Corinthians 12:9).

My Grace Provider, even though I admit I'd rather you just take away this pain in my life, I hear you whisper to me that the grace you will provide for me to endure and emerge from this hurt will be all that I need. I believe.

DIGGING DEEPER

Read 2 Corinthians 12:1-10. What does it mean to you that Paul asked three times for the thorn to be taken away and that the Lord responded the same way each time? How did this word from God transform Paul's perspective?

WEEK 5

SUFFERERS

REFLECTION

What hope, encouragement, or instruction do you find as you look at the lives of some of those in Scripture who suffered?

What has been your response to the suffering in your life so far, and what do you want it to be as you move forward?

MEDITATION

Since Christ suffered physical pain, you must arm yourselves with the same attitude he had, and be ready to suffer, too. For if you are willing to suffer for Christ, you have decided to stop sinning. And you won't spend the rest of your life chasing after evil desires, but you will be anxious to do the will of God. —1 PETER 4:1-2

Read through these verses several times, marking words or phrases that are especially meaningful to you.

Circle each verb and contemplate the action it requires on your part.

Turn these verses into a prayer, telling God what you want to do and what you want from him.

PRAYER

Praise God that he is worthy to be worshiped, no matter how you feel, and choose to worship him now.

Thank God that he hears your cries and sees your pain and that out of his compassion and character he will remember his promises to you.

Intercede for those you know who have been pierced to the very soul, that God would give them relief from the deep hurt they feel.

Confess your resistance to suffering and your desire bordering on demand that God supply you with a comfortable, easy life.

Petition God to give you the grace he has promised in the measure and form needed for your current circumstances.

WEEK 6

WHY?

Suffering is difficult to make sense of, isn't it? And somehow we think that if we can define *why* we are suffering, we will be able to make more sense of it, and perhaps even accept it. So when something bad happens, we want to know why so much pain has invaded our lives.

Part of what we are asking when we ask why is What caused this? Is this my fault? Is God trying to tell me something? Am I being punished?

These were my first thoughts when we received Hope's diagnosis. Quickly I made the assumption: *This is my fault. I didn't pray enough for a healthy baby and now I am going to pay for it.* But is that really how God works? Is the *why* question profitable—or even possible—to answer in regard to the suffering in your life?

To help us lay the groundwork in searching for an answer to the *why* question, we need to look carefully at the causes of suffering.

THIS WEEK'S PASSAGE FOR MEDITATION

As far as I am concerned, God turned into good what you meant for evil. —Genesis 50:20

REAPING AND SOWING

DON'T BE MISLED. REMEMBER THAT YOU CAN'T IGNORE GOD AND GET AWAY WITH IT. YOU WILL ALWAYS REAP WHAT YOU SOW! —GALATIANS 6:7

The other day Matt told me that his youth director has taken up gardening. Evidently, however, he didn't know that he should create certain areas for certain plants and mark what seeds he planted where. So he has no idea what is growing where. But there is no doubt that what grows in his garden will be a direct result of the seeds he has planted.

It works the same way in our lives. We reap what we sow, and often we are surprised and want to blame God for the suffering that grows out of seeds of sin that we plant in our lives. Sometimes when we suffer, we are experiencing the natural consequences of our sinful choices and the sinful choices of others.

How many times has some hurt invaded your life that, if you were honest, you would admit is the fruit of bad choices you have made? God does not always prevent the natural consequences of sinful choices from taking their toll on our lives. The natural consequence of abusing alcohol is often liver disease and the loss of a job. The natural consequence of pride and self-centeredness is frequently broken relationships. But the fact that we may have brought it on ourselves doesn't make it hurt any less.

Unfortunately, sometimes we can even reap what someone else has sown. Sometimes our suffering is the natural consequence of someone else's sin. A parent feeds his perverted passions and causes a child to suffer as a victim of sexual abuse. A driver is drunk and swerves on the road, killing innocent people in the other car. It doesn't seem fair. And it isn't. In fact, I think the unfairness of it adds to the pain. This is a painful aspect of living in this broken world.

As you search for an answer to your *why* questions, consider what has been sown in your life or in the lives of people who have hurt you. Ask God to show you how to sow seeds in your life that will result in joy and peace.

Gracious Father, when I look over my life, I can see that often my hurts have been the natural consequences of my bad choices. Forgive me for blaming you. And help me to forgive those whose sin has brought hurt into my life.

DIGGING DEEPER

Read Romans 6:15-23. In verse 22, what is sown and what is reaped? In verse 23, what is earned and what is given instead? In 2 Corinthians 9:6-15, what is sown and what is reaped?

LIVING IN A BROKEN WORLD

Against its will, everything on earth was subjected to God's curse. All creation anticipates the day when it will join God's children in glorious freedom from death and decay. —Romans 8:20-21

Many people have asked David and me if we believe God "chose" us to have two children with a fatal syndrome, sometimes adding that they believe "God knows whom he can trust with these things." But that has never rung true with me. All I have to do is look around and I realize that human suffering surrounds me—regardless of whether or not those who suffer are people of faith.

While we firmly believe that nothing comes into our lives that does not pass through the sovereign hands of God, we don't believe that God picked us out for this. The fact that we have had two children with this fatal syndrome is the natural result of two parents who have the genetic predisposition for it. We live in a world where sin has taken root and corrupted everything—even our genetic code.

Death, disease, destruction—much of the evil that happens in this world, in your world, in my world—are the results of living in a world that is under a curse. And so some of the suffering that you and I experience is the natural result of living in a fallen, broken world. Faith does not insulate us from this. Romans 5:12 helps us understand: "When Adam sinned, sin entered the entire human race. Adam's sin brought death, so death spread to everyone, for everyone sinned."

This world is broken, and we regularly experience that brokenness in the form of suffering. So we should expect natural disasters, deadly viruses, defective genes—because this world is broken and will continue to be broken until the return of Christ. He will usher in a new era with a new heaven and a new earth that is no longer cursed like the one we are living in now. In your search for a cause for your suffering, could it be simply that the brokenness of this world has touched you personally and painfully?

Creator, I believe that you made this world good and that humanity's choice to sin has corrupted that perfection. Sometimes I hate living in this world of suffering and brokenness. I long for the day when you break the curse and set everything right. Come, Lord Jesus!

DIGGING DEEPER

Read Genesis 3 and Romans 8:18-25. What specific curses are results of Adam and Eve's sin? How does Genesis 3:15 relate to Romans 16:20 and Revelation 12:9? What do you learn about the curse from Romans 8:20-21?

SUFFERING AS SATAN'S TOOL

BE CAREFUL! WATCH OUT FOR ATTACKS FROM THE DEVIL, YOUR GREAT ENEMY. HE PROWLS AROUND LIKE A ROARING LION, LOOKING FOR SOME VICTIM TO DEVOUR. TAKE A FIRM STAND AGAINST HIM, AND BE STRONG IN YOUR FAITH. REMEMBER THAT YOUR CHRISTIAN BROTHERS AND SISTERS ALL OVER THE WORLD ARE GOING THROUGH THE SAME KIND OF SUFFERING YOU ARE. —1 PETER 5:8-9

Did you know Satan has set a goal for you? Satan's goal is to alienate you from God. In fact, according to 1 Peter 5:8, Satan "prowls around like a roaring lion, looking for some victim to devour." And how does he "devour" us? One method Satan employs to destroy us is to bring suffering into our lives.

That is certainly what we see as we read how Satan afflicted Job. Satan asked God for permission to harm Job, and God gave the permission. That's a hard one for us, because it just doesn't fit with our understanding of a loving, protecting God, does it? But it is clear. God gave the permission and set the parameters for Job's suffering. He said, "Okay, you can put him and his faith to the test, but you can only go this far." The first time Satan came to him *asking permission* to harm Job, God told him, "You can bring catastrophe, but you can't harm his body." And the second time Satan came to God asking to harm his body, God said, "Okay, but you can't take his life."

What is it Satan wanted to do? He wanted to go to work on Job's confidence in and commitment to God using the tool of extreme hardship. A hammer can be used to build or to break apart. The difference is in the intent of the person using the tool. Likewise, experiencing suffering can build up your faith and force you to go deeper with God, or it can crush your spirit and squash your soul's longing for God. That is certainly what Satan wants to do with the tool of suffering in your life. He wants to hammer away at your thoughts of the goodness of God and replace them with dark thoughts about God. He wants to chisel away at your confidence in the character of God and cause you to question his authority in your life.

Don't let him do it! Cling to God in your suffering. Refuse to let the devil devour you or destroy your faith.

My great Protector, guard me from the evil one who wants to destroy me by destroying my relationship with you. Help me to trust you and cling to you even when I am tempted to blame you, rather than the devil, for the pain in my life.

DIGGING DEEPER

How do you see both God's sovereignty and Satan's use of suffering in Luke 22:31-32 and 2 Corinthians 12:7?

SUFFERING AS DISCIPLINE

As you endure this divine discipline, remember that God is treating you as his own children. No discipline is enjoyable while it is happening—it is painful! But afterward there will be a quiet harvest of right living for those who are trained in this way. —Hebrews 12:7, 11

God takes no pleasure in the pain of discipline. In fact, he suffers when we suffer, like the parent who says, "This is going to hurt me more than it hurts you." When we truly believe our Father loves us, we can accept the idea that out of that love, sometimes God allows us to suffer so we might be disciplined by it.

It is good for us to learn that sin hurts us, so God might allow us to experience the pain sin causes. It is good for us to learn that disobedience leads to emptiness and regret, so he might allow us to feel the pain of that regret.

The truth is, if God chose not to discipline you, it would mean that he did not love you. He loves you so much that he is not willing to leave you as you are. He wants the pain of his discipline to rub off your rough edges that make you miserable and tone your spiritual muscles so you can carry heavy loads.

The purpose of God's discipline is not to hurt you—the purpose is to help you grow and mature. Learning from God's discipline is no fun at the time, but when you are willing to be trained by it—to be molded and shaped by it—it results in God's richest, most rewarding gift—a peace and joy at your core that comes from knowing everything is right between you and God. This is the kind of inner satisfaction that comes from allowing God's discipline to refine and sharpen you so that you will go around spreading righteousness and peace instead of discord and disobedience.

My perfect Parent, in so many ways I am like a little child always wanting my own way. And I certainly want the easy, pain-free way. But I invite you and trust you to use even hardship to discipline me so that I can know the joy and peace of being right with you.

DIGGING DEEPER

Read Hebrews 12:3-11. According to verses 5-6, what is God's discipline intended to do, and who is it for? What are the two ways we can waste God's discipline? How should we respond instead, according to verses 9 and 11?

SUFFERING REDEEMED

As far as I am concerned, God turned into good what you meant for evil. He brought me to the high position I have today so I could save the lives of many people. —Genesis 50:20

We've seen that suffering can be a natural consequence for our sin or someone else's sin; a result of living in a fallen, broken world; something brought into our lives by Satan; or the hardship of discipline. So where is God in our suffering? *He is redeeming it.* He is taking what is bad and using it for good in your life, if you allow him to. Perhaps this is really the starting place for answering the *why* questions when it comes to the hurts in your life.

It was for Joseph. Sold into slavery by his brothers when he was only seventeen, betrayed, imprisoned, and cut off from his family and their faith, Joseph had every reason to be bitter. But Joseph trusted that God would use every difficulty to make him into the man he needed to be and to put him in the place he needed to be to serve God's unique purpose for his life.

His recognition of God as a redeemer allowed him to overcome the natural and understandable response of hatred and revenge to his brothers' betrayal. Certainly they deserved to be punished for what they had done to him. Joseph did not really excuse or make light of what his brothers had done to him. He recognized that what they did was evil and was meant for evil. But Joseph also saw God's intention to use what was meant to harm him to actually help save the lives of many people. It seems as if Joseph's recognition of God as the One who redeemed all the hurt and pain in his past so settled his question of why it happened that he had no need to make anyone pay and no need for pity.

Do you believe that God intends to use the suffering in your life—no matter what caused it or how awful it is—for good if you allow him to? He can. Invite him to do this in your life, won't you?

My Redeemer, I want to believe that you can use the painful, difficult things in my life for good, no matter what or who has caused them. Would you give me eyes of faith to see that you are making something beautiful out of the brokenness in my life as I invite you to do so?

DIGGING DEEPER

Read Romans 8:28 and rewrite it in your own words. Is this promise universal? If not, who is it intended for? Does the truth that God causes all things to work together for good mean that all things that happen to us are good? What is the difference?

WEEK 6

WHY?

MEDITATION

As far as I am concerned, God turned into good what you meant for evil. —Genesis 50:20

Make a list of some of the suffering you have experienced and continue to experience. Beside each one, tell if you think the cause was (1) natural consequences for your sin or someone else's sin, (2) the result of living in a fallen, broken world, (3) suffering Satan has brought, or (4) discipline through hardship. Then, next to each one, list some of the ways you have seen God redeem that suffering—taking something difficult, painful, or ugly and using it for good in your life or the lives of others. How would you like for him to redeem it?

PRAYER

Praise God for his sovereignty over the universe and his ability to use what is meant for evil in our lives for good.

Thank God for his loving discipline that is never too harsh or inappropriate, but just what we need.

Intercede for those around you who, even now, live every day with pain because of the brokenness of this world that is under a curse.

Confess any sin that results in suffering in your life and the lives of those around you.

Petition God to protect you from the evil one so that he will not be successful in using suffering to drive you away from God.

WEEK 7

LIFE

Many people ask David and me if we were ever pressured to abort when tests revealed that the child I was carrying had Zellweger Syndrome. I know that is common, and we were certainly given that option, but there was no pressure, and for that we were grateful. The medical professionals we were working with had seen for themselves how much we had valued and treasured and been enriched by Hope's limited life, so perhaps that perspective made a difference. Even though Hope and Gabe had a syndrome that is described as "incompatible with life," their lives were no less significant or celebrated. And we just did our best to pack years of living and loving into six short months.

At Gabe's memorial service, David shared a series of lessons that Gabe taught us. One was that the value of a life is not determined by how long a person lives or by how much that person contributes. Every life is valuable because God himself gives life and breath to everything. He is not only the source of life; he is also the source of satisfaction and meaning in life. "In him we live and move and exist" (Acts 17:28).

Second, David shared that Hope and Gabe reminded us that *this life is not all there is*! This life is just a rehearsal for our real life, our forever life in the presence of God. Hope and Gabe will live just as long as David and Matt and I and anyone else who is in Christ—forever. As the song "Glory Baby" by the duo Watermark says, "You'll just have heaven before we do."

THIS WEEK'S PASSAGE FOR MEDITATION

He is the God who made the world and everything in it. Since he is Lord of heaven and earth, he doesn't live in man-made temples, and human hands can't serve his needs—for he has no needs. He himself gives life and breath to everything, and he satisfies every need there is. His purpose in all of this was that the nations should seek after God and perhaps feel their way toward him and find him—though he is not far from any one of us. For in him we live and move and exist. —Acts 17:24-25, 27-28

OH, THAT YOU WOULD CHOOSE LIFE!

TODAY I HAVE GIVEN YOU THE CHOICE BETWEEN LIFE AND DEATH, BETWEEN BLESSINGS AND CURSES. I CALL ON HEAVEN AND EARTH TO WITNESS THE CHOICE YOU MAKE. OH, THAT YOU WOULD CHOOSE LIFE, THAT YOU AND YOUR DESCENDANTS MIGHT LIVE! CHOOSE TO LOVE THE LORD YOUR GOD AND TO OBEY HIM AND COMMIT YOURSELF TO HIM, FOR HE IS YOUR LIFE. —DEUTERONOMY 30:19-20

When she was only twelve, my friend Peggy was walking along the road with her four-year-old sister who was struck by a car and killed instantly. Life as she knew it ended for Peggy that day too. Her mother was so devastated by the loss, Peggy told me, her mother "took to the bed, and she rarely got up again." When her mother died decades later, there was a huge indentation in her mattress left by years of refusing to live in the face of death.

It's not that I am without sympathy. I understand the pull and pleasure of drawing up the covers in an endeavor to sleep away the pain that comes with loss. I understand the numbing effects of refusing to engage or to feel when feeling brings pain. But I also know that refusing to choose life means choosing to die—perhaps not physically, but emotionally and spiritually.

What was it that Moses told the people of Israel is the same as choosing death? "If your heart turns away and you refuse to listen, and if you are drawn away to serve and worship other gods" (Deuteronomy 30:17). Has your heart turned away from God because it is wounded and you believe he is to blame? Have you refused to listen to his promise to be your refuge and strength in times of trouble? Have you chosen to serve and worship the god-of-your-own-making who would never use hardship to refine you, or the idol-of-an-idyllic-life who owes you the comforts of privilege and power?

Oh, that you might choose life, refusing to be enveloped by and eventually destroyed by heart-crushing sorrow and soul-stealing disappointment! To choose life is to turn toward God with all your heart and soul, to open yourself to new joys as well as additional sorrows. It is to choose to live fully for God in recognition that there is no real life apart from him and that anything less is merely existing.

Life Giver, today I choose life! I choose to love you and obey you no matter what disappointments may come from living in this world. I want to occupy the land of blessing you have provided for me, so I turn wholeheartedly to you.

DIGGING DEEPER

Read Deuteronomy 30. What does it mean to wholeheartedly obey God? How does your choice to live for God influence future generations?

ONLY A FEW EVER FIND IT

You can enter God's Kingdom only through the narrow gate. The highway to hell is broad, and its gate is wide for the many who choose the easy way. But the gateway to life is small, and the road is narrow, and only a few ever find it. —Matthew 7:13-14

We live in an age of instant polls. Nearly every day we can look in the newspaper and see what percentage of people engage in a certain activity or have a particular point of view. We read about the latest trend and find ourselves incredibly average or embarrassingly out of step. Being in the majority is often more comfortable than being in the minority, isn't it? Along with the seeming safety of the majority comes strength in numbers and a sense of "rightness." It is the difference between being mainstream and fighting your way upstream.

Jesus' statement that only a few will find their way into the Kingdom of God challenges our assumptions about the soundness of the majority. We wonder how huge numbers of people in our world could be wrong about how to have a life-saving relationship with God and about what makes life worth living. It seems arrogant to believe that a small number of people—people who call themselves by the name of the God of the Bible and Jesus Christ, his Son—have the corner on truth and eternal life. But it is only arrogant if you believe that you are the architect of this plan, that you have done something to make you worthy of being included, or that you have the power to determine who is welcome. The reality is, Kingdom seeking requires that we recognize our complete unworthiness and inability to earn a place in God's family. It requires that we be willing to humbly admit our inescapable need for a Savior. Following the narrow way to life requires humility, not arrogance.

Have you been accused of being small- or narrow-minded because you have gone against the grain of societal thinking, believing that a relationship with Jesus is the only way to know God eternally? Have you felt as if you're out of the "in" crowd, going against the grain of your coworkers or neighbors, out of step within your own family? Then take the words of Jesus to heart. He said that few choose to search for life, but those who do, find it. Are you willing to go through the narrow gate to find life?

The Way, the Truth, the Life, I believe and confess that you are the exclusive way to experience eternal life with God. Help me be openhearted in my walk down your road so that others will want to join me on your road to life.

DIGGING DEEPER

Jesus repeatedly distinguished between those who have eternal life and those who don't. In addition to two gates, two ways, two destinations, and two groups of people in Matthew 7:13-14, what other twos do you find in Matthew 7:13-29?

LOSING YOUR LIFE

IF YOU CLING TO YOUR LIFE, YOU WILL LOSE IT; BUT IF YOU GIVE IT UP FOR ME, YOU WILL FIND IT. —MATTHEW 10:39

Last weekend I called a young woman who wrote to me after losing her firstborn son, who lived two days before dying in her arms. His genetic abnormality is likely to repeat itself in future children she and her husband may have. "I want to be a mother," she wrote to me. "I want to have purpose and meaning in my life. I want to move on with whatever God has for me—but I don't know how to do any of these things. How do I mourn the possibility that I will never have a child of my own, when that has been my heart's greatest desire for as long as I can remember?"

We had a precious conversation, but I could tell that the high cost of what I was calling her to do—no, what Jesus is calling her to do—was staggering. Jesus calls us to abandon our own agendas, what we have deemed will please and fulfill us, so that we can embrace the kind and quality of life that only he gives. This is not about adding Jesus to the life we are living. This is about making Jesus our life. This is about putting our plans for our lives to death so that the abundant life he offers has room to take root and grow. And death is always painful. This is not an extreme brand of discipleship only for go-getters. This is the call for everyone who chooses to be a follower of Jesus.

The problem is, we don't really believe that God's plan for our lives could be better than the one we've crafted. We don't believe we could be as fulfilled by the life he offers as we would be by the one we've planned. It takes a step of faith to believe God will supply satisfying life now and when we die.

"Your son has given you an incredible gift," I told this grieving mom. "He has given you the gift of being forced to reconsider the very purpose of your life. Those who are sailing through a comfortable life at this point have not yet been forced to carefully consider their lives and surrender their dreams. But because you have been shaken to the core, you see clearly that if you cling to your own plans and desires, you will never discover the freedom and joy found in losing your life for Jesus."

Master Jesus, I'm afraid of what may happen and what I may have to surrender if I give up my life for you. Give me eyes of faith to see how beautiful and satisfying my life will be as I die to myself and live to you.

DIGGING DEEPER

What does Jesus expect of his followers, according to Luke 14:25-33?

TO WHOM WOULD WE GO?

At this point many of his disciples turned away and deserted him. Then Jesus turned to the Twelve and asked, "Are you going to leave, too?"

Simon Peter replied, "Lord, to whom would we go? You alone have the words that give eternal life. We believe them." —John 6:66-69

I don't remember a lot about what my pastor, Charles McGowan, said as we stood at the grave, preparing to put Hope's body into the ground. I suppose I wanted to be somewhere else—anywhere else—just not there. But I remember his words were meaningful. The Scripture that pierced me the deepest was: "Lord, to whom would we go? You alone have the words that give eternal life." I suppose I identified with the sense of resignation as well as hope in Peter's words. I craved the comfort of knowing that Hope's life continues beyond the grave in the presence of God. This confidence was and is the only comfort when you stand at the grave.

Jesus had been teaching a large group of followers that if they wanted eternal life, they had to eat his flesh and drink his blood—meaning that they would need to place their faith in his sacrificial death on the cross. But for the Jews, who were entrenched in the Mosaic law that prohibited drinking blood or eating meat with blood in it, this statement was not just unintelligible, it was offensive. It was just too much. Scripture says that "at this point many of his disciples turned away and deserted him."

And we can understand, can't we? Because sometimes what God seems to say about himself through our circumstances is just too hard. We want to turn away. The temptation is to say in our hearts, *What does it matter? God is going to do what he wants, anyway. Why should I pray? Why should I trust him when he has allowed the worst thing I can imagine to become a reality in my life? How can I love a God who would allow this to happen?* We're just offended with God.

We are left with a choice. We can turn from God in the lowest moments of life, allowing our offense to alienate us from God until we are out in the cold, devoid of comfort and hope. Or we can turn toward him, cry out to him, and place our faith in him as our sole source for life.

Lord, in the face of death and disappointment, I yearn for the confidence of life beyond this sorrow-stained world. There is no one else to turn to but you, so I run to you, believing you will welcome me and give me life without end.

DIGGING DEEPER

Read John 6:22-71, noting each mention of eternal life and how to receive it.

SO THAT YOU MAY KNOW

This is what God has testified: He has given us eternal life, and this life is in his Son. So whoever has God's Son has life; whoever does not have his Son does not have life. I write this to you who believe in the Son of God, so that you may know you have eternal life. —1 John 5:11-13

In my town, many people grew up in a church where they were never offered assurance of eternal life. It was dangled in front of them as something they could never be certain of. According to this church, if you forsake the denomination or fail to follow its teaching closely enough, you are out. It is sad to me that believers who have long since left that church and its teachings still wrangle with fear when approaching death because they aren't sure of eternal life.

The town I grew up in had another church with people who could not rest in the confidence of eternal life. But it wasn't faithfulness to the church that was the key issue—it was unconfessed sin. They believed that if there was a sin you neglected to confess and death came, you could be left out.

But the greatest number of people who have no confidence of heaven are those who have accepted conventional wisdom that says heaven is for "good" people—people who haven't murdered anybody or committed any "big" sins. They have believed two lies that have deadly consequences. Lie number one is that being good is what gets you into heaven. Lie number two is that if they try hard enough they can be good enough for God's holy heaven.

The real tragedy is, God never intended that we live in fear and uncertainty, wondering if we will make it to heaven. The equation is simple: "Whoever has God's Son has life" (1 John 5:12). But so many are content just trying to be good enough and thereby deeming Jesus unnecessary. You do not have to wonder about or fear where death will lead you or those you love. Confidence that God has already given you eternal life—not because you have been faithful to a church or because you have confessed every sin or because you have been good enough, but solely because you are hidden in Jesus—this is what offers peace and joy for now and forever.

Son of God, thank you for giving me life and for giving me the confidence that this life in you and with you will last forever.

DIGGING DEEPER

Read John 17. How does Jesus' prayer prior to the Cross affirm the way we gain eternal life and the confidence we can have of eternal life?

WEEK 7

LIFE

REFLECTION

The choice of life in the face of loss is often many smaller choices rather than one determining choice. What are the evidences that you are choosing life?

On what do you base your confidence that you will inherit eternal life, or on what do you base your fears of being excluded?

MEDITATION

He is the God who made the world and everything in it. Since he is Lord of heaven and earth, he doesn't live in man-made temples, and human hands can't serve his needs—for he has no needs. He himself gives life and breath to everything, and he satisfies every need there is. His purpose in all of this was that the nations should seek after God and perhaps feel their way toward him and find him—though he is not far from any one of us. For in him we live and move and exist. —Acts 17:24-25, 27-28

Read the verses slowly several times, noting the words, phrases, and images that speak most to you.

Personalize the passage back to God in the form of a prayer.

Present yourself before God in silence, listening for God to speak to you.

PRAYER

Praise God for giving you life abundantly, now and forever!

Thank God for the words of eternal life only he can offer, words that have given you comfort in loss and hope for the future.

Intercede for those you know who have refused to enter God's Kingdom through the narrow way.

Confess your fear about losing your life for the sake of Jesus, and express your desire for the life he will supply when you let go.

Petition the Holy Spirit to help you truly rest and place your confidence in God's promise of eternal life through Christ Jesus.

SCARED TO DEATH OF DEATH

ONLY BY DYING COULD HE BREAK THE POWER OF THE DEVIL, WHO HAD THE POWER OF DEATH. ONLY IN THIS WAY COULD HE DELIVER THOSE WHO HAVE LIVED ALL THEIR LIVES AS SLAVES TO THE FEAR OF DYING. —HEBREWS 2:14-15

Woody Allen is quoted as saying, "It's not that I'm afraid to die, I just don't want to be there when it happens." The truth is, most of us are scared to death of death. We have a hard time imagining how or why anyone could do anything—even for a noble cause such as defending our country, donating a vital organ, or declining an invasive medical treatment—that could potentially lead to death. Why are we so afraid? Are we destined to be afraid of death?

Some of it, I think, is fear of the unknown. We don't know what it will feel like to die or what will be beyond that threshold. I think Jesus understood this fear, which is why he comforted his disciples by telling them, "I am going to prepare a place for you" (John 14:2). It is not *what* you know but *who* you know that calms the fear of the unknowns surrounding death.

We fear judgment. And it is true that after death comes judgment. But the good news is that there is no condemnation for those who are in Christ. We are judged "not guilty"—not because we have no real guilt, but because Christ has paid the penalty for our wrongdoing. Anticipating freedom from punishment relieves the fear of death.

We also fear the potential pain involved in dying, the separation from those we love, and the loss of control that death brings (since none of us are strong enough to resist death). Perhaps our greatest fear is what it will be like for those we leave behind. It is okay to be afraid of these things. But these fears do not have to consume us, enslave us.

Imagine living in the freedom of no longer being a slave to the fear of death. That is the very purpose for which Christ died. You can rest in the midst of the unknown, trusting God with your future and recognizing that Jesus has removed the sting from death. As you walk in this freedom, you'll be able to give your life away more freely, hold on to your loved ones more loosely, and embrace the adventure of life in Christ more fully.

Freedom Giver, please set me free from the grip my fears about death have on me. Because I know you, I can trust you with my life and my death.

DIGGING DEEPER

What does 1 John 4:13-18 teach us about the antidote to the fear of death?

THE STING OF DEATH

When our perishable earthly bodies have been transformed into heavenly bodies that will never die—then at last the Scriptures will come true: "Death is swallowed up in victory. O death, where is your victory? O death, where is your sting?" —1 Corinthians 15:54-55

I've struggled with these verses. Because I know what it feels like when it seems death has won. Because I have felt the twisting, stinging bite of death-pain on my insides. Have you? How can we ever hope to taunt death and claim victory like Paul does in these verses?

Because death is not the end of the story. Physical death does not speak the final word in the life of the believer and therefore does not declare the ultimate victory. But it requires a step of faith to believe that a day is coming when Jesus' victory over death will come to its complete fruition. And for those who are unable to receive the gift of victory over death by faith, the sting remains, and it is very real and very painful.

My friend Sue is a former hospice nurse, and she has witnessed many different ways patients and families deal with death. She has seen those who peacefully slip away, some completely unconscious of their passage, some clear-minded to the end as they pass from this life, oftentimes even verbalizing glimpses of the next. For those who love them, tears come, but there is also sweetness and even a joy mixed with the tears.

Others are terrorized as death approaches. These people seem to already taste the bitter sting of death, the gripping fear, the fright of the unknown, the anticipation of terror, and the inescapable despair. They are inconsolable, as are those around them when death comes.

As God's child, you can approach death with the confident expectation that God will transform your earthly body into a heavenly body that will never die. Death will be defeated. You will know by experience that the poison sting of death no longer has any power to hurt you.

Death Slayer, your Word tells me that you have taken the poison sting so that those who love you will not have to be injected with its damning toxin. Fill me with confidence in your ultimate victory over death so I can rest in you.

DIGGING DEEPER

Read 1 Corinthians 15:50-58. What is the root of the sting of death, and in what way will there be victory over it? According to verse 58, what impact should this understanding of victory over death have on how we live?

A BETTER DAY

The day you die is better than the day you are born. —Ecclesiastes 7:1

Birthdays. Deathdays. I feel like they are always coming at me. And it is hard to know what to do with these days when you have lost someone you love, isn't it? Letting them just go by doesn't seem right, and yet it can be so hard to work up the energy just to get out of bed, let alone do something constructive or meaningful.

When Hope's and Gabe's birthdays come around, I can usually find some way—sometimes very small and sometimes more significant—to celebrate their lives. I'm grateful they were here if for only a short time, so I can find joy in that. I celebrate the impact they had on other people, even with their significant limitations and the brevity of their lives, and I'm grateful. I remember the joy and richness they each brought to our lives and the gifts they gave us in the form of a deeper understanding of God and deeper relationships with people around us.

But those deathdays are hard. Or, I should say, it is the anticipation of the deathdays that is hard. For me, the day itself is not so bad. It is the days leading up to it, as I have a sense that death is coming again and I can't stop it. I feel a sense of dread and helplessness. Finding a way to "celebrate" a day of death seems absolutely ridiculous and almost like a denial of reality. But is it? Perhaps it is the ultimate embracing of reality.

On the day we are born, we enter a pain-saturated, sin-scarred, darkness-loving, soul-depriving existence for a determined number of years. On the day of our death, if we are believers, we enter a pain-free, perfect place that is ablaze with the glory of Christ, where our deepest longings and joys are fulfilled, not for a number of years, but forever. Think about it. Don't dismiss it because of how much you miss someone who is there or because of your fears of the unknown. Allow this truth to ruminate in your heart and illumine your mind. For you, and for the one you love who knows Christ, won't your deathday be your true birthday?

Lord of life, really believing this requires a radical readjustment to my perspective about this life and the next. Renew my mind and emotions so I can see life on this earth and in eternity with you in proper perspective.

DIGGING DEEPER

According to Philippians 1:20-24, how did Paul view the value of life and the benefits of death? How does a person honor Christ in both life and death?

THE SHADOW OF DEATH

EVEN THOUGH I WALK THROUGH THE VALLEY OF THE SHADOW OF DEATH, I WILL FEAR NO EVIL, FOR YOU ARE WITH ME; YOUR ROD AND YOUR STAFF, THEY COMFORT ME.
—PSALM 23:4 (NIV)

Dr. Donald Grey Barnhouse was one of America's great preachers. His first wife died from cancer when she was in her thirties, leaving behind three children under the age of twelve. Dr. Barnhouse was driving home from the funeral service with his children when a huge truck stopped next to them at a traffic light, blocking the sunlight and covering the car with its shadow. He turned to his children and said, "Death is like that. It blocks the sunshine, but the sun is still shining."

The difference between walking into death and walking in the shadow of death is the difference between finality and a new beginning forever. It is the difference between nothingness and fullness of joy and life. It is the difference between destruction and re-creation for the future. It is ultimately the difference between the darkness of eternal separation from God and the blazing glory of everlasting enjoyment of his presence.

There is no doubt that a shadow is a dark place to be. But when the Lord is our shepherd, we no longer have to fear the dark places that death takes us. In the shadows we reach out to find him beside us, and the fear of the unknown fades. When he gently uses his rod of correction to prod us in the right direction and his staff of compassion to draw us close, we find comfort.

When we are in the fold of God, death is impotent to destroy us. It is depleted of its evil power. The valley where we encounter death is transformed into a place of peaceful comfort; it is in this valley that we are more aware of God's presence than ever before.

My Shepherd, the darkness of the shadow of death has swept over me and at times it feels as if it will crush me. But it is just a shadow because you have taken away its power to destroy me. Walk with me and comfort me in the darkness, and I will not have to be afraid.

DIGGING DEEPER

Recognizing that the prophecies for Israel include those of us who have been grafted in through Christ, what does Isaiah 9:2-5 tell us about our future? What or who is the light? What chains bind us, and what whips scourge us?

REST IN PEACE

THE RIGHTEOUS PASS AWAY; THE GODLY OFTEN DIE BEFORE THEIR TIME. AND NO ONE SEEMS TO CARE OR WONDER WHY. NO ONE SEEMS TO UNDERSTAND THAT GOD IS PROTECTING THEM FROM THE EVIL TO COME. FOR THE GODLY WHO DIE WILL REST IN PEACE. —ISAIAH 57:1-2

When Hope was a couple of weeks old, we went to the Christmas program at our church. As we sat in the balcony, enjoying the beauty of the music and pageantry, it hit me: *I will never get to enjoy music with Hope. She will never sing in the children's choir. We will never sample rich desserts together or explore interesting places, observe amazing art or architecture.* The tears began to drip down my face onto Hope as I started to let go of the dreams I had for sharing with her all the good things life in this world has to offer.

But even as the music swelled, I began to consider what was ahead for Hope. No, she wouldn't enjoy a fine orchestra here with me, but surely the music in the halls of heaven will be finer! As I thought through all of the things I would not be able to share with her, I began to see how much better heaven's version will be.

Over the coming weeks, I also began to consider other earthly things Hope would "miss out on." She would miss out on allergies and acne, fighting weight gain and feeling left out, broken dreams and broken hearts. She would leave a world marked by crime and cruelty, disease and disappointment, for one of wholeness, richness, perfected beauty, and peace.

I began to see that Hope's brief life on earth and quick deliverance into eternal life in the presence of God was not cruel or tragic. It was, in many ways, a gift to her, a protection from the evil to come. Not that it *felt* less cruel or tragic to me. I felt robbed. I felt cheated. Shortly after that I wrote in my journal:

> *I don't want to lose Hope. I would like to see her grow. I would like to know her as an adult. But I also know that this life is filled with pain. And I don't think it is a tragedy that she will have the opportunity to be spared from evil, from the pain of this life, and be in the presence of God. This is what I believe. It is not necessarily how I feel. But believing this makes a difference in how I feel.*

My Protector, I have believed the lie that anything less than a long life on this earth is a tragedy. But death takes people away from an evil world. Use this truth to change how I feel so I can rest in the peace of death.

DIGGING DEEPER

Read in Romans 1:18-32 about the world from which God delivers those who die, and compare that to the world he delivers us to in Revelation 21:1-7.

WEEK 8

DEATH

REFLECTION

Ecclesiastes 7:4 says, "A wise person thinks much about death, while the fool thinks only about having a good time now." How can clear thinking about death prepare us to live and die well?

What fears do you have about your death and the death of those you love? What truths from God's Word can you find to confront those fears?

MEDITATION

To me, living is for Christ, and dying is even better. Yet if I live, that means fruitful service for Christ. I really don't know which is better. I'm torn between two desires: Sometimes I want to live, and sometimes I long to go and be with Christ. That would be far better for me, but it is better for you that I live. —PHILIPPIANS 1:21-24

Read through this testimony of Paul several times, marking words and phrases that are especially meaningful to you.

Ask yourself if you feel the same way Paul did, and if not, why not?

Invite Christ into your conflicting desires and conflicting feelings about life here for Christ and death with Christ.

PRAYER

Praise God for his power over life and death.

Thank God for his provision of a heavenly home where those who love him will spend eternity with him.

Intercede for those you know who have no confidence of life beyond death because they have rejected the love of God in Christ.

Confess your tendency to place more value on a long life on this earth than on eternal life in the presence of God.

Petition God to change your perspective about life and death so that you will be set free from the fear of death and set free to live wholeheartedly for Christ.

WEEK 9

THE LOVE OF GOD

What kind of book would the story of your life be? You might think of it as a tragedy, but in reality, your life is a love story, being written by the hand of God. While some chapters will be more difficult than others, visible in every scene, on every page, is the love of God.

The hurts in your life do not define you. God's love for you determines the course and shape of your life and defines who you are today and who you are becoming. You are enfolded in the love of God now and for eternity, and that love is the cornerstone you can build your life on. It is also your cushion from the blows life inevitably brings.

God loves you simply because he has chosen to do so. He loves you personally. He loves you powerfully. He loves you passionately. He loves you when you don't feel lovable or lovely. He loves you when no one else loves you. Others may abandon or reject you, but God will always love you, no matter what.

This is his promise, on which you can completely rely: "I have loved you, my people, with an everlasting love. With unfailing love I have drawn you to myself" (Jeremiah 31:3).

THIS WEEK'S PASSAGE FOR MEDITATION

I pray that Christ will be more and more at home in your hearts as you trust in him. May your roots go down deep into the soil of God's marvelous love. And may you have the power to understand, as all God's people should, how wide, how long, how high, and how deep his love really is. May you experience the love of Christ, though it is so great you will never fully understand it. Then you will be filled with the fullness of life and power that comes from God. Now glory be to God! By his mighty power at work within us, he is able to accomplish infinitely more than we would ever dare to ask or hope. —EPHESIANS 3:17-20

LOVE DEMONSTRATED

God demonstrates his own love for us in this: While we were still sinners, Christ died for us. —Romans 5:8 (NIV)

David often points out that Hope and Gabe gave us a rare opportunity. Their very lives called us to love on a higher plane and at a deeper level. "Much of what we do for our children is to prepare them for adulthood or to generate gratitude one day," David likes to say. "But in caring for Hope and Gabe, we knew they would never grow up and thank us. We didn't love them for any future reward or result. We simply loved them and cared for their needs. And it was, perhaps, the greatest privilege of our lives."

Don't get me wrong. There was no heroism involved here, no sense of sacrifice on our part. Hope and Gabe were easy to love—perhaps easier to love in their innocence and neediness. We loved them with the same kind of love every parent feels—the kind that wakes you up in the middle of the night to feed a hungry baby and keeps you awake in the middle of the night waiting on a wandering teenager. Parenthood is, perhaps, the closest taste we're given of what it is like to love in a divine way. But even so, we know we fall short. As amazed as we can be at the heroic level of love that seems instinctive as parents, we are equally as surprised by the cruelty we have the ability to inflict.

Divine love is demonstrated in sacrificial dimensions. Ultimate love was expressed in the ultimate sacrifice—the God of the universe on a cross dying for people who don't even care about him or take an interest in him. See him there showing us what it really means to love expecting nothing in return, showing us what real love costs. This is our example to follow, our plumb line to measure our lives against. If we want to love, we must be prepared to demonstrate—not just discuss—sacrificial love.

What is God calling you to sacrifice in order to love others well? Is he calling you out of your comfort zone, up from your self-pity, away from your self-protection? Who are you being called to love in a sacrificial way? Does the example of Jesus compel you to love someone well who does not appreciate the sacrifice inherent in your love?

My divine Lover, knowing how I hate to be inconvenienced, I feel completely incapable of loving at a sacrificial level. Show me the joy of loving in a way that sacrifices and serves, and make my life a demonstration of divine love.

DIGGING DEEPER

Read Titus 3:4-7 and make a list of the ways God demonstrates his love.

NOTHING CAN SEPARATE US FROM CHRIST'S LOVE

Can anything ever separate us from Christ's love? Does it mean he no longer loves us if we have trouble or calamity, or are persecuted, or are hungry or cold or in danger or threatened with death? —Romans 8:35

What does it feel like to be loved by God? It is not a sentimental feeling. Nor is it circumstantial. Feeling loved by God is the deep certainty that the God of the universe is not opposed to me, though I deserve it; he is for me! It is an inner confidence in his loving intentions that gives us the security and strength we need for enduring the difficulties of this life.

But rather than feeling loved by God, you may feel that everything in this life is working against you, and in some ways you would be right. You have an enemy who seeks to destroy you, a flesh that longs to be satisfied, and a life in a world that is under a curse. So when you find yourself on the receiving end of the darkness and the brokenness of this world, it's tempting to assume that you've come to the end of God's loving reach and remembrance. But no power can come between God and his children. His love keeps us safe in him and with him for eternity. God loves us too much to let us slip away or to allow anything to keep us from experiencing his love for an eternity.

Do you want to feel loved by God? Focus on his loving provision for your eternal future, nurturing your confidence to say with Paul, "For I am convinced that neither death nor life [not cancer, a car accident, crime, or calamity], neither angels nor demons [not evil in the media or crazed psychopaths], neither the present nor the future [not any current crisis or any tragedy that may be in my future], nor any powers [not a demanding boss, a cruel dictator, or a blood-thirsty terrorist], neither height nor depth [not winning the lottery or losing my life savings], nor anything else in all creation [not a hole in the ozone, a forest fire or a hurricane, a hungry shark or a killer bee] will be able to separate us from the love of God that is in Christ Jesus our Lord" (Romans 8:38-39, NIV). You can be confident that nothing can keep God's love away from you. When you don't feel it, believe it, rehearse it in your heart and mind, and let your confidence grow.

Everlasting Jesus, the strength of your love binds me to you through life and death, through comfort and calamity, through this world and the next.

DIGGING DEEPER

Read 1 John 4:7–5:5. How is God's love brought to full expression? What is the fear that the love of God takes away?

THE GREATEST LOVER IN THE UNIVERSE

Love is patient and kind. Love is not jealous or boastful or proud or rude. Love does not demand its own way. Love is not irritable, and it keeps no record of when it has been wronged. It is never glad about injustice but rejoices whenever the truth wins out. Love never gives up, never loses faith, is always hopeful, and endures through every circumstance.

—1 Corinthians 13:4-7

We live in a world full of lonely people searching for love. And we don't have to look very far to see intense longing for love—perhaps only as far as the mirror. Neither does it take much searching to find the disappointment insufficient lovers leave behind. We want to love and be loved on a grand scale, yet we are bound by our self-centered tendencies and embittered by broken promises and unmet expectations. Can we ever expect to experience love that will never disappoint, never fade, and never leave?

If a human kiss and the rush of romance is the highest and most satisfying love we can ever expect to know, we are indeed doomed to disappointment, because no human can ever love us fully, completely, faithfully. How many times must our hearts be broken to learn that lesson?

Our brokenheartedness keeps us looking for a grander, surer love. But instead of continuing to look around, we must look up. There we see Jesus, the greatest lover in the universe. He shows us exactly what love looks like. Jesus is patient and kind. Jesus is not jealous or boastful or proud or rude. Jesus does not demand his own way. Jesus is not irritable, and he keeps no record of when he has been wronged. Jesus is never glad about injustice but rejoices whenever the truth wins out. Jesus never gives up, never loses faith, is always hopeful, and endures through every circumstance.

Jesus is not like a human lover who grows weary of our idiosyncrasies. Jesus is patient. Jesus will not bring up our failures of the past and use them against us. He forgives and forgets our sins, casting them away as far as the east is from the west. Jesus will never fail to defend those he loves. Out of his love for us and his hate for evil, he will take up our case and will one day set everything right. Do you think Jesus will give up on you, release his grip on you, and walk away from you? Absolutely not. That's not what Love does.

Lover of my soul, I can't love in the way that you do, but neither can I resist your love. Use even my disappointment in those who fail in loving me well to draw me into the love you so graciously want to shower on me.

DIGGING DEEPER

Examine the example of love Jesus showed us in John 13:1-17. What did this action of love require, and what did it symbolize? What does it teach us?

ENGRAVED ON THE PALM OF HIS HAND

Zion said, "The Lord has forsaken me, the Lord has forgotten me."

"Can a mother forget the baby at her breast and have no compassion on the child she has borne? Though she may forget, I will not forget you! See, I have engraved you on the palms of my hands; your walls are ever before me."
—Isaiah 49:14-16 (NIV)

My mom has carried the same dime in her wallet since 1960. Her sister and sister-in-law tried to use that dime to call her from a pay phone the day my sister, Denise, was born. The phone didn't accept the dime, so they gave it to my mom, and she has kept it in her wallet ever since. Likewise, my dad carries a memento of that important day in his billfold—an old clipping from the *Kansas City Star* with the headline, "Doctor Delivers a Jinks on Friday the Thirteenth." Why would my parents keep an old dime and a faded newspaper clipping so close and so constant? Because they are ready reminders of someone they love, someone who is precious to them.

While carrying a memento of someone we love is meaningful, God has gone even further for his children, the objects of his affection. "I have engraved you on the palms of my hands," he says. It is as if God holds out his open hands to those who wonder if he has deserted and forgotten them, saying, "Take a look. You'll see something—someone—too precious to me to forget." And there, if we will look, we will see ourselves.

The word *engrave* means "to cut into" something. So in a sense, we've been cut into God's flesh. We are engraved into his very person as a permanent reminder of his eternal, unchanging love for us.

Why would God engrave your image onto the palms of his hands? Because he wants to keep you at the center of his attention. He thinks about you all the time. He watches over you. In the palm of his hand is not only your likeness, but your cares and concerns, your weaknesses and wants, your tendencies and traumas. He sees it all and loves you. He cares about what concerns you because he cares for you. You are always before his eyes and on his mind.

Ultimately, it is not the fact that you know God that really matters. What matters is that he knows you and has set his love on you. You are engraved on the palms of his hands—never off of his mind, out of his sight, or away from his loving care.

Loving Lord, I cannot trust my feelings that sometimes tell me I'm forgotten and abandoned by you. I am far too precious to you. Whenever I doubt your love, I need only trace the palms of your hands where I see my own image engraved and the scars from nails that once held you to the cross out of love for me.

DIGGING DEEPER

Read Psalm 31:14-15; 32:4-5; 75:7-8; 119:73; and 139:9-10.What do these verses reveal about the love God expresses to us with his hands?

LORD, THE ONE YOU LOVE IS VERY SICK

A MAN NAMED LAZARUS WAS SICK. HE LIVED IN BETHANY WITH HIS SISTERS, MARY AND MARTHA. SO THE TWO SISTERS SENT A MESSAGE TO JESUS TELLING HIM, "LORD, THE ONE YOU LOVE IS VERY SICK." BUT WHEN JESUS HEARD ABOUT IT HE SAID, "LAZARUS'S SICKNESS WILL NOT END IN DEATH. NO, IT IS FOR THE GLORY OF GOD." ALTHOUGH JESUS LOVED MARTHA, MARY, AND LAZARUS, HE STAYED WHERE HE WAS FOR THE NEXT TWO DAYS AND DID NOT GO TO THEM. —JOHN 11:1, 3-6

"Lord, the one you love is very sick." Mary and Martha were not simply reporting on Lazarus's condition for Jesus' information. Implied in their message is a request for him to come, a plea for him to exercise his power to remedy the situation, to restore Lazarus to health. They seem to be saying to Jesus what we have said many times: "Jesus, if you really love me, then you will prove it by showing up, relieving my pain, and preventing my loss."

I find it interesting that John makes sure that we know that Jesus *loved* Mary and Martha and Lazarus. Perhaps that's because he understood how hard it can be to believe that these two things can both be true: that God loves us and that he allows us to suffer and even die. We look squarely into our suffering and say to ourselves, *If God really loved me, he wouldn't allow this. Therefore, if he does allow it, he doesn't love me.* Our suffering becomes the soil in which our doubts about God's love begin to grow.

But God's love is sure and certain. He is the very definition of love. We tend to interpret God's love by looking at our circumstances. Things-are-good means God loves me. Things-are-bad means God doesn't care. Instead, we must allow the strong and secure love of God to become the lens through which we interpret everything that happens in our lives. When we see our suffering through the lens of God's love, we see that our suffering has meaning and purpose. And while we may never label the suffering as good, we have the consoling confidence that God is going to use it for our good and for his glory. The love of God supports us and sustains us.

Because Jesus loved Mary and Martha and Lazarus, he wanted to deepen their faith. Because Jesus loved them, he turned the most bitter experience of their lives into a blazing testimony to his love and power. And he will do the same for you—because he loves you.

Lord, I want to see everything in my life through the lens of your love in quiet confidence that you are working everything for my good and your glory.

DIGGING DEEPER

Read Matthew 9:9-13. What kind of sickness infected the various people at the dinner? How did Jesus use the situation to explain his purpose?

WEEK 9

THE LOVE OF GOD

REFLECTION

In what situations have you experienced confidence in God's love, and what has caused you to doubt it?

In what ways would you like to experience and cherish God's love in the days ahead?

MEDITATION

I pray that Christ will be more and more at home in your hearts as you trust in him. May your roots go down deep into the soil of God's marvelous love. And may you have the power to understand, as all God's people should, how wide, how long, how high, and how deep his love really is. May you experience the love of Christ, though it is so great you will never fully understand it. Then you will be filled with the fullness of life and power that comes from God. Now glory be to God! By his mighty power at work within us, he is able to accomplish infinitely more than we would ever dare to ask or hope. —Ephesians 3:17-20

Read through this prayer of Paul, hearing him pray it personally for you.

Circle phrases in the passage that offer vivid images to you, and meditate on their meaning.

Turn the passage into a personal prayer, inviting Christ to make himself at home in your heart and to reveal the dimensions of his love to you.

PRAYER

Praise God for his unfailing, eternal, all-encompassing love.

Thank God for loving us so much he gave us his Son and continues to provide everything we need because he loves us.

Intercede for those who are embittered toward God, unwilling to believe that he truly loves them unconditionally.

Confess your disappointment with the form God's love has taken in your life at times.

Petition God to make his love real to you in your daily relationship—that you will feel it as well as know it.

WEEK 10

SOVEREIGNTY OF GOD

To say that God is sovereign is to say that God has the power to do as he pleases in the universe and in my life. To say that God is sovereign is to say that he has the ability and authority to oversee and influence the affairs of governments and kingdoms from the most monumental of events to the smallest detail. God's sovereignty is his absolute independence to do as he pleases and his ultimate control over all his creatures.

When something bad happens, the sovereignty of God is a very hard truth to accept, because if he is in control of everything, we wonder why he has allowed this universe to be ordered in a way that causes us pain. But when we begin to think that "the God I know would never allow this," we have taken our first step toward discovering that God is not who we think he is. That is when we can begin to explore the wonder of his sovereignty.

Though God's sovereignty can be hard to accept, it is also a soft place to land. Without confidence in God's sovereign oversight of the universe, life becomes meaningless, hope for justice fades, and everything seems random. The truth is, if God is not sovereign, we're in trouble. The sovereignty of God is a rock underfoot when the winds blow in our lives. It confronts what seems absurd in our existence. God's sovereignty is our greatest hope as we face an uncertain and unknown future.

THIS WEEK'S PASSAGE FOR MEDITATION

The LORD Almighty has sworn this oath: "It will all happen as I have planned. It will come about according to my purposes. I have a plan for the whole earth, for my mighty power reaches throughout the world. The Lord Almighty has spoken—who can change his plans? When his hand moves, who can stop him?" —ISAIAH 14:24, 26-27

GOD'S SOVEREIGNTY IN SENDING

He called for a famine on the land of Canaan, cutting off its food supply. Then he sent someone to Egypt ahead of them—Joseph, who was sold as a slave. There in prison, they bruised his feet with fetters and placed his neck in an iron collar. Until the time came to fulfill his word, the Lord tested Joseph's character. —Psalm 105:16-19

In Psalm 105, the psalmist serves as our inspired commentator on the story of Joseph. He outlines for us the invisible hand of God at work—in what on the surface seems like a story of evil intentions, false accusations, broken hearts, and wasted years—to show us instead God's sovereignty.

On the surface we see Joseph's jealous brothers' scheme to get rid of the favored son, as they sold him to slave traders. We see Joseph forgotten for years in Egypt's prison. But we also see God with him even there, giving him the ability to interpret Pharaoh's dream, equipping him with the wisdom and opportunity to become second-in-command of Egypt.

The psalmist shows us what we can't see on the surface, clearly revealing God's sovereignty at work. He says that God "called for" a famine. God has the power and authority to use the forces of nature, as well as the actions of people, to accomplish his purposes. The psalmist also tells us that God "sent someone to Egypt ahead of them—Joseph." Though selling Joseph as a slave was a sinful choice made by his brothers, it fulfilled the plans and purposes of God. As John Piper says, "their sinning was God's sending."

I don't know if Joseph could see God's sovereignty as he served as a slave in the house of Potiphar, as he languished in prison, when he interpreted Pharaoh's dream of coming famine. But I do know that eventually Joseph embraced the big picture of God's sovereignty, enabling him to tell his brothers, "Don't be angry with yourselves that you did this to me, for God did it. God has sent me here to keep you and your families alive so that you will become a great nation" (Genesis 45:5, 7). More than saying, "God used it," Joseph says, "God did it." This is the severe and sometimes unsettling sovereignty of God at work. Are you willing to look for the invisible hand of God at work behind the scenes of your suffering and to embrace his sovereign purpose?

Sovereign Sender, I would not have asked for some of what you have sent into my life, but I believe you are at work and you see what I cannot. Give me eyes to see your invisible hand and faith to trust your loving heart.

DIGGING DEEPER

How do these verses in Proverbs show God's invisible hand working behind the scenes: Proverbs 16:1, 9; 19:21; and 21:1?

EVEN THIS DAY?

You saw me before I was born. Every day of my life was recorded in your book. Every moment was laid out before a single day had passed. How precious are your thoughts about me, O God! —Psalm 139:16-17

On the days when life seems good, it is easy to say to God, "Every day of my life was recorded in your book." But on the day tragedy strikes, on the day our lives are changed forever by loss, we wonder, *Was this day of my life written in your book, by your hand? Is this the story you have intended to write for my life, or has there been a terrible mistake?*

On April 20, 2001, missionary Veronica Bowers was in a Cessna over Peru, holding her seven-month-old daughter, Charity, in her lap. With them were Veronica's husband, Jim, and six-year-old son, Cory, when Peruvian authorities mistook them for drug couriers and opened fire on their aircraft. One bullet passed by Jim's head and made a hole in the windshield. Another bullet passed through Veronica's back and stopped inside her baby, killing them both.

We can't help but wonder, *Was April 20, 2001, written in God's book?*

A week later Jim Bowers said at his wife and daughter's funeral, "I want to thank my God. He's a sovereign God. I'm finding that out more now. Could this really be God's plan for Roni and Charity, God's plan for Cory and me and our family? Roni and Charity were instantly killed by the same bullet. Would you say that's a stray bullet? That was a sovereign bullet. . . ."

A sovereign bullet? Think about it. Jim Bowers went on to say that the people who shot the bullet were used by God to accomplish his purpose, comparing them to the Roman soldiers whom God used to put his Son on the cross (Acts 2:23). At first it can seem absurd to label what happened as anything other than a senseless tragedy. But Jim Bowers sees beyond the real culpability of those who fired weapons at their tiny plane and sees instead the sovereignty of God. His words reflect a ruthless trust in God.

Are you willing for your belief in God's sovereignty to permeate your thinking and captivate your heart, enabling you to write across the arrows that pierce your heart and the hurts that invade your life: *sovereign*?

Writer of all my days, it seems a dangerous prayer to invite your sovereignty to rule what is written every day of my life, but knowing how precious your thoughts are about me helps me to trust you and entrust my life to you fully.

DIGGING DEEPER

Read Job 2:10; Isaiah 45:6-7; and Lamentations 3:37-38. How does God use things we would label "good" for his sovereign purpose? What about the "bad" things?

CLAY IN THE POTTER'S HANDS

Lord, you are our Father. We are the clay, and you are the potter. We are all formed by your hand. —Isaiah 64:8

My mother-in-law used to live next door to a potter in Oregon. From the wheel and kiln in his garage, he turned ordinary lumps of clay into things of beauty. But some of his creations were flawed, and he offered them to Rita for next to nothing, several of which she passed along to us. I don't know exactly what went wrong with these pots to cause their imperfections. The potter was out to make a thing of beauty, a piece of art that reflected the design and desire of the artist. Perhaps the clay wasn't pliable enough to take the shape he had in mind, or perhaps a hidden flaw became more pronounced somewhere in the process.

Throughout Scripture, God uses the metaphor of a potter to show us his sovereignty. He sent the prophet Jeremiah to the house of a potter who skillfully shaped a piece of clay with his hands into a beautiful vessel. When another pot he was making was marred, the potter tossed it aside and began a new pot. God said, "O Israel, can I not do to you as this potter has done to his clay? As the clay is in the potter's hand, so are you in my hand" (Jeremiah 18:6).

You are in the hands of God right now, being shaped and formed just as a potter shapes clay. The difficulties you are facing bring you against the pressure of the Potter's wheel, and you are held there by the hand of the Potter. You can resist his shaping through rebellion or resentment. You can become offended with God and determined to shape your life into your image of what is worthwhile and beautiful. Or you can welcome the work of the Potter and allow him to shape your life.

Sometimes we just don't like what the Potter does, do we? "Why did God make me the way I am? Why isn't he using me in the place or position I desire?" So we have to ask ourselves, *Does God have the right to shape my life according to his own wise purpose, or not?* Though we are tempted to resist, we must answer yes!

Potter, I give you this lump of clay called my life. Use whatever pressure is needed to shape me into something of great worth in your sight, something of beauty in your estimation, something fit for displaying your glory!

DIGGING DEEPER

Read about the potter and clay in Jeremiah 18:1-6; Romans 9:16-24; and Revelation 2:26-27. Determine who is represented by the clay and the purpose for which the clay is being shaped.

NO ONE CAN STOP YOU

Job replied to the Lord: "I know that you can do anything, and no one can stop you. You ask, 'Who is this that questions my wisdom with such ignorance?' It is I. And I was talking about things I did not understand, things far too wonderful for me." —Job 42:1-3

A diving accident in 1967 left Joni Eareckson Tada a quadriplegic and introduced her to life in a wheelchair. "I had reasoned it was pure dumb luck that I went to the beach that day," she writes. "And it was my misfortune that I swam out to the raft. It was the law of averages that the tide just happened to be low." That's what she thought until she considered Job's story and saw that God is clearly in charge. "Satan conspires to use everything from the Sabeans to the Chaldeans, from freak storms to fire from the skies . . . but God is the one who ultimately grants the devil permission to harm Job."

Joni figured that if Satan and God were involved in her accident at all, then the devil must have twisted God's arm for permission and God hesitantly agreed. "Then I reasoned that once God granted permission, he nervously had to run behind the devil with a repair kit, patching up what Satan had ruined, mumbling to himself, 'Oh great, now how am I going to work?' Worse yet, I thought that when I became disabled I had missed God's best for me, and the Lord was then forced to go with some divine Plan B."

Do you think that Satan's clever schemes, someone's careless act of violence, or a crushing setback have thrown God's plan for your life off course, caught God off guard? Do you think you are forever relegated to living life in the disappointment of Plan B? Here is the truth: God's plan for your life is unfolding, and nothing and nobody can hinder it—not Satan, not your spouse or your ex-spouse, not your sickness. Whatever is happening in your life, you can welcome it as God's sovereign Plan A. God carries out his own good purposes without mistakes or regrets, and his plan is never thwarted.

Job waved a white flag of surrender, taking back his brash words and harsh questions about God's purposes for the pain in his life. Do you need to pull out your white flag and surrender to God's Plan A?

Lord, you can do anything and no one can stop you. I don't want to stop you from doing what you will for my life. I surrender to anything and everything that is your divine and surely wonderful Plan A for my life.

DIGGING DEEPER

Read Romans 8:29; Romans 15:6; and Ephesians 2:10. According to these verses, what do God's plans for you include?

LIVING WITH THE MYSTERY

Oh, what a wonderful God we have! How great are his riches and wisdom and knowledge! How impossible it is for us to understand his decisions and his methods! For who can know what the Lord is thinking? Who knows enough to be his counselor? For everything comes from him; everything exists by his power. —Romans 11:33-34, 36

I picked up the newspaper this morning and read a story about a boy in our city who was malnourished and chained in his home by his parents. And I can't help but ask, *God, why would you let this happen? What are you thinking?* As much as I've studied about suffering and as long as I've walked with God, there is still so much I don't understand. Frankly, I think that if someone tells you they can completely explain suffering and God's sovereignty, you should probably run in the opposite direction! How could any human ever expect to be able to explain the mind of God in these things?

There is a mystery to suffering and God's sovereignty that can be unsettling and ultimately be the undoing of our faith if we do not make peace with it. There is no explanation for what is or what happens that is more definitive than God. "Everything comes from him; everything exists by his power" (Romans 11:36). It's all his; we are his. So who are we to say that God owes us some answers? Who are we to bargain with God, indignantly demanding an explanation for the circumstances in our lives? Though we may not say it outright, our attitudes say to God, *I don't like the way you run the world; I think you should do things much differently!* Although Paul says we dare not act as if we are the Lord's counselor, we often do this very thing with boldness that borders on self-righteousness. We tell God how he should run the world, and we threaten him with our intentions to reject him if we deem his plan unfair or his performance unfit.

So I suppose the question we must ask is this: Are we willing to make ourselves at home with God in the midst of the mystery? Are we willing to obey and believe him and, most important, love him, even though we may never get all of our questions answered? Oh, my hurting friend, be slow to point your finger at God or to demand that he explain his unfathomable wisdom! Humble yourself and say with Paul, "What a wonderful God you are. How great is your wisdom!" (see Romans 11:33).

Wonderful God, I admit I do not know enough to presume to tell you how to run the world or even how to work in my life. The depths of your wisdom and knowledge are unfathomable to me, and I humble my heart before you.

DIGGING DEEPER

How can Deuteronomy 29:29; Isaiah 55:8-9; and Ephesians 1:9-11 help us accept the mysterious plans of God?

WEEK 10

SOVEREIGNTY OF GOD

REFLECTION

Looking back on your life, in what ways can you trace God's sovereign hand preparing you, shaping you, protecting you?

In what ways do you resist God's sovereignty in your life? In what ways do you welcome his sovereignty?

MEDITATION

The LORD Almighty has sworn this oath: "It will all happen as I have planned. It will come about according to my purposes. I have a plan for the whole earth, for my mighty power reaches throughout the world. The Lord Almighty has spoken—who can change his plans? When his hand moves, who can stop him?" —ISAIAH 14:24, 26-27

Place yourself in the presence of the Lord Almighty and read through these verses several times, listening to the thunder of his voice and the integrity of his oath as he makes these declarations.

Circle the words or phrases that are vivid to you.

Turn the verses into a prayer, welcoming God's plan, purposes, and power.

PRAYER

Praise God for his sovereign power over the universe, which gives us comfort and confidence in a cruel world.

Thank God for his love and his goodness, which help us to trust his sovereignty.

Intercede for a world that rejects the authority of God, for those who reject the reign of God in their hearts and lives.

Confess your reluctance to be shaped by God's hand and your questions about his ways and his work.

Welcome God to accomplish his Plan A in your life and to use it to shape you into a beautiful vessel of honor he can use for his purposes.

WEEK 11

PROTECTED BY GOD

It was a year or so after Hope died, and my assignment for my Bible study group was to read Psalm 91 and express how it had been true in our lives.

> *He will rescue you from every trap and protect you from the fatal plague. . . . He orders his angels to protect you. They will keep you from striking your foot on a stone. . . .*

And I just had to say, "I don't get how this is true. He did not rescue us from a fatal plague. He didn't keep us from striking our feet on a stone but, in fact, allowed much worse than that. It seems to me that God did not protect my family."

Do you ever read a passage like this in the Bible and think, *That's not true!* We believe the Bible is true, but sometimes, based on our experience and our understanding, we can't seem to reconcile it with our experience, with reality.

It is at these points we have to dig in, dig deeper, and seek to understand what God is really saying. And usually truths that are revealed out of frustration and questions mean the most to us. That has been true for me as I've sought to understand God's promises of protection. Perhaps it will be for you, too.

THIS WEEK'S PASSAGE FOR MEDITATION

Those who live in the shelter of the Most High will find rest in the shadow of the Almighty. This I declare of the L*ORD*: *He alone is my refuge, my place of safety; he is my God, and I am trusting him.*

For he will rescue you from every trap and protect you from the fatal plague.

He will shield you with his wings. He will shelter you with his feathers. His faithful promises are your armor and protection.

If you make the L*ORD your refuge, if you make the Most High your shelter, no evil will conquer you; no plague will come near your dwelling. For he orders his angels to protect you wherever you go. They will hold you with their hands to keep you from striking your foot on a stone.*

The L*ORD says, "I will rescue those who love me. I will protect those who trust in my name. When they call on me, I will answer; I will be with them in trouble. I will rescue them and honor them. I will satisfy them with a long life and give them my salvation."*

—PSALM 91:1-4, 9-12, 14-16

PROTECTION FOR YOUR SOUL

DON'T BE AFRAID OF THOSE WHO WANT TO KILL YOU. THEY CAN ONLY KILL YOUR BODY; THEY CANNOT TOUCH YOUR SOUL. FEAR ONLY GOD, WHO CAN DESTROY BOTH SOUL AND BODY IN HELL. —MATTHEW 10:28

Imagine the scene as Jesus prepared to send his disciples out in twos for ministry. Far from a pump-you-up pep talk to reassure them, he seemed to be preparing them for the worst. "When you are arrested, don't worry about what to say in your defense," he instructed. "Everyone will hate you because of your allegiance to me," he predicted (Matthew 10:19, 22). And then he encouraged them not to fear those who wanted to kill them. "They can only kill your body; they cannot touch your soul." *Gee,* I want to say in response, *they can* only *kill my body? And this should be a relief to me?*

Jesus seemed to be preparing them for the worst. And perhaps his words to his disciples have something important to say to you and me as his disciples today—especially as we seek to discover how to understand God's promises of protection. Because we want to know: Can we expect God to protect us?

His words to the disciples and to us reveal that God is much more interested in the life of our souls than the life of our bodies. Your body is going to die. Your soul is going to live forever. God cares more about your spiritual health than your physical health. And his ability to protect your soul from eternal judgment and eternal death is more significant than protection of your body from disease or attack or death. It doesn't always seem more significant to you and me, but it is. Trapped in these bodies and in this time, it is so hard for us to imagine our eternal future with him. And in our desperation amid difficulties, we try to apply his promises of protection for our souls to our bodies, and we're left disappointed. We will continue to be disappointed until our value system lines up with God's, until we value the eternal life of our souls more than the limited life of our bodies.

God has not promised wholesale deliverance in this life for those who place their faith in him. But what he has promised is protection of our souls for eternity—eternal safety and rest in the bosom of Christ.

My Soul Protector, I am beginning to understand that the protection you've promised for my soul is more significant than the preservation of my body. Help me to trust you with my body and my soul and to rest in your protection.

DIGGING DEEPER

Read Isaiah 55:1-7; Matthew 16:26; James 1:21; and 1 Peter 1:9. What do you learn about how God values our souls from these verses?

KEEP THEM SAFE FROM THE EVIL ONE

I'M NOT ASKING YOU TO TAKE THEM OUT OF THE WORLD, BUT TO KEEP THEM SAFE FROM THE EVIL ONE. MAKE THEM PURE AND HOLY BY TEACHING THEM YOUR WORDS OF TRUTH. I AM PRAYING NOT ONLY FOR THESE DISCIPLES BUT ALSO FOR ALL WHO WILL EVER BELIEVE IN ME BECAUSE OF THEIR TESTIMONY. —JOHN 17:15, 17, 20

When we read that Jesus not only prayed a prayer of protection for his disciples but also extended that prayer to all who will ever believe, we can't help but feel privileged and hopeful for the future. Surely God answers the prayers of Jesus with a resounding *Yes! Jesus prayed, "Holy Father, keep them and care for them . . . keep them safe from the evil one" (John 17:11, 15).*

As we listen in on the prayer of Jesus, we can assume that God heard Jesus' prayer and that Jesus always prayed in complete accordance with his Father's will. So we might expect that God's affirmative answer to his prayer would mean that the disciples never faced any harm, right? But we know that isn't what happened. History records that all but one of them were killed for their allegiance to Christ. Only John is said to have lived to old age, and he was severely persecuted for the sake of the gospel. Most of the disciples spent years in prison and were stoned, beheaded, or crucified. So how do we reconcile Jesus' prayer of protection for the disciples with the reality that nearly every one of them died a martyr's death? Is that how God protects those he loves?

Jesus asked his Father to protect the disciples and us from the evil one because he knows that the devil wants to destroy us. In fact, according to 1 Peter 5:8, Satan "prowls around like a roaring lion, looking for some victim to devour." And how does he devour us? Satan, out of his desire to destroy us, brings suffering into our lives in an effort to destroy our faith. Satan wants to alienate you from God and claim you for eternity. But Jesus has prayed for you, asking his Father to protect you from the evil one, and you are not at Satan's mercy. God has answered the prayer of Jesus with a resounding *Yes!* and you are safe from the damning power of the evil one. Satan may win a battle or two in your life, but he will never win the war against your soul. Jesus has prayed for you, and you are protected.

My Protector from evil, how I need you to keep me safe from the evil one who wants to destroy me. Cover me with your strong arms and fill me with your Spirit so I never need to fear Satan's power in my life.

DIGGING DEEPER

Read Genesis 3:14-15; Matthew 25:41; Romans 16:20; and Revelation 20:1-3, 7-10. What do these verses tell you about Satan's ultimate destiny?

KEEP YOU FROM STUMBLING

All glory to God, who is able to keep you from stumbling, and who will bring you into his glorious presence innocent of sin and with great joy.
—Jude 1:24

Watching a montage of highlights from the recent Olympic Games, I couldn't help but identify with some of the competitors in their thrill of victory as well as the agony of their defeat. The feature showed a hurdler who was favored to win but stumbled on the last hurdle, ruining his chances for a medal. We know what it is like to stumble, don't we? Maybe not in the Olympics, but in life. "Little" sins trip us up, and sometimes we fall flat on our faces with enormous failure. Does this mean we are disqualified from the race of faith? Is it over for you if you have failed or fallen?

Perhaps it would be if it were up to you to get yourself across the finish line. But it is not your personal prowess that will keep you from stumbling; it is God's power. "The steps of the godly are directed by the Lord. He delights in every detail of their lives. Though they stumble, they will not fall, for the Lord holds them by the hand" (Psalm 37:23-24).

Not only is God able to keep you from stumbling and falling away, he is able to present you faultless before God, innocent of sin. We know we are not innocent, so we need a miracle of grace to become innocent, and that is part of the protection package God offers to us sinners. When Jesus thinks about the day when he will bring you into God's glorious presence innocent of sin, he can hardly keep the smile off his face. It will not be a solemn occasion; it will be a celebration, filled with great joy.

Do you wonder if you've failed so significantly or fallen so far that you have been disqualified from the race of faith? Has the pain of your fall left you feeling vulnerable to doubts and discouragement, and do you wonder if your drifting away from God will take you away from him forever? If you are in Christ, you are as likely to stumble and fall away as Christ is. And we know that is impossible. God is able to keep you from stumbling. He will protect you and present you faultless, and when he does, it will be a day of great joy.

My Champion, if I'm on my own in this walk of faith, I will never make it. So protect me from anything that would cause me to stumble and fall. Hold me by the hand and bring me home.

DIGGING DEEPER

Read Proverbs 4:11-13; John 12:35-36; 1 Peter 2:8-9; and 2 Peter 1:10. What causes people to stumble, and what keeps them on the right path?

PROTECTION FROM YOUR ENEMIES

You are my strength; I wait for you to rescue me, for you, O God, are my place of safety. In his unfailing love, my God will come and help me. He will let me look down in triumph on all my enemies. —Psalm 59:9-10

I have often been confused when I read the Old Testament talk of enemies, especially in the Psalms. Some of the things the biblical writers ask God to do to their enemies, I wouldn't wish on anyone! To make sense of this, it has helped me to understand that the children of Israel and their God-appointed leaders were God's chosen people. Friends of Israel were friends of God. Enemies of Israel were enemies of God. Through the story of his dealing with his people, God is showing us his power and his will to protect us, his children, from enemies that would seek to do us harm.

God's enemies are those who love themselves more than God, those who reject and refuse the gift of God in his Son, Jesus. So as we seek to understand and apply God's promises of protection from our enemies, the challenge is to figure out: Who are our enemies?

When we think about enemies, we think about bosses who seem out to get us, former spouses who want to ruin us, rivals who want to defeat us, and people who have hurt us. We think of those with ideologies opposed to ours and agendas at cross-purposes with ours. In our self-centered worlds, we are much more concerned about having God on our side to protect our own interests and reputation than we are about being on God's side, seeking after his glory and ultimate victory.

The reality is this: God has not promised to protect you from everyone you would define as your enemy in this limited life. But he has promised you victory over the enemy of unbelief. And he has promised you protection from your ultimate enemy—sin—which no longer has the power to enslave you or determine your eternal destiny. You can entrust yourself to this just, strong God, who will protect you from any and every enemy who would seek to alienate you from God. Run to him who alone is your place of safety.

My Strength, I am weary from the battles of life, and I am vulnerable to attack. Often I see that my own flesh is my worst enemy. Will you show yourself strong in my life and protect me from the enemy who wants to destroy me?

DIGGING DEEPER

Who are God's enemies according to Romans 5:6-11, and what has God done for them? How are we to deal with our enemies according to the following verses: Proverbs 24:17-18; Matthew 5:25; Luke 6:27-36; and Romans 12:20?

PROTECTION FROM WRATH

God has every right to exercise his judgment and his power, but he also has the right to be very patient with those who are the objects of his judgment and are fit only for destruction. He also has the right to pour out the riches of his glory upon those he prepared to be the objects of his mercy.
—Romans 9:22-23

Certainly one of the most politically incorrect words in the English language today is *judgment*. And to say that God will judge sin is considered an old-fashioned, out-of-date scare tactic. But if we are going to believe what the Bible teaches, then we have to affirm that judgment for sin is certain and will be terrifying for those not protected from it.

Paul tells us in Romans, "There is going to come a day of judgment when God, the just judge of all the world, will judge all people according to what they have done. . . . He will pour out his anger and wrath on those who live for themselves, who refuse to obey the truth and practice evil deeds" (2:5-6, 8). One day, the wrath of God against sin is going to be poured out on the earth. In Noah's day, that wrath was poured out in an obliterating flood. A day is coming when "he will come with his mighty angels, in flaming fire, bringing judgment on those who don't know God and on those who refuse to obey the Good News of our Lord Jesus" (2 Thessalonians 1:7-8). But when fire rains down on the earth, those who are in Christ will be protected from the wrath of God by the protective gift of God—Jesus.

My husband is Mr. Johnny-on-the-spot when it comes to having an umbrella. He has one stashed in each car and never fails to have one handy to protect us from the elements. But I'm far too careless and casual. I never seem to have an umbrella when I need it because I rarely want to go to the trouble of lugging one along. I figure I'll take my chances and make a run for it. But this has made for more than one significant bad hair day.

I suppose that is the attitude many people take toward judgment. They are willing to take their chances, hoping to make a run for it when the wrath of God begins to fall, unwilling to go to the "trouble" of accepting God's offer of protection from wrath in the person and work of Jesus. Jesus is your umbrella that will protect you from the wrath of God, but only because there was no umbrella to protect him. As Jesus hung on the cross, he absorbed the wrath of God in our place to protect us from that wrath. "Since we have been made right in God's sight by the blood of Christ, he will certainly save us from God's judgment" (Romans 5:9).

My Protection from wrath, I thank you for pouring out on me the riches of your glory, the fullness of your mercy, not because I deserve it, but because of your patience with me and your love for me.

DIGGING DEEPER

What does 1 Thessalonians 5:4-9 teach us about what God has supplied to protect us and his purpose in protecting us?

WEEK 11

PROTECTED BY GOD

REFLECTION

We have learned that God is more concerned with our souls, which will live forever, than our bodies, which will one day die. How can that knowledge transform your perspective on your current circumstances?

As your understanding grows of God's promises to protect you from the ultimate harm of experiencing his wrath, do you find yourself more fearful or more confident as you face the future? Why?

MEDITATION

Those who live in the shelter of the Most High will find rest in the shadow of the Almighty. This I declare of the LORD: He alone is my refuge, my place of safety; he is my God, and I am trusting him.

For he will rescue you from every trap and protect you from the fatal plague.

He will shield you with his wings. He will shelter you with his feathers. His faithful promises are your armor and protection.

If you make the LORD your refuge, if you make the Most High your shelter, no evil will conquer you; no plague will come near your dwelling. For he orders his angels to protect you wherever you go. They will hold you with their hands to keep you from striking your foot on a stone.

The LORD says, "I will rescue those who love me. I will protect those who trust in my name. When they call on me, I will answer; I will be with them in trouble. I will rescue them and honor them. I will satisfy them with a long life and give them my salvation."

—PSALM 91:1-4, 9-12, 14-16

As you read through this psalm several times and hear the promises of God, let them sink into your heart and soul. Pour out your disappointment to God for the ways in which it seems he has not protected you, and listen for him to respond to your honest questions. Sense his ultimate protection surrounding you, and respond to that reality with praise and thanksgiving.

PRAYER

Praise God for his justice through which he will pour out his wrath.

Thank God for protection from that wrath through the covering of Jesus.

Intercede for enemies of God who refuse his love and protection.

Confess your misappropriation of God's promises of protection and any resentment toward God it may have created.

Petition God to protect you and all who believe from the enemy of God.

WEEK 12

MIRACLES

Whenever the topic of miracles comes up, I must admit I get a little uncomfortable. If I'm honest (and if we define a miracle as a supernatural event that defies the laws of nature), I would have to say that I have not seen many miracles with my own eyes.

I really do believe that God is a God of miracles. I read about them in the Bible, and I don't think they are just devices of literature. The first miracle I believe is found in Genesis 1:1, which tells us that out of nothing, just by the power of his word, God made the heavens and the earth. I believe God parted the Red Sea and sent manna from heaven and closed the mouths of the lions. All of these miracles reveal the power of God and his provision for his people.

And I believe God is still working miracles today; I've heard about them in stories from believers around the world. But in my own life, I've never seen the kind of miracles where people who were physically blind are given sight, where people who have died actually come back to life. It's not that I'm a skeptic of those who claim such miracles today. Okay, maybe I am a bit of a skeptic.

So when I read the Gospels and story after story of the miracles of Jesus, I am left wondering what to do with them. Why did Jesus choose to work a miracle in one setting but not another, for one person but not someone else? I guess deep down I need to understand the purpose and process of his miracles, because I need to know if I can expect him to work a miracle in my life today. Perhaps you do too.

THIS WEEK'S PASSAGE FOR MEDITATION

Jesus' disciples saw him do many other miraculous signs besides the ones recorded in this book. But these are written so that you may believe that Jesus is the Messiah, the Son of God, and that by believing in him you will have life. —John 20:30-31

I NEED A MIRACLE!

There was a woman in the crowd who had had a hemorrhage for twelve years. She had heard about Jesus, so she came up behind him through the crowd and touched the fringe of his robe. Immediately the bleeding stopped, and she could feel that she had been healed! —Mark 5:25, 27, 29

I had never committed to a weekly Bible study because, to be honest, I thought I knew enough about the Bible. Besides, I was far too busy doing "important" things for God. But some health problems and the loneliness of a move made me desperate. So one Wednesday morning I visited a local Bible study class. Little did I know that God would change my life that day.

The lecturer, Sue, was teaching on Matthew 8–9, which includes a series of miracles Jesus performed. She described the woman who had hemorrhaged for twelve years and drew a picture of her as a desperate, destitute outcast, suffering alone and unknown. The life was literally draining out of her. And in her desperation, she reached out to Jesus. With a clasp of faith, she immediately felt her hemorrhage stop. Sue looked up and asked, "Do you feel like the life is draining out of you? Are you desperate for a miracle?" And it was all I could do to keep from raising my hand, because I knew I needed nothing less than a miracle.

Though I grew up in church, worked in Christian publishing, and was a leader at church, my greatest fear was that someone might ask me, "What is God doing in your life right now?" I knew I would have nothing to say. I rarely read my Bible and it had been so long since I prayed, I didn't know where to start. I was embarrassed to start and afraid to fail . . . again. With a heart dulled by years of unresponsiveness, I knew I needed more than a new system or setting; I needed *a miracle* to come alive spiritually, to experience real change. And as I reached out to Jesus in desperate faith that day and in the weeks and months that followed, his power flowed into me, his Word began to change me, his Spirit began to transform me.

Can you relate? Is the life draining out of you, leaving you spiritually limp and dull? Will you reach out to Jesus in your desperation so that he might give you nothing less than a life-giving miracle?

Life Giver, I see myself in the stained robes of this woman. I am broken and desperate for a miracle of life that only you can give. Weary from my failures of the past, I reach out to you in faith once more.

DIGGING DEEPER

Read the story in Mark 5:24-34. What do you learn about the faith of the woman and the power of Jesus?

THE SECRET SHARED WITH SERVANTS

Jesus told the servants, "Fill the jars with water." When the jars had been filled to the brim, he said, "Dip some out and take it to the master of ceremonies." So they followed his instructions. The master of ceremonies tasted the water that was now wine, not knowing where it had come from (though, of course, the servants knew). —John 2:7-9

Most of the miracles Jesus performed were in response to a specific person's request. But when I read about him turning water into wine at the wedding in Cana, I'm left wondering, *Who was this miracle for?* Was it for the bride and bridegroom, who were likely Jesus' relatives? There's no evidence they were ever aware of a wine shortage. Was it for the mother of Jesus, who put pressure on him to *do something*, not wanting her hosts to suffer embarrassment? Mary had waited thirty years for Jesus to publicly demonstrate his authority and power.

Could it have been for the servants? They must have wondered at Jesus' instructions to fill the huge, heavy pots that had everything to do with the rigorous legalism of hand washing and nothing to do with wine making. What good was that going to do? But if they questioned his instructions, they didn't hesitate to obey, filling the jars "to the brim" in overflowing obedience.

And what did they get in return? Jesus shared a secret with them—a secret he was not yet ready to share with the party or with the world—the secret of his power to transform what is ordinary into something extravagantly useful to God. That is a secret I want Jesus to share with me, too. Because I am filled with common concerns, empty promises, unanswered questions, and meaningless religious ritual. Because I need an infusion of life and joy and meaning. And I know only Jesus can transform the ordinary water of my days into something brimming with life.

I'm not sure who this miracle was for, but maybe it was for you and me so it would have the same effect on us that it had on Jesus' disciples that day. "This miraculous sign at Cana in Galilee was Jesus' first display of his glory. And his disciples believed in him" (John 2:11). Have you run out of joy, run out of reasons to celebrate life? Offer him your humble obedience and ordinary self, and not only will he share his secrets with you, he will also gloriously transform you.

Transforming Power, I've run out of joy. So I come to you, willing to do whatever you tell me to do, wanting to drink in the joyous, full life only you can provide. Show me your miraculous power.

DIGGING DEEPER

Read the story in John 2:1-11, noting how different people exhibited faith.

IF YOU WANT TO

A MAN WITH LEPROSY APPROACHED JESUS. HE KNELT BEFORE HIM, WORSHIPING. "LORD," THE MAN SAID, "IF YOU WANT TO, YOU CAN MAKE ME WELL AGAIN." JESUS TOUCHED HIM. "I WANT TO," HE SAID. "BE HEALED!" AND INSTANTLY THE LEPROSY DISAPPEARED. —MATTHEW 8:2-3

I still get a lump in my throat when I read this verse. I remember coming upon it after Hope died. In my sadness, I read this verse and heard Jesus saying to the leper, "I want to." But I also heard its echo in my ears—Jesus saying to me, "I did not want to," and my pain increased. It hurt my feelings as I pictured Jesus refusing me the miracle of giving me a whole Hope.

But even as the words echoed in my head and brought tears to my eyes, I knew something was wrong with that picture. It didn't fit with the Jesus I was discovering in the Gospels. I knew something was wrong with my understanding of this story, so I had to struggle with it until I understood.

I began to examine all the miracles of Jesus' ministry. John especially helped me as he clearly explained the reason that Jesus performed healing miracles: "Jesus' disciples saw him do many other miraculous signs besides the ones recorded in this book. But these are written *so that you may believe that Jesus is the Messiah*, the Son of God, and that by believing in him *you will have life*" (John 20:30-31, emphasis added). I began to see that, while the miracles Jesus performed revealed his love and compassion for hurting people, the greater purpose of each miracle was to show us a picture of a deeper spiritual reality, a greater and more significant spiritual power. And our need for spiritual healing is more significant than our need for physical healing; we just don't realize it.

In Old Testament times God used leprosy to illustrate the spiritual sickness of sin. In reaching out to heal the leper Jesus says, "I can heal you of the most destructive, deadly disease in your life—the disease of sin." You and I have a disease much more deadly than leprosy or Zellweger Syndrome. While Zellweger can kill a person's body, sin can kill the soul. So we come to him with our deadly disease of sin and say, "Lord, if you want to, you can make me well." He turns no one away but looks at us lovingly and says, "I am willing."

Sin Destroyer, I hear you saying, "I want to" to my request for healing my sin-sick soul. Help me to value your power to give life to my soul more than I value your ability to give life to my body.

DIGGING DEEPER

What does John 6:28-40 tell us about what God wants us to do and what Jesus wants to do?

NO NEED TOO GREAT FOR GOD

"THERE'S A YOUNG BOY HERE WITH FIVE BARLEY LOAVES AND TWO FISH. BUT WHAT GOOD IS THAT WITH THIS HUGE CROWD?" THEN JESUS TOOK THE LOAVES, GAVE THANKS TO GOD, AND PASSED THEM OUT TO THE PEOPLE. AFTERWARD HE DID THE SAME WITH THE FISH. AND THEY ALL ATE UNTIL THEY WERE FULL. —JOHN 6:9, 11

Sometimes it seems as if the hurt in a relationship is too deep, the damage to a reputation too pervasive, the need for resources too great for hope to make any sense. Rarely would we dare to say out loud, "This problem is too big, even for God," but if we're honest, we can't help but feel that way at times.

Jesus must have known Philip was thinking that way when he asked Philip where they could buy bread to feed the huge crowd that followed them. "It would take a small fortune to feed them!" Philip answered (John 6:7). He had done the math and it just didn't add up. But Philip left Jesus out of the equation. And Jesus wanted to teach Philip that there is no need so great that he cannot meet it. In fact, Jesus had already determined how he would feed the hungry people, drawing on compassion the disciples could not comprehend and resources they knew nothing of. He multiplied the gift offered by a boy in the crowd, and everyone ate until they were satisfied. Jesus often uses what others offer to meet the needs of those he loves, and by his grace and power he multiplies it in the process.

You may have a problem that is too big for you, but it is not too big for God. He says, "I am the LORD, the God of all the peoples of the world. Is anything too hard for me?" (Jeremiah 32:27). Though your situation may seem impossible, Jesus has resources you know nothing about and compassion you cannot comprehend.

Not only is there no need too great for God to meet it, there is no hunger so deep he cannot satisfy it. The people he fed were hungry the next day. But when we come to Jesus fully aware of our desperate need and fully convinced of his ability and willingness to meet our need, he satisfies and sustains. The Bread of Life that Jesus wants to give you is the only thing that will satisfy your soul. When we eat this life-sustaining Bread, like the people on the hillside that day, we are fully satisfied.

Great Multiplier, the need I have for a miracle seems too big, even for you. But I see your compassion, your power, and your sufficiency, and I believe you will supply all my needs as I depend on you for life itself.

DIGGING DEEPER

Read Matthew 19:23-26; Luke 1:34-37; and Hebrews 11:6. According to these passages, what is possible and impossible with God?

WHAT CAN YOU DO FOR ME TODAY, GOD?

BECAUSE OF THE MIRACULOUS SIGNS HE DID IN JERUSALEM AT THE PASSOVER CELEBRATION, MANY PEOPLE WERE CONVINCED THAT HE WAS INDEED THE MESSIAH. BUT JESUS DIDN'T TRUST THEM, BECAUSE HE KNEW WHAT PEOPLE WERE REALLY LIKE. NO ONE NEEDED TO TELL HIM ABOUT HUMAN NATURE. —JOHN 2:23-25

A friend of mine has a wealthy uncle who never married and has no children. She takes care of him, includes him in family events, and helps him with his needs. I know she does it out of love for him, but I wonder if he is as confident of her motives. Surely he can't help but wonder if she would care for him as attentively if there were nothing for her in his will. It would be only natural, because we know about human nature, don't we? We know our human nature expects something in return for what we give.

Jesus understood human nature too. From the beginning of his ministry he recognized that while many people were willing to believe he was the Messiah, their willingness to believe had more to do with what he could do *for* them than what he wanted to do *in* them. After Jesus fed the five thousand, huge numbers of people began to follow him proclaiming him as Messiah. Jesus bluntly told them, "The truth is, you want to be with me because I fed you, not because you saw the miraculous sign. But you shouldn't be so concerned about perishable things like food. Spend your energy seeking the eternal life that I, the Son of Man, can give you" (John 6:26-27).

Jesus was looking for genuine conversion and not just enthusiasm for the spectacular. Genuine faith is not defined by enthusiastic outbursts, intellectual assent, or even religious-sounding rhetoric, but by wholehearted commitment. It is a response of the mind, heart, and will to the character and nature of Jesus, apart from his miracle-working power. Genuine faith says, "I don't just want what you've got, I want *you*! I don't need a miracle; I have Jesus!"

We might be able to fool others and even ourselves, but we can't fool God. He sees our hearts in reality. When he looks at your heart, does he see the heart of a consumer, not wanting him, just wanting what he's got? Or does he see a heart abandoned to loving him, a heart surrendered to his purpose?

Heart Seer, you know I'm often more interested in what you have to offer me than offering myself to you. Thank you for giving me a new nature that overcomes my human nature so I can love you wholeheartedly.

DIGGING DEEPER

How does God entrust himself to believers today, as evidenced in Romans 8:9; Ephesians 1:13-14; and 1 John 4:11-13?

WEEK 12

MIRACLES

MEDITATION

Jesus' disciples saw him do many other miraculous signs besides the ones recorded in this book. But these are written so that you may believe that Jesus is the Messiah, the Son of God, and that by believing in him you will have life. —JOHN 20:30-31

John included seven miraculous signs in his Gospel. Each has a message that helps us believe God and experience life. Reflect on the meaning or message of the miracles John recorded. How has Jesus worked miracles with similar results in your life? Which ones do you need him to work in your life?

Jesus turned water into wine at the wedding in Cana—

Jesus fills ordinary lives with extraordinary joy.

Jesus healed the son of the Roman officer—

Jesus moves us from using God to believing God.

Jesus healed the lame man—

Jesus offers wholeness to those who will walk in faith.

Jesus fed the five thousand—

Jesus satisfies our deepest desires with himself.

Jesus calmed the storm—

Jesus speaks peace into our desperation and despair.

Jesus healed the man blind from birth—

Jesus is the Light that illumines the darkness of our lives.

Jesus raised Lazarus from the dead—

Jesus brings to life by the power of his Word that which was dead.

PRAYER

Pray through each of these miraculous signs, praising God for his power to work these miracles. Thank him for the miracles he has accomplished in your life and confess your doubt, unbelief, and disobedience that keep him from working. Ask him to work a miracle in your life today.

WEEK 13

HEALER OF MY SOUL

I can't help but write about healing miracles this week because I am in the market for one. As I write, my friend is in his last-ditch effort surgery. All other medical options have been explored.

Lord, I see your miracles of transformation, provision, and healing throughout the Gospels. I see that you heal diseases, you exercise power over natural forces and demonic power, and you restore sight and speech and even life itself. I have no doubt about your power or ability. But I wonder about your will. Will it be your will to exercise your miraculous healing power in my friend today and in the days to come so that his wife will have her husband, his children will have their dad?

As the Author and Sustainer of life itself, you are the ultimate source of healing every time my body has been restored. And I've seen you heal before. I've seen relationships that were over, rekindled. I've seen people who were broken by life seemingly beyond repair, restored. I've seen bodies riddled with disease revived.

But I have also seen relationships fail, people falter, and health fade. I know that you do not always choose to give us the healing we desire. There is a mystery to your miracles we want to understand. Would you help us to understand what your healing is all about? Would you show us what it means to look to you in faith?

THIS WEEK'S PASSAGE FOR MEDITATION

Praise the LORD, I tell myself;
with my whole heart, I will praise his holy name.
Praise the LORD, I tell myself,
and never forget the good things he does for me.
He forgives all my sins and heals all my diseases.
He ransoms me from death and surrounds me with love and tender mercies.
He fills my life with good things. My youth is renewed like the eagle's!

—PSALM 103:1-5

JESUS, OUR COMPASSIONATE HEALER

Wherever he went, he healed people of every sort of disease and illness. He felt great pity for the crowds that came, because their problems were so great and they didn't know where to go for help. —Matthew 9:35-36

What a beautiful picture of Jesus, and what a comfort it is to know that he is moved with compassion as he looks upon people with great problems, people who need healing—people like you and me who don't know where to go for relief of their pain. Out of his compassion, he reaches out to heal them. Jesus, the exact representation of God, shows us what our Jehovah-rophi (the Lord who Heals) looks like and how he responds to hurting people. Healing is not an activity God may choose to do or choose not to do. Healing is who he is; it is his very nature, reflected in his name.

God wants to heal you. He wants to bring you to the complete wholeness he created you for, and he has already begun to do so. It is a work he began at the Cross and will complete when he comes again. He has atoned for sin, which is the deepest, most destructive hurt in your life. He has destroyed its power to rule your life and determine your destiny. But Jesus did not die on the cross simply to save your physical body. He died to save your eternal soul, the essence of who you are. His purpose in your life is not to give you a certain number of days on this earth, but to fit you—body and soul—for an eternity with him.

Some use the Scripture to say that God has promised to heal your body if you pray a certain way or with a certain person. But God has not promised you a long life in this body on this earth. He has promised you a perfected body in a perfect place for an eternity. Would you be willing to stop holding on to this life with such vigor so you can open your hands and heart to welcome the ultimate healing God has promised you?

Do you need the gentle touch of the Healer today? Are you longing to see a relationship restored, a disappointment soothed, a lingering ache relieved? Come to Jesus, who is moved by the pain in your life. Lay it before him and ask him to touch you with his hand of healing.

Gentle Healer, how we need your touch to sooth our ailing bodies, our aching hearts, our troubled minds, and our weary souls. Have compassion on us in our pain, and reach out to us as we reach out for you.

DIGGING DEEPER

Read Matthew 8:1-3; Mark 8:22-25; 10:16; and John 13:3-5; 20:24-28. How did Jesus touch others with compassion according to these verses?

WHAT ARE YOUR MIRACLES ALL ABOUT?

JESUS TOLD THEM, "GO BACK TO JOHN AND TELL HIM ABOUT WHAT YOU HAVE HEARD AND SEEN—THE BLIND SEE, THE LAME WALK, THE LEPERS ARE CURED, THE DEAF HEAR, THE DEAD ARE RAISED TO LIFE, AND THE GOOD NEWS IS BEING PREACHED TO THE POOR." —MATTHEW 11:4-5

I'm relieved that I am in good company when it comes to wondering about the miracles of Jesus. John the Baptist, whom Jesus described as the greatest prophet ever born (see Matthew 11:11), heard what Jesus was doing and sent his disciples to ask, "Are you really the Messiah we've been waiting for, or should we keep looking for someone else?" (Matthew 11:3). John was not wavering in his faith; he was questioning Jesus' agenda. He had expected fire and judgment from the promised Messiah. But instead of judging the house of God, Jesus was far from Jerusalem carrying on a ministry of healing. John came to Jesus with the same question I have: "What is your healing ministry all about?"

Jesus sent John's disciples back as eyewitnesses, instructing them to report to John the Baptist all of the healing miracles they had seen Jesus perform. Why would Jesus answer that way? Jesus knew that John would remember Isaiah's prophecy concerning the Messiah: "And when he comes, he will open the eyes of the blind and unstop the ears of the deaf. The lame will leap like a deer, and those who cannot speak will shout and sing!" (Isaiah 35:5-6).

If we want to understand the nature and purpose of the miracles Jesus performed, we have to hear Jesus' implied message: "I am the one you've been waiting for. I am the one who was promised long ago. I AM." Some say the healing miracles of Jesus are evidence that we can call upon and count on the almighty and all-loving Jesus to touch our bodies and heal our diseases here and now—that God *always* wants to heal our bodies. And I think Jesus might say, "You've missed the point! You're so concerned about getting what you want from me, you've missed *me*."

Do you wonder, like John, what his miracles are all about? Jesus invites you to look closely at his miracles and see who he really is, the gift of God-in-the-flesh who has only just begun fulfilling all his promises to you. Embrace the fullness of who Jesus is—the ultimate answer to your deepest needs.

Promised Messiah, your miracles speak to me of your ability to fulfill your promises and accomplish your purpose in the world. I believe you will also fulfill your purposes in me and promises to me of an eternal future with you.

DIGGING DEEPER

What do the following verses say about the purpose of the miracles of Jesus: John 5:36; 14:11; 20:30-31; and Acts 2:22?

IF IT BE YOUR WILL

How do you know what will happen tomorrow? For your life is like the morning fog—it's here a little while, then it's gone. What you ought to say is, "If the Lord wants us to, we will live and do this or that." —James 4:14-15

When Hope was a month old, the secretary from church called to tell me we were on the church prayer list, that they were asking people to pray that God would work a miracle and heal Hope. I told her, "That is not how we feel led to pray." We didn't ask God for that. It didn't seem right. Or maybe we were afraid to pray that, to expect that, when the diagnosis seemed so sure and so grim. What we did know was that a great deal of damage had already been done to every major organ of her body.

Perhaps because Hope's illness seemed so invisible and mysterious, it was hard for many people around us to understand why we did not cry out to heaven for healing. Because let's face it, in the church, when someone is sick or dying, praying for God to heal is just what we do, isn't it? It was hard for us that some people saw our reluctance to pray in this way as a lack of faith. But it had nothing to do with whether or not God had the power to heal Hope. We firmly believe that God can do anything. For us, it was more a matter of asking ourselves if this was the way we have seen God work. And more important, was it what he had planned for Hope? Did God have in mind for her a short but meaningful life, and would we be open to that as his best?

Often I see the body of Christ put so much into pursuing God for physical healing. With great boldness and passion and persistence, we cry out to God, begging for healing of the body. And in these prayers, there is often a tiny P.S. added at the end where we say, "If it be your will." But shouldn't we switch that around? Shouldn't we cry out to God with boldness and passion and persistence in a prayer that says, "God, would you please accomplish your will? Would you give me a willing heart to embrace *your* plan and *your* purpose? Would you mold me into an instrument that you can use to accomplish what you have in mind?" And then, perhaps, we could add a tiny P.S. that says, "If that includes healing, we will be grateful."

Great Healer, so often I run ahead of you, insistent that I know what is best and what you would want for my life. Teach me to trust in your love for me and your great wisdom so I will want your will for my life, no matter what.

DIGGING DEEPER

Read Matthew 6:10 and 26:36-42. How does Jesus model for us wanting God's will more than anything else?

WE NEED MORE FAITH

One day the apostles said to the Lord, "We need more faith; tell us how to get it." "Even if you had faith as small as a mustard seed," the Lord answered, "you could say to this mulberry tree, 'May God uproot you and throw you into the sea,' and it would obey you!" —Luke 17:6

When I met Diane years ago, she was bright and energetic, but her wig gave away the battle she was fighting—an all-out fight against breast cancer. We asked God to work a miracle in her life and in her body and restore her to health. In her desperation, Diane also drew close to another group of people who encouraged her to surround herself only with people who believed that she was going to be healed. She began to turn away from many of us who wanted to walk with her on this difficult road. If you didn't believe absolutely that she was going to be healed, you were not welcome.

I suppose I understand where some of this comes from. She wanted to surround herself in an atmosphere of faith. But sometimes I wondered, *faith in what*? Faith in God, or faith in faith? Submission to God or insisting on a particular outcome? Sometimes it seems as if people think they feel they must prove to God that they have enough faith and no doubt—that God not only *can* but *will* heal them—in order for God to grant their request for healing.

Does God really set up those kinds of hoops for us to jump through? And in terms of faith, how much is enough? How do you measure it? And how do you get the mountain-moving, mulberry tree–uprooting, demon-removing kind? Rather than giving the disciples a formula for increasing their faith, Jesus told them that it isn't the amount of faith that matters, but the object of faith. In fact, the *only* thing that matters about your faith is its object.

If the object of your faith is your ability to work up enough to impress God, your faith will be as weak as your flesh. If the object of your faith is a particular outcome for your situation, your faith will be as weak as your wisdom. But if the source and object of your faith is Almighty God, even if it is the weak, mustard-seed variety, your faith will be enough for whatever God allows into your life.

Source and Object of my faith, you have given me the gift of faith. I trust you with my life and my death and with the lives and deaths of those I love, knowing you can move mountains of difficulty as I place my faith in you.

DIGGING DEEPER

What do Romans 10:17 and 12:3 tell us about faith and where we can find it?

EYES OPENED

As Jesus was walking along, he saw a man who had been blind from birth. "Teacher," his disciples asked him, "why was this man born blind? Was it a result of his own sins or those of his parents?" "It was not because of his sins or his parents' sins," Jesus answered. "He was born blind so the power of God could be seen in him." —John 9:1-3

My friend Bill Davis, a retired spine surgeon, spends every morning coordinating the phone usage at a downtown homeless shelter. He told me that the people there will rarely look him in the eye because they've learned that people do not want to look them in the eye. This is one of the most painful aspects of being homeless—to be treated as less than a person. They tell of the humiliation of begging and of being avoided at all costs. And most of us would admit that we, too, turn away, hoping to avoid their listless gaze so we don't have to enter into their pain.

Far from avoiding him, John 9 tells us that Jesus *saw* the homeless beggar who had been blind from birth. He saw the man's lifelong suffering and loneliness and felt compassion as he considered the darkness that defined his existence. Jesus recognized not only this man's need to see the world around him, but also his more desperate need to see the Truth.

The disciples looked at the blind man, but they were simply interested in him as an object of theological argument. Jews of the day believed that all personal suffering was the result of personal sin or the sin of one's parents, and some Jewish theologians even taught that a person could sin before birth. But the disciples missed the point just as they looked past the blind man's pain. The issue was not how this man became blind. The issue was his need for Jesus. The disciples wanted to look back and debate the cause of his blindness. Jesus told them to look ahead and delight in the miracle of sight he was about to bestow.

When you look at this blind man, what do you see? If you look closely you may see yourself. We are all born blind, unable to see the things of God until we are touched by the Spirit of Jesus. Only the Spirit can make spiritually blind people see. The Spirit enables us to see beyond our suffering to the glory of God. He transforms us from beggars to believers. Do you find yourself stumbling in the darkness? Jesus sees you, and he reaches out to touch you so you can see how he is working, even now, in your life.

Sight Giver, when you look at me, do you see my desperate need? Reach out and touch me and give me the sight to see you for who you are and the willingness to submit to what you are doing in and through my life.

DIGGING DEEPER

Read John 9:1-41 and note the progression toward spiritual sight and understanding of who Jesus is in verses 11, 17, 33, and 38.

WEEK 13

HEALER OF MY SOUL

REFLECTION

The healing miracles of Jesus reveal God's character of loving compassion toward humanity. In addition, each healing miracle pointed to Jesus' ability to heal a deeper spiritual reality:

Leprosy illustrates the pervasive and fatal nature of sin.

Blindness represents spiritual ignorance.

Deafness represents lack of desire to listen and respond to God.

Demon possession depicts dominating sin.

Paralysis represents permeating, incapacitating sin.

Bleeding typifies waste of spiritual power and life through inward sin.

Dumbness illustrates an inability or refusal to speak for God.

Palsy illustrates spiritual powerlessness.

Fever illustrates the restlessness that sin creates in a person.

Death illustrates spiritual death, an inability to respond to God.

What spiritual sickness do you need healing from through the touch of Jesus in your life?

MEDITATION

Praise the LORD, I tell myself;
with my whole heart, I will praise his holy name.
Praise the LORD, I tell myself,
and never forget the good things he does for me.
He forgives all my sins and heals all my diseases.
He ransoms me from death and surrounds me with love and tender mercies.
He fills my life with good things. My youth is renewed like the eagle's!
—PSALM 103:1-5

Enter into the grateful praise of the psalmist, in a spirit of remembering and valuing what God is doing for you.

Repeat the passage several times as you seek to become "wholehearted" in your praise and thanksgiving.

PRAYER

Praise God for being the Healer of your mind, body, and soul.

Remember and thank God for the healing he has accomplished in your life.

Tell God about the healing you need in your body, your mind, and your soul. Ask him to heal you and to show you how you can cooperate with him in faith.

WEEK 14

THE PRESENCE OF GOD

Brother Lawrence was a French monk who lived during the 1600s. Because his sense of inner peace was so profound, people were drawn to him for spiritual direction. Brother Lawrence would tell them about his efforts to keep his attention riveted on God no matter what he was doing, and how that filled him with peace and joy. He called it the practice of the presence of God.

"We should establish ourselves in a sense of God's Presence, by continually conversing with Him. It's a shameful thing to quit His conversation to think of trifles and fooleries," he said. "We need only to recognize God intimately present with us and to address ourselves to Him every moment." It was this constant conversation with God that not only brought profound communion with God in the ordinariness of life, but also equipped Brother Lawrence to enjoy the presence of God in the pain of life. "God sometimes permits bodily diseases to cure the distempers of the soul," he said. "Have courage then: ask of God, not deliverance from your pains, but strength to bear resolutely, for the love of Him, all that He should please, and as long as He shall please."

God's very presence is his greatest gift to us. And yet I think it is a gift that most of us have never fully unwrapped. We've simply never embraced it for all of the intense joy and comfort it can give us. Maybe it's because we haven't believed the presence of God is enough to soothe and satisfy us. Come, let's learn to welcome his presence and walk in his presence. What could be sweeter?

THIS WEEK'S PASSAGE FOR MEDITATION

I know the LORD is always with me.
I will not be shaken, for he is right beside me.
No wonder my heart is filled with joy, and my mouth shouts his praises!
My body rests in safety.
For you will not leave my soul among the dead or allow your godly one to rot in the grave.
You will show me the way of life, granting me the joy of your presence and the pleasures of living with you forever. —PSALM 16:8-11

LISTENING FOR THE FOOTSTEPS OF GOD

TOWARD EVENING THEY HEARD THE LORD GOD WALKING ABOUT IN THE GARDEN.
—GENESIS 3:8

My college roommate, Stacy, married an Arkansas Razorbacks fan, and they have season tickets that put them at every football game in the fall. Recently some new season ticket holders were seated next to them. Mark, an attorney, introduced himself to Stacy and after some brief conversation asked her what she does. She told him she is a high school Bible teacher. "What is your favorite verse in the Bible?" he asked her. The question caught her a bit off guard, but she told him her favorite verse is Genesis 3:8. "I'm not up on what the Bible says," he said. "What does that verse say?"

"It is when Adam and Eve heard God walking with them in the Garden in the cool of the day," Stacy explained. "It's about God pursuing man, and if he hadn't done that, man would have stayed in the Garden and stayed in his sin."

"Well, I hope God is still pursuing me," Mark responded.

And she replied, "Why do you think he sat you beside a Bible teacher at a Razorbacks football game?"

Can you see it, from the first pages of Scripture through the last—the relentless pursuit of God wanting to walk with us? Can you see it from the earliest days of your life until today, the relentless pursuit of God wanting to walk with you through whatever you face, no matter how dark or difficult? So many people see the Bible as a book of moral teaching used to shore up our good behavior. But the Bible, from beginning to end, is a story of God extending himself, lowering himself, sacrificing himself, so that you and I can know and experience the fulfillment of a relationship with him, the satisfaction and safety of his very presence. It is God telling us over and over again that he wants to be with us. The final words of Jesus before he ascended were the promise, "I am with you always, even to the end of the age" (Matthew 28:20). And his final words in Revelation are, "Yes, I am coming soon!" (Revelation 22:20).

Do you hear the footsteps of God in your life? Will you let him walk with you, or will you run and hide? Won't you slow down and enjoy his presence with you?

God, I have heard your footsteps pursuing me throughout my life. And here in this dark place, I feel you beside me, walking with me.

DIGGING DEEPER

What does the prophecy of the coming of Jesus in Isaiah 35 tell about what God's presence means for us?

WALKING WITH GOD

Enoch walked with God; then he was no more, because God took him away.
—Genesis 5:24 (niv)

Enoch's whole life is told in six verses. We don't know all that much about him except that he is a standout in a long list of genealogy. He stands out for a couple of reasons. First, he stands out because he "walked with God." For all of the others in the long list of descendents from Adam to Noah, we read that so-and-so "lived" X number of years. But it doesn't say that Enoch lived three hundred years; it says Enoch *walked with God* three hundred years. You see, there's a big difference between walking with God and merely living.

The second way Enoch stands out is that for all of the other descendants the text says, "then he died." But for Enoch, we read, "God took him away." He never experienced physical death. He walked with God on the same path, at the same pace, toward the same place. Enoch enjoyed the presence of God so fully, God simply brought him to himself.

We read about Enoch again in the list of heroes of faith found in Hebrews 11. "It was by faith that Enoch was taken up to heaven without dying—'suddenly he disappeared because God took him.' But before he was taken up, he was approved as pleasing to God" (Hebrews 11:5). To be commended as one who pleased God seems out of our reach, doesn't it? When we read of someone who "walked with God," someone "approved as pleasing to God," we quickly dismiss the possibility as available only to an elite super-spiritual few, people who lived in Bible times. We assume that it will never be possible in this life to actually walk with God, to truly be pleasing to God.

But the truth is, you *can* walk with God and please God. As you walk with him in faith, simply and consistently—by talking with him, listening to him, and sharing your life with him; by not running ahead of him or dragging your feet in what he has called you to do; and by diligently seeking him—you bring him pleasure. Are you seeking the approval of God? He is not looking for great feats of faith or some super-self-denying commitment to service. He simply wants to walk with you day by day. He wants to begin and end the day with you, for you to be aware of his presence every moment in between. Won't you keep walking in his direction and enjoying his presence?

God, I don't want to wait for heaven to begin to walk with you and bring you pleasure. And I don't want to merely live. I long to walk with you and experience your presence and pleasure in my life.

DIGGING DEEPER

What does God promise to those who walk with him, according to Isaiah 43?

PREPARE A PATHWAY

Isaiah had spoken of John when he said, "He is a voice shouting in the wilderness: 'Prepare a pathway for the Lord's coming! Make a straight road for him!' " —Matthew 3:3

We may get frustrated with the potholes and patches in our modern-day highway system, but the roads in ancient times were truly terrible. So when a king was preparing to visit a certain area, special roads were created to make his journey as easy and direct as possible. A message was sent to the people to prepare for his coming by repairing "the king's highway."

The prophet Isaiah had this picture in mind as he foretold of John the Baptist who would prepare the way for Israel's coming King, the Messiah. John was the "voice shouting" for people to prepare not their roads but their hearts for the coming of Jesus. Preparing a pathway for this King requires repentance—turning away from everything opposed to God and turning wholeheartedly toward him. If we want to experience and enjoy the presence of God, repentance clears the pathway for him to come to us.

When the people asked John what they should do as a result of their repentance, he was very practical. "If you have two coats, give one to the poor. If you have food, share it with those who are hungry" (Luke 3:11). To tax collectors he said, "Show your honesty" (verse 13). To soldiers, "Don't extort money, and don't accuse people of things you know they didn't do. And be content with your pay" (verse 14). When we truly repent and welcome God into our lives, even what we see as ordinary aspects of life change significantly. Generosity replaces selfishness and greed. Honesty replaces shady business deals. Self-control replaces violence, and a contented spirit replaces complacency.

Do you have mountains of stubborn opinions or valleys of pleasure-seeking habits that need to be removed? Do you need to clear out obstacles of religious ritual or debris from lingering conflict? To experience a breakthrough of intimacy with God, you will need to clear out everything that has cluttered his pathway into your life. God wants to build a highway into your life so he can come and dwell there. Will you clear a pathway for his presence?

King Jesus, I don't want any unconfessed sin or unimportant concerns to obstruct your presence in my life. So with humble repentance and grateful anticipation, I welcome you to come into my life and take your throne here.

DIGGING DEEPER

Compare Matthew 3:1-12 with Luke 3:1-20. What extra details about the message of John the Baptist in Luke's Gospel do you find most interesting?

HEARTBURN

Two of Jesus' followers were walking to the village of Emmaus. Jesus himself came along and joined them and began walking beside them. But they didn't know who he was, because God kept them from recognizing him.
—Luke 24:13, 15-16

As two followers of Jesus walked from Jerusalem to Emmaus, they were joined by a stranger who seemed to know nothing of the recent crucifixion of Jesus or the reports of his resurrection. Something about their exchange with this stranger was unsettling. As they listened to him explain how all the Old Testament Scriptures pointed to Jesus, they fought a burning sensation inside. It was Jesus walking with them, and they didn't even recognize him.

Perhaps these followers didn't recognize Jesus because he simply was not who they were looking for. They had been blinded by disappointment. Luke tells us that sadness was written across their faces. "We had thought he was the Messiah who had come to rescue Israel," they said (Luke 24:21). They were simply too lost in their sadness, too disappointed by his death, and too desperate to make sense of their lives to see Jesus. They were too busy talking about Jesus to enjoy his very presence. Their hearts were burning with the presence of God in their midst, yet they didn't recognize him. It wasn't until Jesus broke the bread and gave it to them that they remembered Jesus breaking the bread on the hillside to feed the five thousand, breaking the bread at the Last Supper. God opened their eyes, and they recognized the presence of Jesus among them. The heartburn of the afternoon gave way to hearts filled with hope for the future because they had experienced the presence of the living God in their lives.

Imagine walking for seven miles with Jesus and sitting down to dinner, never knowing it was he. Yet perhaps that is the way it is with us. He's right here with us, and we don't recognize him. We're so disappointed he has not come through for us in the way we hoped he would that we can't appreciate his presence. We're so sad that we simply can't see him. Beg him to stay with you. See him break the bread for you. Feast upon the truth he tells you and the understanding he feeds you. Don't miss your Savior right beside you.

My heart burns with your presence, Jesus, and I never want to miss you again because I am blinded by disappointment or simply too sad to see you. Open my eyes and my heart to your very presence here with me.

DIGGING DEEPER

Read the whole story in Luke 24:13-34, and imagine what it would be like to have Jesus open the Old Testament to show you everything that points to him.

JESUS AND ME

DRAW CLOSE TO GOD, AND GOD WILL DRAW CLOSE TO YOU. —JAMES 4:8

A couple of my buddies, Bonita and Angela, just got back from a girls' getaway to the beach with several other women (my invitation must have gotten lost in the mail). For Angela, a widow and a single mom, this was her week to relax. But she wanted more than to simply leave behind her heavy responsibilities and walk on the beach. Bonita's and Angela's rooms shared a balcony overlooking the ocean. Through the sheer curtains Bonita could see Angela slip out onto the balcony before everyone else got up in the morning. Angela would put on her headphones and sing to the Lord along with her favorite praise music.

Angela has learned how to welcome and enjoy the presence of God. Bonita could see it and hear it through the curtains as Angela lifted up her arms singing to the Lord, loving him openly and passionately. "I began to look forward to watching her every morning," Bonita told me. Angela told me her favorite day at the beach was the one she spent alone while everyone else went shopping. But she wasn't really alone. "I went for a long walk on the beach, just Jesus and me," she said with delight. "I felt his presence in the waves around my feet and in the sun shining down on me. And I found a place where no one was around where I could shout out loud, 'Jesus, I love you!' "

The road to enjoying Jesus this way has not been an easy one for Angela. "It took me two years after Wes died before I was willing to say to Jesus, in the coldness and loneliness of my bed, 'Jesus, I need you to make your presence known to me, to be a husband and companion to me, to satisfy me,' " she told me. And she admits it is awkward at times to speak out loud to God in the quietness of her room or to wait in silence for him to make his presence known. This is an awkwardness many of us have never been able to overcome. We haven't been quiet enough or patient enough to allow God to meet us. Perhaps what is more deeply true is that we haven't believed that being alone with Jesus will be intimate, intense, or invigorating enough. Are you willing to put Jesus to the test, to invite his presence into your loneliness and need, so you can discover for yourself that he will meet you?

Jesus, I love you, and I want to experience your presence in my life in a very real and natural way. Will you reach out for me as I reach out to you? Will you show me what it really means to enjoy your presence in my life?

DIGGING DEEPER

Read the story of one who openly and passionately expressed love to Jesus in John 12:1-8.

WEEK 14

THE PRESENCE OF GOD

REFLECTION

When have you experienced the presence of God in a meaningful and powerful way? How did this experience change you?

What do you need to clear away and what do you need to embrace so that you can practice the presence of God?

MEDITATION

I know the Lord is always with me.
I will not be shaken, for he is right beside me.
No wonder my heart is filled with joy, and my mouth shouts his praises!
My body rests in safety.
For you will not leave my soul among the dead or allow your godly one to rot in the grave.
You will show me the way of life, granting me the joy of your presence and the pleasures of living with you forever. —PSALM 16:8-11

Read through this psalm several times, marking the words and phrases that are especially meaningful to you.

Pray through the psalm, embracing its promises, protections, and pleasures for yourself.

PRAYER

Praise God for his glorious presence that transforms everyone who comes near.

Thank God for his relentless pursuit of us, his willingness to come down and walk with us.

Intercede for those like Mark (the Razorbacks fan) who have never chosen to pursue God but are hopeful God will not stop pursuing them.

Confess your unbelief that the presence of God in your life will be enough to soothe your fear and bring you comfort and companionship.

Petition God to make his presence known in every aspect of your life, to make your heart burn with awareness that he is there.

WEEK 15

KNOWING GOD

Last night at the football game, another mom expressed something about another person that just didn't sit right with me. "I know him," I said, "and that is just not who he is."

When we really know someone, we are confident he will act according to his character. We can be even more confident this is true of God, because God never has an off day. He is never inconsistent with his character. What he says and what he does are always consistent with who he is. And our understanding of who God is provides the foundation for us to accept what God does even when we don't understand it. When we're confused, we can fall back on what we know about God from his Word, what we've experienced of God in the past, and what we've seen God do in the lives of others.

If you want to make sense of what God is doing in your life, you have to know who God is by studying his nature and his essential characteristics. Each aspect of his character is a window into his beauty, another invitation to trust him, another reason to love him.

THIS WEEK'S PASSAGE FOR MEDITATION

This is what the LORD says: "Let not the wise man gloat in his wisdom, or the mighty man in his might, or the rich man in his riches. Let them boast in this alone: that they truly know me and understand that I am the LORD who is just and righteous, whose love is unfailing, and that I delight in these things. I, the LORD, have spoken!" —JEREMIAH 9:23-24

GOD IS GOOD

Moses had one more request. "Please let me see your glorious presence," he said. The Lord replied, "I will make all my goodness pass before you, and I will call out my name, 'the Lord,' to you. I will show kindness to anyone I choose, and I will show mercy to anyone I choose." —Exodus 33:18-19

No one can see the face of God and live. But Moses just had to push the envelope. He asked for a glimpse of God. So God put Moses in the cleft of a rock and covered him to protect him from the blazing fire of his glory, only lifting his hand for Moses to catch a brief glimpse of his back. And what was the essence of what Moses saw? God's goodness. Goodness is the very essence of who God is, and we can't see God without seeing his goodness. Conversely, if we don't see his goodness, we haven't seen God.

But sometimes a voice deep inside us says, *Something is wrong with this picture! This is not what goodness looks like!* Sometimes our circumstances seem like anything but evidence of God's goodness. But that is because we tend to define God by what *we* have deemed as good. We have to turn that around. We have to learn to define goodness by who God is and what he does. God is eternally, intrinsically, abundantly, infinitely, perfectly good. God himself is the standard by which we should compare anything we want to label as "good." He is the source from which everything that is truly good emanates. God alone is absolutely good. If God ceased to be good, he would cease to be God.

Can God be any less good to you on a dreary and difficult Monday morning than he was on that monumental Friday afternoon when he hung on a cross in your place? Absolutely not! And God will be no less good to you tomorrow either, because God cannot be less than perfectly good. His goodness is not the effect of his disposition but the essence of his character; it is not an attitude but an attribute.

When Moses got a glimpse of God's goodness, he "immediately fell to the ground and worshiped" (Exodus 34:8). As you get a glimpse of the goodness of God and as you enjoy the blessings of God's goodness, will you do the same?

You alone are good, my God. Forgive my self-righteous assumptions that you are anything less than infinitely good in all your ways. Show me your goodness in this land of the living and forevermore.

DIGGING DEEPER

What does God do for you out of his perfect goodness, according to these verses: Psalm 23:6; 25:8; 31:19; 86:5; and 119:40?

GOD IS FAITHFUL

I WILL BE FAITHFUL TO YOU AND MAKE YOU MINE, AND YOU WILL FINALLY KNOW ME AS LORD. —HOSEA 2:20

Imagine that God picked out the person you are to marry, and the reason he wants you to marry this person is because he knows she will leave you for not just another man but for many other men—that she will sell her body to and bear the children of other men even while she is married to you. This is the story of Hosea and Gomer, and it is shocking. When we read it, we're a bit offended that God would ask such a thing of Hosea. God wanted Hosea to understand what it is like to be married to an unfaithful wife before he spoke God's Word to Israel. Through this real-life illustration, Hosea not only understood the betrayal, he felt it. And we do too if we enter into this story, if we look closely enough to see ourselves in it.

We see ourselves in Gomer's unfaithfulness, and we see the faithfulness of God in the love of her husband, Hosea. Or at least we should. But we don't really want to see ourselves this way, do we? It seems too extreme. To describe ourselves as whores is going way too far. But that is what we are. God himself is our spiritual husband and lover. And every time we sin, every time we give ourselves to lesser lovers in this world, we commit spiritual adultery. "The spirit of harlotry has caused them to stray, and they have played the harlot against their God" (Hosea 4:12, NKJV). To fully understand the nature of God's faithfulness toward us, we must see our own unfaithfulness to him for what it is; we must feel his broken heart.

While it is shocking that God would ask Hosea to take a wife he knows will be unfaithful, it is perhaps more shocking that Hosea reclaims Gomer from the auction block, buying back what is already his, taking her back home to start over like young lovers (Hosea 3:2). But once again this is an illustration of what our faithful God does. God woos us tenderly to himself knowing we will fail him; he promises us hope and safety knowing we will not keep our promises; he starts over with any who will come to him; and he offers us the most intimate and pleasure-filled relationship possible. God knows we have sold ourselves to many other lovers in this world, yet he is wooing us to himself where he wants to envelop us in his faithful love, saying, "I will heal you of your idolatry and faithlessness, and my love will know no bounds, for my anger will be gone forever!" (Hosea 14:4).

My faithful, divine Lover, I have known your unrelenting pursuit, your unending patience, and your unflinching acceptance, yet I run to other lovers. I return to you as a harlot, asking you to take me back, to love me once more.

DIGGING DEEPER

Read Hosea 1–3, 14. What do you learn about Hosea, Gomer, and the restoration of Israel?

GOD IS JUST

SHOULD NOT THE JUDGE OF ALL THE EARTH DO WHAT IS RIGHT? —GENESIS 18:25

I've realized recently that there are three little words that are music to my ears. I'm afraid it reveals something rather pathetic about me, but I love it when someone says to me, "You were right." Ahhh. Those three words have an enormous appeal to my ego. And I suppose I'd have to say that some of the most painful words I have ever had to speak are, "I was wrong." And I spit them out less often than they are true. I'm just too flawed as a human to be right all the time. But God is right all the time. He is never wrong.

The Bible uses the same word for righteousness as it does for justice. Justice is the righteous way God governs every part of the universe. Justice is not simply an option God considers, but an unchangeable aspect of his very nature.

When we place our lives in the hands of human judges, we must accept that their justice will be imperfect because their knowledge is limited and our laws are flawed. The righteousness of their decisions is limited by the degree to which they yield to their prejudices and passions. But God has none of these deficiencies in the exercise of justice. He is infinitely wise, and nothing can fool him or escape him. He cannot be anything other than perfectly just. His holiness demands it. We can be confident that when destiny- defining decisions are made, the Judge of all the earth will do what is right.

When the justice of God works its way into our understanding of the painful experiences and circumstances of our lives, we can stand back and say, "God, you were right. Everything you do is right." But this is not what comes naturally to us. It doesn't come naturally to welcome God's way with open arms and worship his righteousness. We're more likely to point our fingers at God, accusing him of unfairness, questioning his timing, and doubting his love.

Are you willing to admit that your understanding is limited and say to God even now, "You are right"? Will you trust that God will always do what is right with you and your life and those you love?

Righteous Judge, you are right. Everything you do is right. Everything you have done in my life is right. I entrust myself to you because I know your love and justice intermingle for my ultimate good.

DIGGING DEEPER

What do the following verses reveal about the quality and nature of God's justice: 2 Chronicles 19:7; Jeremiah 32:19; Zephaniah 3:5; and Colossians 3:25?

GOD IS HOLY

Who else among the gods is like you, O Lord? Who is glorious in holiness like you—so awesome in splendor, performing such wonders? —Exodus 15:11

One day Matt brought home a piece of artwork from preschool. I can't remember what it looked like, but I remember his bewilderment when I told him I thought it was "fine." That wasn't good enough. "You're supposed to tell me it is great," he said. Our culture says that to love a child is to tell him that he is special and unique and that everything he does is wonderful. We're to give him the impression that our world revolves around him. And we've grown up expecting the same of God. We figure if he loves us he will make a fuss over us and celebrate us, only to find ourselves disappointed and disenchanted with God when we discover that we are not at the center of the universe. Instead, the holiness of God is at the center of the universe. His absolute uniqueness and perfection shines bright and beautiful.

If we are going to grow up in God, it is time we learn that God's passion for his holiness is the supreme force and focus in the universe. We often operate under the delusion that he has ordered the universe around us. But the reality is that the world has been fashioned to display his holiness, and we were created to enjoy it. What a satisfying treasure his holiness is if we will indulge in it! "What joy for those you choose to bring near, those who live in your holy courts. What joys await us inside your holy Temple" (Psalm 65:4).

God demonstrated his love for us not by making us the center of his universe, but by going the length of the Cross so that we can enjoy making him the center of our universe and the source of our joy forever. Will you put God in his rightful place—at the center of the universe, at the center of your life—and make his holiness your passion? When we allow ourselves to be consumed by a passion for God's holiness, other passions lose their power over us. Struggles with sexual temptation lose their allure; deep-rooted bitterness, paralyzing fear, and insignificant obsessions cease to be the focus of our energy. See him for who he is—altogether holy—and usher him to the throne of your life.

Holy, holy, holy are you Lord. As I stand in awe of your holiness, my desires to justify myself or to place demands on you diminish. I sense my growing hunger to feast on you, a growing passion to celebrate you.

DIGGING DEEPER

Read 2 Corinthians 6:14–7:1; Ephesians 4:17-24; and Hebrews 12:14. What do these passages teach us about how to respond to the holiness of God?

GOD IS JEALOUS

YOU MUST NEVER WORSHIP OR BOW DOWN TO THEM, FOR I, THE LORD YOUR GOD, AM A JEALOUS GOD WHO WILL NOT SHARE YOUR AFFECTION WITH ANY OTHER GOD!
—EXODUS 20:5

It has never seemed right to me that God would be jealous. Isn't jealousy a bad thing? Doesn't it ruin relationships and poison souls? So how can we say that a perfect God is jealous? We say it because this is how God describes himself. And even if it doesn't sit well with our sensibilities, we want to accept what God says about himself.

In the grand revelation of his nature through the Ten Commandments, God said, "I am a jealous God." In fact, *jealous* is not just a description; God also used it as one of his names, calling himself "the LORD, whose name is Jealous" (Exodus 34:14, NIV). Far from being in conflict with the nature of God, jealousy is the very epitome of it. So what is God so jealous about?

God is jealous for his holy name and reputation. He is jealous for his people, jealous for our sacrifices and devotion. James writes that God "jealously longs for us to be faithful" (4:5). And if God's jealousy is part of his perfection, we know that God's jealousy is not like our jealousy. He is not out of sorts because of envy, but he is zealous out of love. Just as there is an appropriate measure of jealousy that my husband, David, exercises out of his desire to preserve the exclusivity of our relationship, God is right to jealously guard the relationship he has with you. He doesn't see his relationship with you as purely business. He is not going through the motions of religion. This is a love relationship that stirs his deep passions in pursuit of your exclusive devotion and affection. "He is a God who is passionate about his relationship with you" (Exodus 34:14). He does not want you to allow your affections to wander away from him. His jealousy is an appropriate outgrowth of the value he places on his relationship with you.

God is not really interested in your passive, lukewarm love; he wants your passionate devotion. Has hardship dampened the delight you take in your divine Lover? Has it turned you toward another comforter? Hear him call to you from his jealous nature to love him, and let him love you richly in return.

Jealous, this very name for you speaks to me of your passionate love for me, not your demands on me. Stir in me the passion I have had for you in the past. Draw me close and make me the passionate lover your jealousy desires.

DIGGING DEEPER

What do Romans 10:19 and 2 Corinthians 11:2 show about how jealousy provokes and protects us?

WEEK 15

KNOWING GOD

REFLECTION

Which aspects of God's character are hard for you to swallow? Which aspects do you long to know and experience in a fuller way?

As you look at the character of God, in what areas of your life are you challenged to conform your character to his?

MEDITATION

This is what the LORD says: "Let not the wise man gloat in his wisdom, or the mighty man in his might, or the rich man in his riches. Let them boast in this alone: that they truly know me and understand that I am the LORD who is just and righteous, whose love is unfailing, and that I delight in these things. I, the LORD, have spoken!" —JEREMIAH 9:23-24

Quiet yourself to hear the Lord speak through these, his words.

Read the verses several times, marking the words or phrases that especially speak to you or challenge you.

Allow the description of God's character to shape the image of God in your heart and mind.

Ask God to transform your values so that you boast in what is truly valuable.

PRAYER

Praise God for his perfection in character—his goodness, faithfulness, holiness, justice, and jealousy; his graciousness and immutability; his patience and mercy; his omnipotence and omniscience; his wisdom and perfection.

Thank God for how he has exercised each of these attributes in your life.

Intercede for those who, by making a god in their own image, reject the one true God and refuse to embrace his true attributes.

Confess your resistance or questions about what God does and who he is.

Petition God to reveal himself to you in truth and completeness as you seek to know him more fully through his Word.

WEEK 16

GOD'S NAME

From the first verse of Scripture, God begins to reveal who he is by his names. When we read, "In the beginning God created" (Genesis 1:1), we learn the first and one of the most important names for God: the Hebrew word *Elohim*, which reveals his creative power and three-in-one nature. Throughout the Old Testament, God progressively reveals more and more about himself by revealing more of his names. His names depict the resources of his divine character, which are as vast as the needs of his people.

When we are in need and God's resources are at hand, we experience *Jehovah-jireh*: the Lord provides. (See Genesis 22:14.)

When we are sick and God brings relief, we experience *Jehovah-rophi*: the Lord who heals. (See Exodus 15:26.)

When we find ourselves in a spiritual battle and God gives us victory, we experience *Jehovah-nissi*: the Lord our banner. (See Exodus 17:15.)

When we are weary with our own sin and God sets us free, we experience *Jehovah M'Kaddesh*: the Lord who sanctifies. (See Exodus 31:13.)

When our anxiety is overcome by God's peace, we experience *Jehovah-shalom*: the Lord is peace. (See Judges 6:24.)

When God gives victory over evil that threatens us, we experience *Jehovah-tsebahoth*: the Lord of hosts. (See 1 Samuel 17:45.)

When God lovingly brings us back into the fold from our wanderings, we experience *Jehovah-rohi*: the Lord my shepherd. (See Psalm 23.)

When we accept the righteousness of Christ in place of our own sinfulness, we experience *Jehovah-tsidkenu*: the Lord our righteousness. (See Jeremiah 23:6.)

When we are desperately lonely and find God reaching out to us, we experience *Jehovah-shammah*: the Lord who is there. (See Ezekiel 48:35.)

THIS WEEK'S PASSAGE FOR MEDITATION

The LORD is a shelter for the oppressed, a refuge in times of trouble. Those who know your name trust in you, for you, O LORD, have never abandoned anyone who searches for you.

—PSALM 9:9-10

JEHOVAH-JIREH: THE LORD WILL PROVIDE

ABRAHAM LOOKED UP AND SAW A RAM CAUGHT BY ITS HORNS IN A BUSH. SO HE TOOK THE RAM AND SACRIFICED IT AS A BURNT OFFERING ON THE ALTAR IN PLACE OF HIS SON. ABRAHAM NAMED THE PLACE "THE LORD WILL PROVIDE." —GENESIS 22:13-14

After years of longing and waiting, imagine the joy in Abraham and Sarah's household when Isaac was born—even his name means "laughter." And then, imagine how Abraham's heart must have sunk, how he must have felt physically sick when he heard God say to him in essence: "Take your son Isaac and put him to death by your own hand and then burn up his body" (see Genesis 22:1-2).

But early the next morning Abraham got up and saddled his donkey and headed up the mountain with young Isaac at his side. He must have wept as he walked. And yet the writer of Hebrews reveals to us what gave Abraham the strength to keep going, what gave him the confidence to tell his servants, "We will worship there, and then *we* will come right back" (Genesis 22:5, emphasis added). God had said his descendants would come specifically through Isaac, not just any son, so if God was asking him to kill Isaac, Abraham reasoned he must be planning to raise him from the dead (see Hebrews 11:17-19). But Isaac didn't understand. "We have the wood and the fire," he said to his father, "but where is the lamb for the sacrifice?" (Genesis 22:7).

"God will provide a lamb," Abraham answered (verse 8). And on the mountain, as he lifted his knife over Isaac, he heard God call to him to put down his knife. When Abraham looked up, he saw a ram and sacrificed it as a burnt offering on the altar in place of his son. At the lowest moment of his life, Abraham listened for God and looked up to see God at work. Then he celebrated the God in whom he placed all his faith for the future—the God who sees into the future and provides what we need right when we need it.

Has your desperate situation left you wondering if God sees you and your need? Look up and see God at work, foreseeing and providing what you need, when you need it. And realize that he had already provided for your most desperate need long before you recognized it. There was no stay of the knife for his own Son—so that your Jehovah-jireh could provide Jesus as a sacrifice for you.

My Jehovah-jireh, sometimes I wonder if you see me and if you will be on time in supplying what I truly need. Then I look up to you and I see your provision for me in Jesus, reflecting your provision for me in every area of my need.

DIGGING DEEPER

Read Psalm 111:9; Isaiah 61:3; 1 Corinthians 10:13; 1 Timothy 6:17; and 1 Peter 4:10-11. According to these verses, what does God provide for you?

JEHOVAH-ROPHI: THE LORD MY HEALER

If you will listen carefully to the voice of the Lord your God and do what is right in his sight, obeying his commands and laws, then I will not make you suffer the diseases I sent on the Egyptians; for I am the Lord who heals you. —Exodus 15:26

What a celebration it was as the Israelites sang of their freedom from slavery. They had walked through the Red Sea on dry land. Surely they had left their troubles behind in Egypt. But they were immediately plunged into the desert for three days without water. And when they finally found the water they thought would slake their thirst and save them, the water tasted bitter.

Exodus says that Moses cried out to the Lord for help and that the Lord showed him a tree branch. Moses threw the branch into the water, and the water was made good to drink (Exodus 15:23-25). What was bitter became sweet, and what was death-causing became life-giving. Then God laid out for them the conditions for testing their faithfulness in the days ahead, challenging them to listen to him and obey, offering himself to them as "the Lord who heals you."

Have you waded into bitter waters? Did you come thirsty to an alluring pool of sexual satisfaction only to have the bitter taste of shame and regret left in your mouth? Perhaps you believed that just one more drink from the pool of possessions would satisfy, only to find yourself thirsty for more. Or is there a spring of unforgiveness in the interior of your life that has left you neck-deep in a pool of bitterness that is choking the life out of you?

If so, drink deeply of the Lord, who heals you from lust, materialism, unforgiveness, and every sin that makes your soul sick. As you listen to his voice and do what is right, he will purify your body, soul, and mind.

The wood Moses cast into the bitter waters was a foreshadowing of another tree that would bring ultimate healing—the tree of Calvary. "He personally carried away our sins in his own body on the cross so we can be dead to sin and live for what is right. You have been healed by his wounds!" (1 Peter 2:24). Come to Jehovah-rophi, who will heal you and make you whole.

My Jehovah-rophi, how I need the healing in my spirit, mind, and body that only you can provide. Heal the bitter places in my life so that I might experience the sweetness of hearing your voice and obeying your Word.

DIGGING DEEPER

Read this whole story in Exodus 14:21–15:27. What attributes of God do you find in the Israelites' song, and what do they mean for your healing?

JEHOVAH M'KADDESH: THE LORD WHO SANCTIFIES

It helps you to remember that I am the Lord, who makes you holy.
—Exodus 31:13

"God would never want me to spend the rest of my life this miserable. God wants me to be happy." This is a rationalization I've heard many times from people who want to justify walking away from a marriage or toward a questionable endeavor. Maybe you have heard it too. Or maybe you have said it. God does want you to be happy, but he knows that your greatest happiness is found as you pursue holiness. He wants to *be* your happiness, and he wants you to be holy. In fact, holiness is so much a part of who he is and what he wants, it is one of the names he has given himself—Jehovah M'Kaddesh: the Lord who sanctifies.

This name for God not only describes who he is, but what he does. It reflects his purpose and priorities. What does it mean to be sanctified or holy? It is more than just being morally pure. To be holy is to be set apart for God. "Be holy, for I am holy," God said (Leviticus 11:45, NKJV). But truthfully, I can become completely defeated and discouraged with God's expectations for my holiness. I know myself too well. If holiness is the standard, I will never measure up.

Fortunately, God enables us to become what he commands us to be and do what he commands us to do. "May the God of peace make you holy in every way, and may your whole spirit and soul and body be kept blameless until that day when our Lord Jesus Christ comes again. God, who calls you, is faithful; he will do this" (1 Thessalonians 5:23-24). Jehovah M'Kaddesh is not only a revelation of his divine nature, but also an assurance of his divine help.

As we turn away from sin toward our Jehovah M'Kaddesh in worship and love, he will take every part of our lives we offer to him and he will set us apart for himself. He will work in us so that we become closer and closer in reality to what we have already been declared to be through Christ: holy. And in his holiness we will be much more than happy; we will be filled with the overflowing joy of pleasing God.

My Jehovah M'Kaddesh, how I need you to sanctify my spirit to more God-awareness, my soul to less self-dependence, and my body to increasing service to others. May my greatest joy be your holiness growing in me.

DIGGING DEEPER

Read John 17:17; Acts 26:18; 1 Timothy 4:5; and Hebrews 13:12. What agents or instruments does God use to sanctify you?

JEHOVAH-SHALOM: THE LORD MY PEACE

The angel of the Lord appeared to him and said, "Mighty hero, the Lord is with you!"

"Sir," Gideon replied, "if the Lord is with us, why has all this happened to us? And where are all the miracles our ancestors told us about?"

And Gideon built an altar to the Lord there and named it "The Lord Is Peace." —Judges 6:12-13, 24

This morning I got an email from my church asking for prayer for a woman who is preparing for a stem cell transplant in her fight against cancer. She asked us to pray that she and her husband would know perfect peace. God's peace is indeed what we need during difficult times. But is that realistic? Isn't it more realistic that the desperation of her situation would make her question the benefits of a relationship with God? Doesn't she have every right to ask God, "Where is *my* miracle?"

That's how Gideon responded when he heard God proclaim his presence. Years of Midianite cruelty had left the Israelites starving and afraid. So Gideon responded incredulously, questioning why they were suffering so much if God was with them. Gideon also questioned why God would address him as a hero, since he knew he was a nobody from a tribe of nobodies, certainly not strong enough to rescue Israel. Gideon basically said to God, "I'm too offended to believe you and too ordinary to be used by you."

But God transforms ordinary people who feel defeated and full of doubt into mighty heroes of faith as they welcome his presence and power. "Go with the strength you have," the Lord said to Gideon. "I will be with you" (Judges 6:14, 16). We have nothing to offer God but need, but as we give that to him and move forward with our small amount of personal and spiritual strength, we see God begin to work. The revelation and recognition of who God is turns ordinary faith into overcoming faith and helpless people into heroes.

Could you become a hero of faith in your hopeless situation? Could your experience of God be defined by all-encompassing peace? Yes, but you will have to quit being offended with God and welcome him to reveal himself to you as Jehovah-shalom. Peace is not a feeling or possession but a person. Jesus will invade your hopelessness and distress and reveal himself as Peace.

My Jehovah-shalom, you know that my level of anxiety and distress is in a constant state of flux with my circumstances. So I welcome you as Peace personified into my place of despair, and I offer my weak faith to you.

DIGGING DEEPER

Read Judges 6–7. What was Gideon afraid of when he saw God, and how did Jehovah-shalom comfort him? List the ways God made his presence known.

JEHOVAH-SHAMMAH: THE LORD IS THERE

FROM THAT DAY THE NAME OF THE CITY WILL BE "THE LORD IS THERE." —EZEKIEL 48:35

I was walking with a woman at a retreat center, discussing the impossibility of making complete, explainable sense out of suffering. "I think it just comes down to this," she said. "God is with us, and that is enough." And I think she is right. The God who made us walks beside us in the highest and lowest points of life, and even in death. Ultimately, this is God's greatest promise and one of his most precious names, because experiencing the reality of his presence with us is our most profound need.

But I must admit, there have been times the promise of "God with me" hasn't felt like enough for me. It has seemed like the cop-out answer when he wasn't *doing* something for me. I have wanted what he has to offer more than I have wanted him. Part of my problem is that I resist slowing down enough to simply enjoy his presence. I work through my Bible study to get the answers and pray through my list until my mind wanders. Too quickly, I am on to "more important" matters than simply experiencing and enjoying the very real presence of Jehovah-shammah. He is there, but I've missed him.

God's progressive self-revelation through his divine names comes to a climax as Ezekiel described God's future Kingdom city, named for its most distinctive inhabitant, Jehovah-shammah: the Lord is there. Throughout Scripture we see the beauty and feel the comfort of Jehovah-shammah. David found him: "Even when I walk through the dark valley of death, I will not be afraid, for you are close beside me" (Psalm 23:4). Isaiah prophesied, "When you go through deep waters and great trouble, I will be with you" (Isaiah 43:2). An angel proclaimed, "[Mary] will give birth to a son, and he will be called Immanuel (meaning, God is with us)" (Matthew 1:23). Jesus showed us Jehovah-shammah with skin!

So when you are lonely, reach out for Jehovah-shammah. He is there beside you. When you have strayed from God, return to find Jehovah-shammah waiting for you. When you feel surrounded by darkness and evil, look up to see Jehovah-shammah surrounding you with his very presence. He is there.

My Jehovah-shammah, I will stop asking you to "be with me" in my prayers because you are already here! Teach me to enjoy your presence in my home, where I work, everywhere I am. You are here with me, even now.

DIGGING DEEPER

Read Psalm 139. In what phrases do you see "the Lord who is there," and what difference does it make to know he is there?

WEEK 16

GOD'S NAME

REFLECTION

Which of God's names are most meaningful to you right now, and why?

MEDITATION

The LORD *is a shelter for the oppressed, a refuge in times of trouble. Those who know your name trust in you, for you, O* LORD, *have never abandoned anyone who searches for you.*
—PSALM 9:9-10

Enter into this passage as you envision yourself finding shelter from your troubles in the Lord. See yourself searching for God, placing your trust in him, and finding him.

PRAYER

Pray through the names God has revealed in the Old Testament. Praise and thank him for how he has revealed himself personally to you through each name. Confess your tendency to go to other sources to get your needs met rather than coming to him. Ask him to show himself more fully to you and your loved ones through each of his divine names.

Elohim: the Creator

El Elyon: the God Most High

El Roi: the God who sees

El Shaddai: the all-sufficient One

Jehovah: the self-existent One

Jehovah-jireh: the Lord provides

Jehovah-rophi: the Lord who heals

Jehovah-nissi: the Lord our banner

Jehovah M'Kaddesh: the Lord who sanctifies

Jehovah-shalom: the Lord is peace

Jehovah-tsebahoth: the Lord of hosts

Jehovah-rohi: the Lord my shepherd

Jehovah-tsidkenu: the Lord our righteousness

Jehovah-shammah: the Lord who is there

WEEK 17

GIFTS OF GOD

God is the greatest giver in the universe. Do you see him that way? God's abundant generosity prompted Paul to ask the rhetorical question, "Since God did not spare even his own Son but gave him up for us all, won't God, who gave us Christ, also give us everything else?" (Romans 8:32).

Paul takes it for granted that God's greatest gift to us is his Son, and this gift is an indication that God will not be stingy in giving us everything we truly need. You may be tempted to say in response, "I can think of some things God hasn't given me!" If we're honest, we often skip right over the generous gift of God's Son. We simply don't value Christ as God does. We don't appreciate the gift because we've set our affections on so many lesser things than the gift of Jesus. Yet everything we need, everything that is worth desiring, we find in Christ and the gifts that are ours through Christ. In Jesus we find what we need to salve our deepest hurts and solve our most perplexing problems. God, the greatest giver in the universe, wants to give us everything. Will you open your hands and your heart to receive what he wants to give you?

THIS WEEK'S PASSAGE FOR MEDITATION

As we know Jesus better, his divine power gives us everything we need for living a godly life. He has called us to receive his own glory and goodness! And by that same mighty power, he has given us all of his rich and wonderful promises. He has promised that you will escape the decadence all around you caused by evil desires and that you will share in his divine nature. So make every effort to apply the benefits of these promises to your life.

—2 Peter 1:3-5

GRACE SETS ME FREE FROM MY MISERY

SIN IS NO LONGER YOUR MASTER, FOR YOU ARE NO LONGER SUBJECT TO THE LAW, WHICH ENSLAVES YOU TO SIN. INSTEAD, YOU ARE FREE BY GOD'S GRACE. —ROMANS 6:14

In the city of Sao José dos Campos, Brazil, there is a prison run by two Christians. Chuck Colson wrote about it: "When I visited Humaita I found the inmates smiling—particularly the murderer who held the keys, opened the gates and let me in. My guide escorted me to the notorious prison cell once used for torture. Today, he told me, that block houses only a single inmate. Slowly he swung open the massive door, and I saw the prisoner in that cell: a crucifix, beautifully carved by the Humaita inmates—the prisoner Jesus, hanging on a cross. 'He's doing time for the rest of us,' my guide said softly."

We often talk about grace as "undeserved favor," and it is. But it is more than that. Undeserved favor is when someone hands us free tickets to a football game, but that is really just generosity. Grace is favor against merit, favor that goes against what we truly deserve. Mercy says we don't have to do the time. Grace takes our place in the prison cell to do the time we deserve. This is what makes grace amazing.

Grace sets us free from the misery of our painful past and the mastery of sin; it frees us from sin's power to keep hurting us and making our lives miserable. Often we think we are pursuing a joyful freedom only to find ourselves unhappily bound by our bad choices. We just want to exercise self-control and instead find ourselves slaves to an eating disorder; we just want to loosen up and instead find ourselves addicted to alcohol or pills; we just want to spruce the place up and instead find ourselves drowning in debt. Into this prison of our own making, the grace of God appears in the person and work of Jesus. Every taste of goodness and every breath of freedom we enjoy is a gift of grace.

Grace not only sets us free, it shows us how to live in true freedom and points us toward a future to live for. Grace teaches us "to turn from godless living and sinful pleasures. We should live in this evil world with self-control, right conduct, and devotion to God, while we look forward to that wonderful event when the glory of our great God and Savior, Jesus Christ, will be revealed" (Titus 2:12-13).

Gracious Lord, I see you in the cell, upon the cross, bearing my shame and punishment so I can be free. How I want my life to be worthy of such a sacrifice. Show me how to walk in this generous freedom you give by grace.

DIGGING DEEPER

Read Ephesians 2:1-10 and Titus 2:11-14, looking for how we've been set free and what we are to do with our freedom.

MERCY SAVES ME FROM GETTING WHAT I DESERVE

HE SAVED US, NOT BECAUSE OF THE GOOD THINGS WE DID, BUT BECAUSE OF HIS MERCY. —TITUS 3:5

We live in a world that teaches us: "The early bird gets the worm," "No pain no gain," "There is no such thing as a free lunch," and "You get what you pay for." We're comfortable in this world where people get what they deserve, at least in theory. But when pain invades our lives, we quickly say, "I don't deserve this!" and claim our right to justice. Believing we have a right to fairness, we feel violated when we think we haven't gotten what we deserve.

But if we open our eyes to the rest of the world where most people do not live with even the basics of comfort and security that we enjoy, or if we look back on the living conditions and daily-life realities previous generations lived and died with, we realize that to assume we deserve a life free of loss and pain is not only unrealistic, it is arrogant. Our insistence that we don't deserve to suffer betrays our naïveté and narcissism. Just what have we done to deserve the lives we enjoy and the people we love?

On the surface, a perfectly fair world appeals to us. But would we really want to live in such a world? In a perfectly fair world, there is no room for grace—receiving what you don't deserve. Neither is there room for mercy—being spared from receiving the punishment you do deserve. Suffering may be undeserved, but so is our redemption. A fair world might be a nice place for us to live, but it would only be as nice as we are. And we know we're really not that nice. We deserve punishment but receive forgiveness; we deserve wrath but experience love; we deserve death, but God has shown us mercy.

Living in a world where we do not always get what we deserve, and one in which we sometimes get what we don't deserve, means that we will suffer loss. But it also means we will receive mercy. We naturally dread pain, but isn't it worth it if it means we will also experience the gift of grace and the release of mercy?

Merciful Savior, you have forgiven my guilt and pitied my helplessness. Your mercy is the hope I cling to that balances out the pain in this unfair world. Thank you for not treating me as my sins deserve, but for showing me mercy.

DIGGING DEEPER

What are the implications of God's mercy toward us and our mercy toward others in the following verses: Matthew 5:7; 18:23-35; Luke 10:29-37; Colossians 3:12-14; and James 2:13?

FORGIVENESS ASSUAGES MY GUILT

In this man Jesus there is forgiveness for your sins. Everyone who believes in him is freed from all guilt and declared right with God. —Acts 13:38-39

My friend Kate was a "good girl" who grew up in church and found herself pregnant as a senior in college. Wanting to erase the mistake and move on with her life, she had an abortion and promised herself she would not have sex again until she was married. But only two years later she was pregnant again, and once again, she chose to abort the baby. Eventually Kate married and started a family, but she couldn't shake the guilt from her self-centered choices, and for years she was miserable. She believed that God forgave her, but she could not forgive herself.

Kate's eyes were opened, however, when her sister-in-law pointed out that the guilt-inducing voice she heard was not from God but from Satan, who wanted to keep her stewing in her sin rather than enjoying the freedom of God's forgiveness. The Bible says that when God forgives us, he will never again remember our sins. It's not that our all-knowing Father forgets, but rather he chooses not to bring up our sin to hold it against us. It is Satan, the accuser, who brings it back to rub our noses in it and make us feel guilty. Why should you listen to him bringing up your past to accuse you if God does not do so?

The only way to cleanse a guilty conscience is to embrace the absolute and all--encompassing forgiveness of God. Only then can you forgive yourself and make a fresh start. Nothing you try on your own can assuage your guilt—not the mind games to justify your actions, not the escape mechanisms to numb your feelings, not the religious performance to prove yourself worthy. Only the gift of justification and the power of his forgiveness can free you from the prison of regret and shame that holds you hostage.

If God says you are forgiven, who are you to keep punishing yourself? If you refuse to forgive yourself, it's as if you are saying that you are greater than God, that your judgment is higher than his. Will you humble yourself so you can experience the pervasive pleasure of his forgiveness?

Forgiving Father, I am weary of carrying this weight of my guilt and shame, so I bring it to your Cross, where you cover my failure with forgiveness.

DIGGING DEEPER

What do Colossians 1:19-23 and Hebrews 10:1-14 teach us about the sufficiency of Christ's sacrifice in regard to our guilt?

CHRIST RELIEVES MY INADEQUACY

DON'T MISUNDERSTAND WHY I HAVE COME. I DID NOT COME TO ABOLISH THE LAW OF MOSES OR THE WRITINGS OF THE PROPHETS. NO, I CAME TO FULFILL THEM.
—MATTHEW 5:17

Dr. James Rosscup is a simple, studious man who teaches Bible exposition at Master's Seminary. One semester, Dr. Rosscup had a student who depended on his wife to type his papers for class. One evening, the student called Dr. Rosscup to ask for an extension on a paper that was due the next day. He explained that his wife was in the hospital and there was no one to type his paper. He had hoped that Dr. Rosscup would relax his standards and allow him to be late this one time. But the standard was set, and Dr. Rosscup said he could not accept the paper if it was late. "Where do you live?" he asked the student. A short time later, Dr. Rosscup arrived at the student's home, took his place at the typewriter, and began to type. Knowing his student couldn't live up to the standard that was set and unable to lower the standard, he fulfilled the requirements of the standard in his student's place.

This is such a beautiful picture of what Christ has done for us! The standard has been set. And the standard is holiness. It doesn't take too long to realize that we can't meet the standard. We can never be acceptable to God on our own. And while it might seem fair and reasonable to us that God could simply lower his standards to allow for a little sin, a little humanness, we know that to do so would make him less than God. Our pleas of ignorance are inexcusable, our comparisons with others are impermissible, our pious efforts are unacceptable, and the conclusion is unavoidable: We simply can't live up to what God demands. "For no one can ever be made right in God's sight by doing what his law commands. For the more we know God's law, the clearer it becomes that we aren't obeying it" (Romans 3:20).

We can be overwhelmed with our own inadequacy and in a state of constant frustration, or we can call on Jesus to fulfill for us what his righteous law demands. Jesus says to us, "Where do you live? I'm on my way over." That is why he came. He came to live the perfect life you and I cannot live, to die the death we should have died. Love fulfills what the law demands, and we forever benefit.

Holy Jesus, sometimes all I can see is my own inadequacy. Will you lift my eyes to see your sufficiency on my behalf? Will you show me day by day what it means that you have credited your righteousness to my account?

DIGGING DEEPER

According to Romans 4:1-8, how are we declared righteous?

GOD EXACTS VENGEANCE, SO I NEED NOT SEEK REVENGE

Dear friends, never avenge yourselves. Leave that to God. For it is written, "I will take vengeance; I will repay those who deserve it," says the Lord.
—Romans 12:19

Have you been unjustly fired, unfairly criticized, or unceremoniously abandoned? Does the cruelty or thoughtlessness or injustice of it cry out from within you, calling for someone to pay for the hurt inflicted on you?

Into the fury of our righteous demands for revenge Jesus speaks, saying that we should love our enemies. To our ears these words sound like God is asking us to be a pushover, to be the loser once again. To us these words seem to deny the basic sense of justice that is a part of our nature as well as God's. But was Jesus really saying that wrongs do not have to be righted, that no price must be paid for injustice?

Not at all. Jesus doesn't mean justice won't be done; he means God will do it. And this is not just something Jesus talked about; it is what he lived. "[Christ] did not retaliate when he was insulted. When he suffered, he did not threaten to get even. He left his case in the hands of God, who always judges fairly" (1 Peter 2:23). The most innocent man who ever lived suffered the most outrageous injustice ever inflicted, and yet he refused to carry the burden of revenge, turning it over to God because he knew God would settle it in a just way. Do you believe there is a God in heaven? Would you show that belief by allowing him to avenge the evil done against you? Would you release your right of revenge to God?

It's natural to want the people who have hurt us to pay with pain—the same measure of pain they have caused us. This is what comes naturally to us. However, we are not people who live by natural means, but by the supernatural Spirit of God. The Holy Spirit enables us to let go. Letting go of your right to revenge means releasing your hurt, confident that God sees the wrong done to you, that he perceives the motives of those who hurt you more clearly than you do, and that he will settle all accounts with perfect justice. Refusing to seek revenge is not merely a rule we should keep, but a miracle we can experience, a grace we can receive. Are you willing to welcome this grace? Will you surrender your rights and entrust revenge to your God?

Can I truly trust you, my righteous Defender, to take vengeance on my behalf? It seems like a costly surrender to give up my right to revenge. How I need your Spirit to pry it from my hands and entrust it into yours.

DIGGING DEEPER

Read the following verses: Matthew 5:38-42; Luke 6:35; and Romans 12:14-21. According to these verses, what should we do in place of seeking revenge?

WEEK 17

GIFTS OF GOD

MEDITATION, REFLECTION, AND PRAYER

Meditate on the gifts of God revealed in the Scriptures below. Praise God for his generosity and thank him for each provision.

Reflect on your life. Have you accepted these gifts of God? Are you maximizing the blessings of these gifts into your life? Consider how you might enjoy these gifts more fully in the days ahead.

Pray through this scriptural list of God's gifts, asking him to bless you with each gift and committing to be a good steward of each gift God gives you.

> Jesus Christ brought *forgiveness* to many through God's bountiful gift. (Romans 5:15)
>
> We have the free gift of *being accepted by God*, even though we are guilty of many sins. (Romans 5:16)
>
> All who receive God's gracious gift of *righteousness* will live in triumph over sin and death. (Romans 5:17)
>
> A *spiritual gift* is given to each of us as a means of helping the entire church. (1 Corinthians 12:7)
>
> Jesus himself is life, and this life gives *light* to everyone. (John 1:4)
>
> The Holy Spirit gives *new life* from heaven. (John 3:6)
>
> Jesus left us with a gift—*peace of mind and heart*. (John 14:27)
>
> God gives us the gift of *hope*. (Romans 15:13)
>
> God gives us *victory over sin and death* through Jesus Christ. (1 Corinthians 15:57)
>
> God gives us the *ability to stand firm for Christ*. (2 Corinthians 1:21)
>
> Wherever the Spirit of the Lord is, he gives *freedom*. (2 Corinthians 3:17)

The Spirit gives us *desires that are opposite from what the sinful nature desires.* (Galatians 5:17)

Christ gives me the *strength* I need. (Philippians 4:13)

God gives us *special favor* in Christ Jesus. (2 Timothy 2:1)

He gives *life and breath* to everything, and he satisfies every need there is. (Acts 17:25)

WEEK 18

LOOKING TO THE CROSS

I dragged my feet about seeing Mel Gibson's movie *The Passion of the Christ*. I'm not sure I can completely articulate my reluctance except that the movie is very realistic in regard to the Crucifixion, revealing its cruelty and gore. And I guess it is a sight I have not wanted to look at. Besides, I don't do well with movies in which there is great injustice. Oftentimes David has to remind me "it is just a movie; it isn't real." But that is the problem with *The Passion of the Christ*: it is real. The Cross is the most real, most relevant, most revolutionary event in history.

There are benefits to gazing upon the Cross, if not on the big screen, in our own hearts and minds and through the pages of Scripture. The Cross has much to show us and say to us if we will stop long enough to linger and listen. Will you look with me upon the Cross?

THIS WEEK'S PASSAGE FOR MEDITATION

Two others, both criminals, were led out to be executed with him. Finally, they came to a place called The Skull. All three were crucified there—Jesus on the center cross, and the two criminals on either side.

Jesus said, "Father, forgive these people, because they don't know what they are doing." And the soldiers gambled for his clothes by throwing dice.

The crowd watched, and the leaders laughed and scoffed. "He saved others," they said, "let him save himself if he is really God's Chosen One, the Messiah."

By this time it was noon, and darkness fell across the whole land until three o'clock. The light from the sun was gone. And suddenly, the thick veil hanging in the Temple was torn apart. Then Jesus shouted, "Father, I entrust my spirit into your hands!" And with those words he breathed his last.

When the captain of the Roman soldiers handling the executions saw what had happened, he praised God and said, "Surely this man was innocent." And when the crowd that came to see the crucifixion saw all that had happened, they went home in deep sorrow. But Jesus' friends, including the women who had followed him from Galilee, stood at a distance watching. —Luke 23:32-35, 44-49

THE CROSS SHOWS ME THE JOY OF JESUS

He was willing to die a shameful death on the cross because of the joy he knew would be his afterward. —Hebrews 12:2

What joy could Jesus see that enabled him to endure the pain and agony of the Cross? What joy did he know would be his? As Jesus looked ahead, he could see the joy of redemption. By paying the debt for sin, Jesus satisfied justice. It brought him joy to complete the work he was sent to do, which was to pay the price for your sin and my sin. And as he endured the Cross, your face was on his mind, and he was full of joy that the price was now paid so you could spend eternity with him.

Jesus also anticipated the joy of resurrection. He had told his followers numerous times that he would die and that he would also rise again. But they could not imagine the death, nor could they fathom resurrection. His was a shameful death—but not because of his own shame. He had never done anything to be ashamed of. He took the shame of everyone who has ever regretted things they have said or done. Imagine the shame. Yet Jesus could have true joy because he knew he would break the power of shame and death forever and offer abundant life in the place of immobilizing shame.

Occasionally we see on television the return of soldiers who have been away from their families for months or years at a time. And as we watch them run toward those they love, we can feel the sense of joy and release of their reunion, can't we? Now imagine Jesus, who lived in perfect fellowship with the Father from before the foundation of the world. Then he was sent to earth and took on human flesh, with work to do. And as Jesus headed toward the Cross, he began to anticipate the joy of reunion with the Father. Can you just imagine the joy? Jesus returned to heaven having endured the Cross and completed the work, and he is now back in the glory he knew before with the One he loves so dearly.

But Jesus is not content to keep this joy to himself. He longs to share his joy with you and me—as we are redeemed and as we anticipate resurrection—when we will be reunited with him forever. What joy!

Joyful Jesus, I am amazed at your willingness to bear my shame on the cross. Because of you, I can see the joy ahead in redemption, resurrection, and reunion. And I am humbled that you want to share this joy with me forever.

DIGGING DEEPER

What does John 16:16-24 further reveal about the joy Jesus anticipates?

THE CROSS KEEPS ME FROM GIVING UP

Consider him who endured such opposition from sinful men, so that you will not grow weary and lose heart. —Hebrews 12:3 (NIV)

Come and linger with me at the Cross. As we linger and see Jesus there, we find what we need to persevere when things get hard so that we won't grow weary and lose heart. Consider him . . .

When you feel sorry for yourself because your life is hard and you want the easy way out . . . consider him. Consider the difficulty of his life of poverty, never having a home of his own, depending on the kindness of others. See the pain of rejection as those who welcomed him with palm branches later called for his crucifixion. Consider him and do not lose heart.

When you feel forgotten by God and by those you thought cared about you, when you long for the closeness of someone who cares . . . consider him. Consider what it must have been like in those moments on the cross when his Father turned away and he was forsaken. Consider what it was like to be rejected and ridiculed by his own family and the people of his hometown. Consider him and do not lose heart.

When you feel tired and you want to give up . . . consider him. Consider how he spent the whole night in prayer, agonizing over the path he was about to walk. See him sweating drops of blood. Watch him endure the trials and torture after a night of no sleep. Consider him and do not grow weary.

When you feel abused and you want to fight back . . . consider him. Consider his humble responses to those who lied about him and spit on him, ridiculed him, and beat him. Consider him and do not grow weary.

When you feel fearful about the future and you want to find hope . . . consider him, who for the joy set before him endured the Cross. Whenever you are tempted to give up, look to the Cross and see the price Jesus paid so that he might call you his very own.

Faithful, enduring Jesus, in my weariness and discouragement, I often just want to rest and have the hurt and difficulty disappear. But I see you on the cross, and as I consider your courage and commitment in the face of difficulty and even death, you encourage me to never give up.

DIGGING DEEPER

Read about the crucifixion of Jesus in John 19:16-30 or Luke 23:26-49. Consider the details prayerfully and note how they can encourage you when you want to give up.

THE CROSS HELPS ME MAKE SENSE OF SUFFERING

We know that God causes everything to work together for the good of those who love God and are called according to his purpose for them.
—Romans 8:28

It is often a struggle for me to make sense of suffering. I am strongly tempted to label so much of the suffering I see around me as senseless tragedy. Do you ever wonder if there is some other way God could accomplish his purposes in the world that wouldn't have to hurt so many people? More significantly, do you wonder if God could accomplish his purposes in *your* life in a way that wouldn't have to hurt you so much?

It is clear to me from Scripture that God loves us, that his loving plan for us sometimes includes suffering, and that he uses this suffering for our ultimate good and his own glory. I believe that. I accept that. But I can't say that I completely understand that, nor can I definitively explain it.

There's only one thing that enables me to accept what I cannot understand about my suffering and the suffering of this world: the Cross. I look at the Cross and the enormous suffering it represents, and I am humbled and ashamed that I think I could know better than God what is good and right and purposeful. I see that there is a larger plan at work that my heart and my mind can barely comprehend. But mostly I see that the Cross is the ultimate example of God's ability to work all things together for good—even the most wicked deed darkness ever conceived. And if God can work together the cruel death and enormous suffering of his Son on the cross to bring about the greatest good of all time, then perhaps he really can do something good in and through the suffering in our lives too.

Either everything works for good or nothing makes sense. It is the "everything" in Romans 8:28 that is both stumbling block and blessed solace. "Everything" means there is not one thing that falls outside of this promise—not incest, not suicide, not murder, disfigurement, or divorce. I would never say to you that these things are good, and neither does God. But with full confidence I do say to you—if you love God, he will use even the worst thing you can imagine for your ultimate good. And if you doubt that, simply look to the Cross.

My Redeemer, I choose by faith to believe that you are using even the most bitter experiences in my life to bless me. Thank you for the glimpses you give me of your good purposes in my pain.

DIGGING DEEPER

Read Ephesians 1:7; Colossians 1:22; and Hebrews 2:14-15; 9:14. What are the good things resulting from the great evil of Jesus being nailed to a cross, according to these verses?

THE CROSS CALLS ME TO HUMBLE OBEDIENCE

He made himself nothing; he took the humble position of a slave and appeared in human form. And in human form he obediently humbled himself even further by dying a criminal's death on a cross. —Philippians 2:7-8

No one in the first century would have ever believed that the cross would become a fashion statement. No one would have put a cross on top of a building or hung one around her neck. The cross was a shameful, barbaric form of execution reserved for the scum of the earth.

So when we read of the downward spiral Christ chose—making himself nothing, taking the position of a slave, and appearing in human form, we come to the lowest place a person could go. And when we think God has gone as far as he will go, he takes another step downward. "He humbled himself *even further* by dying a criminal's death on a cross." There was no place too low, no service too sacrificial, no loss too great that he would not willingly choose to humble himself in that way so that he might give us life. And in the process, he shows us how to live.

Do you find yourself working hard to be somebody, to prove your own worth, to make a name for yourself? Look at Jesus, who made himself nothing. Isaiah said, "There was nothing beautiful or majestic about his appearance, nothing to attract us to him" (Isaiah 53:2).

Do you think Jesus has called you to a job or role of service that's "beneath you" and an utter waste of your talents? Do you think you deserve better? Look at Jesus and see how he let go of the rights of deity to willingly become a slave.

Do you resent the family God has placed you in, the body he has given you, the way he formed your personality? Look at Jesus and see how he left the glory of heaven to become a baby in a manger, a criminal on a cross.

When you hear the call of Jesus to die to yourself, does it seem too much to ask? Look at the Cross. See the depths to which Jesus sank in obedience to his Father and the lengths to which he went to love. Then make your choice to follow him.

Humble Jesus, I feel trapped by my drive to be important, be noticed, and be served. But I see it is getting me nowhere and I am never satisfied. Help me to keep my eyes on you and follow you in this downward life of servanthood and humility, believing you will satisfy me and lift me up at the right time.

DIGGING DEEPER

What does 1 Peter 2:13-25 reveal about the example of humble obedience Christ set for us?

THE CROSS GUIDES ME HOME

Christ also suffered when he died for our sins once for all time. He never sinned, but he died for sinners that he might bring us safely home to God. —1 Peter 3:18

The day they walked out of a hotel room in Changsha, Hunan, China, with their daughter Shaohannah, their lives were changed forever. Then, a little over two years later at a dedication ceremony for a friend's adopted daughter from China, Steven Curtis Chapman sensed God speaking to him about adopting again. "I felt God speak to my heart so clearly: *This picture you are looking at is a picture of the gospel. I know you have concerns and fears, but if you trust me with these things, I'm inviting you into this adventure again.*" Within days they began the adoption process again and soon went on to complete the adoption of their daughter Stevey Joy Ru Chapman. But they still weren't finished.

The Chapmans' third daughter from China, Maria, made her debut at my son Matt's football scrimmage recently to oohs, ahs, and applause. As I watch Steven and Mary Beth unload the strollers, change diapers, and chase these girls around, I'm touched to witness the lengths this family has gone not only to bring these girls out of orphanages in China, but into their home, into their lives, into their hearts. Their desire was not simply to get these girls out of orphanages, but to bring them safely into their home and make them a part of their family.

It is a beautiful picture of the lengths God has gone to rescue you and me from a lonely life and a fearful death. He was willing not only to take on human flesh, but also to take on your sin and my sin and the sin of the entire world. What would make him, who has no sin of his own, go that far?

He wants to bring us safely home to himself. He wants to dwell with us and in us. He wants to share himself and his home with us. This is the heart of God. And we see it when we look at the Cross. The Cross shows us how far God is willing to go to bring us safely home and make us his own. The home of God is a place of great joy and happiness. There he will parent us with wisdom, care for us with compassion, and give us everything we need. And best of all, he will share that home with us so we can know him. "You will show me the way of life, granting me the joy of your presence and the pleasures of living with you forever" (Psalm 16:11).

My Rescuer, I look at the Cross and see the lengths you will go to bring me safely home to you. I see what it cost you to take my sin upon yourself, and it shows me where I will always find the love I'm looking for: at home with you.

DIGGING DEEPER

Read Psalm 84. Look for attributes of God and the place God dwells, as well as the attitude and activities of the psalmist as he is at home in God's house.

WEEK 18

LOOKING TO THE CROSS

REFLECTION

As you consider the suffering and significance of the Cross, what draws you to Jesus, and what causes you to want to look away?

How do you want careful gazing at the Cross to change you? How do you want it to change the way you relate to other people and the way you relate to Jesus?

MEDITATION

Your attitude should be the same that Christ Jesus had. Though he was God, he did not demand and cling to his rights as God.

He made himself nothing; he took the humble position of a slave and appeared in human form.

And in human form he obediently humbled himself even further by dying a criminal's death on a cross.

Because of this, God raised him up to the heights of heaven and gave him a name that is above every other name,

so that at the name of Jesus every knee will bow, in heaven and on earth and under the earth,

and every tongue will confess that Jesus Christ is Lord, to the glory of God the Father.

—PHILIPPIANS 2:5-11

Read through this passage, stopping to take in the full meaning of each step taken by Christ as he descended to us. Try to explore the full weight of every choice made by Jesus.

Then follow Christ each step upward to heaven, seeking to envision the glory of each honor God has bestowed upon him.

Ask God to show you how your attitude needs to change to more closely align with the attitude of Christ.

PRAYER

Praise God for the magnificence of the gospel of the Cross—his plan that seems foolish to the world but is the power of God for those who are being saved.

Thank God for his willingness to hold nothing back and go to any length to bring you safely home to God.

Intercede for those who have grown weary and lost heart and are tempted to give up on God in their discouragement and disappointment.

Confess your limitations in taking in the full cost of the Cross, and ask God to give you a greater sense of his sacrifice so he might become more precious to you.

Petition God to use your vision of the Cross to help you understand and accept the suffering in your own life.

MEANING IN THE CROSS

What do you think has been the most important day of your life? The day you were born? The day you graduated from high school? Your wedding day? The most important day in your life is the day Christ died for you on the cross. Your connection to the Cross is the most important thing about you.

It also has the biggest impact regarding your future. When you reach heaven, the most essential aspect of your identity will not be the home you grew up in, the friendships that shaped you, or the things you accomplished. None of these things will have made an impression as lasting as the Cross.

If the Cross is the pivotal event of your past and the focal point of your future, shouldn't it have the central place in your life now? Shouldn't we contemplate the implications of the Cross in our lives and the many gifts it bought for us?

> *"Let [the Cross] saturate your soul, let it penetrate your spirit, let it subdue your faculties, let it take the reins of all your powers and guide you whither it will. Let the Redeemer, he whose hands were pierced for you, sway the scepter of your spirit and rule over you this day, and world without end."* —Charles Spurgeon

THIS WEEK'S PASSAGE FOR MEDITATION

We praise God for the wonderful kindness he has poured out on us because we belong to his dearly loved Son. He is so rich in kindness that he purchased our freedom through the blood of his Son, and our sins are forgiven. He has showered his kindness on us, along with all wisdom and understanding. —Ephesians 1:6-8

THE CROSS MAKES IT POSSIBLE FOR ME TO DRAW NEAR

We can boldly enter heaven's Most Holy Place because of the blood of Jesus. This is the new, life-giving way that Christ has opened up for us through the sacred curtain, by means of his death. Let us go right into the presence of God, with true hearts fully trusting him. —Hebrews 10:19-22

First class is nice when you're up front, but there's something annoying about it when you're not—especially when the flight attendant snaps the curtain in place to create a barrier between the privileged few and us peons in coach. Scripture describes a more significant curtain that kept everyone except the high priest out of the Tabernacle's Holy of Holies, where the glory of God dwelled. Literally, no one was good enough to enter because of the offense of their sin. This curtain kept us all out.

But when Christ breathed his last breath on the cross, "the curtain in the Temple was torn in two" (Matthew 27:51). Now we are invited to enter into the holy presence of God, not because we've earned the right, but because Christ has credited his righteousness—or rightness—to us. What an invitation! Not only can you now approach the Creator of the universe, you can also make your home with him and share your heart and your hurts with him. You have the opportunity to get to know God himself! So what is keeping you from it?

Do you think that an intimate relationship with God is something that other people experience but something you can never really expect to experience for yourself? Do you think you just aren't "one of those people" meant to have a meaningful relationship with God? Do you think an intimate relationship with Christ is only for those who always do the right thing, those who never fall into sin, those who seem to have it all together?

He's forgiven you and given you his own holiness. He wants to know you. Christ has set you free from failure, guilt, and shame so that you can be bold enough to get to know God intimately. Wouldn't it be a shame to waste one more year, one more month, one more day on the fringes of real relationship with God because you've believed the lie that you are not good enough or not welcomed enough to boldly approach God and get to know him?

My Barrier Breaker, you have opened the way for me to approach and know God intimately. Keep drawing me close so that I can leave behind my guilt and shame and know the comfort and confidence of life in your presence.

DIGGING DEEPER

Read Exodus 26:31-35 and Hebrews 9:1-15 to learn more about the veil that once separated us from God.

THE CROSS RECONCILES ME TO GOD

Since we were restored to friendship with God by the death of his Son while we were still his enemies, we will certainly be delivered from eternal punishment by his life. So now we can rejoice in our wonderful new relationship with God—all because of what our Lord Jesus Christ has done for us in making us friends of God. —Romans 5:10-11

Unpaid debts, unmet expectations, and unfinished business finally came to a head for my friends—two couples who were estranged from each other after a business venture hit hard times. Feelings were hurt and the friendship was fractured. They met to work it through, but their attempt seemed to only bring more issues to the surface. Then they found themselves standing at Gabe's grave after everyone else had gone, and the four of them embraced. In the sobering reality of that moment, resentment gave way to reconciliation. I've always seen it as a beautiful benediction to Gabe's life, and a blossom of hope growing out of his death.

Reconciliation is close to the heart of God. His desire for reconciliation with those he loves cost him the ultimate price—his Son. The Cross made it possible for you and me to be friends with God. Not merely his servants, but his friends!

Have you been thinking God is mad at you, that he sent difficulties into your life out of anger or retribution for your offenses against him or apathy toward him? God is not mad at you. In fact, he has gone to incredible lengths to restore his friendship with you. He did not wait for you to warm up to him, but in fact, while you were still his enemy, he paid the price of reconciliation with his life. He has taken the first costly step toward you. Won't you take a step toward him and respond to his offer—not just of salvation but also of friendship?

The Cross is the means by which we reconcile not only with God but also with each other. "Together as one body, Christ reconciled both groups to God by means of his death, and our hostility toward each other was put to death" (Ephesians 2:16). When we're standing at the foot of the cross, our disagreements and disappointments with each other don't seem to matter so much. And as we gaze on Innocence upon the cross, we simply cannot hold on to the offenses we've built into walls. Now we can enjoy the depth and joy of friendship with each other that reflects our friendship with God.

Reconciler, I am in awe that God would go to such lengths to be my friend. Remind me to look at the Cross when reconciliation with my brother or sister seems to cost more than I am willing to pay.

DIGGING DEEPER

What does 2 Corinthians 5:18-21 teach us about Christ's role and our role in reconciliation?

THE CROSS PAID THE RANSOM TO SET ME FREE

You know that God paid a ransom to save you from the empty life you inherited from your ancestors. And the ransom he paid was not mere gold or silver. He paid for you with the precious lifeblood of Christ, the sinless, spotless Lamb of God. God chose him for this purpose long before the world began. —1 Peter 1:18-20

At the beginning of their yearlong hostage ordeal in the Philippines, Abu Sayyaf captors told missionaries Martin and Gracia Burnham they believed they could get a million dollar ransom payment for them because they were Americans. But Martin and Gracia knew their mission agency would not pay a ransom, as it would put other missionaries in jeopardy around the world. They also knew their families did not have the means to pay. So as other hostages arranged for ransoms and were released, the Burnhams remained in captivity.

Sitting around the fire in the jungle one day, Gracia told the other hostages, "I'm glad that when Jesus paid a ransom for us, we didn't have to wait for it to arrive or wait for him to decide if he was going to do it. Before the foundations of the world, he knew he would ransom us and that it would cost him everything."

Ransom paying is precious to the believer because we were once captives, existing in a life devoid of meaning and purpose, going nowhere. But we've been bought back. Jesus paid a ransom so we would no longer be enslaved to the emptiness of materialism, the meaninglessness of ritualism, or the insidiousness of cynicism. And this ransom was not paid with mere money. Money could not buy you back. You could only be bought with the costly and precious blood of Christ. The blood of Christ was the purchase price for your freedom so that you can live a life of meaning and purpose. His blood is of infinite value, spilled on your behalf to free you from futility.

Eventually an American philanthropist paid the Abu Sayyaf for Martin and Gracia's release, but their captors decided it wasn't enough and asked for more. You need never fear that the ransom Jesus paid for you is insufficient. The blood of Christ is sufficient to free you from everything in your past that has bound you, and now you can freely enjoy the full life he has bought for you.

My Ransom Payer, how can I ever thank you for paying the ransom that has set me free? I've been set free from the captivity of an empty life so that I can love you and enjoy you. I'm yours.

DIGGING DEEPER

According to Isaiah 53:4-6 and 2 Corinthians 5:21, to whom was the ransom paid for our forgiveness and freedom?

THE CROSS MEANS I BELONG TO GOD

Don't you know that your body is the temple of the Holy Spirit, who lives in you and was given to you by God? You do not belong to yourself, for God bought you with a high price. So you must honor God with your body.
—1 Corinthians 6:19-20

I love watching the Olympic Games. I can't watch the runners compete without hearing in my head the theme from *Chariots of Fire* as well as the voice of Eric Liddell's character saying, "I believe God made me for a purpose, but He also made me fast. And when I run I feel His pleasure." Liddell understood that his body belonged to God, and he wanted to honor God with his body.

When we truly comprehend the painful price paid for us to belong to God, it simply does not fit that we could say with our lives, "I have been bought with a price so I can live as I please." If my body is not my own, if it belongs to God, I have no right to defile my body, waste my energy, or serve myself. If my body belongs to God, every power, every passion, and every ability is altogether God's. But while this is easy to say, it is so hard to live!

A real redemption demands real holiness, and the price paid for us demands from us a practical surrendering of ourselves to the service of others and the pleasure of God. But what a sweet surrender! Belonging to God is full of delight, not demands. Offering God your body and honoring him with the body he has given you is a great joy and privilege of life.

Has God given you energy? Burn your energy in service to God. Has God given you intellectual prowess? Honor God with your mind as you engage an unbeliever in evaluating the claims of Christ. Has God given you a body that is disfigured or disabled? Honor God with your spirit as you display joy in place of self-pity, gratitude in place of resentment. Are your arms empty? Perhaps God has emptied them so you will be able to wrap them around someone who is lonely. Is your heart broken? Perhaps God has allowed your heart to be broken so you will be more sensitive to the hurts of others. Honor God with your heart as you open it to the hurts of others. There is no greater freedom than in belonging to God and no greater satisfaction than honoring God with your body.

Redeemer, you have bought me with your pain and with your death, and I am yours. Such a sacrifice demands that I keep my body from being defiled, my mind from being polluted, and my heart from being corrupted by the world.

DIGGING DEEPER

Read Romans 6:13; 1 Corinthians 6:12-20; 9:27; and Colossians 1:24. What do these verses teach about what you should and should not do with your body?

THE CROSS UNLEASHES THE POWER OF GOD

I KNOW VERY WELL HOW FOOLISH THE MESSAGE OF THE CROSS SOUNDS TO THOSE WHO ARE ON THE ROAD TO DESTRUCTION. BUT WE WHO ARE BEING SAVED RECOGNIZE THIS MESSAGE AS THE VERY POWER OF GOD. —1 CORINTHIANS 1:18

You might as well know: I love to watch the *Dr. Phil Show*, sitting in on his counseling sessions via the magic of television. I love it when he gives a sly smile to someone who is justifying a particular attitude or action and says, "How's that workin' for ya?" It often comes down to people realizing they need to change, but they feel powerless to change. And we know what they feel like, don't we? The power to change is what we want, isn't it? We don't want to be stuck living the same way, haunted by the same insecurities and guilt, enslaved by the same appetites and patterns the rest of our lives. Yet we think, *That is the way I am; I can never change.*

The message of the Cross is good news for people who don't want to keep living the same way they've been living. And bold, expectant faith is the channel through which God pours his supportive power—sin-conquering, life-transforming, courage-generating power. What is the message of the Cross that is the power of God? It is power to change.

The same determination that kept Jesus walking toward the Cross is available to you as you persevere in obedience to God. The same strength that enabled Jesus to withstand ridicule is available to you as you encounter those who belittle your faith. The same ability to forgive that Jesus showed to those who nailed him to the cross is available to you as you seek to forgive those who make your suffering more intense. And the same force that brought Jesus back to life is available to rejuvenate the dead places in your heart where you believe the hurts of life have left you unable to live and love again.

Where do you need the power of the Cross in your life right now? Are you looking for strength to withstand the pull of an addiction, staying power in a marriage, energy to keep putting one foot in front of the other in an unbearable situation? The message of the Cross is the power of God not only for your salvation, but for your transformation.

My Power for change, I am powerless to do what you want me to do and to become who you want me to be. Will you give me your life-transforming, death-conquering power today so I can begin to experience real change?

DIGGING DEEPER

What do you learn about the power of God in John 9:3; Romans 15:13; 2 Corinthians 13:4; 2 Thessalonians 1:11-12; and Hebrews 4:12?

WEEK 19

MEANING IN THE CROSS

REFLECTION

What gifts has the Cross given to you that mean the most to you and why? What do those gifts mean to you today and for eternity?

In what ways does the Cross define your life and serve as the center point of your life? And if it doesn't, how can you move it to a place of greater prominence and appreciation?

MEDITATION

We praise God for the wonderful kindness he has poured out on us because we belong to his dearly loved Son. He is so rich in kindness that he purchased our freedom through the blood of his Son, and our sins are forgiven. He has showered his kindness on us, along with all wisdom and understanding. —Ephesians 1:6-8

Read through the verse several times, turning it into a prayer of praise to God.

Circle each word that indicates a unique gift God has given to you, and thank him for how each gift has been a reality in your life.

Underline each word that describes the measure and generosity of the gifts of God.

PRAYER

Praise God for the wisdom and power and meaning of the Cross.

Thank Jesus for paying your debt, cleansing your conscience, and giving you eternal life through the Cross.

Intercede for those who reject and even ridicule the gifts of the Cross.

Confess your lack of appreciation for the price of pain and death Jesus paid so you would belong to God.

Petition God to deepen your desire to glory only in the Cross.

When I survey the wondrous cross
On which the Prince of Glory died,
My richest gain I count but loss,
And pour contempt on all my pride.
Forbid it, Lord, that I should boast,
Save in the death of Christ, my God;
All the vain things that charm me most,
I sacrifice them to his blood.
See, from his head, his hands, his feet,
Sorrow and love flow mingled down;
Did e'er such love and sorrow meet,
Or thorns compose so rich a crown?
Were the whole realm of nature mine,
That were an offering far too small;
Love so amazing, so divine,
Demands my soul, my life, my all. —Isaac Watts

WEEK 20

HOPE

We had had the name *Hope* in mind for a daughter for years. So when she came, there was no question what we would name her. To me, it was a sweet and simple name, but I could not have told you at the time what the word really means. I had a lot to learn about hope, and really, I think I still do.

When we finally had Hope's diagnosis of Zellweger Syndrome confirmed by a blood test, we sent out a combination birth announcement–Christmas card that was also a desperate act of self-preservation. We didn't want to have to explain it all to everyone we knew one-by-one. It was difficult to say and perhaps more shocking to hear: "This is our daughter, Hope, and she is going to die." So we let the card do it.

Our graphic designer friends Bobby and Kim Sagmiller rose to the occasion to design the card and make it beautiful, and they added something very special—a definition they had discovered of the word *hope*: "the expectation of a favorable future under God's direction." This provided a starting point for my quest to understand what real hope is—especially in the midst of a situation that appeared to be hopeless from a human perspective.

The Scriptures talk a lot about hope. First Peter 3:15 says, "If you are asked about your Christian hope, always be ready to explain it." Perhaps we need to figure out what we're talking about when we use the word *hope*. What is hope—true biblical hope?

THIS WEEK'S PASSAGE FOR MEDITATION

We can rejoice, too, when we run into problems and trials, for we know that they are good for us—they help us learn to endure. And endurance develops strength of character in us, and character strengthens our confident expectation of salvation. And this expectation will not disappoint us. For we know how dearly God loves us, because he has given us the Holy Spirit to fill our hearts with his love. —Romans 5:3-5

MORE THAN WISHFUL THINKING

WHAT IS FAITH? IT IS THE CONFIDENT ASSURANCE THAT WHAT WE HOPE FOR IS GOING TO HAPPEN. IT IS THE EVIDENCE OF THINGS WE CANNOT YET SEE. —HEBREWS 11:1

I recently received a direct-mail advertisement for a magazine called *Hope*, which of course intrigued me. On the inside, they offer a definition of hope from *The Cambridge International Dictionary*: "hope *n.* a desire for the future to be as good as you want it to be." Is that what hope is?

Typically, when we say we "hope" for something, we're saying we're not sure it is going to happen but we want it to happen. We have no sense of confidence that it will come about. We say, "I hope I can lose five more pounds before picture-taking day." "I hope the stock market will turn around so we will have enough money to retire comfortably." "I hope this new treatment will relieve the pain."

But biblical hope is not like that. Biblical hope is much more than wishful thinking. Hebrews 11:1 says that "Faith is being *sure* of what we hope for and *certain* of what we do not see" (NIV, emphasis added). There is nothing uncertain about biblical hope. It speaks of something that is sure but not yet a reality that we can see. Biblical hope is certain but not yet realized. We haven't experienced it yet, but there is no question that it will happen. Hope is like a memory of the future—a God-secured, God-infused, God-glorifying future.

The hope that God provides for you and me as we face an uncertain and perhaps difficult future is not based on wishful thinking that the future will be as good as we want it to be. It is the confident assurance that we can entrust our lives to the One who holds the future no matter what happens. Are you willing to leave behind your wishful thinking and grab on to God-confident hope, believing that your eternal future will be much better than you can imagine?

Faith Giver, so often I settle for the uncertainty of seeking what I want when I want it, and I'm left disappointed. Show me what it means to place all my confidence in you. Fill me with the assurance that my greatest hopes and dreams are fulfilled in you, even when I can't see it for myself.

DIGGING DEEPER

Read Romans 8:23-25. How do these verses reflect the truth that our hope is certain?

HOLD TIGHT TO HOPE

SUCH THINGS WERE WRITTEN IN THE SCRIPTURES LONG AGO TO TEACH US. THEY GIVE US HOPE AND ENCOURAGEMENT AS WE WAIT PATIENTLY FOR GOD'S PROMISES.
—ROMANS 15:4

Do you want to find some evidence that what you are hoping for is going to happen? Your best source for that information and for the encouragement you need as you wait is found in the Scriptures. They were written so that we might have hope.

In Hebrews 10:23 (NIV) we are admonished to "hold unswervingly to the hope we profess." What is the hope that the Hebrews professed and that we profess today? That professed hope is eternal salvation solely through Jesus. The writer to the Hebrews is saying, Don't waver on the source and surety and sufficiency of your salvation.

A couple of years ago, we planted three evergreen trees in our backyard. But one of them just would not stay up—the slightest breeze would blow it down. My dad found an old broom handle in the garage, stuck it deep into the ground, and tied the always-falling-down tree to it. That way, no matter how much the wind blew, the tree didn't fall down again.

When you choose to hold on to the hope of your salvation—Jesus himself—it is as if you drive a stake into the solid ground of God's Word and hold on for dear life. Then, when the wind of adversity or doubt or persecution comes your way, you can hold steady without falling.

You are only foolish to keep holding out hope if the foundation of your hope is insecure. Our confidence in regard to the future is based on the security of God's promises . . . even when we can't see any sign that those promises are being fulfilled. Biblical hope is based on what God has said, not on what we can see. That is the essence of faith—believing when you can't see. Will you drive the stake of your life deep into the Word of God, sinking your most precious hopes in his promises and provision?

Solid Ground of hope, I want to drive the stake of my life deep into your very words of life and eternal hope, knowing that this daily decision will keep my life from collapsing when the wind of adversity blows.

DIGGING DEEPER

Read Hebrews 6:13-20. What makes God's oath that he will fulfill his promise to Abraham reliable? What are two reasons God confirmed his promises with an oath (verses 17-18)?

LIFE FROM DEATH

If Christ has not been raised, then your faith is useless, and you are still under condemnation for your sins. In that case, all who have died believing in Christ have perished! And if we have hope in Christ only for this life, we are the most miserable people in the world. But the fact is that Christ has been raised from the dead. —1 Corinthians 15:17-20

Useless faith. Who wants that? Faith that is just going through the motions of religiosity, that offers no real possibility for the change that we crave, no confidence of a life beyond this one, is useless, powerless, impotent. We want the kind of faith that gives purpose and meaning to our lives now, and we want more than that. We want the confident expectation of salvation from this life into the next—life full of peace and perfection. We want death-defying faith that gives us confident hope!

Death-defying faith is made possible only through the resurrection of Jesus from the dead. If Jesus had just lived a perfect life, it would give us an example to conform our lives to, but it wouldn't supply the resources we need to live a holy life. If Jesus had just died, it would have paid the price to cover our sins so that we would not have to pay, but it would not provide the power to overcome sin and the effects of sin in our lives. It is the resurrection of Jesus that provides not only the power we need to live a life pleasing to God today, but the promise that life will not end when our bodies die. The resurrection of Jesus from the dead is what secures our hope for today and for the future!

If Jesus was not raised from the dead, then placing our hope for now and for the future in his hands is useless and foolish. If the Resurrection didn't happen, our hopes are limited to this life because there is no hope of life to come. But the truth is, the Resurrection is real. Jesus said, "I am the resurrection and the life. Those who believe in me, even though they die like everyone else, will live again" (John 11:25). Life out of death—for Jesus and for us. That's real hope.

Resurrected Savior, though sometimes it seems as if your bodily resurrection was too long ago to have any meaning in my life today, I see that its power reaches through the years to offer me hope for eternal life, and I am grateful.

DIGGING DEEPER

Read Acts 26:1-8. What do verses 6-8 reveal about why Paul is on trial and the basis for his argument?

AN OVERFLOW OF HOPE

I PRAY THAT GOD, WHO GIVES YOU HOPE, WILL KEEP YOU HAPPY AND FULL OF PEACE AS YOU BELIEVE IN HIM. MAY YOU OVERFLOW WITH HOPE THROUGH THE POWER OF THE HOLY SPIRIT. —ROMANS 15:13

How and where do we get the hope to believe something we can't see, promised by someone we have never seen? How can we have that kind of certainty to place our hopes on the Resurrection when we have never seen anyone come back to life? Is hope like this only for optimistic people? Only for those spiritually elite among us who seem to be able to swallow the spiritual realities that get stuck in the throat of some of the rest of us?

The Holy Spirit provides the biblical hope we need to believe. Through the power of the Holy Spirit you can be certain that what you can't see is really true. You can live with the peace and confidence that the salvation Jesus has provided for you is sure and sufficient, no matter what your circumstances. It is as if the Holy Spirit whispers to our spirit: *I am here, and the salvation I provide is not only for eternity but for now. It is bigger than the loss of your job, the addiction of your loved one, the depression that plagues you. You can't see it, but it is sure.*

When you place your faith in Christ, the Holy Spirit makes his dwelling within you, giving you ears to hear what God has said, eyes to see what is certain but not yet realized, and an inner confidence that you can trust what God has done and what he will do to secure your eternal future with him.

People with strong hope are not just those with a natural disposition to believe for the best. People with strong hope are those who are on a continual quest to move out their own agenda and desires and fears so that the Holy Spirit might move in and indwell them more fully, bringing with him an overflow of hope that, according to Romans 15:13, will "keep you happy and full of peace." Isn't that what you want even now? Come Holy Spirit!

Spirit of peace, I just can't do it on my own. How I want to be full of you and the hope only you can provide. Show me what lesser saviors and securities need to be removed so my heart and mind and life can be filled more fully with you.

DIGGING DEEPER

Read Romans 5:3-5. What is the process God uses to strengthen our hope? In addition to hope, what do these verses indicate the Holy Spirit gives us?

ETERNAL PLEASURE

Now we live with a wonderful expectation because Jesus Christ rose again from the dead. For God has reserved a priceless inheritance for his children. It is kept in heaven for you, pure and undefiled, beyond the reach of change and decay. —1 Peter 1:3-4

Perhaps our biggest struggle in regard to hope is not the lack of it but our desire—bordering on demand—that God fulfill what we are hoping for, what we believe he has promised to us, *here* and *now*.

Because we're human, we love pleasure. I love the pleasure of biting into the perfect strawberry, resting after accomplishing a big job, a hot shower on a cold morning. And there is nothing wrong with enjoying pleasure. In fact, the most pleasurable sensations and experiences we have in the here and now are just a taste of what we will experience in the future, on that day when evil is crushed forever and we are joined with God forever in a new heaven and a new earth. Dan Allender says in his book *The Healing Path*, "Think of the finest meal you've ever eaten. Recall the most pleasurable sexual moment with your beloved. Then realize that your memory offers but a glimmer of the glory that awaits you. Hope grows only to the degree that the pleasures of this world serve as a window to the glory of the next."

As believers, we do not want to be willing to settle for the pleasures this world has to offer. We want to live for the ultimate, permanent pleasure. For now, some of our hopes are fulfilled in a partial way. Then, all of our hopes will be completely fulfilled—on that day when eternal life in the presence of God begins. And the source of that pleasure will be Jesus. Biblical hope is not hope for something, but hope in Someone. And that Someone is Jesus. All of our deepest longings will be fulfilled when we are in his presence.

Would you be willing to pull up the anchor of hope that you've plunged into the things of this earth and sink it into the rich and enduring soil of heaven? Keep longing for the ultimate pleasure that is still ahead of us—an eternity spent in the presence of God.

Eternal Father, your promises are so valuable to me, I can't seem to help myself from wanting it all now! Nourish my longing for heaven, and help me to wait well, placing my hope in you.

DIGGING DEEPER

Read Hebrews 11:13-16. What does it mean that these heroes of the faith died without receiving what God had promised to them? What perspective enabled these faith heroes to have hope?

WEEK 20

HOPE

REFLECTION

How does an understanding of biblical hope affect your perspective on your hopes for the future and your expectation that those hopes will be fulfilled?

If hope is based on what God has said, what are some things he has said that give you hope?

MEDITATION

We can rejoice, too, when we run into problems and trials, for we know that they are good for us—they help us learn to endure. And endurance develops strength of character in us, and character strengthens our confident expectation of salvation. And this expectation will not disappoint us. For we know how dearly God loves us, because he has given us the Holy Spirit to fill our hearts with his love. —Romans 5:3-5

Read through these verses slowly several times, taking in the truth phrase by phrase.

Meditate on key words and phrases that are challenging and those that are comforting.

Turn these verses into a prayer back to God, telling him of your desire to have joy in your difficulty and your confidence in how he is using this struggle to strengthen your character and hope.

PRAYER

Praise God for his immutability—his unchanging nature—so that you can wholly depend on his faithful promises.

Thank God for the comfort and refuge we find when we place our hope in Christ for eternal salvation.

Intercede for those you know who feel hopeless, asking God to give them eyes of faith to see the unseen but certain promises of God.

Confess your tendency to build your hopes on lesser things, people, and pursuits rather than on the finished work of Christ.

Petition God to transform your perspective and deepest longings so that you value his eternal provision for you more than comfort in this life.

WEEK 21

THE MYSTERIES OF HEAVEN

Recently I was at the Orlando Convention Center where I saw hundreds of people snaked through ropes, waiting in line for something. "What's going on?" I asked someone. I was told that all the people were in line waiting to buy tickets to a taping of *Crossing Over with John Edward*, the television show in which psychic medium John Edward supposedly connects conflicted people with the spirits of those who have "crossed over to the other side."

As I looked at the crowd, I grieved that so many people in search of answers and peace would not find what they were looking for. And I realized how hungry we as humans are to understand what happens beyond death, how desperate we can become to bring the afterlife into our earthly experience.

Heaven. It is our fondest desire, and yet it is such a mystery, isn't it? So many questions about where it is, what it will be like. Will we recognize those we love? Who will be there? What will we do?

We lack the clarity or vocabulary to understand or describe heaven. The magnificence and marvels of heaven are beyond the capacity of our language and intellect. And really, anything less wouldn't be heaven, would it?

THIS WEEK'S PASSAGE FOR MEDITATION

The wisdom we speak of is the secret wisdom of God, which was hidden in former times, though he made it for our benefit before the world began. But the rulers of this world have not understood it; if they had, they would never have crucified our glorious Lord. That is what the Scriptures mean when they say, "No eye has seen, no ear has heard, and no mind has imagined what God has prepared for those who love him." —1 Corinthians 2:7-9

DOES HEAVEN HAVE A VIEW OF EARTH?

God has made everything beautiful for its own time. He has planted eternity in the human heart, but even so, people cannot see the whole scope of God's work from beginning to end. —Ecclesiastes 3:11

Trent brings home a good report card; Kristen dances beautifully in her recital; Rachel pitches a perfect softball game—and they all wonder, *Can Dad see me?* My friend Angela, who lost her husband, Wes, six years ago whispers, "Dad knows," as a way to reassure them. But we wonder, don't we? Can those who have gone before us see what we are doing now?

Scripture does not tell us plainly, but many point to Hebrews 12:1, which says we are "surrounded by such a huge crowd of witnesses." Does that mean that believers who have died are watching us now? Not necessarily. The writer of Hebrews has just gone through a list of heroes of the faith. When he calls them "witnesses," he does not mean that they are watching us. He is encouraging us to look at their lives and listen to their testimonies of the life of faith. It is as if they are on the witness stand testifying about their experiences of living and dying in faith. Their lives say to us, *Faith works. God keeps his promises. Heaven is worth the wait.* They are examples, not onlookers. They "witness" to us the value of placing all our hopes in God's promises.

Caleb Lee, a friend of Matt's who lost his mom a few years ago, told his dad, Bill, "Everyone says that Mom is watching us, but I don't think Mom can be happy in heaven if she sees how sad we are." Bill reminded Caleb of their Christmas morning tradition of putting presents in unwrapped piles for each family member. They all run into the room to dig into their stash. "Imagine you looked around and there was no pile for you," Bill told Caleb. "You would feel confused and disappointed and sad. But then imagine that Mom is standing back in the hallway looking at you from a distance. Behind her is the coolest go-cart that is everything you ever wanted, and she is laughing while you cry. She knows that what you are about to discover will wipe away the temporary sadness you feel."

Can our loved ones see us from the heights of heaven? I don't know. But if they can, they see us through an understanding of the bigger picture, the grander joy that they know awaits us. And they smile.

Watching Father, whether or not our loved ones see us now, they see you and your gift of heaven clearly. And one day we will too.

DIGGING DEEPER

Read Isaiah 65:17-19 and 1 Corinthians 13:12. What do these passages reveal about what we will see and understand in heaven?

WHOM DO YOU LONG TO SEE?

I HEARD THE SINGING OF THOUSANDS AND MILLIONS OF ANGELS AROUND THE THRONE AND THE LIVING BEINGS AND THE ELDERS. AND THEY SANG IN A MIGHTY CHORUS: "THE LAMB IS WORTHY—THE LAMB WHO WAS KILLED. HE IS WORTHY TO RECEIVE POWER AND RICHES AND WISDOM AND STRENGTH AND HONOR AND GLORY AND BLESSING." —REVELATION 5:11-12

"'I really want to go to heaven to see Johnny, but I'm struck that I want to go almost more to see him than to see Jesus.' I knew how my wife felt. If only we could long for heaven and long for Christ as we long for our son."

When I first read these words in *A Grief Unveiled* by Gregory Floyd, I felt like they gave voice to the conflict I felt inside. Suddenly I was longing for heaven and it seemed so real. And yet, if I was honest, it was not Jesus I was longing to see and enjoy most of all; it was Hope. But I didn't want to admit it. Not to myself, and certainly not to anybody else. It seemed to me a sad commentary on the inferior state of my love for Christ.

Should you feel guilty about wanting to see someone you love in heaven? I don't think so. It is a desire God uses to awaken us to himself. When someone we love is there, heaven becomes more real and our longing more vivid. It is a sacred longing.

If we follow where this longing takes us, we discover that every human love is only a taste of the love and intimacy God wants to share with us. Our sense of loneliness and incompleteness can lead us on a downward spiral of disappointment or on a path toward the satisfaction we seek in loving and being loved in return—a desire that can only be fully satisfied in God himself. Our longings are gifts from God that reveal our inner emptiness and send us on a search for a love that will never leave us or disappoint us.

While people we love are precious to us and our reunions with them in heaven will be grand, the fact that we long for them more than we long for Jesus reflects our current human limitations of taking in the beauty and magnificence of Jesus. In heaven, we will see him in his fullness, and we will not have to choose between focusing on the people we love and loving Jesus with our whole heart. We'll be swept up with the chorus of heaven singing, "The Lamb is worthy" (Revelation 5:12). And together with those we love, we will look to Jesus.

Worthy Lamb, take the limited longing I have for you and deepen and expand it until that day I sing to you in heaven with those I love. You are worthy!

DIGGING DEEPER

What comfort does 1 Thessalonians 4:13-18 offer to those longing to see ones they love who have died?

WHAT WILL OUR BODIES BE LIKE?

We are citizens of heaven, where the Lord Jesus Christ lives. And we are eagerly waiting for him to return as our Savior. He will take these weak mortal bodies of ours and change them into glorious bodies like his own, using the same mighty power that he will use to conquer everything, everywhere. —Philippians 3:20-21

The grave is, for me, a difficult place. Sometimes people have tried to comfort me by reminding me that Hope and Gabe are not in that grave—that they are in heaven. I know what they are saying—but my children's bodies are in that grave and I loved their bodies! Not only are their bodies precious to me, they are precious to God. Bodies must matter to God because he will use the seed of our earthly bodies to make for us bodies fit for heaven. Somehow he will take from the matter that has been long buried or spread on the sea or in the wind and fashion it into something glorious.

In his glorified body following his own resurrection, Jesus defied the natural laws of time and space, and yet he looked like a man—talking, eating, and showing Thomas the nail scars in his hands—the only scars that will still be visible in heaven. While we can't imagine what we will be like when we are given our glorified bodies, we do know that "when he comes we will be like him" (1 John 3:2). We will not float around without a body. Like Jesus' glorified body, we will have all the familiar physical features.

We know that everything will be new and everything will be perfect. Nothing will be broken or decayed or scarred by the injuries and affliction life brings. We will not be limited by old grudges, painful memories, or declining health. Our redeemed bodies will be free of cancer cells, joint pain, unwanted pounds, and disabled limbs. Our bodies will be remade for glorified minds that understand the mysteries of the universe and purified hearts that are free of bitterness and resentment, selfishness and suspicion.

And we can be confident we will recognize those we love. In fact, our perfected hearts and minds will enable us to know them in a richer, fuller way than we ever knew them on earth. We'll have no desire to hide behind masks or barriers. We will see each other as God intended us to be all along, before sin had its way in our hearts and bodies.

Re-Creator, how you will take the bodies we have now and transform them into glorious bodies fit for an eternity in heaven is mysterious, but it is a holy and hopeful mystery.

DIGGING DEEPER

Read 1 Corinthians 15:46-50 and 2 Corinthians 5:1-6. What do you learn from these passages about God's transformation of our physical bodies into heavenly bodies?

WHAT ARE THEY DOING UP THERE?

God raised him up to the heights of heaven and gave him a name that is above every other name, so that at the name of Jesus every knee will bow in heaven and on earth and under the earth, and every tongue will confess that Jesus Christ is Lord, to the glory of God the Father. —Philippians 2:9-11

We don't tend to talk about heaven very much today in our comfortable Western culture. But there is one place where heaven is always talked about—in the pages of a hymnal. Have you ever noticed how most old hymns end with a heaven verse—one that celebrates Christ's coming return or what it will be like to cross death's shores? It was these words from "All Hail the Power of Jesus' Name" that really caught me as I sang them in church one Sunday morning shortly after Hope died:

O that with yonder sacred throng,
we at his feet may fall,
We'll join the everlasting song,
and crown him Lord of all . . .

It was as if I could see through the rafters of the church building and into the heavens. Far, far away, not only could I see that "yonder sacred throng," I could see a familiar face in the midst of the throng! Someone I love is there, worshiping Jesus! It was then I realized that in my desperation to feel close to Hope and Gabe, I am closest to them when I do what they are doing and love whom they are loving—when I fall at the feet of Jesus. I've been singing hymns so long, I'm not sure I had ever considered what the "yonder sacred throng" even was. It is the multitude of believers who have gone before us. And what are they doing? Are they pining to be back on earth with us? Of course not! They are at the feet of Jesus, singing praises to the Lamb who is worthy!

Praising God won't be an unwanted assignment or a boring, repetitive ritual when we are in heaven. We won't be able to help it. As renewed citizens of heaven, together with those we love, we'll just do what comes naturally; we will joyfully sing praise to the King of heaven. But we don't have to wait until heaven to join the everlasting song. We can join in here and now.

Worthy One, as my vision of heaven comes clearer, I see that worshiping you there will far surpass any notion I have now about worship and any reluctance I experience now to worship you freely and passionately. How I long to join the sacred throng in the everlasting song!

DIGGING DEEPER

Read Revelation 4:8-11; 5:9-14; 11:15-18; 15:1-4; and 19:1-7, noting the ways God is worshiped in heaven.

THOSE WHO'VE SEEN HEAVEN

We are fully confident, and we would rather be away from these bodies, for then we will be at home with the Lord. —2 Corinthians 5:8

I went on amazon.com today to look up books about near-death experiences. Wow. Not only are there a lot of people who claim to have had these experiences, it would seem they have all written a book about how it changed their lives! Some say they saw heaven. Some saw hell; some saw loved ones; some saw a light.

There are several people in the Bible for whom God pulled back the curtain to give a glimpse of the reality of heaven. Isaiah described his vision: "I saw the Lord . . . sitting on a lofty throne" (6:1). John recorded his vision of heaven in Revelation. Jesus told him, "I hold the keys of death and the grave. Write down what you have seen" (1:18-19). But one of the most intriguing experiences to me is that of Paul. "I was caught up into the third heaven," he writes in 2 Corinthians. "Whether my body was there or just my spirit, I don't know; only God knows. But I do know that I was caught up into paradise and heard things so astounding that they cannot be told" (12:2-4).

Cannot be told? I can't help but feel disappointed when I read this because I would like to know! Wouldn't you? At least I know that this is a person I can trust when he tells me about heaven. And one of the best things Paul tells us about heaven comes earlier in that same letter, something simple, but profound—that he would rather be absent from the body and home with the Lord (see 2 Corinthians 5:8). Paul's words are precious because knowing a believer is at home once his soul leaves his body makes all the difference when you're sitting at the bedside of one who is taking his or her final breaths on earth, doesn't it?

I love something David said in an interview about the night Gabe died. He said, "While it was one of the most excruciating moments of my life, it also was not hard to envision that he took his last breath here and took his next breath in the presence of God." Don't believe that those who die in Christ linger here, longing to return. Neither are their souls waiting anywhere that is less than the very presence of God. They go home with the Lord, and one day so will you.

My Companion for the afterlife, it seems so natural to cling to this life rather than long for the life to come. Draw back the curtain of my heart so that I will embrace the joy of finally being at home in your presence.

DIGGING DEEPER

Read Isaiah 6:1-8. How was Isaiah affected by his vision of heaven?

WEEK 21

THE MYSTERIES OF HEAVEN

REFLECTION

What common misconceptions about heaven bother you, and which ones do you find tempting to believe?

What practical questions do you still have about heaven? To what extent are you willing to persevere in faith though your questions may linger?

MEDITATION

The wisdom we speak of is the secret wisdom of God, which was hidden in former times, though he made it for our benefit before the world began. But the rulers of this world have not understood it; if they had, they would never have crucified our glorious Lord. That is what the Scriptures mean when they say, "No eye has seen, no ear has heard, and no mind has imagined what God has prepared for those who love him." —1 Corinthians 2:7-9

Read through the verses several times, noting words and phrases that especially speak to you. Seek to weave these truths into the fabric of your understanding of God and your anticipation of heaven.

Pray through the verses, offering praise and thanksgiving for the wisdom of God and the preparation of God for you.

PRAYER

Praise God with the sacred throng of heaven, singing "Blessing and honor and glory and power . . . forever" (Revelation 5:13).

Thank God for the holy heroes who witness to us the value of persevering in the life of faith to gain heaven with God.

Intercede for those whose physical bodies or minds desperately need to be redeemed—those in pain or declining physical health, those suffering disability or handicap.

Confess your questions and doubts about heaven, asking God to give you faith and understanding.

Petition God to transform your longing to see those you love in heaven into a longing for the Lamb.

WEEK 22

HEAVEN: LONGING FOR HOME

From Hope's memorial service program:

> *June 12, 1999*
>
> *When Hope came home with us, we knew she would be with us only a short time. What a gift God gave us to have and hold Hope for over six months. Never could a daughter have been more of a blessing to her parents. Early on, we were tempted to feel sorry for ourselves—that Hope was not a healthy baby who would grow old with us. Certainly that is a loss. But we have come to appreciate the gift of having her just as she was—so innocent and helpless, so precious and sweet, such a joy—for the time that we had her. And quite honestly, we feel so privileged to have been the parents of such a special child. So grieve with us, share our sorrow, but don't feel sorry for us. We are enormously blessed.*
>
> *Now, as we say good-bye to Hope in this life, a piece of us resides in heaven. Her absence leaves a hole in our hearts, but we are comforted to know we will one day see her again. Her life has shown us how temporal this life is, how cruel the effects of sin are in this world, and it has implanted in us a longing for our true home, with him. Hope is there. She's home.*
>
> > *"We've been given a glimpse of the real thing, our true home, our resurrection bodies! The Spirit of God whets our appetite by giving us a taste of what's ahead. He puts a little of heaven in our hearts so that we'll never settle for less." (2 Corinthians 5:4-5, MSG)*

THIS WEEK'S PASSAGE FOR MEDITATION

I heard a loud shout from the throne, saying, "Look, the home of God is now among his people! He will live with them, and they will be his people. God himself will be with them. He will remove all of their sorrows, and there will be no more death or sorrow or crying or pain. For the old world and its evils are gone forever." —Revelation 21:3-4

MY FATHER'S HOME

[Jesus said,] "Don't be troubled. You trust God, now trust in me. There are many rooms in my Father's home, and I am going to prepare a place for you. If this were not so, I would tell you plainly. When everything is ready, I will come and get you, so that you will always be with me where I am."
—John 14:1-3

Walking out of the athletic club, I ran into an acquaintance who began to tell me about a tennis buddy who had just received a terminal diagnosis. Her friend was struggling with questions about eternity as she came face-to-face with death; yet she was resistant to seeing herself as anything other than worthy of heaven, even though she had no relationship with Jesus and no interest in him. To her it seemed simple—everyone goes to heaven when they die. My friend wondered how to make the truth about heaven understandable to her.

I suggested she ask her friend if anybody who comes to her door is welcome inside her home. Most likely, because it is her house, she determines whom she will invite and who will be welcomed. Jesus described heaven as "my Father's home," a place he is preparing for all of God's family where they will live with him forever. Because heaven is his home, the Father has determined who is invited. Actually, he has opened the invitation wide—offering salvation to anyone who will place his or her faith in him through his Son. And he determines who is welcome—only those who have responded to his invitation by faith. Because heaven is his home, he has the right to determine who will be there with him. And if you have responded to God's invitation by faith, there is a room in his home prepared for you.

While it is easy for people to believe there is a heaven that God has created for people to live in when they die, most are not willing to accept what the Bible says about who it is being prepared for. The truth is that because heaven is a perfect place, no imperfection is allowed and no imperfect people are allowed. So who could make it, you ask? None of us can enter God's holy home if we're counting on our own goodness to get us in. "All have sinned; all fall short of God's glorious standard" (Romans 3:23). It is only as we exchange our sinfulness for the righteousness of Christ—not by trying to be good enough but solely by faith—that we become fit for a holy heaven.

Jesus, I trust that you are preparing a place just for me, that you will come for me, and that I will always be with you. Thank you for the gift of your righteousness that has made me fit for your holy heaven.

DIGGING DEEPER

Read Isaiah 61:10; Romans 4:4-8; and 2 Corinthians 5:21. What do these verses tell you about how we obtain the righteousness of Christ?

HEAVEN: THE ULTIMATE REALITY

All these faithful ones died without receiving what God had promised them, but they saw it all from a distance and welcomed the promises of God. They agreed that they were no more than foreigners and nomads here on earth. They were looking for a better place, a heavenly homeland.
—Hebrews 11:13, 16

David often said that Hope and Gabe were not born for this life, but for the next. They were unable to see or hear or function in this world, and they were ushered quickly to the next life, where they will one day receive resurrected and renewed bodies. As we opened our eyes to the reality that this life is preparation for the next, our perspective about the "tragedy" of their short lives was transformed. We decided it was not really so sad that they spent only six months limited by a physical body that was hopelessly flawed. And I ask you, is it really less than the best if the person you love lives less than the eighty to ninety years we have come to define as a lifetime? Not if we see this earthly life as a rehearsal for the real thing.

While most great stories end with "and they lived happily ever after," C. S. Lewis ended The Chronicles of Narnia's *The Last Battle* much differently. As the heroic efforts of the Narnians fail, the storybook ending seems conspicuously absent. But immediately upon their deaths, the Narnians find themselves in a wonderful new land, where they are reunited with those they love and with Aslan himself. C. S. Lewis writes, "They were beginning Chapter One of the Great Story which no one on earth has read: which goes on forever: in which every chapter is better than the one before." Everything that had happened before was put into perspective as their real life and real story began.

So it will be for us when we embark on our real lives—our forever lives—in the presence of God. Then we'll realize that what has gone before was just a shadow of—a prelude to—our real lives in heaven. This life is not all there is, and neither is it the best there is. There is something better, somewhere better, Someone better . . . than any thing, any place, any person who has captured our devotion in the here and now. It is real. And it is forever.

Heavenly Father, help me to see beyond what seems so real in this life into the joyful reality of the next. Give me eyes of faith to see into the distance and welcome the promises of God for a better place, a heavenly homeland.

DIGGING DEEPER

Read Job 19:25-27. What does Job believe is the ultimate reality beyond his current suffering, and how does he feel about this?

LET HEAVEN FILL YOUR THOUGHTS

SINCE YOU HAVE BEEN RAISED TO NEW LIFE WITH CHRIST, SET YOUR SIGHTS ON THE REALITIES OF HEAVEN, WHERE CHRIST SITS AT GOD'S RIGHT HAND IN THE PLACE OF HONOR AND POWER. LET HEAVEN FILL YOUR THOUGHTS. DO NOT THINK ONLY ABOUT THINGS DOWN HERE ON EARTH. —COLOSSIANS 3:1-2

Last year I fulfilled a lifelong dream. I made a trip to Norway that included three days in the home of my best friend from third grade, who is Norwegian. We've kept in touch for over thirty years. One of my favorite things about visiting her is that now when I email her, I can picture her in her neighborhood, in her house, even in her room at the computer from which she emails me. I've been there, so now I can see it clearly in my mind's eye.

But how do I develop a mental picture of heaven when the prerequisite to seeing it is death? How can we "set [our] sights on the realities of heaven" (Colossians 3:1), when it's a place we have never seen and can barely imagine? Heaven can only be grasped by faith, and it can never be completely captured by our finite minds or described in awkward earthly terms. But Scripture provides fodder for filling our thoughts with heaven. The undercurrent of all Scripture—even the passages that give directives for how to live our lives on this earth—is preparation for and longing for heaven. From Genesis 3, in which God's perfect world is first scarred by sin and the Curse, the driving force and beckoning reality for all of history and all of Scripture is *heaven*, a return to the perfect world and perfect fellowship between God and those he loves.

To set your sights on heaven is to choose to anchor your thoughts and your heart's desires beyond the ordinary things of earth. It is to choose to value what is valued in heaven, to be concerned with the concerns of heaven, and to enjoy what is delightful in heaven. No longer will earthbound concerns or values dominate your perspective and priorities. In this world of satellite television, sports schedules, social events, and even church commitments, it takes a concerted effort and solid commitment to let heaven fill your thoughts. While other demands distract us and other delights attract us, God invites you to live on another plane and operate on a different platform from the world as you fill your thoughts with heaven.

Joy of heaven, I so easily feed my mind solely on the entertainment, amusements, and values of this world. Fill my mind with the reality and glory of heaven as I study your Word and nurture my longing for you.

DIGGING DEEPER

Philippians 4:8 provides a description of what we should think about. How does heaven fulfill each word in this description?

SATISFIED HUNGER

You will keep on guiding me with your counsel, leading me to a glorious destiny. Whom have I in heaven but you? I desire you more than anything on earth. My health may fail, and my spirit may grow weak, but God remains the strength of my heart; he is mine forever. —Psalm 73:24-26

Have you ever heard people described as so "heavenly minded" that they are "of no earthly good"? We know what that means. These people are so focused on the next life, they're absent from the reality of this one. Certainly it's not healthy to go to such an extreme, but we can still set our sights on heaven in a way that changes how we interact and what we expect from this world. Longing for heaven is not a form of escapism. It is extreme realism. Those who long for heaven have embraced the reality that their search for satisfaction in this life is insatiable. They have experienced the world's dead ends and examined their own bottomless pit of human desires. They've come to see every innate desire for what it truly is—a longing that will be met only in the completeness of the next life, not this one.

This is the conclusion C. S. Lewis came to, as he wrote about in *Mere Christianity*: "If I find in myself a desire which no experience in this world can satisfy, the most probable explanation is that I was made for another world. . . . I must keep alive in myself the desire for my true country, which I shall not find till after death; I must never let it get snowed under or turned aside; I must make it the main object of life to press on to that other country and to help others to do the same."

Every hunger we have has been placed there by God. Our hunger not only for food, but for sexual satisfaction, for significance and meaning, for adventure and rest—all are God-given, and he is not surprised when we try to satisfy these desires. Neither is he disappointed when we discover that we are never satisfied. We feast and hunger again. We love and are rejected. We excel and someone surpasses our achievement. We experience the ultimate adventure only to become bored in our pursuit. Discovering that we cannot satisfy our longings in the here and now forces us to reckon with the fact that we will never be satisfied in this life. Our disappointment draws us to look forward to the reality of heaven where every hunger will be satisfied, every need will be met—fully and forever.

My eternal Pleasure, behind every pleasure in my life, I see you. With every disappointment in my life, my longing for you grows. You are leading me to a glorious and satisfying destiny. Thanks for the glory glimpses you give me.

DIGGING DEEPER

Read Ecclesiastes 2:1-11. What did Solomon learn about the search for satisfaction and pleasure?

NO MORE

I SAW A NEW HEAVEN AND A NEW EARTH, FOR THE OLD HEAVEN AND THE OLD EARTH HAD DISAPPEARED. AND THE SEA WAS ALSO GONE. HE WILL REMOVE ALL OF THEIR SORROWS, AND THERE WILL BE NO MORE DEATH OR SORROW OR CRYING OR PAIN.
—REVELATION 21:1, 4

Outside on our back patio, looking up into the sky, I said through tears, "I know you are in heaven, but heaven feels so far away from me." *It is the separation that hurts,* I thought, remembering what Anne Graham Lotz had said at Hope's memorial service, in her description of Hope's new home in heaven. She told how she was at first disappointed by one aspect of the description of heaven given in Revelation 21, which says there will be no more sea—because Anne *loves* the beach. Anne looks for any chance she can to steal away for a day in the sun, enjoying the waves and wind. But she said that she realized seas, by their very nature, separate. They separate families and friends and entire continents from each other. In heaven there will be no more separation. There will be *nothing* that separates us from each other or from God ever again.

Not only will there be no separation, but biblical descriptions of heaven also include a long list of "no mores." It is almost as if the biblical writers, in their struggle to describe what heaven *will be*, find that describing what it *will not be* is more instructive. No more night, no more time, no more sun or moon, no more marriage. But each of these have their element of disappointment too, don't they? No more breathtaking sunsets or starlit skies? No more romantic evenings with our life's companion? In reality, however, each "no more" reveals in relief the fullness of heaven.

No more separation—only eternal togetherness with those we love. No more sun or moon, as Jesus will be the only light we will need. No more marriage, as we'll be forever wed to our Bridegroom, Jesus. No more time, as time will no longer be defined by minutes or hours, but only by the richness of Jesus' presence. God knows which "no mores" will mean the most to those of us who hurt. No more sorrow. No more crying. No more pain. No more curse. No more death. "No more" encapsulates some of heaven's sweetest gifts.

Designer of heaven, I can hardly imagine the joy of no more separation, no more sorrow or pain or death. You know what will make up heaven's perfection and what to wipe away. I cling to your promises of "no more."

DIGGING DEEPER

Read Isaiah 25:7-8 and Revelation 21:1-4, 22-27. What do these visions of heaven indicate will be no more?

WEEK 22

HEAVEN: LONGING FOR HOME

REFLECTION

What experiences, pleasures, or disappointments has God used to increase your desire for heaven?

What reading, viewing, or listening habits do you need to change so that you might be better able to "let heaven fill your thoughts" (Colossians 3:2)?

MEDITATION

I heard a loud shout from the throne, saying, "Look, the home of God is now among his people! He will live with them, and they will be his people. God himself will be with them. He will remove all of their sorrows, and there will be no more death or sorrow or crying or pain. For the old world and its evils are gone forever." —Revelation 21:3-4

Read through these verses, placing yourself in the scene. Hear and see Jesus speak from the throne of heaven, and imagine a reality where God lives with his people in a place where there is no more death, sorrow, crying, pain, or evil.

Pray through the passage, praising God on the throne. Thank him in advance for what he will do, and welcome him to come quickly.

PRAYER

Praise God as the architect and builder of heaven, where Jesus sits at God's right hand in the place of honor and power.

Thank God for the disappointments in your life, which reinforce that you will never be satisfied here and now.

Intercede for those who have not responded to God's invitation to live forever with him on his terms, those who believe they are good enough to get into heaven on their own merit.

Confess your contentment with and investment in earthly things that dampen your desire for heaven.

Petition God to increase your yearning for and hope in the ultimate reality of heaven.

WEEK 23

RESURRECTION

We sensed one night that Gabe was fading. Matt had already gone to bed, so we woke him and told him we thought Gabe might die during the night and we wanted him to have the chance to say good-bye. Then we put Gabe in our bed between us and thanked God for his life. I pulled out my Bible and turned to 1 Corinthians 15 in *The Message* and said, "Gabe, do you want to hear about the Resurrection?"

When we face the grave, as we all will, all this religious talk about resurrection becomes more than just talk. It was all too real for me in that moment, and of supreme importance. In those hours of saying good-bye to Gabe, I needed to reaffirm that the Resurrection is real, and our only hope. So I began to read out loud: "If corpses can't be raised, then Christ wasn't, because he was indeed dead. And if Christ weren't raised, then all you're doing is wandering about in the dark, as lost as ever. If all we get out of Christ is a little inspiration for a few short years, we're a pretty sorry lot. But the truth is that Christ has been raised up, the first in a long legacy of those who are going to leave the cemeteries. It's resurrection, resurrection, always resurrection, that undergirds what I do and say, the way I live" (verses 13-14, 19-20, 32).

THIS WEEK'S PASSAGE FOR MEDITATION

But tell me this—since we preach that Christ rose from the dead, why are some of you saying there will be no resurrection of the dead? For if there is no resurrection of the dead, then Christ has not been raised either. And if Christ was not raised, then all our preaching is useless, and your trust in God is useless. And we apostles would all be lying about God, for we have said that God raised Christ from the grave, but that can't be true if there is no resurrection of the dead. If there is no resurrection of the dead, then Christ has not been raised. And if Christ has not been raised, then your faith is useless, and you are still under condemnation for your sins. In that case, all who have died believing in Christ have perished! And if we have hope in Christ only for this life, we are the most miserable people in the world. —1 Corinthians 15:12-19

DO YOU BELIEVE?

JESUS TOLD HER, "YOUR BROTHER WILL RISE AGAIN." "YES," MARTHA SAID, "WHEN EVERYONE ELSE RISES, ON RESURRECTION DAY." JESUS TOLD HER, "I AM THE RESURRECTION AND THE LIFE. THOSE WHO BELIEVE IN ME, EVEN THOUGH THEY DIE LIKE EVERYONE ELSE, WILL LIVE AGAIN. THEY ARE GIVEN ETERNAL LIFE FOR BELIEVING IN ME AND WILL NEVER PERISH. DO YOU BELIEVE THIS, MARTHA?" —JOHN 11:23-26

Jesus often asked penetrating questions. He asked the man by the pool of Bethesda, "Do you want to get well?" He asked the woman caught in adultery, "Where are your accusers?" He asked Peter, "Who do you say that I am?" And he asked Martha, "Do you believe?"

The questions Jesus asks echo through the ages, gently but firmly requiring an answer from each of us. They are penetrating and personal and, most important, purposeful. His purpose in asking Martha if she believed was to move her from a vague belief in a resurrection to a firm confidence that he is the Resurrection, her only hope.

Martha, in the midst of her grief and despair, affirmed her belief, saying, "Yes, Lord . . . I have always believed you are the Messiah, the Son of God, the one who has come into the world from God" (John 11:27). Jesus shifted her focus from her suffering to her Savior. His words of resurrection can do the same for you and me, depending on how we answer his question, "Do you believe?" But before we can answer it, perhaps we need a clearer understanding of what it means to believe. Paul wrote, "If you confess with your mouth that Jesus is Lord and believe in your heart that God raised him from the dead, you will be saved" (Romans 10:9). So what does it mean to believe in your heart that God raised Jesus from the dead? It can't be merely a mental assent to this historical fact, because the Bible says even Satan acknowledges that. Believing in your heart that God raised Jesus from the dead means trusting in all the promises it represents: newness of life, hope for the future, and the power for living. It means being so confident in God's power and love that nothing can tempt you to trust in a lesser savior. This is resting in his resurrection, believing in it in a saving way. To believe is to leave your cynicism behind and enter into the resurrected Jesus as the very atmosphere in which you live, where he becomes your treasure, your satisfaction, your life.

Resurrected Jesus, I believe; help my unbelief. Work this belief from my head into the recesses of my heart. Shift my focus from my suffering to my Savior.

DIGGING DEEPER

How does Jesus' identification of himself as the resurrection and the life echo what he said in John 5:24-30?

EXPERIENCING RESURRECTION POWER

I CAN REALLY KNOW CHRIST AND EXPERIENCE THE MIGHTY POWER THAT RAISED HIM FROM THE DEAD. I CAN LEARN WHAT IT MEANS TO SUFFER WITH HIM. —PHILIPPIANS 3:10

Sometimes I try to listen with uninitiated ears to the phrases we Christians say all the time. What must it sound like to someone who has never heard the gospel for someone to suggest they should "ask Jesus into their heart"? I often wonder what it means to those who are skeptical of Christians when they hear us say we have a "personal relationship" with Jesus. I can't help but wonder if they think we're a little off upstairs. How can a human have a "personal relationship" with a deity?

It is obvious from the passion of his words that Paul wanted far more than to simply know about Jesus. He wanted to know him by *experiencing* him. He wanted to experience his pain and his power—he wanted it all. No holding God at arm's length—he wanted to get personal. And getting personal with God means experiencing his power in the present tense. Paul reached for the ultimate highs and lows that are required for knowing someone in a full and complete way. He wanted to go to the depths with Christ to have fellowship with him there in his suffering, and he wanted to go to the heights with Christ to experience the power of his resurrection. Paul had already experienced the power of God in his salvation. Everyone who comes to Christ in faith experiences this resurrection power. But Paul wanted more, and I have to say, I do too. I desperately need the power of God to resist the temptations that entice me, to persevere in the pain that afflicts me, and to serve in spite of the ease that attracts me. Only as we experience his resurrection power can we endure the fellowship of his suffering.

To experience the power that raised Christ from the dead is to lay hold of everything Christ holds out to us and to anticipate the day that awaits us when "the Lord himself will come down from heaven with a commanding shout, with the call of the archangel, and with the trumpet call of God. First, all the Christians who have died will rise from their graves. Then, together with them, we who are still alive and remain on the earth will be caught up in the clouds to meet the Lord in the air and remain with him forever" (1 Thessalonians 4:16-17).

My Power Source for salvation and in suffering, I don't want to settle for just being an acquaintance of the Almighty. I want to know you personally and powerfully. I want to share in your life and in your death, and I want to be changed.

DIGGING DEEPER

What do you learn about the power of Christ from each of the following verses: Ephesians 1:15-23; Colossians 1:16-18; and 2:13-15?

THE SPIRIT GIVES LIFE

The Spirit of God, who raised Jesus from the dead, lives in you. And just as he raised Christ from the dead, he will give life to your mortal body by this same Spirit living within you. —Romans 8:11

When David and I share our story, we often save time at the end in case people have questions. Invariably, one of the first questions is, "How is Matt?" I have always answered this question thinking the person is wondering how he is doing emotionally, having lost two siblings. Only recently did I figure out that sometimes people are wondering if there is any chance Matt might die too as a result of Zellweger Syndrome. I was telling Matt about this when we returned from a recent speaking engagement. "What did you tell them?" he asked when I explained my new understanding of the question. "I said that you're going to die too, but hopefully no time soon!" I told him with a smile. "Then I reminded them that eventually we're all going to die."

Sometimes we live in a dream world in which we deny death. But those of us advancing in years need no one to remind us that the process of physical death is even now at work in us, and we can't stop it, although we try. We try so hard because we've believed the world's lie that being truly alive means being thin, beautiful, sexually active, and young-looking. But if this is true, why are so many thin, beautiful, sexually active, young-looking people so unhappy and unfulfilled? Our bodies are not what make us happy. It is the Spirit who dwells within us that makes us truly alive. We can look good on the outside, but when we are cut to the core by the sharp edge of pain, our inner life is revealed. Unless the Spirit has made his home in us, what is revealed will be only emptiness. When the Spirit is living within us, those around us see the imprint of the supernatural in the interior of our lives when we suffer.

Our only hope in a world of pain is the life of God in our very souls. As God fills us with his Spirit, he touches us at the deepest level of our being and begins his work of transformation, leading up to the day when our very bodies will be transformed. On that day when he "will give life to your mortal body" (Romans 8:11), you're going to be better than you ever were—even when you were at your best. What the Spirit of God did for Jesus on that first Resurrection day, he will do for us on the next.

Indwelling Spirit, you give me life and meaning and joy on the inside! Even now you are renewing me and remaking me as I anticipate the day you will resurrect my earthly body.

DIGGING DEEPER

Read the story of the Spirit giving life to dry bones in Ezekiel 37:1-14.

NO ONE CAN ROB YOU OF THIS JOY

You will grieve, but your grief will suddenly turn to wonderful joy when you see me again. You have sorrow now, but I will see you again; then you will rejoice, and no one can rob you of that joy. —John 16:20, 22

Life is fragile. Our lives can change in an instant when a driver swerves on the interstate or the phone rings in the middle of the night. Very little in this life is secure, and that can make us feel very vulnerable. Into the insecurity and instability of this world Jesus comes, offering us a promise with amazing absoluteness rooted in his resurrection: "No one can rob you of that joy" (John 16:22).

Jesus was speaking to his disciples on the night before he faced the Cross. He was trying to help them understand what was ahead for them. "In just a little while I will be gone, and you won't see me anymore. Then, just a little while after that, you will see me again" (John 16:16). He knew the disciples were going to be sad when they lost the leader they loved, but he wanted them to know that the pain would pass, he would rise from the dead, and he would "see you again" (John 16:22). Jesus makes the promise of unending joy to those whose hearts rejoice in being with him. And if you do not rejoice in being with Jesus, then this promise is his invitation to you to make him the center and source of your joy. Jesus is the only permanent joy in this world and the next. If your joy is not found in Jesus, then your joy can be taken from you. And the truth is, we make so many other things the source of our joy, don't we? We lose a job, a romance ends, our youth fades, and we think we can never be happy again.

The reason our joy is secure and will last forever is because Jesus has been raised from the dead and will never be cut off from us again. By defeating death and holding the keys to death in his hands, Jesus will never die, and we don't have to die either. The resurrection of Jesus means that not only will he live forever as the source of our joy, but we also will live forever if he is the source of our joy. This solid joy enables us to say, "Disease can destroy my health, another lover can steal my spouse, a business failure may take my life's savings, but because my joy is not rooted in these temporal things, nothing can take my joy." This is freedom. This is rest. This is forever joy.

Source of joy, your promise gives me confidence in a world where so much has been and can be taken from me. Your resurrection assures me that no one and nothing can take away the joy I share with you now and forever.

DIGGING DEEPER

Read how and why the psalmist found joy in God's presence: Psalm 16:9-11; 28:7; 34:5; 43:4; and 63:5-7.

A BETTER RESURRECTION

Women received back their dead, raised to life again. Others were tortured and refused to be released, so that they might gain a better resurrection.
—Hebrews 11:35 (niv)

At a recent Just Give Me Jesus revival in Seattle, a woman was found on the floor of a bathroom, an apparent victim of a heart attack. She was not breathing. When the paramedic arrived, he was hesitant to begin working to revive the woman because he was confident she was past the point of resuscitation. But my friend Leigh O'Dell said, "You can't do nothing; you've got to try!" To the utter amazement of the medic, the resuscitation worked. In fact, before he left, he told Leigh that in his twenty years as a paramedic, he had never seen someone so far gone come back to life.

What could be better than having someone you love who has died raised back to life again? Hebrews 11 tells us in the middle of a long list of people who had amazing faith experiences: "They shut the mouths of lions, quenched the flames of fire, and escaped death by the edge of the sword. Their weakness was turned to strength. They became strong in battle and put whole armies to flight. Women received their loved ones back again from death" (verses 33-35). But then the list changes dramatically, and when I read it, the awful reality takes my breath away. "But others trusted God and were tortured, preferring to die rather than turn from God and be free. They placed their hope in the resurrection to a better life. Some were mocked, and their backs were cut open with whips. Others were chained in dungeons. Some died by stoning, and some were sawed in half; others were killed with the sword. Some went about in skins of sheep and goats, hungry and oppressed and mistreated" (11:35-37).

What could be better than being raised back to life again or escaping being tortured for your faith? I'll tell you—a resurrection that is more than merely resuscitation. Those who were raised back to life again still died eventually. But these faith-filled people had their hearts set on a better resurrection, a resurrection that would be forever; not just a temporary fix to the problem of death, but an eternal one. What could be better than seeing the one you love walk again or work again or wake up again? Resurrection. A *better* resurrection. It's the miracle we truly long for.

Lord of life, give me the faith of these followers who were willing to trust you in spite of persecution and torture and death. With them, I want to place my hope in a better resurrection rather than settle for temporary resuscitation.

DIGGING DEEPER

Read stories of Jesus restoring life in Matthew 8:5-13; Luke 7:11-15; 8:41-56; and John 11:38-44 and consider how resurrection will be even better.

WEEK 23

RESURRECTION

REFLECTION

As you consider the day of resurrection in the distant—or perhaps not too distant—future, what do you look forward to most?

In what way would you like to experience the resurrection power of Christ right now in your life? What is dead in or around you and needs the life-giving touch of God?

MEDITATION

Tell me this—since we preach that Christ rose from the dead, why are some of you saying there will be no resurrection of the dead? For if there is no resurrection of the dead, then Christ has not been raised either. And if Christ was not raised, then all our preaching is useless, and your trust in God is useless. And we apostles would all be lying about God, for we have said that God raised Christ from the grave, but that can't be true if there is no resurrection of the dead. If there is no resurrection of the dead, then Christ has not been raised. And if Christ has not been raised, then your faith is useless, and you are still under condemnation for your sins. In that case, all who have died believing in Christ have perished! And if we have hope in Christ only for this life, we are the most miserable people in the world. —1 Corinthians 15:12-19

Follow Paul's train of thought in this passage, seeking to understand the argument he is making and the implications of his point.

Consider what it would mean for the world and for you if Jesus had not been raised and there were no resurrection of the dead.

PRAYER

Praise Jesus as the Resurrection and the Life!

Thank Jesus for overcoming the power of death to become the firstfruits of all who will rise from the dead—including you.

Intercede for those who have not yet experienced the resurrection power of Christ, the indwelling of the Holy Spirit, and the joy Jesus gives.

Confess your misplaced value on resuscitation in this life rather than placing all your hopes and desires on a better resurrection.

Petition God to demonstrate his resurrection power in your relationships, your emotions, your body, and your mind. Ask him to fill your life with his Spirit.

WEEK 24

REWARDS

"Great is your reward in heaven" (Matthew 5:12, NIV). No matter how difficult your circumstances may be right now, don't these words sweep over you with a sense of relief and anticipation? Jesus knows that living for him in this world is not easy. He understands the power a promised reward has to fill us with courage and inspire our perseverance.

But some of us are uncomfortable with the idea of being rewarded for what we do for God. We want to serve Christ out of our love for him, with pure hearts and motives. And that's what Jesus wants too. He said, "When you obey me you should say, 'We are not worthy of praise. We are servants who have simply done our duty' " (Luke 17:10). But out of his grace and generosity, he is letting us know in advance that everything we do for him will be rewarded richly. His plan to reward us, like his provision to save us, is a display of his grace and mercy. It is an extension of his character as "a rewarder" (Hebrews 11:6).

To say that reward or punishment should have no place in motivating us as Christians is to be more spiritual than Jesus himself! He often spoke of rewards. And throughout the New Testament, God's reward is presented as an honorable motive for serving him and living a pure life. To diminish God's promise of present and future reward and punishment is to eliminate the security of justice and love and to rob life of meaning.

God notices and rewards your attempts, no matter how small, to serve him. Jesus said, "If anyone gives you even a cup of water because you belong to the Messiah, I assure you, that person will be rewarded" (Mark 9:41). Your reward will be sure and satisfying, profound and personal, given by God himself. The psalmist wrote: "Because I have done what is right, I will see you. When I awake, I will be fully satisfied, for I will see you face to face" (Psalm 17:15).

THIS WEEK'S PASSAGE FOR MEDITATION

It is impossible to please God without faith. Anyone who wants to come to him must believe that there is a God and that he rewards those who sincerely seek him. —HEBREWS 11:6

I AM YOUR VERY GREAT REWARD

The word of the Lord came to Abram in a vision: "Do not be afraid, Abram. I am your shield, your very great reward." —Genesis 15:1 (NIV)

It was my first day back to my weekly Bible study after Hope's birth. My heart was heavy, my emotions were raw, and I felt desperate to hear God speak to me. And he did! From the first book of the Bible—written by Moses so long ago—the words spoken to a fearful Abram seemed to be just for me. "Don't be afraid, Nancy. I am your shield, your very great reward." That day I wrote in my journal, "This was timely for me as various fears creep up on me—fear of what Hope's seizures will be like, fear of her pain, fear of loneliness and heartache when she's gone. I know God is my shield right now and he is protecting me, so I need not be afraid. God himself is my very best reward. An intimate relationship with him is the most valuable thing I can possess."

God knew the fears and questions in the heart and mind of Abram as he lay in the dark in his tent. And God came to him, beckoning him not to be afraid, promising him the resources of the Great I Am for his protection and blessing, saying, "I am the sufficient answer to all of your fears!"

Likewise, God knows the fears and faith struggles that keep you awake in the night. And while you might not hear an audible voice, God's words come to you with the same sure promise and soothing power as they came to Abram: "Do not be afraid." God beckons us to leave fear behind as he offers himself to us as an invisible shield of protection. With him as our shield, we know that nothing can touch us or hurt us except by his permission. We are safe.

But God does not just want to protect us; he wants to bless us. And he knows just what is worthy of being prized above anything or anyone else. *He* is our very great reward—our most precious treasure, our most satisfying joy. The reward of believing God and trusting him with our fear is the security and sufficiency of God himself on our side, in our corner. God has many good things he wants to give to you, and he will give you everything he has promised. But the most valuable reward you will receive for believing God and obeying God is God himself. *He* is your very great reward. Enjoy him.

My great Reward, what a relief to know I can trust in your protection and treasure your very presence in my life. Help me not to trust in lesser saviors or treasure lesser rewards.

DIGGING DEEPER

What do the following verses reveal about the reward of God himself: Psalm 16:11; John 12:26; 14:3; Romans 5:2; and Philippians 1:23?

PLEASING GOD OR IMPRESSING PEOPLE?

WHEN YOU GIVE A GIFT TO SOMEONE IN NEED, DON'T SHOUT ABOUT IT AS THE HYPOCRITES DO—BLOWING TRUMPETS IN THE SYNAGOGUES AND STREETS TO CALL ATTENTION TO THEIR ACTS OF CHARITY! I ASSURE YOU, THEY HAVE RECEIVED ALL THE REWARD THEY WILL EVER GET. GIVE YOUR GIFTS IN SECRET, AND YOUR FATHER, WHO KNOWS ALL SECRETS, WILL REWARD YOU. —MATTHEW 6:2,4

A few years ago, Matt was basking in the glow of having the funny lines and amusing costume in the children's musical at church. Not wanting to leave the party afterward, he said, "This is what it feels like to be a star!"

Let's just be honest, the admiration of others feels really good, and the applause of others sounds really good. We all want to be admired and applauded, and Jesus understands this. He understands that we are especially tempted to practice our faith and do our good works in a way that will capture the attention of others. That's why he points specifically to the sacrifice of giving, the practice of prayer, and the discipline of fasting, saying that if the applause of people is what we're giving for and living for, then we'd better enjoy it thoroughly, because it's all we can expect to get. But if our motive is to please *him*, he will reward us fully and eternally.

My former Bible study teacher, Diane Cobb, explained it this way: We have a closet in our hearts—a place where the things done solely for God's glory are deposited. Over the course of a life sold-out to pleasing God, the shelves become full and glowing. But if the real purpose of our righteous deeds is to impress people, nothing is deposited for us to enjoy in God's presence on that day when the closet is opened and its contents are revealed. When we rob God of the glory and indulge in it for ourselves, it is devoured and disappears. But when we shun the public applause of people for the private approval of God, we enjoy the secret satisfaction of his pleasure now and the ultimate reward of hearing him one day say, "Well done, my good and faithful servant" (Matthew 25:21).

Our reward from people comes from their view of our performance. God's reward comes from seeing our hearts. Are you seeking his eternal applause or settling for fleeting fame?

Secret Seer, you not only know everything I do, but you see my heart and know my motives. Purify my heart and implant within me a longing to please you that will make me patient for your reward, your "well done."

DIGGING DEEPER

Read 1 Corinthians 4:1-5. How does Paul exemplify a desire to please God more than men? How does he demonstrate his faith in God's reward?

PUT THROUGH THE FIRE

ANYONE WHO BUILDS ON THAT FOUNDATION MAY USE GOLD, SILVER, JEWELS, WOOD, HAY, OR STRAW. BUT THERE IS GOING TO COME A TIME OF TESTING AT THE JUDGMENT DAY TO SEE WHAT KIND OF WORK EACH BUILDER HAS DONE. EVERYONE'S WORK WILL BE PUT THROUGH THE FIRE TO SEE WHETHER OR NOT IT KEEPS ITS VALUE. IF THE WORK SURVIVES THE FIRE, THAT BUILDER WILL RECEIVE A REWARD. BUT IF THE WORK IS BURNED UP, THE BUILDER WILL SUFFER GREAT LOSS. THE BUILDERS THEMSELVES WILL BE SAVED, BUT LIKE SOMEONE ESCAPING THROUGH A WALL OF FLAMES.
—1 CORINTHIANS 3:12-15

Buried in the rubble of the World Trade Center after the September 11 attack was a vault filled with silver, gold, platinum, and palladium estimated to be worth at least 230 million dollars. But while officials were concerned about theft in the aftermath of the tragedy, they knew the gold and silver would have survived the incinerating fire of the attack. Gold, silver, and precious stones are quality materials that are not destroyed by fire.

When we serve out of love for God, Scripture likens that service to gold and silver. Likewise, shallow activities devoid of eternal value (though not necessarily evil) are compared to wood, hay, and straw, which are consumed by flames. A day is coming when each of us will give an account of what we did while we were alive on earth. The fire will test and reveal not only what we did, but also why we did it. If our works survive the fire because they are empowered by God and done to the glory of God, then we will be rewarded. If our works are consumed because they were done for our own selfish reasons, then there will be no reward.

Your eternal future will not be in jeopardy on this day. Your salvation is a gift of God by grace through faith in Jesus. You cannot earn or deserve it. But rewards are different. Rewards will be given according to our works. "See, I am coming soon, and my reward is with me, to repay all according to their deeds," Jesus promises in Revelation 22:12. This is a day to anticipate, not to dread. The day of the fire will be a day of celebration, not disappointment or shame. As my college Bible professor Jim Walters once explained to me, "Everyone's cup will be filled to overflow, but we will have different sized cups." We will not experience the pain of regret, only the joy of reward. And we will be fully satisfied.

Righteous Judge, what a joy it will be to receive your reward! Show me how my heart needs to change so I will do what is pleasing to you in a way that is pleasing to you.

DIGGING DEEPER

What do the following verses teach about what will cause your works to endure or burn: Matthew 6:1; Luke 6:35; 14:12-14; and 1 Corinthians 13:3?

TREASURES IN HEAVEN

DON'T STORE UP TREASURES HERE ON EARTH, WHERE THEY CAN BE EATEN BY MOTHS AND GET RUSTY, AND WHERE THIEVES BREAK IN AND STEAL. STORE YOUR TREASURES IN HEAVEN, WHERE THEY WILL NEVER BECOME MOTH-EATEN OR RUSTY AND WHERE THEY WILL BE SAFE FROM THIEVES. WHEREVER YOUR TREASURE IS, THERE YOUR HEART AND THOUGHTS WILL ALSO BE. —MATTHEW 6:19-21

David's uncle Bernard made a fortune as an entrepreneurial inventor, using wood by-products to make roofing material. Bernard and his wife, Loene, were known for being pack rats. One day Bernard decided to clear out years' worth of old newspapers from the basement while Loene was away. What he didn't know until after the paper was destroyed was that Loene had stashed thousands of dollars worth of cash in the paper stacks for "safekeeping."

So much of what we value is so vulnerable—our possessions and wealth, our families, our health, our abilities and reputations—it is all vulnerable to loss and destruction. Is there anything we can't lose? Only what we send ahead for storage in heaven is protected for our eternal enjoyment. So how do we store our treasures in heaven?

We must ask ourselves, *What treasure has God given to me, and what is God asking me to do with it?* The treasure you value most might not necessarily be money. It may be your athletic ability, your academic prowess, or your career potential. How can you give it away to build God's Kingdom? God might be asking you to surrender your child to ministry or sacrifice your leisurely Saturdays to mentor a needy child. God wants you to use what you value most to serve his Kingdom. That's the way you spend your financial and personal capital in a way that ensures it will be returned to you later.

The same Aunt Loene who stashed cash in newspapers stipulated in her will that David should receive one of her three grand pianos after her death. And sure enough, one day a truck pulled up in front of our house and off came a Steinway grand piano. But sticky stars from years of piano lessons and dust from disuse had taken their toll, making the piano unusable. Everything of value here is vulnerable to decay, but only those things that we give away for the glory of God are secure. What we treasure here is fleeting, but our treasure in heaven is forever.

My Treasure Keeper, how I love and hold tightly to the treasures of this earth! Help me to loosen my grip with a vision for the future and a confidence in your faithfulness to reward me for everything I give away for your glory.

DIGGING DEEPER

What do the following verses teach about how we can store up treasure in heaven: Luke 12:33; Galatians 6:7-10; and 1 Timothy 6:18-19?

EVERYTHING IS OURS

Since we are his children, we will share his treasures—for everything God gives to his Son, Christ, is ours, too. But if we are to share his glory, we must also share his suffering. Yet what we suffer now is nothing compared to the glory he will give us later. —Romans 8:17-18

I hassled my parents in jest recently when they went on an extended exotic cruise, telling them they are spending my inheritance! My dad loves to say that he wants to do what his father did—die broke. So I guess I shouldn't count on getting rich someday from any earthly inheritance.

But my eternal inheritance is sure and secure, and so is yours if you are a child of God. God has made up a will that provides for the future of his children. Scripture says we will inherit a home in heaven, an eternal body made for us by God himself, God's promises, and the riches of heaven. We don't know exactly what the essence of our inheritance will be, but we can be confident that heaven will not disappoint us like life does. And when we truly value what we have to gain there, we no longer sulk over what we've lost here. God himself becomes our dearest desire and greatest inheritance.

Does it sometimes seem as if you've lost everything dear to you, and do you wonder what else is going to be taken from you? Someday each one of us will leave this earth and let go of everyone we have loved and everything we have enjoyed. We'll be left with only our eternal inheritance. But Paul has done the math, and by his careful calculations he assures us that what we suffer here is *nothing* compared to the glory of our eternal inheritance. Nothing. It seems a stretch to us from where we sit. But if you don't trust his calculations, if you do not highly value your eternal inheritance, you will overvalue what God has given you on earth and your grip on it will become a tyranny to you. But as you value the privilege of being an heir with Jesus, you will begin to live like the glory he will share with you one day is worth everything it may cost you. You will see your suffering as a severe mercy that keeps you from falling more deeply in love with the comforts, securities, and pleasures of this world so you can anticipate more fully a rich and rewarding inheritance in the next.

My generous Father, you have provided abundantly for me and my future by making me one of your heirs, and I am grateful. Looking forward to my eternal inheritance helps me to loosen my grip on the things of this world.

DIGGING DEEPER

According to Galatians 5:19-21 and Ephesians 5:5, what actions are evidence that a person is not a child of God and therefore not an heir of God?

WEEK 24

REWARDS

REFLECTION

How have you undervalued the eternal rewards Christ has promised you? How can you nurture more longing for those rewards?

What have you done for the glory of God that is stored in the secret place of your heart, and what would you like to do?

MEDITATION

It is impossible to please God without faith. Anyone who wants to come to him must believe that there is a God and that he rewards those who sincerely seek him. —HEBREWS 11:6

Add to and adjust your view of God so that you can see him as a rewarder. Imagine the joy he expresses in rewarding those he loves, including you.

Bring him your limited faith and insincere seeking and ask him to enlarge and transform it.

Linger over these words of Jesus in the following verses, seeking to hear his voice as he describes and assures you of his reward:

Matthew 6:3-6

Matthew 16:24-27

Matthew 19:29

Matthew 24:45-47

Mark 9:41

Luke 6:22-23, 35

PRAYER

Praise God for being a rewarder out of his generosity and grace.

Thank God for the reward of living a life in which you can experience his blessing now and for the calm confidence of his reward in the future.

Intercede for those who are undergoing significant suffering and persecution for their faith in Christ, that they will find peace in their confidence of eternal reward.

Confess your love of the admiration and applause of people, and ask God to help you value his approval even more.

Petition God to give you more of his presence and more of his power, to be your very great reward, even now.

WEEK 25

ANGELS

A reporter for *Life* magazine visited a conference for angel enthusiasts and wrote that the angels described to him at the conference were "cuddly as a lap dog, conscientious as a school crossing guard." He wrote, "I heard angels likened to spiritual kissing cousins, flower delivery messengers, and just a nice feeling of warmth and love that washes all over you. Today's angels seem to spend a lot less time praising God than serving us." While they are still making superhero, nick-of-time rescues, they are also showing up in less dire emergencies to track down a set of lost keys or make a chicken casserole more flavorful.

Why are angels so popular? I think it is because we all want to have a personal experience with the supernatural. And to many, angels seem to offer protection and comfort while making no demands.

But just as it is inappropriate to focus on or worship angels or to allow the world to define them, it is also wrong to ignore them. Angels are far more involved in our world than most of us realize, intervening both visibly and invisibly. Angels are referred to 108 times in the Old Testament and mentioned in the New Testament 165 times. To know who angels are and what angels do, we must listen carefully to Scripture. The Word of God must always be our source for evaluating the spectacular and exposing mere sentimentality.

THIS WEEK'S PASSAGE FOR MEDITATION

That night some shepherds were in the fields outside the village, guarding their flocks of sheep. Suddenly, an angel of the Lord appeared among them, and the radiance of the Lord's glory surrounded them. They were terribly frightened, but the angel reassured them. "Don't be afraid!" he said. "I bring you good news of great joy for everyone! The Savior—yes, the Messiah, the Lord—has been born tonight in Bethlehem, the city of David! And this is how you will recognize him: You will find a baby lying in a manger, wrapped snugly in strips of cloth!" Suddenly, the angel was joined by a vast host of others—the armies of heaven—praising God: "Glory to God in the highest heaven, and peace on earth to all whom God favors." —Luke 2:8-14

ANGELS SHOW US WHO TO WORSHIP

God's Son is far greater than the angels, just as the name God gave him is far greater than their names. When he presented his honored Son to the world, God said, "Let all the angels of God worship him." —Hebrews 1:4, 6

I can't claim to have ever seen an angel, but from reading Scripture, I know angels must be awesome. They are described as gleaming and bright—perhaps reflecting some of the brilliance of God's glory. Often their first words to those they visit are "Don't be afraid," so there must be something about them that is startling and intimidating. Holy angels in Scripture are so bright and beautiful that humans are tempted to worship them. At least the apostle John was. Late in his life, while in exile on the island of Patmos, he was given the vision recorded in the book of Revelation, a vision filled with angels. At one point, John bowed down to worship an angel, but the angel promptly rebuked him, saying, "No, don't worship me. I am a servant of God, just like you and your brothers the prophets, as well as all who obey what is written in this scroll. Worship God!" (Revelation 22:9).

Perhaps that is one reason we can't see angels—so we are not so tempted to worship them. It is God who is worthy of our worship, and that is why angels always point us toward him. Psalm 89:7 says, "The highest angelic powers stand in awe of God. He is far more awesome than those who surround his throne." The angels look around the landscape of heaven and see nothing and no one that remotely approaches the awesomeness and beauty of God. Angels help us to lift our eyes from this troubled and temporal earth, always drawing our gaze to the Lord, not to themselves. They help us say with the psalmist, "Whom have I in heaven but you? And earth has nothing I desire besides you" (Psalm 73:25, NIV).

In a culture that considers talking about Jesus a bit pushy and worshiping him a bit extreme, an interest in angels is acceptable and even fashionable. Angels seem like a safe form of spirituality. People who want a spiritual placebo are quick to bring their search for God to a dead end and search instead for angels. But what a tragedy if we worship the created instead of worshiping the Creator. Don't settle for the sentimental and shallow spirituality of angel worship and miss the glory of God.

Jesus, King of angels, you are the light and joy of heaven, and I have no desire to worship any other. With the angels, I will worship you forever!

DIGGING DEEPER

Read Hebrews 1, noting all the ways Jesus is superior to angels.

ANGELS SHOW US HOW TO WORSHIP

Hovering around him were mighty seraphim, each with six wings. With two wings they covered their faces, with two they covered their feet, and with the remaining two they flew. In a great chorus they sang, "Holy, holy, holy is the Lord Almighty! The whole earth is filled with his glory!" —Isaiah 6:2-3

What would we be like if we camped each night beside God's throne in glory and were able to stay full of his presence even when we went out into the world to do his work? I've been around people who just seem to radiate love for and joy in God. They talk about God continually, and their relationship with him sounds so real and natural that I've wanted to learn from them. Likewise I can learn from angels by watching what they do and by listening to what they say. Revelation says that the angels "keep on saying, 'Holy, holy, holy is the Lord God, Almighty' " (Revelation 4:8). If these holy creatures, awesome as they are, cry out in praise of his holiness day and night, if they fall down before God again and again, how much more should we? Angels show us how to worship in fear and freedom, in faithfulness and fullness.

We might think that angels would grow comfortably familiar with being in the presence of God, but they are eternally in awe of him, filled with holy fear. However, they are not frozen with fear. They're free to worship God the way he wants to be worshiped. They shout and sing and fly. This freedom is what we, too, were made for! Angels show us what wholehearted, all-the-time worship looks like—gazing at Jesus on the throne, responding to him with reverent fear, enjoying him with great freedom, obeying him with genuine joy, and inviting the whole world to gaze on his beauty.

Our lesson from the angels begins when we recognize God's holiness. His holiness is untouchable, unknowable, fiery, and consuming, and we simply cannot be casual and carefree and comfortable around it, demanding that our needs be met. His blazing holiness brings us to our knees, and we bow low before him. His holiness blinds us to our petty concerns and bids us to let go of lesser cares. As we enter his presence now, day-by-day, we become fitted for the day when we will unite in perfect praise with the angels, together forever in the presence of God.

Holy, holy, holy are you Lord God Almighty! I'm only beginning to learn what it means to praise you as you deserve, but how I want to learn! How I long to worship you in appropriate fear and freedom, beginning today.

DIGGING DEEPER

Compare the four living creatures in Revelation 4:6-8 and Ezekiel 1 and 10.

GUARDIAN ANGELS?

He orders his angels to protect you wherever you go. They will hold you with their hands to keep you from striking your foot on a stone.
—Psalm 91:11-12

"I feel like Ben is my little angel taking care of me," a grieving mom said to me about her son who had died. The idea gave her comfort, and I didn't want to steal that away from her, but I wanted to direct her to a more solid and significant Comforter. I wanted to tell her that her child did not become an angel when he died, and neither is he burdened with the responsibility of looking after her. People don't become angels. Angels are their own created order, created by God to serve his saints.

Throughout Scripture we find angels personally involved in protecting God's people in times of great need. But while angels serve us, they are not our servants. God alone is their Master. When they minister to us, it's because God has directed them. Our God uses his awesome power in a compassionate, loving way to help those in need. There's great hope and comfort in knowing that he is concerned about people who hurt, and that he has the power to dispatch one angel or an army of angels to meet our urgent needs. While we have no way of knowing how often our feet are directed onto right paths or how often we are guarded from harm, our invisible companions are ever at hand. They form a protective shield, and over and above them is the everlasting God and Father they serve, the one whom we love, our one and only true source for help and protection.

The Bible gives no indication that angels will respond if we pray directly to them for help. In fact, there are no instances in Scripture of people even asking God to send an angel to protect them. The only person in Scripture who tried to persuade someone else to seek help from an angel was Satan, who quoted Psalm 91 about angelic protection while tempting Jesus in the wilderness (see Matthew 4:5-6). And Scripture gives no basis for assuming angels will serve and help those who are not in God's family. The Bible describes angels as "spirits sent from God to care for those who will receive salvation" (Hebrews 1:14).

When we focus only on angels and what they can or cannot do, it takes our focus off Jesus. As you think of guardian angels watching over you, be sure to keep your eyes on the one who sent them. Put your trust in God, not in angels.

Guardian of my soul and body, I trust you to take care of me as you see fit, using an army of angels or your own strong arm of protection.

DIGGING DEEPER

Read about angels God sent to guide, instruct, protect, and judge in Acts 8:26-40; 10:1-48; and 12:6-25. What do these appearances of angels reveal about God's priorities?

THE ANGEL OF THE LORD

In all their distress he too was distressed, and the angel of his presence saved them. In his love and mercy he redeemed them; he lifted them up and carried them all the days of old. —Isaiah 63:9 (niv)

God created all the angels, including Satan and his demons, except for one. The "angel of the Lord" is clearly distinguished from all the angelic beings in a number of ways, and yet he is called an angel. Hagar met this angel in the desert, and he comforted her with predictions concerning the future. Abraham heard the angel of the Lord's voice on Mount Moriah telling him not to kill his son Isaac. Jacob spent the night wrestling with the angel of the Lord. Moses saw and heard the angel of the Lord in the form of a burning bush. This angel of God was in the pillar of cloud and the pillar of fire that led Israel through the wilderness.

This angel seems to be not just *from* the Lord, but actually to *be* the Lord. Though the angel of the Lord seems in some ways to be *distinct* from God, he clearly is God—and therefore not at all like other angels. Who is this angel who is sometimes called God and who ministered to people by giving them directions and prophecies that were later fulfilled? Though nowhere does Scripture spell it out absolutely, it seems to indicate that the angel of the Lord was none other than the preincarnate Son of God. Centuries before Jesus was born in Bethlehem as a baby, he walked the earth manifesting himself as a ministering angel. God was there in the form of his angel, providing his loving guidance and careful protection, actively involved in the cares and affairs of men. It is almost as if he can't help himself. His love for us means that he cannot remain uninvolved and aloof from us. He sees our need and he condescends to us. He cares. He comes.

The angel of the Lord's appearances ceased after the birth of Jesus—further evidence that he was that angel. He has come to us in the person of Jesus, he has given us the Holy Spirit, and he has spoken to us in the revelation of Scripture. His very Spirit lives with us and in us.

Angel of the Lord, Holy One from God, keep coming down! How I need you in my distress. Come down and speak to me. Come down and walk with me. Come down and save me. Visit me with your holy presence and carry me.

DIGGING DEEPER

Read about other manifestations of the angel of the Lord in Numbers 22:21-41; Judges 6:1-24; 13:1-22; and Hosea 12:2-6.

DON'T BE AFRAID; JESUS IS COMING

As I was praying, Gabriel, whom I had seen in the earlier vision, came swiftly to me at the time of the evening sacrifice. He explained to me, "Daniel, I have come here to give you insight and understanding."
—Daniel 9:21-22

We struggled in the process of naming our son Gabriel. We wanted his name to be as significant and meaningful as *Hope* had been for our daughter, but uniquely his own. David sent out an email the day Gabriel was born, saying, "We chose his name because we believe that he, like the angel Gabriel, is sent from God. We will not be surprised if he has heavenly messages for us to hear, if we will listen. And significantly, whenever Gabriel appeared in the Bible, he reassured his stunned audience: 'Don't be afraid!' "

In the Old Testament book of Daniel, God sent the angel Gabriel to explain to Daniel the meaning of a vision. Gabriel explained the imagery in the dream and the future restoration of God's people, which included the coming of the Anointed One—Jesus. Then, in Luke 1, Gabriel came to Zechariah, an elderly priest in the Temple, telling him that his wife would bear a son, John, who would "precede the coming of the Lord, preparing the people for his arrival" (1:17). And again in Luke 1, God sent the angel Gabriel to Mary, telling her that she would have a son, Jesus, who would be "very great and will be called the Son of the Most High" (1:32).

Gabriel's message is always the same. It's Jesus. "Don't be afraid; Jesus is coming." For Daniel and his people, held captive in a godless land, hope was found in the revelation that Jesus was coming. For Zechariah and his wife, Elizabeth, disappointed and disgraced by life, hope came in the angel's promise that Jesus was coming. And Mary, confused, disturbed, and frightened about the future, was filled with hope in the holy confidence that Jesus was coming. And for you and me, as we listen for God in the midst of our pain, the message is the same: Jesus. Don't be afraid as you face the future. Jesus is coming.

I suppose some had hoped for some supernatural message from our little angel, Gabriel—perhaps something we'd never heard before. But because God has a message he wants us to hear, he sent more than an angel or a baby—he sent his own Son. "The Word became human and lived here on earth among us" (John 1:14). Jesus is the ultimate articulation of God's love for you and me. Jesus is everything God wants to say to us.

Jesus, I believe you are coming, and it takes away my fear.

DIGGING DEEPER

Read the stories of Gabriel's messages in Daniel 9 and Luke 1. What similarities do you find?

WEEK 25

ANGELS

REFLECTION

Have you paid too much attention to angels or perhaps too little?

How does an examination of the message and the mission of angels challenge you? How does it change you?

MEDITATION

That night some shepherds were in the fields outside the village, guarding their flocks of sheep. Suddenly, an angel of the Lord appeared among them, and the radiance of the Lord's glory surrounded them. They were terribly frightened, but the angel reassured them. "Don't be afraid!" he said. "I bring you good news of great joy for everyone! The Savior—yes, the Messiah, the Lord—has been born tonight in Bethlehem, the city of David! And this is how you will recognize him: You will find a baby lying in a manger, wrapped snugly in strips of cloth!" Suddenly, the angel was joined by a vast host of others—the armies of heaven—praising God: "Glory to God in the highest heaven, and peace on earth to all whom God favors." —LUKE 2:8-14

Place yourself in the fields outside Bethlehem. Seek to see what the shepherds saw, hear what they heard, and feel what they felt.

Read through the message of the angel carefully, examining each word for its special meaning and promise to the people of that day and to you today.

PRAYER

Praise God for his absolute holiness.

Thank God for creating and sending his angels to protect us, guide us, and meet our needs.

Intercede for those who have been deceived by Satan, who disguises himself as an "angel of light."

Confess your fascination with the spectacular and pseudo-spiritual that reveals a lack of faith in God's Word.

Petition God to help you give angels their rightful place in your worship and in the world.

WEEK 26

THE ENEMY

Bring up the topic of the devil and most people will look for a way to turn the matter into a joke. The myth of horns and a tail leads people to associate everything they hear about the devil with superstition and humor. But they confuse fact with fiction. The devil is very real; he is our invisible adversary.

He is called many things throughout Scripture, and just as the names of God reveal much about God's character and conduct, so do the names for Satan. He is called the great blasphemer, a murderer from the beginning, the father of lies, a roaring lion, the evil one, the dragon, a serpent, the prince of this world, the enemy, an accuser of the brethren, our adversary, a liar, the power of darkness, the tempter, and the wicked one.

To laugh off the reality of Satan is to open the door for his lies to deceive you, his accusations to assault you, and his evil to overpower you. He wants to trick you and tempt you, to destroy and devour you. So "put on all of God's armor so that you will be able to stand firm against all strategies and tricks of the Devil" (Ephesians 6:11). Satan is very real and very powerful, but Christ in you is the power that will spell his defeat.

THIS WEEK'S PASSAGE FOR MEDITATION

Be strong with the Lord's mighty power. Put on all of God's armor so that you will be able to stand firm against all strategies and tricks of the Devil. For we are not fighting against people made of flesh and blood, but against the evil rulers and authorities of the unseen world, against those mighty powers of darkness who rule this world, and against wicked spirits in the heavenly realms. Use every piece of God's armor to resist the enemy in the time of evil, so that after the battle you will still be standing firm. Stand your ground, putting on the sturdy belt of truth and the body armor of God's righteousness. For shoes, put on the peace that comes from the Good News, so that you will be fully prepared. In every battle you will need faith as your shield to stop the fiery arrows aimed at you by Satan. Put on salvation as your helmet, and take the sword of the Spirit, which is the word of God. Pray at all times and on every occasion in the power of the Holy Spirit. Stay alert and be persistent in your prayers for all Christians everywhere. —Ephesians 6:10-18

SATAN WANTS TO DRIVE A WEDGE

Satan replied to the Lord, "Yes, Job fears God, but not without good reason! You have always protected him and his home and his property from harm. You have made him prosperous in everything he does. Look how rich he is! But take away everything he has, and he will surely curse you to your face!" —Job 1:9-11

In the story of Job, Satan comes before God after roaming around the earth. What has he been looking for? He's been looking for an opportunity . . . an opportunity to defeat God, to prove himself more powerful than God, to be worshiped as God. And it was God who brought up the name of Job. Why? Because Job is such a beautiful example of what pleases God—a person above reproach. I think Job must have had an incredible track record of faithfulness in the face of difficulty as well as success (and success can be as much a test of our godly character as difficulty, can't it?). Evidently Job had proven over and over again that he would be faithful to God no matter what.

But Satan was skeptical. He accused Job of loving God only for what he could get from him. Satan thought Job was in a relationship with God only because Job was supernaturally protected by God and had a comfortable life. He figured that if Job's comfortable life was taken away from him, he would turn on God. You see, Satan recognizes that if we are in a relationship only for what we can get, at the first sign of difficulty, if we're not getting what we want, we're out of there. He understands our consumer mentality toward the things of God—a mentality that is sometimes stronger than our commitment to the person of God.

Satan wanted to drive a wedge between God and Job. That was the big goal, the big question. Would Job reject God when trouble came, or would he be faithful to God no matter what, thwarting Satan's plan and supposition? And the question is the same in your life. Satan wants to alienate you from God, and he will use whatever means possible to accomplish that goal, including suffering. Will you allow Satan to use your suffering to drive a wedge between you and God, or will you determine to be faithful, no matter what?

Lord, I don't want to let anything come between me and you—not the hurts in my past or the pain in my future. Give me the strength and grace I need to keep cleaving to you in the midst of my suffering.

DIGGING DEEPER

Read how Satan was seeking to drive a wedge between man and God in Genesis 3. What did he use to drive a wedge, and was he successful?

SATAN HAS TO SEEK PERMISSION

"All right, you may test him," the Lord said to Satan. "Do whatever you want with everything he possesses, but don't harm him physically." —Job 1:12

I find this verse troubling, and maybe you do too. Satan has come to God and asked permission to harm Job, and God has given the permission! That's a hard one for us, because it just doesn't fit with our understanding of a loving, protecting God, does it? But it is clear. God gives the permission and sets the parameters for Satan to bring pain into Job's life. God says in essence, "Okay, you can put his faith to the test, but you can only go this far." This reveals something very important about Satan and, ultimately, about God.

Satan has to ask permission because Satan has no power that is not given to him by God. You know God is powerful, and you believe that God is more powerful than Satan, right? But the bigger truth is that Satan has absolutely no power that God does not grant him. That is how sovereign God is over the universe and how limited Satan is in the world. He can go only as far as God will allow him in inflicting suffering on this world and in your life. God and Satan are not two ultimate powers in the universe battling to determine a winner. There is only one ultimate power, and that is God.

In Luke, we read again of Satan asking permission to harm one of God's own. Jesus says, "Simon, Simon, Satan has asked to have all of you, to sift you like wheat. But I have pleaded in prayer for you, Simon, that your faith should not fail" (22:31-32). The "all of you" Satan wants to sift includes you and me. Satan's sifting is an effort to destroy our faith. If he can do it by shaking you in the sieve of suffering, then he will try that. If he can do it through amusement or ease, he may try that. But while God may give Satan permission to harm us or sift us, he will never allow our faith to fail permanently or our hope to be destroyed ultimately. God's confidence that Job would pass the test and Jesus' expectation that Peter's faith would not fail utterly was not dependent on Job or Peter, but on God's power. And your ability to endure the tests hardship brings is not determined by the amount or quality of your faith, but by the object of your faith. The almighty God will never grant Satan permission to destroy the faith that makes you his and keeps you his forever.

Almighty God, it is hard to grasp that you have granted Satan permission to bring pain into my life, but I believe that your ultimate purpose is for my good and your glory. Your shield of faith gives me courage and comfort.

DIGGING DEEPER

Read about demons asking permission from Jesus in Luke 8:27-33.

RESIST THE DEVIL

He gives us more and more strength to stand against such evil desires. As the Scriptures say, "God sets himself against the proud, but he shows favor to the humble." So humble yourselves before God. Resist the Devil, and he will flee from you. Draw close to God, and God will draw close to you.
—James 4:6-8

I was shocked when I heard it, and to be honest, I'm still shocked. How could my lifelong friend leave her husband and children and move in with another man? She's always been a person of integrity, a pillar of the church. It breaks my heart and it shakes me up because I want to think there are some sins I am above, things I would never do. But I realize that this attitude is not only prideful, it's dangerous.

Even when we remember the things we've done that have caused us to hide our faces in shame and shake our heads in amazement, we think to ourselves, *How could I have done that? That isn't like me!* We're so full of pride; we don't realize we should instead be thinking, *This is exactly like me! This just reveals the core of who I am. I am a sinner who desperately needs the grace of God to do anything good.* We can keep holding on to our pride, our sense of self-confidence that we would *never* do what we see others do, or we can humble ourselves before God and admit our evil desires and our vulnerability to the devil's seduction. As we humble ourselves before God, we lay before him our desperate need for the strength to turn away from what we don't have the strength in ourselves to resist.

You should know that God doesn't want you to resist the devil merely so you can be good. He knows that what the devil offers will hurt you, and he wants you to turn away from the devil so you can draw close to him. He doesn't want to share you. He wants to love you. As we draw close to God, we find the comfort we crave and the love we've been longing for. With every step you take toward him, the pleasures of the world lose their appeal, the emptiness of its entertainment is exposed, and the words the devil has whispered in your ear—tempting you to doubt God's love and faithfulness in the face of suffering and disappointment—will be recognized as lies.

Draw me close to you, God, as I humble myself before you and draw near to you. Give me the strength to resist what the devil has convinced me will fulfill and please me. Nothing in this world can give me the pleasure that being close to you brings.

DIGGING DEEPER

Read Hebrews 4:12-16 to see how drawing close to God helps us to resist temptation and to see ourselves for who we are.

TEMPTED TO AVOID THE CROSS

Jesus was led out into the wilderness by the Holy Spirit to be tempted there by the Devil. —Matthew 4:1

Recently I discovered something surprising in this verse. What surprised me was that it was the Holy Spirit who led Jesus into the wilderness to be tempted. While Jesus may have purposed to pray and prepare for fulfilling the plan of God through his ministry, the Holy Spirit led him there to be tempted. God wanted his Son to be tempted in his human body just as you and I are tempted. This would prepare him not only for his ministry on the earth, but his priestly ministry in heaven. Once again we see God using what Satan intended for evil to accomplish his own good purpose.

We might think it was easy for Jesus to resist the temptation Satan threw at him because, after all, he's God. But Jesus didn't exploit his inherent deity to overcome temptation. He faced it in his full humanity, using only the same weapons that we have at our disposal: the Word of God, the Holy Spirit, and absolute trust in his heavenly Father.

Since he was a boy lingering in the Temple, Jesus had maintained his focus on completing the work his Father had sent him to do. He had waited until God's appointed time until, at the age of thirty, Jesus was stepping out of the shadows, each day taking one step closer to the Cross. Satan tempted Jesus to use spectacular signs to please the Jewish masses who were looking for a Messiah to save them from their Roman occupiers, not from their sin. He tempted Jesus to compromise on God's plan to gain his most noble desire—to gather Jerusalem to himself as a hen gathers her chicks (Matthew 23:37). Satan's temptation was to induce Christ to finish the work without the suffering, without the personal humiliation of obedience and self-denial, without the rejection and misunderstanding of people—in a word, without the Cross.

Satan tempts us in the same way, trying to convince us that we can experience the glory of God without the suffering of Christ, that we can accomplish a great work for God without the cost of carrying our cross. Would you refuse to give in to the temptation to avoid suffering at the cost of rejecting the Cross? Would you use Scripture as your shield against Satan?

Sinless Savior, you understand the intensity of the temptation I face, and you show me how to withstand it through the strengthening power of your Word.

DIGGING DEEPER

Read how the temptation of Jesus helps him understand our struggles and shows us how to overcome in Hebrews 2:17-18; 4:15-16; 5:7-9; and 7:25.

SATAN'S ULTIMATE DESTINY

THE LORD GOD SAID TO THE SERPENT, "BECAUSE YOU HAVE DONE THIS, YOU WILL BE PUNISHED. FROM NOW ON, YOU AND THE WOMAN WILL BE ENEMIES, AND YOUR OFFSPRING AND HER OFFSPRING WILL BE ENEMIES. HE WILL CRUSH YOUR HEAD, AND YOU WILL STRIKE HIS HEEL." —GENESIS 3:14-15

Why does God allow evil? We know that God created the universe, including the angels, some of whom rebelled against him. So why did he let it happen? Wouldn't the world be a better place if he had never allowed Satan to rebel and evil to run loose? These are philosophical questions for some, but for those of us who've been hurt by the evil and brokenness of this world, the question is personal, and our pursuit of an answer is pivotal.

The Bible begins and ends by addressing God's battle with Satan. We see the beginning of the story in Genesis 3, as God curses the serpent Satan, pronouncing his punishment—that the seed of the woman, the coming Christ, will one day crush him. And we are not left to wonder how the story of history will end. Revelation 20 tells us that at the end of this age, when Christ returns, judgment will rain down. Satan will be thrown into the lake of fire along with his demons. Can you almost hear the sighs of relief and shouts of victory from God's people as Satan goes down in the sulfur inferno for the last time? He will be destroyed forever, never again to terrorize us with evil or tyrannize us with sin.

We're glad to hear it, but we can't help but ask, *Why not now? God, why would you permit Satan to inflict so much pain in the world for so long?* Ultimately, we must trust the wisdom, goodness, and timing of God, but he has given us clues in his Word. God permits Satan to work in the world because in the end it will be good for the church he loves and it will bring him more glory. Through the suffering sent by Satan, we are drawn to rely more heavily on God. Satan fans the flames of God's refining fire, which we know God is using for good in our lives. And so God waits. And we wait.

When you become discouraged and defeated by the evil that surrounds you and the sin that has stolen so much from you, and when you're tempted to think wickedness has won, remember that the devil's days are numbered. Find hope in the truth that when all is said and done, the devil will be defeated and you'll be safe in the arms of God.

Conquering Savior, how we long for that day when you serve Satan the final blow and we are free of his influence forever. Come quickly, Lord Jesus!

DIGGING DEEPER

Read the whole story of Satan's final defeat in Revelation 20:1-10.

WEEK 26

THE ENEMY

REFLECTION

In what ways have you made yourself vulnerable to the devil by not taking him seriously? In what ways have you failed to resist him?

What troubles you and what encourages you as you consider Satan's purposes, the expanse and limitations of his power, and his ultimate destiny?

MEDITATION

Be strong with the Lord's mighty power. Put on all of God's armor so that you will be able to stand firm against all strategies and tricks of the Devil. For we are not fighting against people made of flesh and blood, but against the evil rulers and authorities of the unseen world, against those mighty powers of darkness who rule this world, and against wicked spirits in the heavenly realms. Use every piece of God's armor to resist the enemy in the time of evil, so that after the battle you will still be standing firm. Stand your ground, putting on the sturdy belt of truth and the body armor of God's righteousness. For shoes, put on the peace that comes from the Good News, so that you will be fully prepared. In every battle you will need faith as your shield to stop the fiery arrows aimed at you by Satan. Put on salvation as your helmet, and take the sword of the Spirit, which is the word of God. Pray at all times and on every occasion in the power of the Holy Spirit. Stay alert and be persistent in your prayers for all Christians everywhere. —EPHESIANS 6:10-18

Read through this passage several times, taking seriously the power of the devil and taking stock of your spiritual armor.

Allow your mind to meditate on the Lord's power provided to you for battle against spiritual enemies.

Work your way through the passage, underlining all the action words of instruction. Ask God to give you insight into what each instruction means for you.

PRAYER

Pray through the passage, asking God for his power and protection and thanking him for each piece of armor and every promise of victory.

WEEK 27

THE SCHOOL OF SUFFERING

The prophet Isaiah told God's people, "Though the Lord gave you adversity for food and affliction for drink, he will still be with you to teach you. You will see your teacher with your own eyes, and you will hear a voice say, 'This is the way; turn around and walk here' " (Isaiah 30:20-21).

Adversity and affliction are not necessarily our idea of a feast, yet deep down we know that suffering nourishes even as it causes pain. We want to learn and we want to grow, but we really don't want to suffer. And yet to grow in God is to enroll in a difficult school where character is built out of persevering through difficulty.

Larry King interviewed Billy Graham in the days following the announcement of his Parkinson's disease. "You pray not to be in pain, don't you?" Larry asked.

"Not at all," Graham responded. "I pray for God's will." Graham explained that he was more than willing to suffer if God had another lesson for him to learn. Billy Graham wants to learn the lessons God has for him, even if it requires pain.

Do you want to learn the lessons only suffering can teach you? Would you say to God even now, "If I have to go through this, then give me everything. Teach me everything you want to teach me through this. Don't let this incredible pain be wasted in my life"?

THIS WEEK'S PASSAGE FOR MEDITATION

Since Jesus went through everything you're going through and more, learn to think like him. Think of your sufferings as a weaning from that old sinful habit of always expecting to get your own way. Then you'll be able to live out your days free to pursue what God wants instead of being tyrannized by what you want. —1 Peter 4:1-2 (MSG)

DON'T RUN FROM SUFFERING; EMBRACE IT

ANYONE WHO INTENDS TO COME WITH ME HAS TO LET ME LEAD. YOU'RE NOT IN THE DRIVER'S SEAT—I AM. DON'T RUN FROM SUFFERING; EMBRACE IT. FOLLOW ME AND I'LL SHOW YOU HOW. —LUKE 9:23-24 (MSG)

Nobody wants to suffer. I sure don't. In fact, most of us would have to admit that we have spent most of our lives doing everything we can to *avoid* suffering. In our modern world, we expect a cure for every illness, a replacement for every loss, a fix for every failure. We are shocked and shaken when unexpected, unwanted pain interrupts our lives. None of us have to go looking for suffering. Suffering intrudes uninvited into our safe existence, and we are never the same.

Jesus must understand our natural inclination, and yet he tells us not to run from suffering. To run from suffering is to refuse to see God's hand at work in the midst of it. To run from suffering is to reject the lessons God has for you in it. It is to resent the plan and purpose of God that is being accomplished through the suffering.

While Jesus tells us not to run from suffering, he suggests we do more than simply endure it. He admonishes us to embrace it. He wants us to stop feeling sorry for ourselves and to focus on what there is to learn in the suffering. He invites us to draw closer to him in the midst of our suffering. There's freedom there, and he's inviting us into the glory and joy of it.

To embrace suffering is to welcome God's work in your life even in the most unimaginable circumstances. To embrace suffering is to enjoy God's presence in your life even when you are filled with questions for him. To embrace suffering is to enter into a deeper relationship with God that you could not have enjoyed without experiencing penetrating pain. The suffering not only makes you crave such a relationship, it gives you the capacity to savor it. Ultimately, to embrace suffering is to allow your now broken heart to be more easily rebroken by the things that break the heart of God. To embrace suffering is to become more aware of and more apt to engage with the suffering in the world around you. Don't run from suffering; embrace it and find yourself enriched and renewed.

My Teacher in suffering, everything in me tells me to run from the hurt in my life, and yet you bid me to linger and even embrace it. Allow me to feel your embrace as I open myself to the hidden gifts of suffering.

DIGGING DEEPER

What do the following verses say we should run from and toward: Psalm 119:32; 143:9; Proverbs 5:3-8; 18:10; and 2 Timothy 2:22?

THE REFINER'S FIRE

I have refined you but not in the way silver is refined. Rather, I have refined you in the furnace of suffering. —Isaiah 48:10

In ancient times, a workman would take a piece of ore hewn from the earth, crush it into pieces, and place it in a piece of pottery that he would then thrust into a fire. The refiner carefully tended the fire, knowing just how intense the flame needed to be to soften the ore and cause the impurities to rise to the top so they could be skimmed off, leaving a bubbling treasure of molten metal. The refiner was patient, knowing just how long the metal should stay in the fire so that more and more dull impurities would rise to the surface until finally he could look into the liquid silver and see what he had been working for and waiting for—his own reflection.

We, too, are being refined in the fiery crucible of suffering and pain. Our Refiner knows just how hot to make the fire so that our impurities will rise to the top to be lifted away. He does the careful work of removing from our lives what is unfit and impure, transforming the ordinary ore of our lives into a shining treasure. The fiery flames of distress and difficulty are much too hot for our liking, but the refiner's fire is not a cause for fear. It burns for our good. His purpose in plunging you into the fire is not to *disfigure* you, but to *mold* you into a person who thinks and acts and looks like Christ. Every sorrow that has singed you has been for the supreme purpose of transforming your character into the likeness of Jesus.

But it is possible to resist God's refining process. The prophet Jeremiah described what happens when God's people resist: "The bellows blow fiercely. The refining fire grows hotter. But it will never purify and cleanse them because there is no purity in them to refine. I will label them 'Rejected Silver' because I, the Lord, am discarding them" (Jeremiah 6:29-30). Impure, unusable, rejected, discarded. Can you imagine anything worse than being deemed unusable by God because you've resisted his refining process? Welcome the work of the Refiner. Allow him to plunge you into the fire so he can form you into his image, making you a shining treasure that reflects his own glorious character.

My careful Refiner, how I resist the fire of suffering and long for relief from the flames. But I want to be useful to you, a beautiful reflection of you, so plunge me into the fire, if you must, to make me into your image.

DIGGING DEEPER

Christ's coming is likened to what two purifying agents in Malachi 3:2-3? What does 1 Peter 1:7 say is revealed through suffering, and for what benefit?

KEEP ON DOING WHAT IS RIGHT

If you are suffering according to God's will, keep on doing what is right, and trust yourself to the God who made you, for he will never fail you.
—1 Peter 4:19

We have a hard time believing that it could ever be "God's will" for us to suffer. And yet if we embrace God's sovereignty over the universe and accept that nothing happens apart from his power and control, we know our suffering must ultimately be according to God's will. So then what do we do?

The intensity of suffering can put us in a place where we are tempted to compromise, where we can easily justify an attitude or action we never would have considered before pain invaded our existence. Fear and pain can cause us to lose sight of the guiding force in our lives: pleasing God.

In your search for answers in the midst of your suffering, have you resolved to live a pure and holy life? It's tempting to "give yourself some space," to "cut yourself some slack" since everything in life is hard. Have you rejected this temptation? Have you determined to be faithful to do what God has clearly asked you to do or not do through his revealed moral will (his Word)? When you are in the midst of difficult circumstances and you aren't sure what to do, hold tight to what you do know. Obey God's clear commands without compromise.

Sometimes it is difficult to know what is right, but more often we do know the right thing to do; we just don't want to do it. It costs us something we don't want to pay. We make matters more complicated than they are, straining for the gray in what is clearly black and white. And really our reluctance to do what we know is right is a lack of faith. Our reluctance to obey God's clear commands is our way of saying to God, "You may have made me, but you don't know me well enough or understand the situation well enough to know what is best for me. I know best what is best for me."

He's the one who made you. He knows best what you need and what will make you eternally happy. So keep on doing what is right, no matter what people around you say. Entrust yourself to him through your wholehearted obedience, confident that he knows best.

Maker, I want to suffer in a manner that pleases you, and I am determined to keep on doing what is right. I entrust myself to you by obeying your Word.

DIGGING DEEPER

Read Deuteronomy 5 and Matthew 5:21-48 to examine your life in light of God's clear commands.

CALLED TO SUFFER

This suffering is all part of what God has called you to. Christ, who suffered for you, is your example. Follow in his steps. When he suffered, he did not threaten to get even. He left his case in the hands of God, who always judges fairly. —1 Peter 2:21, 23

Wanted: Disciples who are willing to leave everything familiar to follow Jesus. Carrying a cross is required. Following may result in death.

Who would answer a call like that? We have, if we call ourselves Christians. But most of us really only wanted to sign up for Christianity lite. We wanted the version in which we go to church and maybe teach Sunday school, the kind of Christianity that helps us to clean up our act and be nice, and in return we get a sense of respectability now and heaven when we die. We didn't really hear God calling us to suffer for his sake. And if we had, we certainly would not have answered.

Maybe you came to Christ because someone told you that "God loves you and has a wonderful plan for your life." It was true then and it is still true. But if you've never made the transition from a life focused on pleasing yourself to a life of obedience focused on pleasing God, then you will forsake faith at the first sign of adversity. We often hear people talk about the "victorious Christian life." But isn't the life of a Christian really more about bending the knee, humbling ourselves, and taking up a cross? Jesus said it is. "If any of you wants to be my follower, you must put aside your selfish ambition, shoulder your cross, and follow me" (Matthew 16:24).

I don't know what the cross will look like for you. I just know it will require a death to your earthly desires and earthbound dreams to carry it. And I know it won't be easy. But I also know that as you die to yourself, God's life will take root and grow within you. And as you die to your dreams, his dreams can flourish. He will give you new desires and then fulfill them completely.

God calls us to bow the knee, whether or not we have it figured out, whether or not we agree. Jesus shows us how to do that. Follow in his steps. He shows us how to suffer without becoming resentful or revengeful. He shows us how to entrust our reputation and vindication to God, how to leave our very lives in the hands of God. This is what God calls you to. Will you follow?

My Example in suffering, I want to follow close behind you, learning from your purity, your forgiveness, your submission. Following in your footsteps, I place my life in your hands, trusting in your wisdom and love.

DIGGING DEEPER

What else has God called believers to, according to the following verses: Romans 1:6-7; Galatians 5:13; Colossians 3:15; and 1 Thessalonians 2:2; 4:7?

WHAT DOES GOD WANT TO DO IN YOU OR THROUGH YOU?

If we are to share his glory, we must also share his suffering. Yet what we suffer now is nothing compared to the glory he will give us later.
—Romans 8:17-18

One afternoon Anne Graham Lotz and I were having lunch in a hotel, and she was telling me the story of how she came home one day to find all of the doors of her house flung open and everything valuable in the house gone. Anne's mother and grandmother had marked special occasions in her life with pieces of jewelry, and it was all gone. Her children's silver baby cups and spoons—gone. That night, as she replaced the pillowcase that had been taken by the thieves to haul away so many things that were precious to her, and as she wiped away tears, she asked God, "What is it you want to do in me or through me that would have to cost me this much?"

And then she looked at me and said, "I look at what you have lost, and I wonder, *What is it that God wants to do in you or through you that would possibly have to cost you this much?*"

In the months to come, her words echoed in my mind and framed my loss with meaning—a meaning I wanted to embrace and fulfill. Early on I had told God that I did not want the pain of loving and losing Hope to be wasted in my life, and that desire had not diminished but grown. I realized that the only thing that could balance out such significant suffering is substantial glory. The only thing that could make my loss and your loss bearable is for it to result in greater glory to God. Because God's glory is the only thing that really matters; it is the only thing that really lasts.

Have you come to the place where you believe the glory of God is worth what it has cost you or may cost you in the future? Have you embraced the foundational truth that your life is not about you and your pain, but that you exist to display and enjoy the glory of God? All of history and every aspect of your life have been designed by God to display his greatness and his beauty. And so I pass along this question for you to ponder, this endeavor for you to embrace: *What is it that God wants to do in you or through you that would have to cost you this much?* Whatever it is, I assure you it will be glorious.

Glorious God, how I want to reflect your glory and make it shine brighter to the world around me even now in the midst of my loss. I offer myself to you, asking you to do something glorious in me.

DIGGING DEEPER

What do 1 Peter 1:11 and 4:13 add to your understanding of the relationship between suffering and glory?

WEEK 27

THE SCHOOL OF SUFFERING

REFLECTION

What important and life-altering lessons have you learned from the school of suffering? How have these lessons changed you?

In what ways have you run from your suffering, and how have you embraced it?

MEDITATION

Since Jesus went through everything you're going through and more, learn to think like him. Think of your sufferings as a weaning from that old sinful habit of always expecting to get your own way. Then you'll be able to live out your days free to pursue what God wants instead of being tyrannized by what you want. —1 PETER 4:1-2 (MSG)

Since Christ suffered physical pain, you must arm yourselves with the same attitude he had, and be ready to suffer, too. For if you are willing to suffer for Christ, you have decided to stop sinning. And you won't spend the rest of your life chasing after evil desires, but you will be anxious to do the will of God. —1 PETER 4:1-2 (NLT)

Read the passage several times in both translations, allowing the differences and similarities to make the meaning clearer to you. Circle words and phrases that are especially meaningful to you.

Offer the passage back to God in the form of a prayer, asking for his attitude and way of thinking about suffering, expressing your desire to be free to pursue what he wants.

PRAYER

Praise God for the magnificence of his glory that outshines our suffering and makes it worthwhile.

Thank God for lovingly and carefully refining you, though the process is sometimes painful.

Intercede for those around the world who have been called to suffer and are experiencing real and significant persecution for their faith.

Confess your reluctance to embrace suffering, and confess your resentment toward God.

Petition God to show you what it is he wants to do in you or through you uniquely because of your suffering.

WEEK 28

MY SOUL SOURCE

I don't know if they are still around, but there used to be stores in some malls called Just Ties. I had a friend in college who thought it was great fun to go into a Just Ties store and say to the salesperson, "Do you sell suits here?" or, "Do you have any shirts?" He would go on and on, asking for everything other than ties until the irritated salesperson would say something like, "This is *Just Ties*. We just sell ties!"

Much of our frustration and disappointment with living in this world comes from the fact that it simply does not and cannot offer what we are desperately looking for, what our souls hunger for. We keep asking and expecting the world to supply the inner resources our souls crave, but we've gone to the wrong source. When will we learn that the deepest needs of our souls can only be met by the One who created our souls, the One who values our souls so much that he has gone to the lengths of the Cross so that those souls can be safe and secure with him for eternity?

Jesus says, "Come to me . . . and you will find rest for your souls" (Matthew 11:28-29). Jesus invites you to come. He is your source for everything your soul longs for.

THIS WEEK'S PASSAGE FOR MEDITATION

May God bless you with his special favor and wonderful peace as you come to know Jesus, our God and Lord, better and better. As we know Jesus better, his divine power gives us everything we need for living a godly life. He has called us to receive his own glory and goodness! And by that same mighty power, he has given us all of his rich and wonderful promises. He has promised that you will escape the decadence all around you caused by evil desires and that you will share in his divine nature. So make every effort to apply the benefits of these promises to your life. Then your faith will produce a life of moral excellence. A life of moral excellence leads to knowing God better. Knowing God leads to self-control. Self-control leads to patient endurance, and patient endurance leads to godliness. Godliness leads to love for other Christians, and finally you will grow to have genuine love for everyone. The more you grow like this, the more you will become productive and useful in your knowledge of our Lord Jesus Christ. —2 Peter 1:2-8

CHRIST: MY SOURCE FOR COMPLETENESS

It is in [Christ] that God gives a full and complete expression of himself in bodily form. Moreover, your own completeness is realised in him.
— Colossians 2:9-10 (Phillips)

Incomplete. That is the only way I know to describe how our family feels at times. The three of us have a great time together and our house is full of joy, but at times we are painfully aware that Hope and Gabe are missing, and we feel the void.

Hope's birthday falls the week of Thanksgiving, so in a desire to create a new memory and escape the emptiness at home that first Thanksgiving, we decided to take a trip to the Blue Ridge Mountains. I dropped by a friend's house shortly before the trip in an effort to reconnect. I was telling her about our plans to stay in a bed-and-breakfast and visit the Biltmore mansion. "It should be fun," she said, "won't it?"

Yes, I thought, *but not like you're thinking.* Honestly, I can't remember what I said out loud, but I remember thinking that if she and her family went off to a ski lodge for the holiday without one of their sons, she might better understand how I felt. They would have a great time, but as they sat by the fire playing cards, they would think to themselves, *This is fun, but it would really be fun if Peter were here, if our family were complete.* I wished she could understand that in every experience we have—good or bad—there is an aching awareness that we are not complete.

But I know better than to think that if Hope and Gabe were here, their presence would assure a sense of completeness. That would be foolishly sentimental. While the void created by the losses in our lives is very real, it only punctuates the deeper void we feel when we realize that no person can make us feel whole and complete. We can never feel completely safe or completely satisfied unless we nestle ourselves in the bosom and being of Christ, where we find the completeness we lack. In him we find full confidence, complete understanding, total acceptance. "For in him we live and move and exist" (Acts 17:28). Won't you give up looking for completeness in anyone or anything other than Christ?

Christ, you are the One who completes me, and without you I would be eternally and hopelessly incomplete. Use the losses in my life to show me that you are my only source for the completeness I crave.

DIGGING DEEPER

Read Colossians 2:6-15. How does our union with Christ complete us?

MY ROCK OF TRUTH IN TRAUMA

Do not snatch your word of truth from me, for my only hope is in your laws. —Psalm 119:43

I was sad to get this email recently from Michelle Alm, one of my friends from Tyndale House Publishers, with the subject line "Holding on to Hope!"

DEAR NANCY:
Early in the morning on Saturday, October 9th, my son, Vince, was in a serious car accident. As a result of his injuries, he is a C6 quadriplegic. This tragedy has rocked my world in a way I did not even know was possible. I am very thankful that you have gone ahead of me in sadness. Seeing that you survived it is the hope I need to move ahead.

DEAR MICHELLE:
The words "he is a C6 quadriplegic" don't seem to do justice to the immensity of this trauma. I can't imagine how hard this has been and how hard the future must look for you and for Vince. I went for a walk after I got your email to talk to God. Sometimes I have to check in with him to make sure it is all still true—his goodness, his sovereignty, his purpose in suffering, his desire for our ultimate good, his love, heaven. Because if it isn't true, we are completely without hope in this life, and it is all meaningless. If it isn't true, then pointing hurting people toward him is actually very cruel. But if it is true, then we can trust him; we can love him, no matter what happens. And I firmly believe it is true; he is true! In these days, as your world has been rocked so significantly, grab on to what is true and determine to hold on to it even as the winds of doubt and despair blow over you. It is not necessarily great faith or great courage that will get you through this (although that is what others no doubt will see). It is holding on to what you know is true about God and refusing to let go.

DEAR NANCY:
"The LORD's loving kindnesses indeed never cease, for his compassions never fail. They are new every morning." My pillow at the end of these long days is my greatest friend. It means that enough suffering has gone on for today, and even though I know there will be new opportunities to feel the sadness of this loss the next day, I have suffered enough for today.

Michelle's source for hope and strength is the Truth. Will you hold on to this hope along with her, regardless of what rocks your world?

Rock of truth, I run to hide in you and be strengthened by you as everything in my world quakes around me. I'm holding on to you and never letting go.

DIGGING DEEPER

What do you learn about where truth comes from and what truth does from John 8:32; 12:48; 14:6, 17; 16:13; 17:17; and 18:37?

MY TEACHER IN CONTENTMENT

I HAVE LEARNED HOW TO GET ALONG HAPPILY WHETHER I HAVE MUCH OR LITTLE. I KNOW HOW TO LIVE ON ALMOST NOTHING OR WITH EVERYTHING. I HAVE LEARNED THE SECRET OF LIVING IN EVERY SITUATION, WHETHER IT IS WITH A FULL STOMACH OR EMPTY, WITH PLENTY OR LITTLE. —PHILIPPIANS 4:11-12

"Whatever my lot, thou hast taught me to say, it is well, it is well, with my soul." You've likely heard how Horatio Spafford wrote these words on an ocean liner at the place where his four daughters had perished when their ship sank. The reality of our similar sorrow hit me as I prepared to lead worship with this hymn one week. I wondered at his ability to say that, no matter what, all was well. As I read, "thou hast taught me to say," I wondered, *How did God teach you?* I don't know enough about Spafford to know what lesser hurts God had used as lessons in contentment. But evidently Spafford learned well from them so that when sorrow rolled over him, rather than being crushed by it, he was content in it; he was at peace in God and with God.

We might like to think that contentment comes naturally to some, and if we are not content, we just blame it on our personality. But contentment isn't a gift or a personality trait; it's a learned trait, a response we can choose to nurture or neglect. Paul said he had "learned" to be content. How did he learn contentment? By being inconvenienced, impoverished, encroached upon, unfed. He determined to find his contentment in God regardless of his circumstances. To be content doesn't mean that you don't care what happens, that you are indifferent to your surroundings or your suffering. To be content means that you are at peace in the sufficiency of Christ, regardless.

We think we'll be content when we finally get what we want, but real contentment is when we accept less than or something other than what we want. Jesus is our source for the spiritual strength we need to live with what we didn't ask for and less than we want, to be satisfied even when our stomachs or our hearts are empty. Do you have an unmet need, an unfulfilled desire, an unresolved injustice, or an unrelieved pain? Could this be God inviting you into the classroom of contentment? Would you allow him to teach you to find your contentment in him?

Teacher, I want to learn to be content in you rather than constantly comparing my lot to that of others and collapsing under waves of disappointment and discontentment. Will you teach me?

DIGGING DEEPER

What does 1 Timothy 6:6-10 teach about what results from contentment and a lack of contentment?

MY SOURCE OF STRENGTH IN SUFFERING

My life is an example to many, because you have been my strength and protection. —Psalm 71:7

One of the most amazing aspects of our experience with Hope and Gabe was how it brought people into our lives and gave us an almost instant closeness with them because of the intensity and intimacy of the experience. Julie Dilworth came every Monday, and she sent me this email the Monday after Hope died:

> NANCY:
> Well it is Monday and I miss Hope, and I know by next week it will be much worse. I want to thank you for giving me the privilege of knowing her. I feel like I am one of the privileged few who really miss HER. I barely even knew you all, and you let me have a piece of your time with her. I am very grateful to you and humbled by that.

Later Julie told me that a lasting impact of spending time with us during those difficult days was that she came away with less fear about the future. "I saw that you are an ordinary person and that God gave you the strength you needed. So I now believe that if I have to go through something like that, he will give me the strength I need when I need it."

I love that! This is part of the privilege given to those of us who suffer under scrutiny. We have the opportunity to put the faithfulness of God on display to those around us—not because we are strong people with strong faith, but because we are weak in courage and weak in faith. God gives us *his strength* in our weakness, so "that everyone can see that our glorious power is from God and is not our own" (2 Corinthians 4:7). Our lives become the canvas on which God draws a picture of these words (originally given to the hurting apostle Paul): "My power works best in your weakness" (2 Corinthians 12:9). Are you physically weak, emotionally spent, spiritually insufficient for what you are facing? God delights in supplying his strength to weak people. Won't you ask him to fulfill his promise of sufficient grace and supernatural strength for whatever may come?

Spirit of strength, my strength has run out, and I am weak and vulnerable. Would you give me the supernatural strength only you can provide? Would you give me what I need to persevere in hardship with joy and peace so that those around me are amazed by your faithfulness and sufficiency?

DIGGING DEEPER

Where does strength come from and what is it to be used for, according to 1 Corinthians 1:8; Colossians 2:19; 2 Thessalonians 3:3; and 1 Peter 1:7?

MY SOURCE OF MEANING IN FUTILITY

"Everything is meaningless," says the Teacher, "utterly meaningless! Everything is so weary and tiresome! No matter how much we see, we are never satisfied. No matter how much we hear, we are not content."
—Ecclesiastes 1:2, 8

David, Matt, and I went to Santa Fe, New Mexico, over the holidays last year. We read about the art, culture, shopping, and skiing, but we went to an expert to learn about the dining. I called my college professor Mike Flynn, who spends lots of time in Santa Fe. He gave us his top restaurant choices, and we ate our way through the list! His experience made him a credible source for advice.

The book of Ecclesiastes allows us to consult a credible source on finding meaning and purpose in life, as it was written by a man with extraordinary wisdom and extensive experience. King Solomon went on a search for satisfaction. He sought satisfaction through pleasure, but found it empty and fleeting. He tried philosophy, but it ended in confusion. He pursued wealth, and even though he was the wealthiest man alive, he found what he had was never enough. Solomon's journey toward fulfillment left him deflated, depressed, and disillusioned. And we know what it feels like, don't we, to have high expectations for life and to be continually disappointed?

As our credible source who tried everything, Solomon reported that life is meaningless, that seeking satisfaction in this life is "like chasing the wind" (Ecclesiastes 1:14). "Here is my final conclusion," he said. "Fear God and obey his commands, for this is the duty of every person" (Ecclesiastes 12:13). As I read these words, I feel a sense of relief that in the absence of meaning in earthly pursuits, he found it in pursuing God. I can do that. And yet I'm uneasy because I know that I can never fear God fully. I can never obey God completely. I need more than earthly wisdom and more than expert advice on life. I need a Savior. My only hope is to hide myself in the One who fears God perfectly and obeys completely. There's a reason our lives on this earth are so devoid of purpose and meaning. It sends us searching and leads us to the One who not only saves us, but satisfies us. Nothing under the sun satisfies, so heaven came down to earth. In Jesus we find our salvation and our satisfaction.

My Meaning for living, everywhere I turn I come up short. The emptiness of it has left me disillusioned and disappointed. But I see that is exactly where you want me to be so I will see that you are my only source for satisfaction. You are my only Savior, and you are enough.

DIGGING DEEPER

Read about Solomon's search for satisfaction by skimming through Ecclesiastes 1:1–6:9.

WEEK 28

MY SOUL SOURCE

REFLECTION

What have you been searching for and been frustrated trying to find? Have you gone to the right source? Would you be willing to lay that need before Jesus and ask him to fulfill it?

How have you found Jesus to be the source for the completeness, truth, contentment, strength, and meaning your soul desires?

MEDITATION

May God bless you with his special favor and wonderful peace as you come to know Jesus, our God and Lord, better and better. As we know Jesus better, his divine power gives us everything we need for living a godly life. He has called us to receive his own glory and goodness! And by that same mighty power, he has given us all of his rich and wonderful promises. He has promised that you will escape the decadence all around you caused by evil desires and that you will share in his divine nature. So make every effort to apply the benefits of these promises to your life. Then your faith will produce a life of moral excellence. A life of moral excellence leads to knowing God better. Knowing God leads to self-control. Self-control leads to patient endurance, and patient endurance leads to godliness. Godliness leads to love for other Christians, and finally you will grow to have genuine love for everyone. The more you grow like this, the more you will become productive and useful in your knowledge of our Lord Jesus Christ. —2 PETER 1:2-8

Read through this passage several times, marking the words or phrases that are especially meaningful to you.

What benefits and promises do these verses describe?

What instructions do they give?

Pray through the passage, making it into a personal conversation with God.

PRAYER

Praise God for being the provider of everything your soul truly longs for.

Thank God for what he has given you and for making available to you everything you will need for the future.

Intercede for those who are trying to satisfy their longings but are searching from sources that lead only to disappointment and dissatisfaction.

Confess your unbelief that God can really supply what will satisfy your soul.

Petition God to give you everything he has made available through Christ, showing you how to apply the benefits of his promises.

WEEK 29

I AM

We use the words *I am* all the time. *I am* hungry. *I am* Matt's mom. *I am* going to the grocery store. But there is something unique about the *I AM* utterance when it comes from the mouth of God. When God says "I AM WHO I AM," he puts an end to our inflated view of ourselves, our notion that God is whoever we want him to be. God is not limited to our understanding of who he is, nor is he vulnerable to the latest fad in God-consciousness. He is I AM, the eternal, self-existing One.

In John's Gospel, the words *I AM* come from the lips of Jesus no less than twenty-one times as he makes incredible statements about himself. We can completely miss the meaning of these statements unless we understand the implications of I AM. The people of Jesus' day were not so dull. They understood the implications when Jesus said, "Before Abraham was born, I am!" (John 8:58, NIV). They recognized he was claiming to be God, and it was such an offense, such seeming blasphemy, that they picked up stones to throw at him.

We were made for knowing God in the expanse of who he is. Do you want to strive to know him for who he really is instead of simply who you would like him to be? Then listen closely as he tells you who he is: I AM.

THIS WEEK'S PASSAGE FOR MEDITATION

I am the living bread that came down out of heaven. Anyone who eats this bread will live forever. —JOHN 6:51

I am the light of the world. If you follow me, you won't be stumbling through the darkness. —JOHN 8:12

I am the gate. Those who come in through me will be saved. Wherever they go, they will find green pastures. —JOHN 10:9

I am the good shepherd. The good shepherd lays down his life for the sheep. —JOHN 10:11

I am the resurrection and the life. Those who believe in me, even though they die like everyone else, will live again. JOHN 11:25

I am the way, the truth, and the life. No one can come to the Father except through me. —JOHN 14:6

I am the true vine, and my Father is the gardener. —JOHN 15:1

I Am Who I Am

God replied, "I Am the One Who Always Is. Just tell them, 'I Am has sent me to you.'" —Exodus 3:14

I have memories of mistakes I've made that cause me to flinch when I remember. I work hard to keep my mind from going there because of the pain of regret. I wonder if that's how Moses felt when God called to him from the burning bush, telling him to go back to Egypt. He'd spent forty years forgetting, or at least trying to forget, his failed effort to save the Hebrew people—an outburst of violence that had resulted in murder. A death warrant was still on his head in Egypt, and that's where God told him to go. He may have been successful in putting the pain of Egypt behind him until God called, but now his pain seemed like a worthy excuse to avoid God's unwanted instructions. Perhaps flinching as he remembered the ridicule and rejection of the Hebrew slaves who had witnessed his crime, Moses responded to God by asking, "Who am I?" (Exodus 3:11). In Moses' mind, he was a washed-up former royal, a murderer, a sheepherder, and a nobody—definitely not a deliverer.

God responded not by answering Moses' question, but simply by letting Moses know who God is: I Am. Moses had made the mistake of believing that his success as a deliverer would be about him—his abilities, his credentials, his reputation. But God was saying to Moses, *I am eternally everything you need. This is about me, not you.* I Am is your resource for facing a regret-ridden past. I Am is your reserve to keep facing the day when the day is hard. I Am is the answer to your immobilizing fear about where your future will take you. I Am is your authority for demanding deliverance from what has enslaved you and those you love.

Is God asking you to face something painful from your past? Is he asking you to go somewhere you don't want to go, to do something you believe is beyond your ability and credibility? If so, God offers you what he offered to Moses: himself, I Am. God says to you, *I Am a Redeemer who has orchestrated every aspect of your life to prepare you to serve others. I Am with you wherever you go, leading and guiding you. I Am the One who will enable you to do what I've called you to do. I Am everything you need.*

Great I Am, my Deliverer, this is holy ground because you are here offering me the vast resources that are so much a part of you that even your name reflects them. I receive you. I will obey you.

DIGGING DEEPER

How does God reveal himself in Exodus 3 as the covenantal God of the past, the compassionate God of the present, and the caretaking God of the future?

UNLESS YOU BELIEVE

[JESUS SAID,] "UNLESS YOU BELIEVE THAT I AM WHO I SAY I AM, YOU WILL DIE IN YOUR SINS." —JOHN 8:24

Shortly after *Holding on to Hope* was released, I received a letter from a woman who took issue with what I wrote:

> *What really turned me off was when you claimed the only way to know God is through Christ, dismissing all other faiths. All religions and sacred texts have men of God who spoke and taught his word. We are all God's blessed children—no matter what faith we practice, what we believe or do not believe. Gandhi did not find it incompatible to follow Christ's precepts and practice his Hindu religion. There is mystery in the many faiths and religious practices of this world. God created it all.*

It took me a while to formulate my answer and respond. I wanted to be kind, but I needed to correct her drastic and potentially fatal error—that Jesus is one of many religious options, all leading to the same end. I wrote to her in part:

> *I'm sorry that you were turned off by my presentation of Jesus as the only way to know God. That is what he said about himself. It is impossible to embrace his moral teaching and ignore this, his most important teaching. I would disagree with you that all people are God's blessed children regardless of what they believe, not because I think it should work that way, but because of what Jesus said. He told people who claimed to be God's children, "If God were your Father, you would love me" [John 8:42]. A relationship with Jesus is required to be in God's family. John 1:12 says, "But to all who believed him and accepted him, he gave the right to become children of God." Becoming a child of God has everything to do with what we believe and our willingness to receive Jesus. While there is mystery in the many faiths, God did not create them all. Man created most of them in an effort to make his own way toward God in rejection of the way God prescribed that we come to him, which is only through his Son, Jesus.*

Have you planted your faith so firmly in Jesus alone that you are willing to stand up against expectations of religious tolerance? Has Jesus captured your heart so completely that you want to love him and lift him high?

Jesus, I believe you and therefore receive you as the unique and holy Son of God, the only Savior of the world. You are high and lifted up above all the philosophies and religions of man, and I worship you alone.

DIGGING DEEPER

Read John 8:12-59. Look for the evidences Jesus gives of a true child of God.

I AM THE BREAD OF LIFE

YOUR ANCESTORS ATE MANNA IN THE WILDERNESS, BUT THEY ALL DIED. HOWEVER, THE BREAD FROM HEAVEN GIVES ETERNAL LIFE TO EVERYONE WHO EATS IT. I AM THE LIVING BREAD THAT CAME DOWN OUT OF HEAVEN. ANYONE WHO EATS THIS BREAD WILL LIVE FOREVER; THIS BREAD IS MY FLESH, OFFERED SO THE WORLD MAY LIVE.
—JOHN 6:49-51

Shortsighted and simpleminded. That describes the crowd waiting to see Jesus, wanting him to do an instant replay of the previous day's miracle of feeding five thousand. Their hungry stomachs sent them chasing after Jesus in hopes that he would feed them again. But Jesus could see they were shortsighted, looking only to have their stomachs filled temporarily rather than their souls satisfied eternally. They were content to settle for earthly nourishment that would last only a day rather than pursue the Bread from heaven that would last forever. They were shortsighted in their willingness to settle for mere bread when Jesus was offering himself, the true Bread of heaven, a gift of God.

At Jesus' suggestion that he was Bread from heaven, the crowds showed that they were simpleminded as well as shortsighted. "This is Jesus, the son of Joseph," they said. "We know his father and mother. How can he say, 'I came down from heaven'?" (John 6:42). They simply couldn't wrap their limited minds around the reality that Jesus was the Son of God sent from heaven, because they had seen him grow up as the son of Joseph. And when they asked Jesus, "What does God want us to do?" (verse 28), Jesus replied, "Believe in the one he has sent" (verse 29). But they were too simpleminded to think that deeply about the call of God, too hard-hearted to turn from their miracle seeking, too shortsighted to choose life everlasting over their next meal.

Can you see yourself in that crowd, wanting Jesus to fill your physical cup, to miraculously meet your immediate need? Are you promising to really believe in him if he comes through for you? Can you see that your ultimate Provider is holding out the nourishment you need for life now and life everlasting, offering you Jesus, the true Bread from heaven? Will you feast on him, or will you reject his offer of himself if he does not deliver the miracle you crave?

My ultimate Provider, I don't want to be shortsighted and simpleminded, unable to see the magnitude of what you are offering to me in Jesus. I don't want to be unwilling to think deeply about the implications of God holding out life to me for believing. Feed my hunger with the true Bread.

DIGGING DEEPER

Read about God's provision of manna in Exodus 16. What aspects of God's provision point to the true Bread that God would provide in Jesus himself?

THE WAY, THE TRUTH, AND THE LIFE

Jesus said to him, "I am the way, the truth, and the life. No one comes to the Father except through me." —John 14:6 (NKJV)

David occasionally goes on a Google search for our names just for the fun of it. He once found a church newsletter in which the pastor described me as "decent" but my theology as "poor and damaging." He had read an article in *USA Today* that quoted me as saying that a saving relationship with God must come through his Son. The pastor wrote in response, "At the heart of the tragic incomprehension among Christians is the assertion that the only hope for us all is in Jesus." I was stunned that the leader of a church would assert that hope can be found anywhere other than Jesus until I read the church's belief statement on their Web site: "We believe in one God, known to us in Jesus Christ, also known by different names in different traditions."

Honestly, I wasn't offended by their criticism of me, but I was saddened that they diminished Jesus so significantly, reducing him to one of many religious options and robbing him of his unique deity and saving power. What other names do they think Jesus is known by? Muhammad? Buddha? Have they rejected what Acts 4 says about Jesus? "There is salvation in no one else! There is no other name in all of heaven for people to call on to save them" (verse 12).

When Jesus declared that he is the way, the truth, and the life, that no one comes to the Father except through him, Jesus was not threatening or warning or bragging. He was not setting up a hurdle for us to overcome, but pointing us in the right direction and offering himself to get us there.

His disciples were confused and disturbed. They didn't understand nor did they want to understand Jesus' talk of impending death and departure. So Thomas, as spokesman for the group, bluntly said in desperation, "Lord, we don't know where you are going, so how can we know the way?" (John 14:5, NIV). Jesus did not want them to be confused or disturbed or lost. So he pointed out the way by pointing to himself. Jesus is *the way* to know God, experience God, go to God. Don't be offended by his exclusivity; enter into it. The way to God is not mysterious or out of reach; it is knowable and attainable. Jesus is the way to God. And he has given himself for you and to you.

My Way, my Truth, my Life, you have made the pathway clear to me so that I can follow you to your Father's house. The way is narrow, so I must stay close to you, following only you and trusting only you. You are my only hope.

DIGGING DEEPER

How do Colossians 1:15-17 and Hebrews 1:3 affirm Christ's unique deity?

WHO DO YOU SAY I AM?

[JESUS ASKED,] "WHO DO PEOPLE SAY THAT THE SON OF MAN IS?" "WELL," THEY REPLIED, "SOME SAY JOHN THE BAPTIST, SOME SAY ELIJAH, AND OTHERS SAY JEREMIAH OR ONE OF THE OTHER PROPHETS." THEN HE ASKED THEM, "WHO DO YOU SAY I AM?" SIMON PETER ANSWERED, "YOU ARE THE MESSIAH, THE SON OF THE LIVING GOD."
—MATTHEW 16:13-16

Occasionally we get a flier in the mail inviting us to some fancy resort, offering us several days and nights for an incredibly low price. There's just one catch: You have to be willing to sit through a sales presentation for buying into the property. And it just isn't worth it to me. Even though there is "no obligation," I know they will put on the hard sell at some point, and we'll have to either buy in or walk away. They will want a decision.

In some sense that is what Jesus was doing with the disciples. But he wasn't selling them something; he was offering himself freely. The disciples had walked with him for three years, seeing the miracles, hearing him teach, enjoying his presence, and now it was time to declare a decision. Jesus is not content with a vague form of followership. He calls for a confession and a commitment of faith, because he knows we'll need it to follow where he leads—to the Cross. He knows that recognizing who he is will empower and sustain us as we follow. So he forced a crisis, asking his disciples the question that is the crisis question in all our lives: "Who do you say I am?"

Whether you know it or not, there is a crisis in your life deeper than any crisis lurking on the surface. Or perhaps the surface crisis has been brought about by God to bring you to a place of confession and commitment. Each of us faces the same deep inner crisis of faith, demanding that we declare where we stand with Jesus. Is he merely an object of fascination, a source of inspiration, or is he much more to you? The most critical question of your life is this: *Who is Jesus to the world, and who is Jesus to me personally?* Can you see that he is the focal point of all of history, and more important, are you willing to make him the centerpiece of your life, the source from which you draw your identity and security and serenity? Are you willing to confess him and commit to him?

Father in heaven, thank you for revealing Jesus to me and for being unwilling to accept anything less than a clear confession and commitment on my part. This clarity brings me closer to you and gives me security in you.

DIGGING DEEPER

Read the confessions and commitments about who Jesus is in Matthew 3:17; Luke 22:70; and John 1:49.

WEEK 29

I AM

REFLECTION

In what ways has your understanding of God been too limited, too small, too powerless, too fluctuating? What impact has this had on your relationship with the I Am?

Which of Jesus' I Am statements is most meaningful in your current circumstances? Which do you long to know more fully?

MEDITATION

I am the living bread that came down out of heaven. Anyone who eats this bread will live forever; this bread is my flesh, offered so the world may live. —John 6:51

I am the light of the world. If you follow me, you won't be stumbling through the darkness, because you will have the light that leads to life. —John 8:12

I am the gate. Those who come in through me will be saved. Wherever they go, they will find green pastures. —John 10:9

I am the good shepherd. The good shepherd lays down his life for the sheep. —John 10:11

I am the resurrection and the life. Those who believe in me, even though they die like everyone else, will live again. —John 11:25

I am the way, the truth, and the life. No one can come to the Father except through me. —John 14:6

I am the true vine, and my Father is the gardener. —John 15:1

PRAYER

Praise the great I Am and humble yourself before him.

Thank God for each of the I Am gifts you've received in the person of Jesus.

Intercede for those who have not yet seen and understood the glory and gifts of Jesus, the I AM in our midst and on the Cross.

Confess how you have diminished the greatness and glory of Jesus through your unwillingness to proclaim him as God's unique Son and our only Savior.

Petition God to keep revealing more of himself to you in unmistakable and meaningful ways.

WEEK 30

STORMS

Have you ever seen one of those specials on the Weather Channel or the Discovery Channel about storm chasers? They thrill at the threat of a tornado and race toward it rather than running for cover. What are these people thinking?

My dog, Pepper, could never be a storm-chaser dog. She seems to have supersonic hearing when it comes to thunder. Long before a rumble reaches my ears, she is darting under our bed or under my feet—wherever I am. Her instincts tell her to look for protection when a storm is threatening. I suppose mine do too.

Storms are scary because they are so powerful, so unpredictable, and often so destructive. And they respect no one. Jesus said that the Father in heaven "gives his sunlight to both the evil and the good, and he sends rain on the just and on the unjust, too" (Matthew 5:45).

Perhaps you find yourself watching the storm clouds gather in the distance, or maybe you feel yourself swirling in the center of a storm. Or perhaps the storm has come and gone and you are picking up the pieces of your life. God often speaks to us through the storms in our lives.

It's likely that we will never become storm chasers, seeking out turmoil and trials in life. But we can become God chasers—recognizing that, if we listen, in the midst of the most violent storm we can detect the still, small voice of God, calling us to greater faith in him.

THIS WEEK'S PASSAGE FOR MEDITATION

Anyone who listens to my teaching and obeys me is wise, like a person who builds a house on solid rock. Though the rain comes in torrents and the floodwaters rise and the winds beat against that house, it won't collapse, because it is built on rock. —Matthew 7:24-25

SAFETY IN THE STORM

LOOK! I AM ABOUT TO COVER THE EARTH WITH A FLOOD THAT WILL DESTROY EVERY LIVING THING. EVERYTHING ON EARTH WILL DIE! BUT I SOLEMNLY SWEAR TO KEEP YOU SAFE IN THE BOAT, WITH YOUR WIFE AND YOUR SONS AND THEIR WIVES. —GENESIS 6:17-18

It was the storm of all storms. There had never been one like it before nor has there since, and according to God's promise, there never will be again. This was a storm of judgment that was sent by God to destroy every living creature on the earth—except for Noah and his family.

Hebrews 11 says that Noah was warned about things not yet seen. He had never seen a flood. He had never seen a thunderstorm. He may have never even seen a raindrop. But he believed God. Even though he had never seen rain, he took God at his word that there would be judgment on the earth by a flood. He also believed that God would provide a way for him and his family to escape judgment. Noah had confidence in God's provision of an ark that would protect him from the judgment that was about to fall upon the earth in the form of raindrops.

It can be easy to assume that some of the storms that crash into our world are also God's judgment. Knowing the wrong things we have done and the wickedness in our hearts that we try to keep well hidden, we wonder if the hurts in our lives are God finally giving us what we deserve: judgment.

But that is the beauty of the gospel! Even though we all deserve judgment because of our sin against a holy God, that same God has provided an ark of safety where we can take refuge from the storm of judgment. Jesus himself is the ark in which all who believe can take refuge. Make no mistake: Even though it is unpopular to talk about it today, judgment will once again fall on the earth. The next time it won't be rain; it will be fire. But God has provided Jesus—our ark of safety—so that we might be saved and the storms of life will never destroy us.

Jesus, you are my only Savior. I can't save myself or justify myself before a holy God. Thank you for your provision for me so that I no longer have to fear the storm of judgment by flood or by fire.

DIGGING DEEPER

Read 2 Peter 3. What do you learn about when judgment will come and what it will be like? Who will it be for? What should we do because it is coming?

CRYING OUT TO GOD

The sailors picked Jonah up and threw him into the raging sea, and the storm stopped at once! The sailors were awestruck by the Lord's great power, and they offered him a sacrifice and vowed to serve him. —Jonah 1:15-16

"But Jonah got up and went in the opposite direction in order to get away from the Lord" (Jonah 1:3). Who of us has not, at one time or another, clearly heard God's instruction and run in the opposite direction? That was the case with the prophet Jonah, who boarded a ship hoping to escape from the Lord. But the story says that "as the ship was sailing along, suddenly the Lord flung a powerful wind over the sea, causing a violent storm that threatened to send them to the bottom. Fearing for their lives, the desperate sailors shouted to their gods for help" (1:4-5).

Jonah finally fessed up and told them that the storm was his fault, that he was running away from God. Then the rugged sailors "cried out to the Lord, Jonah's God" (1:14), they were "awestruck by the Lord's great power, and they offered him a sacrifice and vowed to serve him" (1:16).

Crying out to God. We just don't do it when we are sailing along under sunny skies, do we? We're complacent and comfortable and blissfully unaware of our desperate need for God. But then a storm hits and our cries to God come from deep within us as we beg God to show his power in our situation. And usually we are not alone. When the storm hits the hardest, we find that those around us are drawn in as well, creating a chorus of cries to the Almighty to save us from the storm.

I've heard it in the waiting room of hospitals after an accident, during a surgery. I've heard it in the prayers of parents whose children are walking on a path toward destruction. I've heard it from children desperate for their parents to claim Christ before they slip into eternity.

God uses storms in our lives to cause us and those around us to cry out to him. All pretense is gone and we throw ourselves at the mercy of our only source of hope. And when we cry out to him, he bends down to listen.

Only Savior, we cry out to you to save us! We are powerless to save ourselves from the fury around us and desperate to see you reveal yourself in the midst of the storm.

DIGGING DEEPER

Read Jonah 1. List the ways you see God's sovereignty in this storm. What stands out to you when you read Jonah's words in 1:9?

DON'T YOU EVEN CARE?

Soon a fierce storm arose. High waves began to break into the boat until it was nearly full of water. Jesus was sleeping at the back of the boat with his head on a cushion. Frantically they woke him up, shouting, "Teacher, don't you even care that we are going to drown?" —Mark 4:37-38

Jesus and his disciples were on a boat crossing the Sea of Galilee when a windstorm came up. For many of Jesus' disciples, being on a boat on the sea was a familiar place. They had lived on the sea. And they also knew many who had died on the sea in just such a sudden storm.

Obviously, their fears were well founded. The boat was nearly full of water and sinking quickly. Frantically, they woke Jesus up, shouting, "Teacher, don't you even care that we are going to drown?"

I know what it is like to feel as if I am sinking and to wonder if Jesus even cares. Do you? *Don't you even care that my child is dying? Don't you even care that my business is failing? Don't you even care that the one I love is suffering?*

When I read that Jesus questioned their faith, I wonder if he was just a little cranky from being awakened from his nap. Didn't they have every right to be afraid? The boat was sinking and he was sleeping!

Perhaps Jesus was frustrated that everything the disciples had already seen and heard had not seemed to penetrate deeply enough to become belief. Perhaps by calling him "Teacher" they revealed their view of him as only a teacher and their lack of faith in him as God. Perhaps by expressing their confidence that they were going to drown, they revealed their doubt in his ability to save. I'm not sure.

But I do know that they lost sight of what it meant to simply have Jesus on the boat with them in the middle of a storm. Having God with us makes all the difference, no matter what swirls around us. We know God cares for us because he is with us in the storm, speaking peace.

Lord of the wind and waves, would you speak peace into my life even now? I'm afraid my boat is sinking, and I so easily forget that your presence with me makes all the difference. Give me the faith to believe I can rest in you.

DIGGING DEEPER

Compare Mark's version of this story in Mark 4:35-41 with Matthew 8:23-27. What details does Mark offer that Matthew does not? What does the question "Who is this man?" reveal about the disciples' faith?

WALKING ABOVE THE WAVES OF OUR CIRCUMSTANCES

"All right, come," Jesus said. So Peter went over the side of the boat and walked on the water toward Jesus. But when he looked around at the high waves, he was terrified and began to sink. "Save me, Lord!" he shouted.
—Matthew 14:29-30

Jesus had sent the disciples ahead in a boat while he went up on a mountain to pray. Suddenly a strong wind came up, and the disciples were struggling against heavy waves. Jesus came to them walking on the water. Peter said to Jesus, "If it's really you, tell me to come to you by walking on water" (Matthew 14:28). Peter stepped out of the boat and miraculously began to walk toward Jesus, but when he turned to look at the waves, he became afraid and began to sink, crying out, "Save me, Lord!" (verse 30).

The very week I was studying this story, a storm blew into our lives in the form of a phone call. Having discovered I was pregnant again a year and a half after Hope died, we had been waiting for the prenatal test results that would tell us whether or not the baby I was carrying would have Zellweger Syndrome. Finally the geneticist called, telling us we would, indeed, have a second child with the fatal syndrome.

We were still feeling battered from the last storm, and another one was now sweeping into our lives! We wondered if we would be able to endure it. But Jesus was walking toward us in our distress, urging us not to be afraid. In a sense we heard him calling us to get out of the boat and trust him. We knew that if we looked at the wind and waves of the sorrow and difficulty that was sweeping into our lives, we would surely sink. But if we reached out to Jesus and kept our eyes focused on him, he would empower us to walk above the waves of our bitter circumstances.

Storms give us the opportunity to step out in faith. We can look down on the hurt and uncertainty that threaten to overtake us, or we can look *up* at the Savior. He will empower us to walk and live in a way that transcends the natural world. As we focus on him, he provides what we need to keep walking toward him when the winds of adversity are whipping all around us.

Savior, I hear you calling me to step out of the boat and trust you. But I'm afraid. Keep reaching out to me as I seek to keep my eyes focused on you.

DIGGING DEEPER

Read Matthew 14:22-33 and Mark 6:47-52. What differences and similarities do you see in these accounts? What effect did watching Jesus and Peter walk on water have on the disciples?

BUILDING A LIFE THAT WON'T COLLAPSE

ANYONE WHO LISTENS TO MY TEACHING AND OBEYS ME IS WISE, LIKE A PERSON WHO BUILDS A HOUSE ON SOLID ROCK. THOUGH THE RAIN COMES IN TORRENTS AND THE FLOODWATERS RISE AND THE WINDS BEAT AGAINST THAT HOUSE, IT WON'T COLLAPSE, BECAUSE IT IS BUILT ON ROCK. —MATTHEW 7:24-25

When I was growing up, I sang the classic Sunday school song, "The Wise Man Built His House upon the Rock." And as we learned from the song, when the rains came down and the floods came up, the house on the rock stood firm, while the house on the sand went *splat*.

So really, what was the difference between the wise man and the foolish man? When we read the parable Jesus told, we see that they had many things in common. Both of them heard God's Word. In modern terms, it is as if they were both churchgoers who sat through the sermon Sunday after Sunday. Both of them experienced the storm. The torrential rain and rising floodwaters came upon both. But the story tells us that the wise person's house did not collapse because it was built on a rock, while the foolish person's house fell with a mighty crash because it was built on sand.

What does it mean to build your house on the solid rock versus unstable sand? The difference is in the way the builders responded as they heard God's Word. One translation says that the wise person not only hears God's words but that he "puts them into practice" (Matthew 7:24, NIV). The foolish man heard God's Word, but he ignored it. It is as if he thought being in church was good enough, and he didn't allow the truth of God's Word to change and shape him, to strengthen and prepare him.

Do you wonder how you can withstand the storms that are coming into your life? The secret is choosing now to live out all that God has taught you. Begin to put God's Word into practice through obedience. Then you'll be ready when the storm comes, and you will not be destroyed by it.

Teacher, there is so much truth I have heard but have not yet begun to live. Show me how to put your Word into practice in my life so that through the power of your Word I might be ready to withstand the storms that come.

DIGGING DEEPER

Read Matthew 7:24-27 and Luke 6:46-49. Think through these key words: *hearing, listening, obeying, standing firm*, and *falling*. What does each mean in practical terms?

WEEK 30

STORMS

REFLECTION

In what ways have you been called to exercise faith in the midst of the storms in your life? What have the results been?

What are you doing now to build your life on a solid foundation so that when storms come in the future, you will not be destroyed?

MEDITATION

Anyone who listens to my teaching and obeys me is wise, like a person who builds a house on solid rock. Though the rain comes in torrents and the floodwaters rise and the winds beat against that house, it won't collapse, because it is built on rock. —MATTHEW 7:24-25

Read these verses several times, attempting to hear them as from the lips of Jesus, delivered on the hillside to the multitude.

Think about the teachings you've received in the past few weeks, and then about the time you have known Christ and have been reading God's Word. Value this gift and determine to obey. Thank God for the gift of wisdom that enables you to listen and obey.

PRAYER

Praise God for his unlimited power over the natural world he created.

Thank God for his provision of an ark of safety—Jesus—and for the confidence we have that Jesus is with us in the storms of life.

Intercede for specific people you know who have not accepted God's provision of safety from the coming judgment.

Confess the unbelief and fear that keep you from stepping out of your boat, so that you can experience the supernatural ability to walk above the waves of difficulties in your life.

Petition God to show you areas of your life in which you have heard God's clear teaching but have not put it into practice, so that the foundation of your life will become firm and secure in him.

WEEK 31

PARABLES

Jesus preached in the synagogues at the beginning of his ministry, but as opposition to his teaching increased, he began to preach mostly outside the synagogues—on the seashore, in the desert, in homes, and on the road. Matthew 13:34-35 says, "Jesus always used stories and illustrations like these when speaking to the crowds. In fact, he never spoke to them without using such parables. This fulfilled the prophecy that said, 'I will speak to you in parables. I will explain mysteries hidden since the creation of the world.' "

Because of their hidden meanings, parables draw out a person's desire to discover truth personally instead of being spoon-fed. So by speaking in parables, Jesus gave those close to him an opportunity to draw closer as they listened carefully to his words and pondered their implications. Likewise, his parables are an invitation to us to draw close and be changed.

Parables have a unique ability to reveal who we are as we see ourselves in them. Some are humorous and others are tragic; they are all simple yet provocative. The parables have their deepest meaning and significance in what they tell us about the Storyteller and his kingly reign. At the same time they seem to nail us for who we are and how we live. When we read a parable, we are sometimes bothered, sometimes baffled, and sometimes encouraged, but always profoundly challenged.

THIS WEEK'S PASSAGE FOR MEDITATION

His disciples came and asked him, "Why do you always tell stories when you talk to the people?" Then he explained to them, "You have been permitted to understand the secrets of the Kingdom of Heaven, but others have not. To those who are open to my teaching, more understanding will be given, and they will have an abundance of knowledge. But to those who are not listening, even what they have will be taken away from them. That is why I tell these stories, because people see what I do, but they don't really see. They hear what I say, but they don't really hear, and they don't understand." —MATTHEW 13:10-13

SEARCHING FOR THE KINGDOM

One day the Pharisees asked Jesus, "When will the Kingdom of God come?" Jesus replied, "The Kingdom of God isn't ushered in with visible signs. You won't be able to say, 'Here it is!' or 'It's over there!' For the Kingdom of God is among you." —Luke 17:20-21

Jesus often used parables to teach about the mysteries of the Kingdom. He often began his parables with, "The Kingdom of Heaven is like . . ." But I sometimes get confused about what he really meant. Is the Kingdom of God a future reality to be hoped for or a present reality to be experienced now? The answer is yes. What is mysterious about the Kingdom is that it has come partly but not fully. Many of the blessings of God's Kingdom are a reality we enjoy now, but many are not yet here. While the fulfillment of the Kingdom came in the person and work of Jesus, the consummation of the Kingdom will be when Jesus comes again.

We experience some of the Kingdom's power now, but not all of it. Some of the curse and misery of this world can be overcome now by the presence of God's Kingdom, but only some of it. While our King has fought and won the decisive battle against sin and Satan, sickness and death, the war is not over. We must still battle sin. We must still resist Satan. We must still pray and groan over sickness. And we must still face physical death. But the day is coming when the King will return, and his Kingdom will be a reality on earth. This makes us want to say, "Lord Jesus, come quickly!"

Understanding what Jesus meant when he talked about the Kingdom helps us with the disappointment we feel about living in a world where things are not yet as God promised they will be. It keeps us from insisting that God demonstrate now the dimensions of the Kingdom he has reserved for the future. It helps us celebrate the current fulfillment of God's Kingdom. The King's righteousness is now ours by faith, and his Spirit is living inside us. His holiness is being produced in us, and we experience his joy and peace in a world where sin, pain, and sorrow prevail. The Kingdom of God is a reality in your life to the extent to which Jesus reigns in your heart. His Kingdom comes to you like a mustard seed, not a military coup. Will you let him reign and rule in your life even as you wait for his Kingdom to be consummated?

Lord, make my heart your throne and rule in me. My passion is to seek first your Kingdom here and now as I anticipate the glory of your future Kingdom.

DIGGING DEEPER

Read Matthew 12:22-30 and Luke 19:11-27. What do these verses reveal about the fulfillment and consummation of the Kingdom?

THE SOIL OF YOUR HEART

A farmer went out to plant some seed. As he scattered it across his field, some seed fell on a footpath, where it was stepped on, and the birds came and ate it. Other seed fell on shallow soil with underlying rock. This seed began to grow, but soon it withered and died for lack of moisture. Other seed fell among thorns that shot up and choked out the tender blades. Still other seed fell on fertile soil. This seed grew and produced a crop one hundred times as much as had been planted. —Luke 8:5-8

How is the soil of your heart? When you read or hear God's Word, does the seed take root and grow into fruit in the good earth of your life? Or is the seed falling on a hard heart, a shallow heart, or a distracted heart?

For some of us, the soil of our hearts has been hardened by disappointment and cynicism. Our hearts become calloused when they are pricked over and over by the truth but we fail to respond. For many, the seed of God's Word falls on a heart with shallow, stony soil. These responded enthusiastically to God initially but have never allowed his Word to run deep and take root in their lives. When the heat of hardship beats down on them, there is no deep inner strength to face it. All of us find the soil of our hearts infected at times with thorns and weeds. Our lives become so easily cluttered with time-wasting and soul-absorbing things. We find ourselves sitting in church thinking about our plans for the afternoon or rushing through our devotions so we can get on with "more important things." This type of soil is dangerous and deceiving as we may hardly notice the weeds of pleasure and empty activity growing up around us. Then we awaken to find a hollowness within. The weeds' roots have choked out the true seed of God's Word before it could grow into something beautiful and fruitful in our lives.

Is the soil of your heart receptive to the seed? Are you willing to allow God to plow up your heart so his Word can take root? Only the Divine Gardener can break up the hard ground in your heart, uproot the rocks, and remove the weeds and thorns. That is your only hope—not your efforts, but the work of the Gardener. He promises, "I will give you a new heart with new and right desires, and I will put a new spirit in you. I will take out your stony heart of sin and give you a new, obedient heart" (Ezekiel 36:26).

Sower, plow up the ground of my heart. Remove the rocks of indifference and the weeds of worldly wisdom so that your Word will run deep in my life and blossom into beautiful fruitfulness for your glory.

DIGGING DEEPER

According to Matthew 13:39, what other sower is planting seeds, and what form do they take? How does this relate to Genesis 3:15?

A PRECIOUS PEARL

THE KINGDOM OF HEAVEN IS LIKE A PEARL MERCHANT ON THE LOOKOUT FOR CHOICE PEARLS. WHEN HE DISCOVERED A PEARL OF GREAT VALUE, HE SOLD EVERYTHING HE OWNED AND BOUGHT IT! —MATTHEW 13:45-46

It is interesting that Jesus used a pearl in this parable since the Hebrew people did not consider pearls precious or valuable. That fact makes this brief parable even more revealing about them and challenging to us. It shows us how we take Christ for granted, how we often prefer spiritual poverty to the riches of Christ.

The pearl merchant was a man on a search for satisfaction. He found it in the pearl that was so magnificent, so valuable, that it was worth selling everything he owned so he could buy it. But our problem with this story is the same as that of the Hebrews who heard it. We don't value the Pearl, at least not according to its true worth. If we truly valued the Pearl, if we recognized what Christ is truly worth, we wouldn't find it so difficult to let go of what we are called to sell off in order to treasure Christ. Embracing Christ requires that we let go of things that have been valuable to us—the religion of our parents, our past way of thinking, our sinful pleasures, and our self-righteousness. To claim Christ requires that we see him as everything we need and desire; it requires that we say, "Whatever it may cost me, I must have Christ!"

This is what David was saying when he wrote, "I would rather be a gatekeeper in the house of my God than live the good life in the homes of the wicked" (Psalm 84:10). Paul also recognized the value of Christ: "Everything else is worthless when compared with the priceless gain of knowing Christ Jesus my Lord. I have discarded everything else, counting it all as garbage, so that I may have Christ and become one with him" (Philippians 3:8-9). To treasure Christ requires a change in our value system so we see the uselessness of everything in this world in comparison to the splendor of Christ. Is there anything you treasure so much that you would say, "I love this too much; I will not pay this to gain Christ"?

If you have renounced everything else for Jesus, do you think you will one day find yourself disappointed at what will have proved to be a bad bargain? No way. You will not find yourself wanting anything back. It is the exchange of your life, and it will make you eternally happy.

Pearl of great value, you are beautiful and worthy of whatever it may cost me to have you as the center of my life. Show me what needs to go so that I may have more of you.

DIGGING DEEPER

Read about the hidden treasure in Matthew 13:44. What is the difference between the man and the merchant in verse 45? What is the same?

THE SINNER GOD HEARS

Jesus told this story to some who had great self-confidence and scorned everyone else: "Two men went to the Temple to pray. One was a Pharisee, and the other was a dishonest tax collector. —Luke 18:9-10

If only we could hear the parables of Jesus with the fresh ears of those to whom they were spoken. Many of us have heard them so many times as Sunday school stories that we don't realize how shocking they are, how they turn our understanding upside down, how they show us what we don't want to see about ourselves. Sunday school handouts gave those of us who grew up in church a fuzzy picture of what a Pharisee is—something like a cross between Snidely Whiplash and a member of the Taliban, and certainly someone evil. But in reality, Pharisees were the middle-class pillars of society in their day. Far from being the wicked people we envision, they were the highest moral ideal in their culture.

We've learned to view the tax collector with a sympathetic eye because we know how his story ends. But to the original hearers of this story, the tax collector was the evil one, a traitor who sold out to the Roman occupiers and lined his pockets with the hard-earned money of the Hebrews. They had no sympathy for him, only contempt.

As Jesus' hearers listened to this story, they were surprised that the tax collector had the guts to even enter the Temple, while the Pharisee seemed right at home there. The Pharisee prayed, "I thank you, God, that I am not a sinner like everyone else, especially like that tax collector over there!" (Luke 18:11). They weren't sure what to think when they heard that the tax collector "stood at a distance and dared not even lift his eyes to heaven as he prayed. Instead, he beat his chest in sorrow, saying, 'O God, be merciful to me, for I am a sinner' " (Luke 18:13).

We are tempted to read this parable and feel relieved that we are not like the Pharisee. But self-righteousness comes to us so naturally, we don't even see it. Do you see yourself as a self-righteous Pharisee or a humble tax collector? Perhaps a bit of both? A contradiction of faith and repentance mixed in with unbelief and pride? We might as well admit it, because we can't hide it from God. Won't you humble yourself and ask God to show you the reality of who you are on the inside? That's a prayer he bends down to hear, a person he turns toward.

Merciful God, keep me looking in the mirror to see my sin and need, instead of looking down my nose at others.

DIGGING DEEPER

Read the warnings Jesus gave the Pharisees in Matthew 23:1-36.

WHAT HAS GOD PLACED IN YOUR HANDS?

The servant with the one bag of gold came and said, "Sir, I know you are a hard man, harvesting crops you didn't plant and gathering crops you didn't cultivate. I was afraid I would lose your money, so I hid it in the earth and here it is." But the master replied, "You wicked and lazy servant!"
—Matthew 25:24-26

Since I've worked in publishing for years, many people asked me after Hope died if I was going to write a book. I thought about it, but honestly I was afraid. Over the years I had seen many people have incredible experiences and then seem to exploit them through the pages of a book. The idea that I might do that with the precious experience God had given me with Hope, and the awareness that I was not above it, kept me from it.

Then one day, Diane Cobb, teaching on the parable of the talents at Bible Study Fellowship, said, "What God entrusts to us is valuable to him. He requires that we do all we can with what he has given us—time, talents, gifts, energy, personality, life experience, material resources." Then she asked the question, "Will you invest or squander what you've been given?"

Suddenly I saw myself in the story. I was the servant who had buried what God had put into my hands, so afraid of doing the wrong thing that I didn't do anything. That day I saw all that God had placed into my hands—my knowledge of the publishing industry, an understanding of Scripture, communication gifts, and an experience that gave me insight and credibility. I realized that God wanted me to invest it, to use what he placed in my hands for his glory. So I went home and began to write. Four months later I sent my manuscript for *Holding on to Hope* to the publisher.

Once I realized that it was all about being a faithful steward of what God had placed into my hands and not about exploitation, everything changed. It might look the same on the outside, but inside me, in the area of my motives and methods, it is all about stewardship. God has taken what I offered up to him and used it in the lives of others for a spiritual return far beyond what I could have ever imagined. So I must ask you: What abilities, opportunities, and resources has God placed in *your* hands? Will you invest them for his glory? Now is not too late.

Master, I realize that I am accountable for everything you have given to me. How I long to hear you say, "Well done, my good and faithful servant."

DIGGING DEEPER

Read Matthew 25:14-30. What was the basis for distribution of the talents? What reward was given to the wise investors?

WEEK 31

PARABLES

REFLECTION

Recognizing that God reveals more truth to those who respond to what he has already given them, how are you doing on responding to the truth God has revealed to you?

What parable speaks most powerfully to you, and how has it changed you?

MEDITATION

His disciples came and asked him, "Why do you always tell stories when you talk to the people?" Then he explained to them, "You have been permitted to understand the secrets of the Kingdom of Heaven, but others have not. To those who are open to my teaching, more understanding will be given, and they will have an abundance of knowledge. But to those who are not listening, even what they have will be taken away from them. That is why I tell these stories, because people see what I do, but they don't really see. They hear what I say, but they don't really hear, and they don't understand." —MATTHEW 13:10-13

Sit with Jesus on the hillside and listen to him share with you the secrets of the Kingdom. Open yourself to his teaching and ask him to give you an abundance of knowledge and understanding. Ask him to give you ears that hear and eyes that see.

Read through some of the parables in Matthew 13 and Luke 17–18, asking God to make them a mirror into your soul.

PRAYER

Praise God as the hidden treasure, the pearl of great price, the Good Samaritan, the merciful creditor, the generous employer, the searching Father, the vineyard owner, and the host of the wedding feast.

Thank God for being willing to share the secrets and mysteries of the Kingdom with those who lean close to listen.

Intercede for those whose hearts have become dull by unresponsiveness to truth, those whose ears do not hear, those whose eyes are veiled.

Confess your self-righteousness and unwillingness to see yourself through the lens offered in the teaching of the parables.

Petition God to reveal who he is through the parables and to show you who you really are so that he can do his work in and through you.

WEEK 32

PARADOX

"The world is crazy." Occasionally David and I remember and repeat this statement we heard from our psychologist friend Roy Austin. Sometimes it is the only thing that explains the upside-down values and inexplicable realities of the way people think, the way this world works. Likewise, our pastor Ray Ortlund often refers to the gospel as counterintuitive. He says living in light of the gospel goes against everything our natural way of thinking tells us.

God's Kingdom is dramatically different from the kingdom of this world. In reality, the Kingdom of God is the creation of God right side up while the world at large is the creation of God upside down. When we see this reality, we suddenly understand that the gospel is true, sound, and sane, while the world is crazy.

To make our home in the Kingdom of God, we must make some sense of its paradoxes. We must come to accept that our way of thinking and valuing and enjoying this life will never make sense to the world. As A. W. Tozer said, "A real Christian is an odd number anyway. He feels supreme love for One whom he has never seen, talks familiarly every day to Someone he cannot see, expects to go to heaven on the virtue of Another, empties himself in order to be full, admits he is wrong so he can be declared right, goes down in order to get up, is strongest when he is weakest, richest when he is poorest, and happiest when he feels worst. He dies so he can live, forsakes in order to have, gives away so he can keep, sees the invisible, hears the inaudible, and knows that which passeth knowledge."

What a way to live.

THIS WEEK'S PASSAGE FOR MEDITATION

In everything we do we try to show that we are true ministers of God. We patiently endure troubles and hardships and calamities of every kind. We serve God whether people honor us or despise us, whether they slander us or praise us. We are honest, but they call us impostors. We are well known, but we are treated as unknown. We live close to death, but here we are, still alive. We have been beaten within an inch of our lives. Our hearts ache, but we always have joy. We are poor, but we give spiritual riches to others. We own nothing, and yet we have everything. —2 Corinthians 6:4, 8-10

THE GRAND PARADOX

It pleased the Lord to bruise Him; He has put Him to grief. —Isaiah 53:10 (NKJV)

It is hard to imagine how a parent could be pleased when his child suffers. So we can't help but be baffled when we read that God was *pleased* to see his Son's bruised and broken body on the cross. On the surface, something seems terribly wrong here. Or perhaps there is something we can't see. When we do get it all in proper perspective, maybe everything that has confused us will make some sense.

A paradox is a statement that is inherently self-contradictory but is true nevertheless. A self-contradictory statement can only be true if the basis of the statement is solid. The foundation of every Kingdom paradox is the Cross of Christ, the most solid and true reality in the universe. The profound truth of the Cross makes the seemingly self-contradictory statements in the gospel profoundly true and helps us accept what we find difficult to understand. What more amazing yet perplexing paradox is there than Christ, the perfect Savior of the world, on the cross dying in my place? An innocent man laden with my guilt and shame, bound so I can be free, dying so I can live? Somehow it seems appropriately paradoxical that this dark day would be called "Good Friday."

The Cross is the grand paradox that provides the foundation for the unsettling paradoxes of the gospel—Jesus' teachings that we must be poor if we want to be rich, mourn if we want to be happy, give everything away if we want to be rich, die so we can live. Only in the shadow of the Cross do these paradoxes begin to make sense to us. We rest in knowing that one day the Cross, which the world views as foolish, will be lifted high as the soul of common sense rather than the absence of it. Finally, the truth that has been rejected will be irrefutable.

Can you see that when your life doesn't seem to make sense, it's the Cross that gives it meaning and clarity? In your confusion, will you look at the Cross and see a love for sinners so big that God would be *pleased* to sacrifice even his own Son so that we, who deserve to die, might live? A love so big that we, who have earned no place in his presence, might boldly enter and make ourselves at home? Sinners purified, dead people made alive is the paradoxical beauty of the Cross—our only hope for healing in this hurting, confusing world.

Beautiful Savior, only your Cross and the coming victory of your Cross could make living in a world gone crazy bearable and even beautiful. You told us that when you were lifted up you would draw all people to yourself. You have drawn me to your Cross, and there I find perspective for living in this world.

DIGGING DEEPER

According to Galatians 2:14–3:14, how did the Cross help Peter, Paul, and the Galatians make sense of our intuitive law-keeping and natural exclusivity?

BECOME A FOOL SO YOU CAN BECOME WISE

Stop fooling yourselves. If you think you are wise by this world's standards, you will have to become a fool so you can become wise by God's standards. For the wisdom of this world is foolishness to God. Everything belongs to you, and you belong to Christ, and Christ belongs to God.

—1 Corinthians 3:18-19, 22-23

Driving a car full of kids on a field trip is an education in itself. I'm never quite sure if I should try to be a hip and cool mom or simply keep my mouth shut. The kids' conversations are a constant stream of attempts to one-up each other. They've all seen or done something more interesting, more daring, or more expensive. It is a less sophisticated version of the conversations we have as adults in our futile attempt to cover up deep-seated insecurities and shore up our worldly securities.

We all have a built-in sense of insecurity that comes from living in a world that is beyond our control. At the same time, we've fooled ourselves into believing that we have everything under control, that we know enough to solve our own problems or know someone who can. We're a mixture of self-sufficiency and insecurity, and our big talk covers up our profound need and paralyzing fear. Both sides of this paradoxical self- deception are an affront to God. One side tells God we have no need for him. The other says we believe our needs are too great for him to meet. One appears strong and the other weak. But both require the grace of God in order to humble ourselves. God hears us talking big in the backseat of this ride through life, and he knows we are not as smart or self-sufficient as we think we are. Neither is he as powerless as we sometimes think he is. To our self-sufficiency, he says we must give up our own wisdom and embrace his. To our insecurity, he reminds us that because we are in Christ, everything that belongs to him belongs to us. We can be secure in his sufficiency.

God is not out to be impressive on the world's terms, nor is it his goal to make you merely impressive. In this world, the wisdom and power of God come across as weak and foolish, and God wants it that way. Are you willing to humble yourself to enter into his sufficiency and security? Are you willing to become foolish in the eyes of the world so that you might become truly wise in the estimation of God?

Wisdom of God, you are everything I need. In the foolishness of the Cross, you are wiser than the wisdom of this world. You show me how to become a fool so I can gain life-giving, soul-sustaining wisdom.

DIGGING DEEPER

Read 1 Corinthians 3 to see what the Corinthians were boasting about and what Paul wanted them to boast about instead.

BROKENNESS IS THE PATHWAY TO USEFULNESS

JESUS TOOK A LOAF OF BREAD AND ASKED GOD'S BLESSING ON IT. THEN HE BROKE IT IN PIECES AND GAVE IT TO THE DISCIPLES, SAYING, "TAKE IT AND EAT IT, FOR THIS IS MY BODY." —MATTHEW 26:26

Putting up Christmas lights at our house has not always been marked by holiday mirth. We would plug in the lights and sure enough, one or two bulbs would be broken so the whole string wouldn't work. The time-consuming quest to find and replace the offending bulb generated large amounts of crankiness. So we developed a new policy at our house to ensure domestic tranquility. If a string of lights doesn't work, we simply put it in the trash and pull out a new, never-used set purchased at last year's post-Christmas clearance sale. Joy to the world!

In this world, when something is broken, we throw it away and consider it useless. But in God's economy, brokenness is not cause for being cast aside. It is our brokenness that actually makes us useful. In fact, brokenness is required in order to be pleasing to God. "The sacrifice you want is a broken spirit," David wrote (Psalm 51:17). If brokenness makes us useful and pleasing to God, what does it mean to be broken? Do we qualify if our hearts are broken by the hurts of life?

The truth is, you can be brokenhearted and not be broken. You can experience a breakdown of your health, the breakup of a marriage, broken dreams, and broken promises and not become a broken person in the process. Brokenness is not the automatic result of experiencing deep hurts. Brokenness is a lifestyle of agreeing with God about the true condition of our hearts. It is shattering our self-will so that the life of Jesus might spill out of our lives. It is continually responding to conviction in humility and obedience.

Jesus said that if a grain of wheat does not fall into the ground and if its outer shell is not broken, it does not produce a harvest. He was speaking of his own brokenness, the brokenness of his body that would demonstrate his supreme usefulness in the work of salvation. Jesus has shown us what it means to be broken and to be used by God in painful but beautiful ways. Do you want to simply be brokenhearted and broken down, or do you want to be truly broken before God and thereby useful to him?

Broken Savior, used by God, as I remember your body, broken for me, I begin to see my heart the way you do, and I fall in brokenness and repentance before you. Use me in my brokenness as only you can.

DIGGING DEEPER

Explore the usefulness that came from brokenness in Exodus 17:1-7; Judges 7:16-22; Matthew 26:26-30; and Mark 14:1-9.

WHOEVER WANTS TO BE A LEADER MUST BE A SERVANT

WHOEVER WANTS TO BE A LEADER AMONG YOU MUST BE YOUR SERVANT, AND WHOEVER WANTS TO BE FIRST MUST BE THE SLAVE OF ALL. FOR EVEN I, THE SON OF MAN, CAME HERE NOT TO BE SERVED BUT TO SERVE OTHERS. —MARK 10:43-45

A few weeks ago our choir sang the beautiful anthem "The Majesty and Glory of Your Name." The choir loft was full and their voices were strong. It reminded me of the choir's musical gift at Hope's memorial service. My heart seemed to break all over again as I remembered the desperation and emptiness of that day, and I wept through the rest of the service. When it was over, two women were waiting to talk to me—one who wanted to tell me about a friend who had lost a child and a recent widow who needed to talk to someone who could understand her persistent tears. A voice inside me said, *Can't I just nurse my own wounds today? Do I always have to set myself aside to care for others?*

Just when I think I'm too stressed to serve, too needy to meet another's needs, too empty to give again, I catch a glimpse of Jesus, the night before his crucifixion. He knew his time had come and what was ahead. The pressure must have been enormous and the stress overwhelming. He had every reason and right to focus on his own suffering, to expect others to tend to his pain. And what did he do? He washed his disciples' feet. When they entered the room for the Last Supper, they were too busy being important to pick up the bowl and the towel. So Jesus did. Full of anguish over what lay ahead he "took the humble position of a slave," serving others when he deserved to be served (Philippians 2:7). "I have given you an example to follow," he told the disciples. "Do as I have done to you. . . . That is the path of blessing" (John 13:15, 17). Jesus knows that our greatest happiness comes from serving others in his shadow, even when we need to be served ourselves. He knows we will experience a breakthrough of joy by listening to others when we want to be listened to, by giving to others while our needs go unmet, by caring for others when we want to be cared for. Does it seem unfair that Jesus would ask you to extend compassionate care to others just when you need it yourself? Jesus has walked this way before you, and he beckons you to pick up the towel.

Son of Man, my Servant, just when I think I cannot keep on giving, your example inspires me to give myself away once again. Your Spirit empowers me to put aside my own problems to ease the pain of others.

DIGGING DEEPER

How is this paradox of serving when you need to be served illustrated in the following verses: Luke 18:12-14; Philippians 2:5-11; James 4:10; and 1 Peter 5:1-6?

GAINING THROUGH LOSING

IF YOU TRY TO KEEP YOUR LIFE FOR YOURSELF, YOU WILL LOSE IT. BUT IF YOU GIVE UP YOUR LIFE FOR ME, YOU WILL FIND TRUE LIFE. —MATTHEW 16:25

I think we are all a little superstitious when it comes to suffering. We would rather not get too close to someone who has suffered or is suffering lest it rub off on us. Likewise, we are a little suspicious of God. We have a deep-seated suspicion that God wants to hurt us or deprive us. We're afraid to trust God with all we are and all we call our own, fearing he will take it away just to make us prove it. Perhaps our suspicions stem from our belief that the gains Jesus offers cannot be worth our losses.

My friend, God does not want to take away all that you hold dear; he simply wants to become your most prized possession. He wants you to see that he is more precious and more satisfying than anything or anyone else, and he wants to give himself to you. To follow Jesus is to prize him above all else. And the measure of your prizing is in your losing. Prizing Jesus makes everything else in this life negotiable. This is how it was for Paul, who wrote, "I once thought all these things were so very important, but now I consider them worthless because of what Christ has done. Yes, everything else is worthless when compared with the priceless gain of knowing Christ Jesus my Lord. I have discarded everything else, counting it all as garbage, so that I may have Christ" (Philippians 3:7-8). Paul had come to see that the things he had held on to his whole life were actually depriving him of what he really wanted. So he moved what he had seen as assets into the liability column in his life. He reordered his entire life in order to get what he valued most. He wasn't content with just enough of Jesus to save him from the fires of eternal damnation. He wanted Christ in his fullness to save him from the futility of comfort fixation. And he didn't feel sorry for what he had left behind. No regrets over what he'd lost, only rejoicing over what he had gained: Christ.

When we truly recognize how much Christ is worth, our superstitions dissolve into sweet sacrifices. Our suspicions are replaced by surrender. And in the process, we discover the gain found in abandoning ourselves to God, even in—perhaps especially in—the sufferings of this life.

My prized Possession, I see that losing what I love in this life does not mean losing out. I see that you are turning my temporary losses into eternal gains, and I am glad.

DIGGING DEEPER

Read 2 Corinthians 12:7-10; Philippians 1:12-13; and 1 Thessalonians 1:6-7. In these passages, what did believers lose? What did they gain?

WEEK 32

PARADOX

REFLECTION

What upside-down logic of the gospel is hard for you to understand? What do you understand but find difficult to embrace? What gift of grace is to be found and enjoyed if you can learn to live in this paradox?

How have you experienced joy and freedom through Kingdom living—through finding comfort and meaning by living in the gospel paradoxes?

MEDITATION

In everything we do we try to show that we are true ministers of God. We patiently endure troubles and hardships and calamities of every kind. We serve God whether people honor us or despise us, whether they slander us or praise us. We are honest, but they call us impostors. We are well known, but we are treated as unknown. We live close to death, but here we are, still alive. We have been beaten within an inch of our lives. Our hearts ache, but we always have joy. We are poor, but we give spiritual riches to others. We own nothing, and yet we have everything. —2 CORINTHIANS 6:4, 8-10

Read through the passage several times, exploring the paradoxes and embracing the gift of grace in each one.

PRAYER

Praise God for his wisdom and ways that are inexplicable to the world.

Thank God for inviting you into his Kingdom and for opening your eyes to his way of living and dying.

Intercede for those who are blinded to the truth and the joys of Kingdom understanding and Kingdom living.

Confess your slowness to serve others when you want to be served, your self-sufficiency that keeps you from admitting your need, your resistance to brokenness that keeps you from repenting, and your suspicion of God that keeps you holding tight to what you don't want to lose.

Petition God to change your perspective and enable you to live and walk in this crazy world through the sanity of the gospel.

WEEK 33

THE GOOD SHEPHERD

Do you ever wonder how God feels about people with problems? Does he get tired of listening? Does he reach his limit of sympathy? Does he just want to fix them and be done with them?

Matthew 9 tells us exactly how God feels about these kinds of people—people like you and me. "He felt great pity for the crowds that came, because their problems were so great and they didn't know where to go for help. They were like sheep without a shepherd" (Matthew 9:36). Jesus has compassion for those of us who struggle and stray and suffer, because he has the heart of a shepherd who lovingly cares for his sheep.

Jesus has always had the heart of a shepherd. Isaiah prophesied about the Messiah this way: "He will feed his flock like a shepherd. He will carry the lambs in his arms, holding them close to his heart. He will gently lead the mother sheep with their young" (40:11). What a promise to those of us with problems! He will tenderly carry us through the wilderness, not out of duty or obligation, but out of love, holding us close to his heart because we are precious to him.

THIS WEEK'S PASSAGE FOR MEDITATION

The LORD is my shepherd; I have everything I need. He lets me rest in green meadows; he leads me beside peaceful streams. He renews my strength. He guides me along right paths, bringing honor to his name. Even when I walk through the dark valley of death, I will not be afraid, for you are close beside me. Your rod and your staff protect and comfort me. You prepare a feast for me in the presence of my enemies. You welcome me as a guest, anointing my head with oil. My cup overflows with blessings. Surely your goodness and unfailing love will pursue me all the days of my life, and I will live in the house of the LORD forever.

—PSALM 23

THE LORD IS MY SHEPHERD

The Lord is my shepherd; I have everything I need. He lets me rest in green meadows; he leads me beside peaceful streams. He renews my strength. He guides me along right paths, bringing honor to his name. —Psalm 23:1-3

If anyone was an expert on shepherds, it was David, the author of this psalm, the shepherd boy who became king. David knew from experience that a sheep's quality of life was dependent on the character and commitment of the shepherd. Most likely he had seen neglected, suffering sheep in the care of lazy shepherds. And he had seen flocks flourishing in the care of good shepherds. And because he was confident in the character, commitment, and compassion of God, being under the care of the Good Shepherd was where he wanted to be.

What may be more difficult to understand in this psalm is that David could say, "I have everything I need." This is the man who had been hunted and attacked not only by King Saul, but also by his own estranged son, Absalom. He had known his share of deprivation and defeat as well as shame and sorrow. And yet he expressed complete contentment. How could he do that?

David recognized that being content in the Good Shepherd's care is not defined by having our physical, financial, or material needs met at every juncture, but rather by our dependence on his loving care.

Have you ever known people who have experienced hardship and disaster, and yet their lives and their countenances exude deep contentment and quiet joy? Regardless of their circumstances, they entrust their lives to the care of their Shepherd without complaint or consternation. These people radiate humble satisfaction. Their experience has been one of rest and renewal as God leads them every step of the way. Don't you want to live like that? I do. And yet, so often, we don't.

The Good Shepherd cares for us lovingly, completely, and purposefully. We can be content with what he provides and where he leads.

My Shepherd, I am so easily discontented with my circumstances and with myself. Help me see that because I am in your loving care, I have everything I need. I trust you to guide me on the right path for your glory.

DIGGING DEEPER

Read Psalm 23, noting what the Lord does as our Shepherd and the benefits to those who are in his flock. How have you already experienced these benefits? How will you experience those benefits in eternity?

THE SHEPHERD WHO SEEKS

If you had one hundred sheep, and one of them strayed away and was lost in the wilderness, wouldn't you leave the ninety-nine others to go and search for the lost one until you found it? —Luke 15:4

I know what it feels like to fail and to agonize with the anxiety and regret and embarrassment that inevitably follow. Remembering can cause me to cringe. But I have been fortunate (so far) that most of my most painful mistakes have not been in full view for all to see.

It wasn't like that for a friend of mine. Her private indiscretion became headline news, a public scandal. It was painful and humiliating and scary. Many who were hurt and disappointed by her sin turned their backs on her, which added rejection and isolation to her pain.

Disillusioned by believers who failed her, broken by her own failure and shame, and filled with doubts about whether or not the gospel she had claimed to build her life around is really true and reliable, she simply walked away from her faith. She still lingers there outside the fold, walking away from God rather than toward him, a thoroughly entrenched skeptic.

When I see her or think of her, my heart breaks because I love her and because I see her for who she is—a lost lamb. I want her to know that the joy and rest the Good Shepherd provides are real. I've experienced them. I know the heart of the Good Shepherd is broken for her, too, and that he cannot rest until the one who has strayed is safely returned. He doesn't seek her so that he can punish her or pass judgment. He wants to lavish his love on her and lead her to a place of safety and rest and joy.

Isn't it good to know that is the heart of our Good Shepherd? Out of his great love, he pursues those who stray away from his loving care and he rejoices when they return. He takes the first step to pursue the one who is lost and is persistent until he brings the lost one safely home. And the one who was lost is not greeted with a lecture but with a celebration.

Seeker and Savior of the lost, implant within me your heart for those who have wandered away from you. Rid me of my religious elitism that implies you are lucky to have me in the fold and that ignores those who are lost.

DIGGING DEEPER

Read Psalm 119:169-176. What does this "lost sheep" think, feel, do, and want from God so that he might return to the fold?

I AM THE GATE

Yes, I am the gate. Those who come in through me will be saved. Wherever they go, they will find green pastures. My purpose is to give life in all its fullness. —John 10:9-10

As part of our trip to Norway, David and I visited a Christian bookstore in the heart of Oslo in which the owners have put together an amazing "walk through the Bible" display and experience. As our host walked us through the exhibit, he came to a sheepfold with an opening just big enough for sheep to enter, and he sat down, blocking the entrance and exit of the fold. He explained that this is what the people pictured when Jesus said to the people of his day, "I am the gate for the sheep." Middle Eastern shepherds would oftentimes sleep in the gateway to guard their sheep, and Jesus used this image to assert his loving care for us as well as his being the only way "in" to true life with God. Jesus, the Good Shepherd, is the only way into the fold of forever life.

But our Good Shepherd doesn't just give us life that lasts forever. When we allow him to become the "gateway," submitting to his control, we discover what a full life is all about. When we are in his fold, we can be freed from our striving and the self-centered pursuits of life. We are ushered into a life of deep joy and satisfaction, made so because he is there with us, enjoying us, directing us, filling us, using us. He is the Good Shepherd who longs to give us a quality of life that is beyond our human ambitions. This is not a life reserved for only the super-spiritual few who have the right spiritual genes or impulses or disciplines. This day-by-day, hour-by-hour, minute-by-minute enjoyment of the presence of Jesus is a habit that must be nurtured in our lives. Here we discover the peace of his presence and power in every detail of our day. Here we can rest in the green pastures he provides for us.

So why do we think that giving God control of our lives will diminish our freedom and joy? When we give the Good Shepherd control and begin to cherish his constant presence, we'll find an abundance of rest and freedom and absolute joy from living within his fold.

Guardian and Keeper of my soul, you keep me safe and content as I trust you to care for me. You give me peace and joy as I choose to welcome your presence in every detail of my life.

DIGGING DEEPER

Read John 10:1-18, noting the difference in actions and purpose between the Good Shepherd and the thief or hired hand. Who is the thief and who is the hired hand?

I KNOW MY SHEEP

I AM THE GOOD SHEPHERD; I KNOW MY OWN SHEEP, AND THEY KNOW ME, JUST AS MY FATHER KNOWS ME AND I KNOW THE FATHER. AND I LAY DOWN MY LIFE FOR THE SHEEP. MY SHEEP RECOGNIZE MY VOICE; I KNOW THEM, AND THEY FOLLOW ME. I GIVE THEM ETERNAL LIFE, AND THEY WILL NEVER PERISH. NO ONE WILL SNATCH THEM AWAY FROM ME. —JOHN 10:14-15, 27-28

"I know my own sheep." God knows me. He knows it all. He knows my public persona and my private pettiness. He knows what lights the fire of my soul and what dampens the flame within me. He knows how I struggle, even now, between self-pity and self-sacrifice. Even if I want to hide my inner thoughts and motives from him, I can't. He knows. I might be able to write revisionist history for you, but he knows my past as well as my future, and he sees me more clearly than I see myself.

Oh, how painful and at the same time pleasurable it is to be fully known! Such a relief that I do not have to put on pretenses, yet such a rub to have all my weaknesses exposed. And then I remember that he is the Good Shepherd. His full knowing of me doesn't cause him to recoil; it reminds him of why he came—to lay down his life for me. Knowing I've done nothing to deserve it, and knowing that at times I will stray from his flock, he has chosen to lay down his life for me and he invites me to know him in an intimate way. Even though he knows the real me, he wants me to follow him now and for eternity. He wants to be with me! He jealously guards me so that nothing and no one can snatch me away from him.

He knows me to the core, and what he has seen is not pretty. I am infected by sin, but because he is the Good Shepherd, he has done what is required to remedy this fatal malady. He laid down his life for me. If he loves me so much that he is willing to die for me, why do I try to hide and why do I run? There is rest in remembering that he is the Good Shepherd who knows me thoroughly and loves me unendingly.

Shepherd of my soul, I hear your voice and I recognize it because I am yours. Speak to me, and remind me that being fully known by you and following you is the safest place I can be.

DIGGING DEEPER

Read Psalm 139. List the ways God knows you. What does he think about you? What are the benefits of praying the way David prayed (verses 23-24)?

FEED MY SHEEP AND FOLLOW ME

Jesus said, "Then feed my sheep. The truth is, when you were young, you were able to do as you liked and go wherever you wanted to. But when you are old, you will stretch out your hands, and others will direct you and take you where you don't want to go." Jesus said this to let him know what kind of death he would die to glorify God. Then Jesus told him, "Follow me."
—John 21:17-19

Jesus told Peter something most of us want to know and at the same time don't want to know—how he would die. Jesus had just finished questioning him about whether or not Peter genuinely loved him. Then, after instructing Peter on how that love should be expressed, Jesus revealed where a life of fishing for men and shepherding the flock of God would lead—to a cross.

Is that really where a life of loving obedience should lead? Somehow it doesn't seem to square with our modern sensibilities, does it?

Jesus had certainly been calling Peter to a life of loving obedience, or rather, a life of obediently serving others out of love for Christ. Three times he told Peter that talk of loving God is cheap. Real love for God is expressed by feeding lambs with the nourishment of God's Word—taking care of sheep who are vulnerable to attack and dressing their wounds. The same is true today. Real love for God is expressed by caring for the flock of God, a humbling, tiring job because people in God's flock are often like stupid, smelly sheep. We are needy and dependent.

The Good Shepherd has shown us how to become his undershepherds. We are to follow the example he gave us as he said, "I lay down my life for the sheep" (John 10:15). Caring for his beloved flock is his most desired expression of our love for him. It is what we do as we follow him. Just as it did for Peter, a life like this may take us where we do not want to go. We may be called to lay down our leisure time, our lifestyle, or like Peter, our very lives so we can feed his sheep and follow him.

Great Shepherd, you have done more than tell me what a Good Shepherd does, you have shown me by laying down your life. But honestly, I resist the demands that feeding your sheep requires. It is inconvenient and uncomfortable. Give me a heart to follow you this way, to love you this way.

DIGGING DEEPER

Read 1 Peter 5:2-5. Who among the flock has God entrusted to your care? What are the hallmarks of how you should tend to them, and what can you expect in return?

WEEK 33

THE GOOD SHEPHERD

REFLECTION

How does seeing the shepherd-heart of God affect your view of God and your understanding of how he views your current situation?

What kind of a sheep are you? Have you strayed? Do you hear and know your Shepherd's voice? Do you allow him to lead you to safe places and green pastures?

MEDITATION

The LORD is my shepherd; I have everything I need. He lets me rest in green meadows; he leads me beside peaceful streams. He renews my strength. He guides me along right paths, bringing honor to his name. Even when I walk through the dark valley of death, I will not be afraid, for you are close beside me. Your rod and your staff protect and comfort me. You prepare a feast for me in the presence of my enemies. You welcome me as a guest, anointing my head with oil. My cup overflows with blessings. Surely your goodness and unfailing love will pursue me all the days of my life, and I will live in the house of the LORD forever.
—PSALM 23

Turn this psalm into a personal prayer to your Shepherd, changing "he" to "you."

PRAYER

Praise God for his loving compassion as our Good Shepherd.

Thank God for showing us what a good shepherd does—lays down his life for his sheep.

Intercede for those you know who have strayed from the fold of God, and begin to see them as lost lambs whom the Shepherd is seeking.

Confess your hesitancy to love God the way he desires—by feeding his sheep. Confess also your fear of following him in a way that requires you to lay down your life.

Petition God to transform your view and understanding of God so that you may see him for who he truly is—a good and gentle Shepherd who longs to carry you in his arms, close to his heart.

WEEK 34

JOY

You may have sung this song like I did while growing up: "I've got the joy, joy, joy, joy down in my heart, down in my heart, down in my heart. I've got the joy, joy, joy, joy down in my heart, down in my heart to stay!"

That's fine, but then something goes wrong with this song. "And I'm so happy, so very happy! I've got the love of Jesus in my heart. And I'm so happy, so very happy! I've got the love of Jesus in my heart!"

The truth is, it is possible to be filled with joy and still not be described as "happy." Sometimes we're just plain sad, not only down in our hearts, but down to our toes. Have you found that to be true? Have you experienced joy in the midst of your great sadness?

The Bible says, "A joyful heart is good medicine" (Proverbs 17:22, NASB). As we savor the joy we have in Christ, we feel the healing power of that medicine. In fact, our joy should be as consistent as God is. It doesn't have to be tied to the turbulent conditions of our feelings and moods. Our joy is grounded in God. It flows from him and back to him. Joy is not something we can generate with positive thinking or a bit of humor. It is a fruit of the Holy Spirit's work in our inner lives. Joy shines forth from the life of the true believer, no matter how dark the circumstances. Joy in God deserves our constant, courageous pursuit. Will you seek God with this expectation and lay hold of him for this reward?

THIS WEEK'S PASSAGE FOR MEDITATION

Dear brothers and sisters, whenever trouble comes your way, let it be an opportunity for joy. For when your faith is tested, your endurance has a chance to grow. So let it grow, for when your endurance is fully developed, you will be strong in character and ready for anything. God blesses the people who patiently endure testing. Afterward they will receive the crown of life that God has promised to those who love him. —James 1:2-4, 12

GENUINE JOY

ALWAYS BE FULL OF JOY IN THE LORD. I SAY IT AGAIN—REJOICE! —PHILIPPIANS 4:4

I spent plenty of after-school afternoons with *Batman*, *That Girl*, *Speed Racer*, *The Munsters*, and *The Partridge Family*. Remember that *Partridge Family* theme song, "C'mon, Get Happy"? Don't you sometimes wish that "getting happy" were as easy as lip-synching along with David Cassidy? The truth is, a person can't just decide to have joy. Genuine joy is not an act of willpower or positive thinking. It is a spontaneous, soul-level response to the most solid, satisfying joy in the universe.

And while we could never expect to always be full of joy on our own, it is not unrealistic to always be full of joy in the Lord if he is the source of our joy. This is what Paul tells us, and he has tremendous credibility in the matter. Paul writes these words from a jail cell—a jail cell in which he endured the cold, encountered mistreatment, and experienced hunger—the kind of suffering that, on the surface, would seem to justify a joyless existence. But over and over in his letters, Paul writes of joy in the midst of suffering in the lives of believers. In Romans 5:3 he said, "We can rejoice, too, when we run into problems and trials, for we know that they are good for us." In his letter to the Thessalonians he wrote, "You received the message with joy from the Holy Spirit in spite of the severe suffering it brought you" (1 Thessalonians 1:6). To the Corinthians he wrote about the churches in Macedonia, "Though they have been going through much trouble and hard times, their wonderful joy and deep poverty have overflowed in rich generosity" (2 Corinthians 8:2).

How could Paul have joy in his jail cell? And how can you have joy in your dysfunctional family, with your deteriorating health, or in your dire circumstances? You can rejoice in the Lord at all times, in any situation, because he is always who he says he is. If you have God, you have a durable, rugged joy that cannot be diminished by anyone or anything. It is not superficial or flimsy, but deep and firm. You can rejoice in pain and in poverty and in problems. True joy is your abiding possession if you are in Christ.

Perhaps my joy is not as fragile as I think it is, Lord. I know that you never command me to do anything that I cannot do, and you are my resource for what I need to obey your command to rejoice.

DIGGING DEEPER

Read the following verses in Philippians, looking through the lens of Paul's emphasis on joy: 1:4, 18, 25; 2:2, 17-18, 28-29; 3:1; 4:1, 4.

GOOD NEWS OF GREAT JOY

THE ANGEL REASSURED THEM. "DON'T BE AFRAID!" HE SAID. "I BRING YOU GOOD NEWS OF GREAT JOY FOR EVERYONE!" —LUKE 2:10

Many people see God as a cosmic killjoy. They suspect that he needlessly limits our enjoyment of life. Because of this misunderstanding, they view anything having to do with God as infinitely boring. Their view of God is grim, and their expectation of any experience with God is gloomy. What a tragedy that so many people cannot see that God is full of joy, that he is in fact overflowing with joy. This is the good news the angel brought to the shepherds that night. "The Savior—yes, the Messiah, the Lord—has been born tonight in Bethlehem, the city of David!" (Luke 2:11). Jesus is good news of great joy. Jesus is the joy overflow of heaven spilling upon us the very joy of God. Jesus is not a bummer or a bore or a burden. He is a great joy, our greatest joy.

Certainly the announcement of his coming and the experience of his glory were both exciting and terrifying to the shepherds. Their response to the great news the angel proclaimed was utter fear. And the truth is, because God is holy and sin is consumed in his presence, they had reason to be afraid. And so do we. But that's why the angel's message was such good news for them and for us. Jesus wasn't coming to consume them, but to save them. Jesus replaces our fear with joy. He doesn't want to take away our joy in living. He wants to *be* our joy. Jesus is good news of great joy because he is the answer to our deepest need. We think we need a physical cure, a financial windfall, a relational breakthrough, a political upset. But God knows that what we really need most is a Savior. We can point out the problems of the world all around us. But God knows that you and I are the problem. We have good intentions, but they are not strong enough or pure enough to overcome our evil impulses. We need a Savior to rescue us from ourselves. So he sent his Son to save us.

Won't you embrace Jesus as the best news you've ever heard, the highest joy you will ever experience? Matthew says that when the wise men saw the star that would lead them to Jesus, "they were filled with joy!" (Matthew 2:10). Hear the good news; seek out Jesus in your darkness. Let Jesus fill you with his joy!

Joy of heaven and earth, what good news of great joy you are. If I have you in my life, I need nothing else in order to be filled with joy.

DIGGING DEEPER

See the focus on joy in Luke 1–2, noting 1:14, 44; 2:10, 34.

RESTORED JOY

Oh, give me back my joy again; you have broken me—now let me rejoice. Restore to me again the joy of your salvation, and make me willing to obey you. —Psalm 51:8, 12

I tried to share my M&M's with a friend at yesterday's middle school wrestling match, but she had spent the afternoon trying on pants. And every woman knows there's nothing like spending a few hours trying on clothes to make you want to watch what you eat and hit the gym. In the mirrors of the dressing room, the truth is revealed, and all our efforts to camouflage that truth are useless.

Just as we have become experts at covering up our figure flaws, so have we become adept at covering up the ugly realities of our inner lives. But then the day comes when we're broken by our sinful choices, undressed before the eyes of God, unable to hide. This is where King David found himself after his affair with Bathsheba and murder of Uriah, her husband. He had tried to cover it up and justify it, but he found himself exposed by the truth and exhausted by guilt. As he looked into the mirror of the law and love of God, the reality of what he had done broke him and humbled him. David cried out to be cleansed, asking God to wash away his sin, relieve him of his guilt, and replace it all with joy—the joy he had known before, when everything was right and open between him and God.

There's a direct correlation between our sorrow over sin and our capacity for joy. The reason we don't have more joy is because we're just not that sorry over our sin. We don't see it as that big of a problem. It's like this: If you have a hangnail and it is cured, you are happy. But how much greater is your joy to find out you've been cured of heart disease? Likewise, if you're cured from what you consider a small sin problem, your joy is small. But when you see yourself in the mirror of the holiness of God and recognize the enormity of your sin problem, and you find out that God has cured you, your joy is great, overflowing, unspeakable.

Perhaps it's time you stopped avoiding the mirror. Bring everything out into the open before him. As you see your sin for the big problem it really is, ask him for forgiveness and restoration. God will show you his mercy and fill you with his joy.

My Restorer, I want to let go of this guilt and shame and feel the smile of God on my life. Restore me and renew me. Give me back my joy.

DIGGING DEEPER

Read David's prayer of repentance and restoration in Psalm 51.

JOY IN HEARTACHE

Our hearts ache, but we always have joy. We are poor, but we give spiritual riches to others. We own nothing, and yet we have everything.
—2 Corinthians 6:10

My friend Mary Bess arranged for meals for our family during most of Hope's life and again during Gabe's life. Often, when people would bring us a meal, we would ask them to bring enough for their family, too, and invite them to stay to eat with us. We quickly discovered that one of the gifts Hope and Gabe gave to us was a richness of relationships. When they were there, the conversation simply couldn't consist of triviality. Having people in our home during those difficult but rich days was a blessing to us—and to them, I think. We got to know people we had not known well before. They got to know and enjoy our children in our home, which had preciousness to it that I can't quite put into words.

I remember at times saying good-bye and closing the door behind visitors and wondering if they walked away thinking, *That's weird. They sure don't seem very sad.* The truth was, while there were lots of tears of sadness in our home, there was also a great deal of joy. Hope and Gabe were here and we were making the most of it! And even in the difficult and empty days following their deaths, sadness did not always define the atmosphere in our home. Joy was always peeking its way through the curtain of sorrow.

To experience sorrow does not eliminate joy. In fact, I've come to think that sorrow actually deepens our capacity for joy—that as our lows are lower, so are our highs higher. Deep sorrow expands our ability to feel deeply. We feel sadder than we ever knew we could, sadder than we think we can survive. But our sorrow prepares us to experience a more satisfying and solid joy than we've ever known before. When joy surfaces, it allows us to see that deep beneath the chaos and catastrophe is the strong current of confidence that we can be content in the sovereign hands of God. It's just not natural to experience profound joy in the face of heartache. It is supernatural; it is spiritual. This is the kind of joy God has for you. It is not produced by the human spirit in response to pleasant circumstances, but by the Holy Spirit in spite of difficult circumstances. It is the very joy of Christ fulfilled in us.

Jesus, I know you understand heartache, so can you show me how I can experience profound joy even though my heart is breaking? Will you give me your supernatural joy that is solid and satisfying?

DIGGING DEEPER

In 1 Peter 1:5-9, how does Peter echo Paul's words in 2 Corinthians 6:3-10?

LAUGHTER

Weeping may go on all night, but joy comes with the morning. —Psalm 30:5

TO: DAVID GUTHRIE
RE: TYPO
DATE: THU, 24 JUNE 1999, 08:19:08
I took a peek at our girl on the Web site tonight. What a beautiful daughter we had! Imagine that!
And I found a typo. Goodness is spelled goodnes. Just a little short on the s's.
I love you, dear husband.
NANCY

Thank, honey, i didn't even notice. Gues i wan't paying attention. I'll fix it a oon a i can!
DG

David makes me laugh. He always has. There have been times I've been mad that he made me laugh—like the day Gabe died. I can't remember now what he said. I just remember bending over the bed saying, "How dare you make me laugh today?!" Laughter seems off-limits or certainly inappropriate in some situations, on some days. I remember being afraid that some people might think I was either in complete denial, or worse, that I didn't really care about Hope if I laughed out loud during her life or following her death.

Sometimes we are afraid to laugh lest people think our pain has passed or that our sorrow has been a sham. But just as tears give vent to the deep sorrow we feel inside, laughter is evidence of the deep joy that abides, even in the midst of sorrow, when our hope is in Christ. Mysterious and amazing joy that has nothing to do with denial is part of what it means to grieve differently from those who have no hope. Laughter reveals that while grief may have a grip on us, it has not choked the life out of us. Laughter takes some of the sting out of hurt. It gives us perspective and relieves the pressure. In fact, laughter helps control pain, not just emotionally but physically. It increases the production of endorphins, our bodies' naturally produced painkiller. It gives us a mini-vacation from our pain. And don't you sometimes feel as if you would like to take a day off from your sorrow? Won't you give yourself permission to laugh a little and enjoy some relief from the pain?

Spirit of joy, I can't generate the kind of joy that will bubble up into holy laughter. Only you can give me that joy. Will you give it to me now? Will you fill me with your joy so the world will see that my hope is in you?

DIGGING DEEPER

Check out what David recently shared with his Sunday school class regarding Nehemiah's favorite composer (Nehemiah 1:1, NIV), preferred hotel (3:26), and car of choice (2:1).

WEEK 34

JOY

REFLECTION

How have you experienced joy in God in the midst of the difficult circumstances you face?

What could you do to open the way for more experiences of the joy of God in your life?

MEDITATION

Dear brothers and sisters, whenever trouble comes your way, let it be an opportunity for joy. For when your faith is tested, your endurance has a chance to grow. So let it grow, for when your endurance is fully developed, you will be strong in character and ready for anything. God blesses the people who patiently endure testing. Afterward they will receive the crown of life that God has promised to those who love him. —JAMES 1:2-4, 12

Read through this passage several times, jotting down the progression that James suggests leads us toward joy in the midst of trouble.

Mark the words and phrases that are especially meaningful to you.

Accept the admonitions in the verses and savor the promises.

PRAYER

Praise God for being the great Joy in the universe, worthy of our delight.

Thank God for the gift of forgiveness that restores the joy of salvation and the gift of laughter that relieves the pressure of problems.

Intercede for those who have never heard the good news of great joy that is for them in Jesus.

Confess your tendency to base your joy on your circumstances or your mood swings rather than on the consistency of God.

Ask God to restore your joy, to fill you with his joy, and to use the overflow of his joy in your life to bless those around you.

WEEK 35

JOY ROBBERS

Some people think feelings are like sneezes, that they are neither right nor wrong, they just happen. They believe that feelings are what they are, that we have no control over them. Based on this belief, many of us, while we may pursue God to shape and change our will, never expect him to transform how we feel.

When we come to Christ, he changes our hearts and renews our minds. This change doesn't just cause us to think and act differently, it causes us to feel differently. God's transforming power changes how we think about God, and therefore how we feel about our circumstances. The clearer our view of God becomes, the more our feelings are centered in joy. And while our negative emotions that threaten joy may never completely disappear, they will lose their power over us.

THIS WEEK'S PASSAGE FOR MEDITATION

If your faith remains strong after being tried by fiery trials, it will bring you much praise and glory and honor on the day when Jesus Christ is revealed to the whole world. You love him even though you have never seen him. Though you do not see him, you trust him; and even now you are happy with a glorious, inexpressible joy. Your reward for trusting him will be the salvation of your souls. —1 Peter 1:7-9

ANXIETY AND WORRY

Don't worry about anything; instead, pray about everything. Tell God what you need, and thank him for all he has done. If you do this, you will experience God's peace, which is far more wonderful than the human mind can understand. —Philippians 4:6-7

Do you know what it is like to wake up with a sick feeling of anxiety in the pit of your stomach? to have a sense of dread when the phone rings? to feel at the mercy of anxious thoughts about your life and the lives of those you love? I do. Sometimes I find myself churning with anxiety even as I know that this is not what God wants for me as his child. For many of us, worry and anxiety are enemies we consistently struggle against.

But some of us have given up the struggle on this one, believing that we are natural-born worriers who can never change. We've forgotten that Jesus is all about change, about breaking us free from the natural tendencies that enslave us and rob us of the joy he has for us. We do not have to stay stuck in the pit of worry, bound to the painful uneasiness of a mind that continually feeds on impending fears. When Paul wrote, "Don't worry about anything," the word he used for worry indicates choking or strangling. And that's what anxiety does, doesn't it? It doesn't solve any of our problems. It just strangles the life out of us, leaving us gasping in fear, devoid of joy. In its mildest form, we simply churn. In its most severe form, we panic. This is no way to live.

We really don't have to keep living in a world dominated by anxiety and worry. As we leave our old lives behind and enter into new life in Christ, he offers those who suffer from worry and anxiety a new atmosphere of serenity in which to live and breathe. Rather than fret and fear, those who live in the serenity of Christ choose to apply their energy toward prayer, believing there is no concern too small and no situation too big that God cannot dissolve their worry over it into peace. They feel safe, no longer wasting energy on trying to anticipate and compensate for every imaginable outcome. Their hearts are guarded by the peace of God; their emotions are guided by belief in God. Though we're invited into this beautiful place of serenity, we have to choose to enter in. Refusing to enter in is choosing to be emotionally bankrupt and spiritually immobilized. Won't you enter into the peace of God by surrendering your worries and entrusting your cares to him?

My Burden Bearer, I've lived in anxiety so long, I can hardly believe I don't have to anymore. But you've given me a vision of the serenity you want me to live in, and it is an irresistible offer. I give you my worries, and I accept your peace.

DIGGING DEEPER

What do the following verses teach about how to handle worry and anxiety: Psalm 55:22; Matthew 11:28; and 1 Peter 5:7?

FEAR

HAPPY ARE THOSE WHO FEAR THE LORD. THEY DO NOT FEAR BAD NEWS; THEY CONFIDENTLY TRUST THE LORD TO CARE FOR THEM. THEY ARE CONFIDENT AND FEARLESS AND CAN FACE THEIR FOES TRIUMPHANTLY. —PSALM 112:1, 7-8

Recently, when David and I were sharing our story in front of a group, I got a question that stumped me. A woman asked me, "How did you deal with your fear?" All I could think to say in response was, "I felt afraid."

But the more I thought about it, I realized that while we may feel afraid, fear does not have to have the final word on our emotions and outlook. It doesn't have to deaden our capacity for joy. In Isaiah 41:10, God says, "Don't be afraid, for I am with you. Do not be dismayed, for I am your God. I will strengthen you. I will help you. I will uphold you with my victorious right hand." Can you step back from your fearful situation to see what God wants you to see about him here? Can you see his all-encompassing presence and hear his unfailing promise? This vision is our secret weapon in the battle against overwhelming fear.

"I am with you." He is by your side in the operating room, at the graveside, in the courtroom, in your aching loneliness.

"I am your God." He is over you, watching carefully, covering you, caring for you personally.

"I will strengthen you." He makes his presence known within you as his Holy Spirit gives you supernatural courage and strength to face what you never wanted to face and what you never dreamed you could face.

"I will help you." He is all around you, holding you up in your weakness, lifting you up from your hopelessness, and carrying you through your crisis.

"I will uphold you." He is the sure and solid foundation underneath you, the strong arms that will never let you fall.

Can you see him? Embracing this reality of his presence in and around you is the secret to facing a fearful future with godly courage. As God becomes larger in your estimation and closer in your experience, fear will lose its power and loosen its grip. Paralyzing fear and genuine faith simply cannot coexist. It's not the amount of faith that gives us confidence in crisis, but the object of our faith that calms our fears. Faith enables us to say with the psalmist, "When I am afraid, I put my trust in you" (Psalm 56:3).

Ever-present God, my eyes have been opened to see you over me, around me, beside me, inside me, and underneath me. The reality of your presence calms my fears and gives me courage.

DIGGING DEEPER

Read Exodus 20:18-21. How does fearing God help us with our other fears?

JEALOUSY

ONCE WE, TOO, WERE FOOLISH AND DISOBEDIENT. WE WERE MISLED BY OTHERS AND BECAME SLAVES TO MANY WICKED DESIRES AND EVIL PLEASURES. OUR LIVES WERE FULL OF EVIL AND ENVY. BUT THEN GOD OUR SAVIOR SHOWED US HIS KINDNESS AND LOVE. HE WASHED AWAY OUR SINS AND GAVE US A NEW LIFE THROUGH THE HOLY SPIRIT. —TITUS 3:3-5

I finally identified the root of the problem I'm having with someone. I'm jealous, and it is so hard and so humbling to admit. So many little things have been rubbing me the wrong way and I've found myself constantly churning and complaining. Then I realized it wasn't so much about her doing or saying the wrong things as much as my attitude toward her, an attitude that has been warped by envy. I am envious of her gifts that dwarf mine and of her opportunities that eclipse mine. I feel jealous as she moves into territory that I've considered mine. (Did you catch the mine, mine, mine theme here?) But I'm finding that just by naming it for what it is, seeing it for the sin it is, jealousy is losing its power over me. I want to celebrate her accomplishments and speak well of her whenever I have the opportunity. I don't want to listen to the voice of insecurity that tells me her successes will diminish me, that those who care about her will forget me. I want to be free.

Those of us who have experienced loss are especially prone to jealousy and envy. We're painfully aware of what others have that we do not—those who have complete families while ours is fractured, those who have financial security while ours is shattered, those who seem to have rosy futures when ours is threatened. We can't help but notice, but we can guard our hearts from souring with jealousy and simmering with envy. Is the anger you feel toward others in your life due to envy over the abilities they have that you do not have, advantages they have that you were not given, admiration they enjoy that you have always wanted? Are you jealous, fearing that the affection of someone you care about or the attention from people you respect will go to someone else? Would you cleanse your heart from envy by choosing to unselfishly and sincerely celebrate the joys of those who inspire jealousy rather than ignore or undermine them? Would you thank God for what he has given to you and seek to find full satisfaction in him?

Kind Savior, you provide everything I need and enjoy. Help me to stop looking around at others, feeding my envy of who they are and what they have. Help me to live out my satisfaction in you by dying to jealousy and envy.

DIGGING DEEPER

According to the following passages, what companions come with jealousy: 2 Corinthians 12:20; Galatians 5:19-21; 1 Timothy 6:4; James 3:16; and 1 Peter 2:1?

GUILT

God can use sorrow in our lives to help us turn away from sin and seek salvation. We will never regret that kind of sorrow. But sorrow without repentance is the kind that results in death. —2 Corinthians 7:10

Guilt seems like a constant companion to grief. The "if onlys" that plague our thoughts can leave us swimming in a pool of regret. Our binges and blowups, compromises and capitulations can so fill us with guilt, there is no room left for joy.

The truth is, we're all guilty. But our very real guilt has been dealt with at the Cross. We know that in our heads, don't we? Our problem is that we still *feel* guilty. These feelings of guilt are our warped way of trying to pay for our sin ourselves. It just seems too good to be true that Jesus has paid the debt we owe, so we continue to try to pay by tormenting ourselves with self-condemnation. Our unwillingness to let go of guilt feelings reveals that we don't really believe Jesus' payment for our sin was adequate.

Wouldn't you like to begin living in the reality that your sin has been paid for completely by Jesus? Guilt loses its destructive power in our lives when it is exposed to the light and truth of God. But you should know that there is a good kind of guilt. This is the guilt we experience when we are under conviction, and this kind of guilt is not to be rejected, but welcomed. Conviction is the work of the Holy Spirit in our lives to reveal to us our ongoing sin. But the Holy Spirit doesn't convict us so we will feel guilty. He convicts us so we will confess our sin and change our behavior. Conviction is what God uses to correct and protect us, not to burden us with feelings of guilt. Conviction is the gift of God that clears the way for our joy to be restored.

Is the guilt you feel conviction from the Holy Spirit—godly sorrow that leads to repentance and restoration? Or is it false guilt—self-condemnation that has filled you with the pain of regret and keeps trying to make you pay? Ask God to show you. Confess your sin and stop punishing yourself. Ask God to restore the joy that guilt has stolen from you.

Gracious Savior, I'm tired of living with this regret, under this guilt. Send your Holy Spirit to convict me so I can repent and be set free. Remind me of your sufficient sacrifice for sin so I won't allow false guilt to rob me of joy.

DIGGING DEEPER

How did Peter deal with his guilt appropriately (Matthew 26:69-75), and how did Judas deal with his inappropriately (Matthew 27:3-5)?

ANGER

My dear brothers and sisters, be quick to listen, slow to speak, and slow to get angry. Your anger can never make things right in God's sight.
—James 1:19-20

Am I the only person in the world who practices my arguments with people? I doubt it. When I'm angry, I often find myself rehearsing a confrontational conversation, and I'm good! I want to be ready to win in the war of words! When I'm angry I have such a sense of self-righteousness. I easily fool myself into believing that I am an innocent victim, a force for all that is good and right, when oftentimes I'm really just angry because I didn't get my own way.

Anger is a natural reaction when our desires for security, significance, or satisfaction are not being met. As we brood over our hurt, we churn and plot and imagine how delicious it will be to put the people we're mad at in their place. But we should be wary of our anger. It is powerful and most often powerfully destructive. Anger is a potential poison in our souls that not only spoils our own joy, but also spills out on those around us.

Some might say it is unrealistic to think that we won't get angry and that it is unhealthy or dishonest *not* to express our anger. Everybody gets angry, right? But while anger may be a natural reaction to not having our needs met, and may even be justified by our circumstances, our lives as believers are all about being transformed on the inside so that we are no longer bound to do what comes naturally or demand what we think we deserve. The Holy Spirit in us empowers us to respond supernaturally. The truth is, we do not have to let our anger control us when someone does something that hurts us. We will be tempted, but we can refuse to give in to that temptation.

I'm not talking about feeling a flash of anger. Anger becomes sin as we entertain it, as we stir it up and allow it to drive our emotions and steer our actions. The Scripture says, " 'Don't sin by letting anger gain control over you.' Don't let the sun go down while you are still angry, for anger gives a mighty foothold to the Devil" (Ephesians 4:26-27). So don't let your anger linger. Let it go. Hasn't anger done enough damage to your relationships? Hasn't it robbed you of joy long enough? Will you release it to God?

Gentle Jesus, my simmering anger feels so delicious to me, and yet when I look at it through your eyes, I'm ashamed. I want to get rid of anger so that joy can take its place directing my emotions and my actions.

DIGGING DEEPER

According to Ephesians 4:17–5:2, why is a believer unable to justify deep-seated, lingering anger?

WEEK 35

JOY ROBBERS

REFLECTION

What negative emotions have robbed you of joy? On what misbeliefs about God are these emotions based?

What truths about God's power and goodness and sufficiency need to make their way from the pages of Scripture into the recesses of your heart so that nothing can steal your joy?

MEDITATION

If your faith remains strong after being tried by fiery trials, it will bring you much praise and glory and honor on the day when Jesus Christ is revealed to the whole world. You love him even though you have never seen him. Though you do not see him, you trust him; and even now you are happy with a glorious, inexpressible joy. Your reward for trusting him will be the salvation of your souls. —1 PETER 1:7-9

Read through these verses several times, marking the words and phrases that are especially meaningful to you.

Envision yourself in the presence of Jesus on that day when he is revealed to the world. Feel the joy of seeing your faith in trials bringing praise, glory, and honor to Jesus. Feel the joy of receiving your reward for trusting him.

Focus on the foundation of those joys. Pray through the passage, asking God for what you need to make it a reality in your life.

PRAYER

Praise God as your strength and as your refuge from emotions that rob you of joy.

Thank God for sending us the Holy Spirit to convict, comfort, assure, and empower us so we are not helpless in our negative emotions.

Intercede for those who have made you angry or who inspire jealousy and envy.

Confess your misbeliefs about God that provide the foundation for anxiety and fear.

Petition God to transform your feelings and protect your joy by showing you his power, assuring you of his presence, and giving you faith to believe his promises.

WEEK 36

FINDING PURPOSE IN PAIN

Teach me everything you have for me—just don't let this pain be wasted in my life! I don't remember much about praying during the short six months of Hope's life. Perhaps because we hardly knew how to pray. But I do remember this prayer—a desperate request that God would use this dreadful experience in my life for some sort of good.

It is the seemingly senseless suffering, the wasted pain, the meaningless loss that is so difficult to get past, isn't it? We are desperate to believe that even if we could never label what has happened to us as good, we could point to something good that has come out of it.

David read Philip Yancey's book *Where Is God When It Hurts?* during Hope's life, and I'll never forget his explanation of an important point from the book. Yancey suggests we replace the question "Why?" with the question "To what end?" Another way to ask the same question might be, "For what purpose?"

That is the real question, isn't it, when the worst thing we can imagine becomes a reality in our lives? Is there some purpose to this suffering, or is it simply random and meaningless? Finding meaning helps with acceptance.

There is purpose and meaning in suffering for the child of God. Our Redeemer is able to take evil and pain and use them for a good purpose in our lives and the lives of others. This week, let's consider some of the good purposes for which God uses suffering in our lives.

THIS WEEK'S PASSAGE FOR MEDITATION

We know that God causes everything to work together for the good of those who love God and are called according to his purpose for them. —Romans 8:28

TURNING TO GOD

THE PAIN TURNED YOU TO GOD. —2 CORINTHIANS 7:9 (TLB)

"I can't feel my boo-boos," five-year-old Ashlyn Blocker said through missing baby teeth she'd knocked out without a tear. Ashlyn is among a tiny number of people in the world known to have congenital insensitivity to pain. It's a rare genetic disorder that makes her unable to feel pain.

"Some people would say that's a good thing, but it's not," her mom said. "Pain's there for a reason. It lets your body know something is wrong and needs to be fixed. I'd give anything for her to feel pain." Ashlyn's baby teeth posed big problems. She would chew her lips bloody in her sleep, bite through her tongue while eating, and once stuck her finger in her mouth and stripped flesh from it.

We tend to think of pain as our great enemy, the source of our unhappiness, and we assume that if we could just get rid of pain, we would truly be happy. But in reality, physical pain is a gift—an internal warning signal that tells us something has gone wrong and needs our urgent attention. Similarly, our emotional, relational, and spiritual pain is a gift, warning us that an area of our lives needs urgent attention to bring about healing. So perhaps the secret to happiness is not so much figuring out how to avoid all pain, but learning how to respond to it.

C. S. Lewis said, "God whispers to us in our pleasures, speaks in our conscience, but shouts in our pains: it is His megaphone to rouse a deaf world." God uses the physical pain that does not subside, the relational pain that puts us on edge, the emotional pain that brings us to tears, to get our attention and to turn our attention toward him. Is that how God has used pain in your life? Do you find yourself praying more often, thinking more deeply, searching more urgently for the truth? When pain invades the busyness of our routine existence, it insists that we reexamine our assumptions and reevaluate our appetites and affections, doesn't it? Pain often affords us—or imposes on us—time for reflection. If we will accept it, pain can give us the gift of reconnection with God, a fresh intimacy with him, a passionate nearness to him. Pain brings us to our knees. We begin with prayers for our pain to be removed. And as he works in us, our prayers change so that we begin to ask that the pain will be redeemed.

My Pain Redeemer, you have my attention! This pain has brought me to my knees and bid me turn to you. You are the pleasure I find in this pain. So speak to me and show me how I need to change. Heal the hurt in my life as I turn wholeheartedly toward you.

DIGGING DEEPER

Read Psalm 119:71 and Luke 13:1-5. What role does pain play in getting us to turn toward God?

FAITH PROVED GENUINE

Be truly glad! There is wonderful joy ahead, even though it is necessary for you to endure many trials for a while. These trials are only to test your faith, to show that it is strong and pure. It is being tested as fire tests and purifies gold—and your faith is far more precious to God than mere gold.
—1 Peter 1:6-7

Why is it that over and over again the biblical writers suggest that we have joy in the midst of suffering? What could make you or me joyful when our worst nightmare becomes our reality? The joy is in finding out that faith works. The joy is in discovering that when the rubber hits the road, the faith you have given lip service to is now put into action. It is the joy of discovering that your faith is genuine—the real deal.

To experience this joy of knowing your faith is genuine, it must be put to the test. When we think about a test, most of us think about the kind of test in which you can either pass or fail. But this is different.

Recently, my car died after twelve years of faithful service, so we went to various dealers and took cars for test drives. Were we looking to see if the car passed or failed? No. We were allowing the car to show us how it works and what it feels like, to demonstrate how it operates. The car was put to the test—not in an effort to see if it would pass or fail, but so it could show us its stuff! When God puts us to the test, he is giving us the opportunity to experience and demonstrate what it is like to live out our faith in the most difficult of circumstances. It is the chance to live what we say we believe.

When a friend of mine was recently let go from her high-profile job, I shared the above verses from 1 Peter with her. "It is like you are on a stage and the curtain has been pulled back and now the world will see if your faith is for real," I told her. It is in the midst of suffering, when we choose to trust instead of fear, that we reveal genuine faith. To accept rather than complain. To forgive rather than seek revenge. To choose humility instead of proving we were right. The curtain is pulled back and we have the opportunity for our faith to be proved genuine.

Faith Revealer, how I long to know the joy of being tested by you and having my faith proved genuine. Test me so I can show the world that faith in you works.

DIGGING DEEPER

How did Abraham demonstrate faith through his test, according to Hebrews 11:17-19? Was the test for God's benefit or for Abraham's?

GROWING UP IN GOD

Dear brothers and sisters, whenever trouble comes your way, let it be an opportunity for joy. For when your faith is tested, your endurance has a chance to grow. So let it grow, for when your endurance is fully developed, you will be strong in character and ready for anything. —James 1:2-4

I'm sure you know people who have claimed to have a relationship with Jesus for many years, and yet it seems that there has never been much transformation of their character or growth in their lives. They are still "babies" when it comes to matters of faith. But then you also probably know people who seem to have gone so far with God even though they've known him only a short time. This causes us to wonder, *What is the secret to becoming spiritually mature?*

Is it based on how long we have been a Christian? I don't think so. Is it as simple as going to church or attending a Bible study or reading books that increase our knowledge of spiritual things? Surely those things can help us grow, but are they the tools God uses to help us "grow up" in faith?

God's method of choice to help us to grow spiritually is suffering. But suffering itself doesn't do the job. It is how we respond to the suffering that determines if the pain will take us deeper in our walk with God. Paul said in Romans 5:3-4: "We can rejoice, too, when we run into problems and trials, for we know that they are good for us—they help us learn to endure. And endurance develops strength of character in us, and character strengthens our confident expectation of salvation." Both passages have the same formula: Responding to suffering in faith builds endurance, which develops character and results in spiritual maturity.

We grow when we persevere in faith through difficulties. Just experiencing the pain will not produce growth. But growth follows when we respond to the difficulties with an attitude of endurance that says, "This will not diminish my faith or trust in God. It will only cause me to dig deeper in my faith and seek to trust him more fully." Are you ready to go deeper with God as you grow older? Are you willing to suffer well, if that is what is required?

Lord, help me to see the difficulties in my life as opportunities to learn to persevere so that I will be strong in character and ready for anything.

DIGGING DEEPER

According to Ephesians 4:12-16 and Hebrews 5:12–6:3, what are the traits of a mature believer?

DISPLAYING THE GLORY OF GOD

"Teacher," his disciples asked him, "why was this man born blind? Was it a result of his own sins or those of his parents?" "It was not because of his sins or his parents' sins," Jesus answered. "He was born blind so the power of God could be seen in him." —John 9:2-3

Shortly after Hope's birth, we realized that it was going to be very difficult to explain her condition and our thoughts and feelings about it over and over. So we sent out a card to everyone we knew, explaining that her life would be very short. We closed by saying, "Our desire is that God would be glorified in our lives and in Hope's life in the months and years to come." From what I knew of Scripture, I believed that we had the ability to bring glory to God in how we responded and dealt day by day with this difficulty. I believed that the purpose of Hope's short life and my life was and is to glorify God.

But that belief became more real to me a few months later at the Good Friday service at our church, as David and I read the same lines we read each year, retelling the story of Creation and Redemption and the ancient prophecies fulfilled by Jesus. That year the words seemed to leap off the page. No longer was it necessary for me to interpret the whole of Scripture in my efforts to understand God's purpose in Hope's life. That night I read it clearly in Jesus' own words, spoken in response to the disciples when they asked why a man was born blind.

"Neither this man nor his parents sinned," said Jesus, "but this happened so that the work of God might be displayed in his life" (John 9:3, NIV).

Are you looking for purpose in your suffering? Would you be willing to make it your purpose to allow the work of God to be displayed in your life? The very glory of God can be displayed in your life in a way that is unmistakable. How? You can reflect the character of God in your response to suffering. Instead of demanding that God explain himself and his purpose, you can decide to trust him, recognizing that your circumstances provide an unparalleled opportunity to glorify God just by trusting in his purpose, even when you can't see that purpose.

Glorious God, it seems unimaginable that you would choose to reveal your glory through my life. But what a privilege! Would you show me what needs to be cleaned away so I might be a faithful reflection of who you are?

DIGGING DEEPER

According to 2 Corinthians 3:13-18, where is God's glory now seen? According to John 15:8, how do we bring glory to God?

TURNING MISERY INTO MINISTRY

When we are weighed down with troubles, it is for your benefit and salvation! For when God comforts us, it is so that we, in turn, can be an encouragement to you. Then you can patiently endure the same things we suffer. We are confident that as you share in suffering, you will also share God's comfort. —2 Corinthians 1:6-7

It was literally the Mother's Day of a lifetime. The only Mother's Day I would have with Hope. She was five months old, and I wanted to enjoy the gift of having her for this Mother's Day rather than focus on the reality that it would be our only one together, which it was.

As that day approached, and as I anticipated the mixture of joy and pain the day would bring for me, I began to think of people around me—people I knew who had lost their mothers that year and faced their first Mother's Day without their mother. I thought of those who had lost children and felt the void especially on that day. There were those who, like me, had children who would not live until the next Mother's Day and those who had never been able to conceive or carry a child successfully.

So I made a list and went to the store to buy Mother's Day cards. It's not easy to find a selection of cards for men who've lost their mothers or mothers who've lost children, so I had to improvise. But I sent out a big stack. Early Mother's Day morning, I called a woman in my church whose mother had died of breast cancer the month before. Then at church that morning, I looked over and saw a woman with four small children whose husband had recently left her. I walked over and wished her happy Mother's Day, telling her that I thought she was an incredible mother to her children. It seemed to matter. And my sorrow seemed to lift.

God often uses sorrow in our lives to open our eyes to the pain of others and to equip us to comfort them. Something good happens when we get our eyes off our own pain and minister out of it to hurting people. In the midst of comforting others through the power of the Holy Spirit, we find the comfort we crave.

Comforter, sometimes I feel so desperate to find something to soothe my heart and mind but I find no relief. Open my eyes to the hurts of those around me so that I can turn the misery in my life into ministry by comforting others.

DIGGING DEEPER

What does 2 Corinthians 1:3-7 teach us about the source and purpose of real comfort?

WEEK 36

FINDING PURPOSE IN PAIN

REFLECTION

How has suffering allowed your faith to be proved genuine? How has it revealed a lack of faith in your life?

Are you content to stay where you are, or do you really want to grow up in your faith? How will you need to adjust your attitude toward suffering to allow it to help you become more spiritually mature?

MEDITATION

We know that God causes everything to work together for the good of those who love God and are called according to his purpose for them. —Romans 8:28

Read through this verse slowly several times, carefully considering the meaning each word adds to the whole.

Insert into the verse specific circumstances and experiences from your life in place of the word *everything.*

PRAYER

Praise God the Redeemer for his ability to infuse the most seemingly senseless suffering with meaning and purpose.

Thank God for the gift of pain that causes us to turn to him.

Intercede for those around you who are hurting. Pray that they would experience the joy of discovering that faith works and that their faith is the real thing.

Confess your tendency to look for comfort in other places, people, and pursuits rather than in God himself. Confess your unwillingness to make comforting others in pain a priority.

Petition God to meet you where you are right now, and commit to see the difficulty in your life as a tool he wants to use to help you mature spiritually.

WEEK 37

FRUITFULNESS

What does it mean to be fruitful? You bear inner fruit when you allow God to nurture in you a new, Christlike quality. Bearing inner fruit can be as simple as new growth of contentment and gratitude where there once was only a grumbling and complaining spirit, as profound as forgiveness flowering in a field of bitterness.

You bear outward fruit when you allow God to work through you to bring him glory. It can be something as simple as painting the house of a disabled neighbor out of love for Jesus or as all-encompassing as giving your life as a tribal missionary out of obedience to Jesus. Outward fruit appears when your inner motive is to bring glory to God.

God created you to bear fruit . . . to be his hands and feet on earth. And in complete contrast to what the world tells us, a life of joy and fulfillment doesn't come from looking out for ourselves. The abundant life comes from bearing fruit for Christ. Jesus wants to transform the landscape of our lives from bleak to beautiful, from barrenness to bounty.

THIS WEEK'S PASSAGE FOR MEDITATION

I am the true vine, and my Father is the gardener. He cuts off every branch that doesn't produce fruit, and he prunes the branches that do bear fruit so they will produce even more. You have already been pruned for greater fruitfulness by the message I have given you. Remain in me, and I will remain in you. For a branch cannot produce fruit if it is severed from the vine, and you cannot be fruitful apart from me. Yes, I am the vine; you are the branches. Those who remain in me, and I in them, will produce much fruit. For apart from me you can do nothing. Anyone who parts from me is thrown away like a useless branch and withers. Such branches are gathered into a pile to be burned. But if you stay joined to me and my words remain in you, you may ask any request you like, and it will be granted! My true disciples produce much fruit. This brings great glory to my Father.

—John 15:1-8

FRUITFUL IN THE LAND OF SUFFERING

JOSEPH NAMED HIS OLDER SON MANASSEH, FOR HE SAID, "GOD HAS MADE ME FORGET ALL MY TROUBLES AND THE FAMILY OF MY FATHER." JOSEPH NAMED HIS SECOND SON EPHRAIM, FOR HE SAID, "GOD HAS MADE ME FRUITFUL IN THIS LAND OF MY SUFFERING."
—GENESIS 41:51-52

The first time I heard Pastor Jim Cymbala preach, he preached on these verses. That day, his message seemed to be just for me. The process of leaving a job I loved had left me ripe for bitterness. Pastor Cymbala described what it meant for Joseph, who had so many justifiable reasons to hold a grudge against his brothers, to experience the forgiving power of God in his life to the extent that he would name his firstborn son "God has made me forget all my troubles and the family of my father." Giving his son this name was his way of celebrating a supernatural work of God in the interior of his life. I don't know how anyone can truly forgive others for significant betrayal without a work of God. God not only enabled Joseph to forgive, but also helped him to forget. While I imagine Joseph had memories of the hurt, when he thought of what had been done to him, it no longer brought a sting in his soul.

Years after that sermon, a friend sent me a note after listening to a tape of me speaking to a group of women about what God was teaching me, recorded when Hope was about five months old. She told me she saw in my life what Joseph experienced in his: "God has made me fruitful in this land of my suffering" (Genesis 41:52).

It is one thing to experience significant suffering and to see with hindsight what God has done and how he has used it for good. It's far more thrilling when we begin to allow God to use the suffering in our lives even while we are in the midst of it. God does not want to wait until everything is perfect in your life to begin to use you. He wants you to be fruitful right now, in the midst of your pain . . . perhaps uniquely because of your pain. Would you be willing to ask God to begin to use you even now as you live in a land of suffering? You may have to surrender your own agenda and set aside your self-pity, but the fruit will be so sweet.

Oh God who makes me forget my sorrow and makes me fruitful in my suffering, how I want to celebrate the birth of a Manasseh and an Ephraim in my life. You are the power behind that possibility, but how I need you to plow up my life so you can do your work.

DIGGING DEEPER

What three kinds of fruit do you find in John 4:36; Romans 7:4; and Philippians 1:11?

PRUNED FOR GREATER FRUITFULNESS

I AM THE TRUE VINE, AND MY FATHER IS THE GARDENER. HE CUTS OFF EVERY BRANCH THAT DOESN'T PRODUCE FRUIT, AND HE PRUNES THE BRANCHES THAT DO BEAR FRUIT SO THEY WILL PRODUCE EVEN MORE. YOU HAVE ALREADY BEEN PRUNED FOR GREATER FRUITFULNESS BY THE MESSAGE I HAVE GIVEN YOU. —JOHN 15:1-3

One Saturday morning all our neighbors met in our front yard to plant a tree in honor of Hope. Their desire was that its blossoms would serve as a reminder of her life. Each spring the blossoms on Hope's tree come and go quickly (which somehow seems appropriate). But the tree has been looking a little sickly of late (which also seems appropriate). One large branch is producing no new growth and is going to have to be removed. Other healthy parts of the tree need to be pruned so that all the branches will have more blossoms.

Just as our "Hope Tree" needs the careful cutting of an expert gardener if we want to enjoy its blooms, so our lives need the attention of our Father, the gardener, if we want to be fruitful. God's strategy for coaxing a greater harvest out of his branches is not the one you and I would prefer. His plan is to prune, which means to thin, reduce, and cut away. But he is an expert pruner. He never pinches or cuts too soon lest he damage a tender branch. He knows exactly which of our parts need to be pruned and exactly how much.

Have you asked God to make you more like him and to use you in a significant way? His pruning is his answer to your prayers. In pruning, God cuts away commitments that would sap you of time and energy for him. He severs relationships that are not nourishing your growth. He clips your wings so in the stillness you can hear his voice. His careful pruning clears away the things that keep you from becoming all he means for you to be.

Pruning is cutting, and cutting hurts. In fact, God's pruning may have left you feeling like a bare, bleeding stump, wondering what he is going to cut away next. He will not stop tending your life, and really, you don't want him to. The fact that he is cutting away things in your life reveals that he is carefully cultivating you for growth. How much more fruit would you produce if you were to submit more fully to the pruning of the Gardener's shears?

Master Gardener, how I want your careful tending of my life, and yet I flinch at the sound of your shears. But do your pruning. Cut away anything and everything that keeps me from bearing more fruit for you.

DIGGING DEEPER

What do Isaiah 42:3 and Hebrews 12:11 reveal about God's motive and method in pruning?

FRUIT PRODUCED BY THE SPIRIT

When the Holy Spirit controls our lives, he will produce this kind of fruit in us: love, joy, peace, patience, kindness, goodness, faithfulness, gentleness, and self-control. —Galatians 5:22-23

I've been making an unofficial list for a while now—a list of songs I can go my whole life without ever hearing or singing again. At the top of the list is "For Those Tears I Died" (sorry if you wrote it or love it). Although I'm not sure it is officially on the list, another song I grew to dislike from overuse in youth ministry settings was "Peace like a River."

At church one Sunday about ten years ago, I looked over the order of worship and saw we were going to sing the familiar chorus. I wondered why we had to drag that meaningless oldie out. But then we began to sing. Tears come even now as I remember. The preceding months had brought about significant change in my life. I was studying the Bible for myself as I never had before, and it was doing its work; it was changing me. And it felt great! As the Holy Spirit spoke to me through the pages of Scripture to convict me of sin, I began to repent—not just feel bad, but to really turn away from my old ways and welcome the fresh air of the Spirit of God into new areas of my life.

That morning, as I began to sing, "I've got peace like a river, I've got peace like a river in my soul . . . I've got joy like a fountain," I began to weep because I realized that it was true! No longer was I simply going through the motions of religion as I had done for so long. I had a peace I had not known before, a joy that was fresh and new, and I was falling in love with Jesus in a way I never had before.

That's fruitfulness. It's not simply a work he wants you to do. It is a work he wants to do *in* you, in the interior of your life, in the transformation of your character. It is not a matter of working harder to be more loving or more joyful. The fruit of the Spirit is not a to-do list; neither is it a menu of options. It is more like a portrait that shows us what a life looks like when God is at work. We can never expect to be perfectly patient or exercise perfect self-control, but isn't this fruit of the Spirit what we want to see growing in our lives? Isn't this the kind of fruit you want to see flourish?

Cultivator of peace and joy, how I want to see your Spirit at work in the barrenness and brokenness of my life, blossoming forth in beauty. I'm tired of trying to change on my own. I want to give you control and let you do your work.

DIGGING DEEPER

Read what Jesus said in Matthew 7:15-20 about good fruit and bad fruit.

FIRSTFRUITS

As you harvest each of your crops, bring me a choice sample of the first day's harvest. It must be offered to the Lord your God. —Exodus 23:19

"Why does God always get the old piano?" This is a question I heard Jill Briscoe ask in a message years ago. It is a question she had first asked when there was a need for a piano at her church and someone donated an old piano that had seen better days. She couldn't understand why we offer God our castoffs and leftovers rather than our very best. It is a worthwhile question. I think of it every time I am tempted to feel noble and generous when giving away something of value that I no longer use or need.

In the annual firstfruits offering of grain or fruit initiated in the Old Testament, God's people were to bring to the Temple the very best of their harvest. But it was even more than that. They were not to wait until the full harvest was done; they were to bring the very best of what was first, before they even knew if more would be harvested. Firstfruits means "a promise to come." The firstfruits offering was a step of faith, trusting God with their first and best, trusting that he would take care of them whether the rest of the harvest was plenteous or scarce.

In this Old Testament shadow, we see what God wants from us. He is pleased when we offer up to him our firstfruits, when we give him the best of our day rather than giving him only what we can squeeze in around other appointments. He smiles when we write out our tithe check at the beginning of the month rather than waiting to see if the cash is on hand after other bills are paid. God wants the best of our creativity, the best of our energy. He wants us to "seek first his kingdom" (Matthew 6:33, NIV).

Do you feel that you have been called to sacrifice what is most precious to you? Do you wonder if God appreciates your extra effort, if he notices when you go the extra mile out of love for him? This is a special offering to God, and because what you have given is precious to you, it is precious to him.

Lord of the harvest, I see I have dishonored you with my halfhearted giving—offering to you the leftovers of my time, energy, and other resources. I want to give to you my firstfruits, knowing it will be a sacrifice for me but that it will be especially pleasing to you.

DIGGING DEEPER

According to Romans 8:29 and 1 Corinthians 15:20, what firstfruit did God give out of love for us? According to James 1:18, who are his firstfruits now?

LEAVES THAT NEVER WITHER

DAY AND NIGHT THEY THINK ABOUT [GOD'S] LAW. THEY ARE LIKE TREES PLANTED ALONG THE RIVERBANK, BEARING FRUIT EACH SEASON WITHOUT FAIL. THEIR LEAVES NEVER WITHER, AND IN ALL THEY DO, THEY PROSPER. —PSALM 1:2-3

While many people ask Anne Graham Lotz what it is like to be the daughter of Billy Graham, she will tell you that being the daughter of Ruth Bell Graham is far more intimidating. Her mother is witty and wise, creative and kind. Anne remembers how her mother would put all of the children to bed and then spread out several translations of the Bible to study into the night. Early in the morning Anne would awaken to find her mother reading her Bible. Living the life of a single parent while her husband traveled the world to preach, Ruth found her source of strength in God's Word.

This is the kind of person the writer of Psalm 1 had in mind, a person whose thoughts are drawn day and night to God's Word, not out of obligation, but because the pages of Scripture offer the nourishment we need. People who are drawn to God's Word are fruitful even when the hot winds of adversity blow and even while they wait for the gentle rain of relief. Their fruitfulness is not dependent on the proper atmospheric conditions but on being planted in the right place—a place where their roots can go deep into God's Word, which feeds them in the deepest places of their thirsty souls. People who have deep roots in the soil of God's Word are steadily nourished by its life-giving streams. They overflow with deep-seated joy and contentment; they flower with green goodness, fed by an inner spring of delight in God's Word. They are renewed and refreshed by the truths of Scripture. In its pages they find life-giving insight, an alternative to the life-draining triviality of the world.

Is it really possible to bear fruit *without fail* and to prosper in *all* you do? It is absolutely possible to the extent that you stay connected to your source, drinking up the living water of the Word. You do not have to give up on fruitfulness in the dry seasons of life, as long as you continue in consistent contemplation and internalization of God's Word. What a rich and rewarding life awaits us as our roots go deeper into God's Word.

River of life, how I long for my roots to drink steadily of your living water so I need never wither in the dry and difficult seasons of life. Your Word is life, and it is the ultimate source for never-fading, ever-flowering fruitfulness.

DIGGING DEEPER

What does Isaiah 55 say about where to find the nourishment that produces fruit?

WEEK 37

FRUITFULNESS

REFLECTION

What inner fruit is growing in your character, and what outer fruit is evident in your good deeds?

What can you do so that you will be more firmly planted in the Word of God? How can you be more open to the Holy Spirit to fill you so that you can bear more fruit?

MEDITATION

I am the true vine, and my Father is the gardener. He cuts off every branch that doesn't produce fruit, and he prunes the branches that do bear fruit so they will produce even more. You have already been pruned for greater fruitfulness by the message I have given you. Remain in me, and I will remain in you. For a branch cannot produce fruit if it is severed from the vine, and you cannot be fruitful apart from me. Yes, I am the vine; you are the branches. Those who remain in me, and I in them, will produce much fruit. For apart from me you can do nothing. Anyone who parts from me is thrown away like a useless branch and withers. Such branches are gathered into a pile to be burned. But if you stay joined to me and my words remain in you, you may ask any request you like, and it will be granted! My true disciples produce much fruit. This brings great glory to my Father.

—John 15:1-8

Enter the garden with Jesus and see the vines he uses as an illustration of his invitation for you to abide in him.

Read through his words several times, marking the phrases that speak to you most, noting especially the action words.

Meditate on his words, seeking to be joined to him and to have his words remain in you.

PRAYER

Pray through the passage, praising God for being the true and living vine.

Thank him for his promise to remain in you and to work through you.

Confess the areas of your life that are unproductive, and ask him to prune from your life whatever hinders your fruitfulness.

Intercede for those who have no connection to the vine, no source for the nourishment they need for life.

Ask him to keep you abiding in him so that you can produce much fruit and bring him great glory.

WEEK 38

PEOPLE

One of the best things and one of the worst things about going through a significant trial is people. We were often utterly amazed and deeply touched by the kindness shown to us by people we knew well, people we barely knew, and complete strangers. To feel the tangible love of others, the love of God with human skin, in the low points of life is an indescribable comfort and joy.

However, people sometimes magnified and added to our suffering. Their difficult questions, unwanted advice, and thoughtless comments left us reeling to find our balance. The awkward silences and averted eyes magnified our loneliness even in a crowded room.

So what are we going to do with people? Can't live with 'em, can't live without 'em, right? It's going to take a lot of grace to get through this. It's going to take a lot of courage to rise above this. It's going to take a lot of forgiveness to get past this.

But people are worth the pain. God gives us people to help soften the pain.

THIS WEEK'S PASSAGE FOR MEDITATION

All praise to the God and Father of our Lord Jesus Christ. He is the source of every mercy and the God who comforts us. He comforts us in all our troubles so that we can comfort others. When others are troubled, we will be able to give them the same comfort God has given us. You can be sure that the more we suffer for Christ, the more God will shower us with his comfort through Christ. So when we are weighed down with troubles, it is for your benefit and salvation! For when God comforts us, it is so that we, in turn, can be an encouragement to you. Then you can patiently endure the same things we suffer. We are confident that as you share in suffering, you will also share God's comfort.

—2 Corinthians 1:3-7

ONE THING TO HELP THE PAIN

DON'T THINK ONLY ABOUT YOUR OWN AFFAIRS, BUT BE INTERESTED IN OTHERS, TOO, AND WHAT THEY ARE DOING. —PHILIPPIANS 2:4

The week after Hope died, I was sitting on the couch reading a book by a man who had lost a child. He wrote, "There's only one thing I've found that helps with the pain." You would have thought I was in the desert and he was telling me where to find water. I wanted to skip ahead. I wanted to know, *What is it that will soothe this enormous ache inside me?* Then I read it: "serving others." Honestly, I felt disappointed. *That's it?* I thought. A part of me said he was just a preacher who was giving me the party line. But I also thought that someone who has hurt like he had hurt would not lie to me about where to find comfort. And so even though I didn't really believe him, I decided to put what he said to the test. I was desperate.

My friend Angela had just moved into a house in our neighborhood. The house had been empty for a while. The landscaping was badly in need of attention, and I knew she, as a widow, was overwhelmed with moving into a new house. So we loaded up our lawn tools and went to her house. We pulled weeds and trimmed hedges—and we wept, for ourselves and for her. As I exerted energy in serving someone else, and more significantly, as I thought about what it was like for her to move away from the home she had lived in with her husband to set up a new home without him, my focus moved from my pain to hers. And it was a relief. It was a distraction. It was an outlet. It was a step toward healing. That day I discovered the secret of serving for myself.

You may be skeptical as I was. But would you consider putting this to the test? Some people have told me they simply can't start reaching out to other people until their load of grief lightens. But it is the reaching out to others in the midst of your pain, uniquely because of your pain, that is the secret to lightening your unbearable load. You can keep sitting around waiting to feel better, or you can get up, look around, and seek out someone to serve. Prove me wrong on this. I dare you.

I am overwhelmed with my pain, Lord, and I find it hard to believe that I could find the strength to serve someone else or that it would make any difference. But I want to step out in faith, believing you will meet me there and ease my pain.

DIGGING DEEPER

What do we learn from Jesus' example and instruction about serving others in Matthew 20:25-28 and 25:31-36?

MISERABLE COMFORTERS

What miserable comforters you are! Won't you ever stop your flow of foolish words? What have I said that makes you speak so endlessly? —Job 16:2-3

We have a friend who was recently diagnosed with breast cancer, and in the days following the dreadful diagnosis, many people were anxious to tell her the stories of people they know who have faced breast cancer. There is just one problem—many of the women in the stories died, and the storytellers were so excited to relate to her how happy the cancer victims' husbands were with their new wives! *Gee, thanks so much for telling me!*

David and I have a theory about this. We've decided that when people hear about the difficulty in your life, their brain, like a computer, goes on a search, looking for a connection. Because they don't know what else to say and in an effort to fill up the awkward silence, people tend to say the first thing that comes up as a connection. "I knew a family who had this happen . . ." Sometimes it feels like a subtle effort to diminish our suffering, as if because the same or worse has happened to someone else in the world, it shouldn't hurt us quite so much. I'm not sure why, but people have this tendency to want to compare pain. *This is harder than that; that would be worse than this.* But you can't really compare pain. It all just hurts.

People are so quick to tell stories about other people who have faced similar losses. It makes them feel better to suggest a solution, a book, an expert, but it doesn't always make us feel better, does it? People are hoping to be helpful, trying to let us know that they can relate. If we put ourselves in their shoes, we realize that it is really hard to know what to say to someone who is suffering, isn't it? So we can be prickly and sensitive about the things people say to us that we wish they hadn't. Or we can choose to see their brains at work searching for a connection, their hearts wanting to show us they care even though they simply don't have the words to express it well. Won't you decide to give people grace and determine not to make the same mistake yourself when you encounter people who are hurting?

My best Comforter, I feel hurt and disappointed by the thoughtless things people have said to me in my pain and by those who have said nothing at all. Will you give me the grace to lower my expectations and let go of my hurt?

DIGGING DEEPER

What do you learn from the following verses about what we should and shouldn't say to others: 1 Corinthians 2:6-13; 1 Thessalonians 2:4; and James 4:11?

SHARING JOY, SHARING SORROW

When others are happy, be happy with them. If they are sad, share their sorrow. —Romans 12:15

I pulled up behind my friend Jan in front of the school, and when she got out of her SUV there were tears on her face—tears for me. She felt bad that her tears might make me hurt worse (as if that were possible at the time), but their impact was just the opposite. In those days, it was as if David and I were carrying a heavy load of sorrow, and when she cried, it was as if she were taking a bucket load of sorrow and carrying it for us. It was a relief. Her tears revealed how deeply she shared my sorrow, and they helped me not feel so alone. This is the beauty of having friends who are willing to let us be sad without trying to fix us, people are willing to simply share our sorrow.

When we are hurting, we like the part of the verse that tells people to "weep with those who weep." But we think that we're exempt from the first part, "Rejoice with those who rejoice" (Romans 12:15, NKJV). Those of us who are sad find it very difficult to be happy with others when they are happy, to enter into the joys of their lives. It is painful and costly to celebrate the joys and successes of other people when we are weighed down by our own sorrows, losses, and failures—especially when their gain is exactly what we've lost. The ugly truth is, while we don't think their happiness should keep them from sharing our sorrow, we see our sadness as an adequate excuse for refusing to enter into their joy.

Do you think your suffering provides an excuse for you to step back from others, unwilling to feel what they feel, whether it is joy or sorrow? Must your suffering and sorrow continue to be at the forefront of your mind and the determining factor of your give-ability? Have you allowed yourself to become that self-centered? If so, aren't you ready to break free from it? What a relief, really, to not make everything about you anymore, to no longer have everyone tiptoeing around your feelings and sensitivities. There is something that feels better than sympathy: admiration. When you genuinely share the joy of someone who is happy, someone who is celebrating a joy that has been taken from you, it does not go unnoticed. Others will see and admire you. More important, God will see and applaud you.

Man of Sorrows, Source of joy, it is your Spirit inside me that enables me to share the joys and sorrows of those around me. Let me feel your pleasure in my life as I abandon my excuses and enter into the feelings of others.

DIGGING DEEPER

Explore and apply the other practical life instructions in Romans 12.

BLESSED GIVERS, GRACIOUS RECEIVERS

YOU SHOULD REMEMBER THE WORDS OF THE LORD JESUS: "IT IS MORE BLESSED TO GIVE THAN TO RECEIVE." —ACTS 20:35

After Hope was born, as my first-rate friends circled around us and began making meals, washing clothes, even putting up our Christmas tree, I was very aware of all that people were doing for us. I began to wonder how I was ever going to pay everyone back. For a while, at least, I held on to the folly that I would one day return the favors. But I quickly figured out I would never be able to repay all that people were doing for me and for my family. I was bankrupt to repay them. I had to surrender to receiving from others. And for us list-keepers and fairness-watchers, that's not easy. It is much more comfortable for someone to owe us a favor than to be in another person's debt. It is humbling to receive—to really receive with grace, with no thought of trying to pay back.

But as it began to dawn on me that nobody wanted me to pay them back, I began to learn to receive gracefully. Nobody was keeping score. They wanted the joy and delight—the blessedness—of giving to me. I began to see that people wanted to find some way to help us in our helpless situation, and that when they did, they experienced the blessing of giving. I came to truly believe that it is more blessed to give than to receive—that all the people who did my laundry and made my family a meal, those who helped with Hope or gave Matt rides, were blessed by it. They were blessed by doing for us, giving to us. What a freedom there is in becoming comfortable receiving and therefore allowing others the blessedness of giving.

By the time Gabe came to us I was free. When people expressed a desire to do something for us, I looked for something for them to do rather than dismissing their offers, because I wanted them to experience the blessing of giving. Have you learned yet how to receive from others who want to reach out and serve you or give to you? Will you humble yourself and receive graciously?

Great Giver, I have so much to learn about what it means both to give sacrificially and receive graciously. Thank you for blessing the people who have reached out and served me. Help me not to rob them of that blessing by refusing to humble myself and receive.

DIGGING DEEPER

Read Acts 20. What was Paul's situation, and what point was he trying to make to the Ephesian Christians by quoting these words of Jesus?

MAKING PEACE WITH PEOPLE

TAKE A NEW GRIP WITH YOUR TIRED HANDS AND STAND FIRM ON YOUR SHAKY LEGS. MARK OUT A STRAIGHT PATH FOR YOUR FEET. THEN THOSE WHO FOLLOW YOU, THOUGH THEY ARE WEAK AND LAME, WILL NOT STUMBLE AND FALL BUT WILL BECOME STRONG. TRY TO LIVE IN PEACE WITH EVERYONE. —HEBREWS 12:12-14

A few weeks after Hope died I was walking from one building at our church to another. My timing was bad. As I came out the door, four or five women emerged from the nursery building walking toward me with babies in their arms. I'm not sure who was more alarmed, them or me. I wanted to turn and run, to not have to face them or the awkwardness, but I also knew this was my chance—my chance to set these women at ease with me and my grief.

You see, I figured out early on that on top of being the one to bear the grief, I also bore most of the responsibility for making things okay for the women around me with babies. They felt awkward that they had children in their arms while mine were empty. Now it didn't seem fair to me that this was up to me, but one thing we've figured out by now is that life isn't fair, right? I realized that I could do what seemed natural—avoid these women and perhaps even resent them—or I could step up to the plate and seek to overcome the hurdle of awkwardness with each one and set us both free to enjoy each other. That Sunday morning I stopped to greet the first woman I came to, smiling and stroking the hair of her daughter, Joy, born eight days before Hope, as all the other women filed by. Then I went to my car and cried.

If you've lost something—be it your spouse or your house or your health—everywhere you look, you see people with loving partners, beautiful homes, and healthy bodies. And even though you don't begrudge them the joy of these things, they are a reminder of what you've lost. Let's face it, we're human and it's hard. So you have a choice. You can let everyone walk on eggshells around you. You can wait for them to do or say the right thing (if there is a right thing) that will make it okay with you. You can give in to your fear that things will never be normal with certain people again. Or you can extend yourself and do your part to set things on the pathway toward normalcy and wholeness. You can overcome the awkwardness and live in peace. This is what you want and what God wants for you.

Peace Maker, I'm so tired of avoiding people and feeling awkward around people. I want to knock over the barriers that have built up between me and people around me. Give me the grace and strength to live at peace with everyone.

DIGGING DEEPER

Read what it means to love each other well in 1 John 3:11-20 and 4:7-21.

WEEK 38
PEOPLE

REFLECTION

What have others done or said that has been helpful to you? What have they said or done that has been hurtful?

In what ways could you serve others out of your suffering? How could you become a better receiver and barrier breaker?

MEDITATION

All praise to the God and Father of our Lord Jesus Christ. He is the source of every mercy and the God who comforts us. He comforts us in all our troubles so that we can comfort others. When others are troubled, we will be able to give them the same comfort God has given us. You can be sure that the more we suffer for Christ, the more God will shower us with his comfort through Christ. So when we are weighed down with troubles, it is for your benefit and salvation! For when God comforts us, it is so that we, in turn, can be an encouragement to you. Then you can patiently endure the same things we suffer. We are confident that as you share in suffering, you will also share God's comfort.

—2 Corinthians 1:3-7

Read through the passage several times, marking the words and phrases that are most meaningful to you.

Embrace the beautiful purpose of suffering revealed in these verses, and envision yourself fulfilling this purpose in comforting others with the comfort you've received.

PRAYER

Praise God as the Source of every mercy and for being the God who comforts us.

Thank God for the people around you who have graciously and generously shown you the love and comfort of God in your suffering.

Intercede for those who suffer as you do but do not have the resources of friends and family that you have.

Confess your self-centeredness and sensitivity over what people have said and done or *not* said and *not* done, as well as your resistance to receiving from others graciously.

Ask God to set you free from such high expectations of others and to show you who you can serve and how to do it well.

WEEK 39

SELF

I have had a great fear while working on this book. I've been afraid that you will get completely sick of me, weary of my story, and irritated by my style. The reason I fear this is because I get so sick of myself! Sick of hearing myself talk, sick of stories about myself. Sick of my thoughts and ideas.

At the same time, I love to talk about myself. I love to give my opinion. I thrill at the sound of my own voice.

Sick of ourselves and yet so in love with ourselves. Isn't that how we are? This life is an unending battle between our flesh that cries out to be served and the Spirit that calls for us to deny ourselves. Somehow, I know deep down that if my flesh wins, I lose. And I know that as I focus more fully on Jesus, I'm simply not so enamored with myself. *So Spirit, have your way in me! Quiet me, control me, and humble me. Fill me so I won't be so full of myself.*

THIS WEEK'S PASSAGE FOR MEDITATION

Jesus said to the disciples, "If any of you wants to be my follower, you must put aside your selfish ambition, shoulder your cross, and follow me. If you try to keep your life for yourself, you will lose it. But if you give up your life for me, you will find true life. And how do you benefit if you gain the whole world but lose your own soul in the process? Is anything worth more than your soul?" —MATTHEW 16:24-26

SELF-PITY VS. SELFLESSNESS

I am disgusted with my life. Let me complain freely. I will speak in the bitterness of my soul. —Job 10:1

There have been plenty of days when I have wanted to do nothing more than indulge in an enormous pity party, feeling that I've earned it. And there's no question that self-pity feels good . . . for a while. At first it feels warm and comforting, but it quickly becomes cold and corrosive. It's like a little monster from a Saturday afternoon movie—if you feed it at all, it becomes bigger and bigger until it overpowers you. In reality, the self-pity we think will salve our wounds only serves to keep opening them.

We think that the sympathy of others is the antidote to our misery. So we invite guests to our pity party. And when they arrive we derive sadistic satisfaction from seeing them shake their heads at how hard our life is and from hearing them agree that we've set a new record for personal pain. But this satisfaction is short-lived. After a while we become sickened by a steady diet of sympathy.

Indulging ourselves in the luxury of misery requires a convenient amnesia of the provision of God's grace and riches in our lives. It puts our own self-interests on the throne of our lives so that we worship them rather than God. It blinds us to seeing that God has used difficulty to bring us to the entryway of his purpose for our lives. So we collapse in a heap, and if we do not get up and enter into what God wants to do in our lives, our spirits begin a slow death. The sympathy we engender from those around us simply tucks us comfortably into our deathbed.

Are you about ready to call it quits on your personal pity party? There is a simple cure for self-pity. It is selflessness—caring for someone else's needs more than your own. This is the only cure that works for me. So when I feel myself spiraling downward, I pick up the phone—not to complain to someone who will pity me, but to care for someone else who is hurting. When tempted toward self-pity, would you take your eyes off your troubles and look around for someone to serve? Would you offer a helping hand and a listening ear, the selfless fruit of your own broken heart?

God, I have become sickened by the sympathy of others and by my own self-pity. Will you save me from myself? Draw my eyes toward you and my heart toward the needs of others.

DIGGING DEEPER

What happened when God showed up at pity parties in Jonah 4 and 1 Kings 19?

SELF-FORGETFULNESS VS. SELF-PROMOTION

HE MUST BECOME GREATER AND GREATER, AND I MUST BECOME LESS AND LESS.
—JOHN 3:30

I'm a publicist by profession. Publishing companies hire me to get coverage in the media for their books and authors. And I love it . . . usually. Actually, I've learned that the authors I love to publicize the most are those who want it the least. Some authors have seen it as my job to make them a star, to make sure they get noticed, and when the media or the public doesn't respond, they are sure something has gone wrong somewhere. I've always been drawn to people who shun the spotlight, or better said, the ones who simply want to use the platform God has given them to shine the spotlight on Jesus.

These are people who impress me not with their ability or promotability but with their humility. And I know this desire doesn't flow out of insecurity but out of sincerity. They desire for God to be glorified and shudder at the thought of stealing God's glory for themselves. But that doesn't mean they don't sometimes struggle or that such self-deprecation comes easily or naturally. Self-promotion comes naturally to most of us, and my humble clients are no different. But they've decided they want their lives to reflect the desires of John the Baptist, who said about Jesus, "He must become greater and greater, and I must become less and less."

That's what it is all about, isn't it? Shouldn't this be the joy and passion of our lives? For Jesus to become bigger in our estimation and in the eyes of the world? For Jesus to shine brighter than any other star in the universe, including our own? For Jesus to take the throne he deserves in the heavens and in our hearts? It's what we want and yet there's a rub. For Jesus to become greater, we must become less. Our agenda must become less important so his agenda can chart our course. Our earthly appetites must be subdued so our appetite for him can be unleashed. Our afflictions must leave center stage so that his love for the world can be made visible in us and through us.

First Peter 5:6 in *The Message* reads, "So be content with who you are, and don't put on airs. God's strong hand is on you; he'll promote you at the right time." Aren't you ready to stop promoting yourself so you can enjoy the freedom of forgetting about yourself? Won't you let his star shine bright?

Beautiful Jesus, you are the brightest star in the heavens, and I worship you. As you become greater in my life, I'm finding joy and freedom in forgetting about myself. You must become even greater, and I, less and less.

DIGGING DEEPER

Read John 3:22-36 to see the ways John the Baptist considered Jesus superior.

SELF-CONFIDENCE VS. GOD-RELIANCE

We were crushed and completely overwhelmed, and we thought we would never live through it. In fact, we expected to die. But as a result, we learned not to rely on ourselves, but on God who can raise the dead.
—2 Corinthians 1:8-9

I was in a conversation with a woman who is grieving for all the ways caring for her hydrocephalic daughter has affected her family and especially her marriage. She was especially dreading the increase in seizures the medical experts had told her to expect over the coming months. And then she said something I've heard many times: "But I know God will not give me more than I can handle."

"I don't think that's true," I told her. "That little quip is based on a misunderstanding of 1 Corinthians 10:13, which says that God will not allow us to be tempted beyond what we can withstand, but God never promised not to give you more difficulty or distress than you are able to handle on your own. In fact, I think he often gives us much more than we can handle so our eyes will be opened to how desperate we are for him."

The ethos of our world is to bury our natural sense of inadequacy and inability in an avalanche of pep talks, telling ourselves, *I can do it. I just need to believe in myself.* Although we're aiming for increased self-confidence, most of us fail in our efforts to appear self-reliant and self-assured, cool and in control (which is why falling or failing in public is so humiliating). But this failure is good for us. It helps us to stop kidding ourselves. Rather than seeking to become more self-confident, we need to strive to become more God-reliant, and if we want to do that, we have to root out our desire to appear all together and in control. This desire has deep roots. As we see in 2 Corinthians 1, it was so deeply rooted in Paul that God was still using hardship to increase his God-reliance twenty years into his missionary ministry.

What difference would it make in your attitude toward your struggles if you saw them as valued lessons in God-dependency? When you come to the end of your rope, can you see that you've finally arrived just where God wants you? At the end of your own intellectual, physical, and emotional resources, you can more fully depend on his. This is what he wants for you.

All-sufficient Savior, here I am at the end of myself, and now I find out this is just where you want me to be. Here I find you. Use the struggles in my life to make me less self-confident and self-reliant and more God-dependent.

DIGGING DEEPER

Read 2 Corinthians 1:8-11. What role did intercessory prayer play in Paul's challenges?

SELF-CENTERED VS. SELF-SACRIFICIAL

LIVE A LIFE FILLED WITH LOVE FOR OTHERS, FOLLOWING THE EXAMPLE OF CHRIST, WHO LOVED YOU AND GAVE HIMSELF AS A SACRIFICE TO TAKE AWAY YOUR SINS.
—EPHESIANS 5:2

It was an uncanny turn of events. The Saturday before Gabe was born we found ourselves in the neonatal ICU at the hospital. A virus had infected the heart of our pediatrician's newborn son, and at just three weeks old, he was in desperate need of a heart transplant. As we talked with Dr. Ladd in the corridor, he explained that the typical waiting time for a heart to become available was six weeks and that his son, Luke, had just two or three weeks to live without a new heart. It looked as if our doctor, who had taken such sweet care of Hope in life and death, might be facing the death of his own child.

Miraculously, a heart became available the next day, and Luke had his transplant surgery that Sunday night. Gabe was born the next morning, and we were amazed when Dr. Ladd came to see us and check up on Gabe. We were touched by his willingness to leave his own son to see ours, but it wasn't until days later that I learned the true extent of our doctor's selflessness. One of the NICU nurses, who attends the same church as Dr. Ladd, told me that on that Sunday morning, while they were still waiting for a heart for their son, Dr. Ladd submitted a prayer request. But it wasn't for Luke. It was for us.

I'm still touched and amazed when I remember—touched that we would be on the forefront of his mind, amazed that he found room in his heart for us when the need of his family was so great and his burden was so heavy. His simple prayer request is such a beautiful picture of what it means to live a life full of love for others, to make room for the concerns of others in our hearts.

Christ has set the example for loving each other in this self-sacrificial way. He has shown us the extent love goes to, how much love gives. We simply can't wait until all our needs are met and our comforts are secure to follow his example. To love others in a sacrificial way means coming alongside others even when we are looking for support; it means lifting others up even while we are sinking. Love lays down its life for the lives of others.

My Example in self-sacrifice, I am so full of my own concerns I sometimes feel I have no time or energy, and honestly, little genuine compassion for the needs of others. Help me to follow your example of self-giving. Show me how to live a life filled with love for others.

DIGGING DEEPER

What do Romans 8:3; Hebrews 9:14; and 1 John 2:2 tell us about the willingness of Jesus to sacrifice himself and what that sacrifice accomplished?

SELF-MINISTRY VS. SELF-MEDICATION

LET'S SEE IF YOUR IDOLS CAN DO ANYTHING FOR YOU WHEN YOU CRY TO THEM FOR HELP. THEY ARE SO HELPLESS THAT A BREATH OF WIND CAN KNOCK THEM DOWN! BUT WHOEVER TRUSTS IN ME WILL POSSESS THE LAND AND INHERIT MY HOLY MOUNTAIN.
—ISAIAH 57:13

"Now I understand why people take drugs," I said to David the Sunday afternoon following Hope's burial and memorial service on Saturday. Honestly, I had never understood it before, because I had never felt that much pain before. And now the pain I felt was consuming, and I just wanted it to go away. So that Sunday afternoon I went to bed hoping to sleep it away. But that day, and in the days that followed, I discovered I couldn't sleep it away, eat it away, drink it away, shop it away, travel it away, or busy it away. I just had to feel it. And it hurt. Physically.

I had to do my best to confront my pain with the truth of God's Word, to comfort myself with the promises of God. But the pull toward self-medication rather than self-ministry is strong when we are tempted, discouraged, angry, guilty, or sad, and most of us have never learned how to minister to ourselves. In our pain we turn too quickly to the telephone or the bottle or some other quick but ineffective fix. Even though we may say we believe Jesus is the answer, we often turn to earthly idols to meet our needs. So we must learn how to minister to ourselves. When we sense our spirits beginning to sink, when the pulse of pain awakens a desire that demands to be placated, we need to reject any and all lesser comforts than Christ alone. We must choose to cover ourselves with his kindness. We have to remind ourselves of his promises. *Jesus, you understand what pain feels like. You are here with me to comfort me and empower me. I can enjoy you right now and welcome your peace and your presence. You are doing good things in my life even with the hurt I am feeling.**

Do you feel the pull of the bottle or the refrigerator or the mall or the television or the computer screen, offering you numbness to the pain? Will you reject the invitation of idols and accept the invitation God holds out for you? Will you bring him your pain and hide yourself in him, nestling close to his heart, finding your solace in him alone?

God of all comfort, I abandon false comforters and run into your arms of safety and solace. Your truth, your very presence, soothes my pain.

DIGGING DEEPER

Read about the false comfort of idols in 1 Samuel 12:21; Isaiah 41:21-29; 57:3-13; Jeremiah 10:14-16; and Hosea 14:8.

*We are blessed to have modern drug therapies that many of us need for the short or long term. Using prescribed drug therapy is not a failure of faith, but a helpful tool for healing.

WEEK 39
SELF

REFLECTION

How are you doing in your battle against self-centeredness and self-satisfaction? What victories do you need to celebrate? What defeats do you need to determine to turn around?

What have you lost in this life by trying to please yourself? What have you gained by making God the focus of your life?

MEDITATION

Jesus said to the disciples, "If any of you wants to be my follower, you must put aside your selfish ambition, shoulder your cross, and follow me. If you try to keep your life for yourself, you will lose it. But if you give up your life for me, you will find true life. And how do you benefit if you gain the whole world but lose your own soul in the process? Is anything worth more than your soul?" —MATTHEW 16:24-26

Place yourself in the presence of Jesus and hear him speak these words to you.

Read through the verses several times, soaking in his instructions and interacting with his questions.

Turn the passage into a prayer, telling Jesus that you want to follow him. Tell him what you want to lose for him and what you believe in faith you will gain.

PRAYER

Praise God for being the center of the universe, worthy of all praise, glory, and honor.

Thank God for freeing you from slavery to yourself, from being driven to always think of yourself and serve yourself first.

Intercede for those who are unwilling to humble themselves and give God his rightful place on the throne of their lives.

Confess your self-centeredness and lack of self-control.

Petition God to become greater and greater in your thoughts and emotions and actions while you become less and less.

WEEK 40

SUBMISSION

In her book *A Vision of His Glory*, Anne Graham Lotz tells the following story about her brother Franklin:

> *One morning when my mother called us all to come sit at the table for breakfast, Franklin refused. My mother repeated her invitation, which had now become a command: "Franklin, sit down."*
>
> *Again he refused emphatically: "No, I won't!"*
>
> *At that point my mother began to count to three. We all knew what that meant. If she got to three and Franklin had not obeyed, judgment would fall! So she began, "Franklin, one, two, th—"*
>
> *He quickly sat down then glared up at her defiantly and said, "I may be sitting down on the outside, but I'm standing up on the inside!"*

Can you relate to little Franklin? I can. Most of us really don't even like the word *submission*, let alone the practice of it. We rebel against the very idea. But we need to learn to submit. You see, there's a difference between merely surviving your suffering and submitting to it. C. S. Lewis wrote, "There are two kinds of people: those who say to God, 'Thy will be done,' and those to whom God says, 'All right, then, have it your way.' " What a joy to say to God, "I'm yours. Have your way with me." What a relief to stop fighting and start submitting.

THIS WEEK'S PASSAGE FOR MEDITATION

Your attitude should be the same that Christ Jesus had. Though he was God, he did not demand and cling to his rights as God. He made himself nothing; he took the humble position of a slave and appeared in human form. And in human form he obediently humbled himself even further by dying a criminal's death on a cross. Because of this, God raised him up to the heights of heaven and gave him a name that is above every other name, so that at the name of Jesus every knee will bow, in heaven and on earth and under the earth, and every tongue will confess that Jesus Christ is Lord, to the glory of God the Father.

—Philippians 2:5-11

I AM THE LORD'S SERVANT

MARY RESPONDED, "I AM THE LORD'S SERVANT, AND I AM WILLING TO ACCEPT WHATEVER HE WANTS. MAY EVERYTHING YOU HAVE SAID COME TRUE." —LUKE 1:38

"Greetings, favored woman! The Lord is with you!" (Luke 1:28). These were the first words of the angel Gabriel to Mary, the mother of Jesus. I can't help but wonder if Mary felt God was showing her his disfavor rather than his favor that day. "Don't be frightened, Mary," the angel told her, "for God has decided to bless you! You will become pregnant and have a son, and you are to name him Jesus" (verses 30-31). From our perspective, two thousand years later, it seems like great news! Immanuel, God with us! But imagine how it must have sounded to a teenage girl living in Hebrew culture, a betrothed woman with dreams of her own, a woman living a pure life of devotion to God. Surely what seems to us to be good news must have sounded, to her, like the worst news possible.

And we know what it is like to get bad news—news from the doctor that the test results are not good, bills in the mail that are bigger than our bank account, a phone call that begins, "There's been an accident," an angry voice mail from a child saying she doesn't want to live by your rules anymore.

There were many ways Mary could have responded to the news she received. Selfishness: "God, you have to change this because this is not what I have planned for my life!" Self-pity: "God, this is not fair. My life is ruined." Self-righteousness: "God, I've been a very good girl, and I certainly don't deserve this!" But Mary chose none of these responses. Instead she said, "I am the Lord's servant, and I am willing to accept whatever he wants." Mary submitted, welcoming the mysterious and unsettling plan God had for her life. Oh, how her ready submission must have pleased the heart of God!

I don't know what news you've received or what news is coming, but I do know you have a choice in how you respond. You can choose selfishness, self-pity, self-righteousness. Or like Mary, you can see yourself as the Lord's servant and choose to submit to whatever your Lord allows into your life. Would you choose to believe that God has decided to bless you even though, from your limited perspective, God's plan for your future may seem like the worst news possible?

Lord, you are with me, and because I know you want to bless me, I want to trust you and your plans for my life that seem anything but favorable. Whatever you want, Lord, I'm your servant.

DIGGING DEEPER

Read Mary's song of praise, celebrating the plan of God in Luke 1:46-55.

MESSAGE TO A RUNAWAY

The angel said to her, "Hagar, Sarai's servant, where have you come from, and where are you going?"

"I am running away from my mistress," she replied.

Then the angel of the Lord said, "Return to your mistress and submit to her authority." —Genesis 16:8-9

I've never seen an angel or heard the audible voice of God, but I've clearly heard God speak to me. In the early weeks of Hope's life, he spoke to me the way he always does, through Scripture. I was looking at the story of Hagar, who had run away from Abram and Sarai due to Sarai's harsh treatment. Hagar wanted to escape her difficult situation, but God spoke to her in the desert, telling her to "return and submit." My Bible study leader seemed to be speaking right to me, asking, "What is God calling you to submit to?" And I knew. I knew God was calling me to submit to the journey we were facing with Hope—not to fight it or cry out to him to change it, but to submit to his plan and his purposes, to walk through it in a way that brought him glory, a way that exemplified what it means to trust him in the midst of sorrow and difficulty and disappointment.

For me, submission has meant a quiet, though sorrowful, acceptance of God's plan and God's timing. It has meant giving up the plans I had for my family and for my life and bringing them all under submission to God. And the call to submission hasn't stopped. Every day, as I let go of my dreams and desires, I'm once again called upon to submit. And honestly, some days I do better than others. But because I believe God's plans for me are better than what I could plan for myself, rather than running away from the path he has set before me, I want to run toward it. I want to submit.

Do you find yourself wanting to run away, and do you hear God calling you to submit? Is it a difficult situation, a demanding person, an unfulfilled dream, a separation, a limitation, a loss? Are you willing to submit? Submission frees us to embrace God's plan for our lives, a plan he has put together with our very best interests in his heart and mind. Instead of running away from the unfair expectations, unfit authority, and unsettling situation in your life, will you listen for the Word of God speaking to your soul, asking you to trust him, calling you to submit?

God, I hear you calling to me in this desert of difficulty and I'd really like to keep running, but I don't want to run away from you. I want to run toward you. I want to submit.

DIGGING DEEPER

Read Genesis 16 and discover the special revelation God gave to Hagar.

ANGRY WITH GOD

THE PEOPLE WILL DECLARE, "THE LORD IS THE SOURCE OF ALL MY RIGHTEOUSNESS AND STRENGTH." AND ALL WHO WERE ANGRY WITH HIM WILL COME TO HIM AND BE ASHAMED. —ISAIAH 45:24

In the radio interviews I did when my book *Holding on to Hope* came out, I could always count on one question coming up: Didn't you get angry with God? Some interviewers seemed very frustrated with me when I told them that I really didn't get angry. I think they thought I was either being dishonest or trying to be too good to be true.

When we face a devastating loss, fellow believers sometimes encourage us to express our anger freely toward God, assuring us that God understands and accepts our honest emotions. It is a natural response to be angry when you don't get your way, when something or someone you love is taken away. And God is the easy target for that anger. Because our understanding of his sovereignty is shallow, we reason that if God is in charge of everything, then our suffering must be his fault, and therefore we see our anger as justified.

But wait a minute, where is our fear of God? Why do we think we have a right to be angry with our Creator? Who do we think we are to suggest that God owes us an explanation? What arrogance for us as finite, sinful creatures to disapprove of what God does and what he permits. The fear of God holds our tongue when we want to accuse God of wrongdoing; it halts our defiant finger-wagging; it humbles us in the midst of our self-righteous anger.

Am I saying that being honest with God about how you feel is sinful? No. When we feel it, we might as well admit it since he knows anyway, and hypocrisy only adds to our sin. Am I saying you should never feel angry? No. What I'm saying is that as you work through your feelings about what has happened, and as you inform your feelings by what you know to be true about God, you can reject the temptation to turn your back on God. You can refuse to point a finger in the face of God saying, "You are not good." Instead of pointing a finger toward God, won't you open your hands, asking him to meet your desperate need? Won't you lift your hands to praise him?

Source of all my righteousness and strength, I'm ashamed at how quickly and easily I grow angry and stay angry with you. What arrogance on my part! I humble myself before you and open myself to you.

DIGGING DEEPER

Read Psalm 37:8 and Proverbs 29:22. What are some of the results of giving in to and holding on to anger?

MEEKNESS, NOT WEAKNESS

He was oppressed and treated harshly, yet he never said a word. He was led as a lamb to the slaughter. And as a sheep is silent before the shearers, he did not open his mouth. —Isaiah 53:7

I sometimes find myself squinting to see something in the distance that I can't quite make out clearly. But it wasn't physical squinting that allowed the prophet Isaiah to see into the future and catch a glimpse of the Messiah. He saw into the distant future through the inspiration of the Holy Spirit. Although he could not make Jesus out in total clarity, he saw that Jesus did not have physical beauty that people found attractive or a worldly charisma that people admired. Through the distance of years, he could also see the inner quality of Jesus that left him vulnerable to oppression and harsh treatment. In describing him as a sheep silent before the shearers, Isaiah peered into the person of Jesus and saw his meekness.

Isaiah was not the only person to describe Jesus as meek. In one of the few times Jesus spoke about his own personal character, he described himself as "meek and lowly" (Matthew 11:29, KJV). He is our example for what it is to be meek. It was his meekness—his strong submission to the plan of God—that led him to the Cross. At the Cross, we see clearly the epitome of meekness.

So why would anybody want to be meek? What child says, "When I grow up, I want to be meek"? Meekness goes against everything the world tells us about getting what we want. We think we get what we want by asserting ourselves and promoting ourselves. But Jesus said that meek people will inherit the earth (Matthew 5:5, KJV). They get it all. The only people who will get anything lasting out of this life are people who learn to be meek.

Meekness has to be learned; it isn't something that comes naturally to some personality types and not to others. We think of meek people as those who are timid and quiet and never have an opinion. But strong, outgoing people can learn to be meek. Meekness is something God works into us as we welcome him to do so. Meekness is what makes submission possible. Without a spirit of meekness, it is impossible to submit to the work of God in our hearts and the plan of God for our lives. Are you going to keep fighting and wrestling for control, or are you going to pursue meekness? Will you stop trying to manipulate and maneuver your way so you can learn what it means to be meek?

Gentle, lowly Jesus, give me the strength I need to be meek. Bring my will under your control so that I am directable, teachable, and moldable.

DIGGING DEEPER

Examine the portrait of meekness in Psalm 37.

UNJUST SUFFERING

God is pleased with you when, for the sake of your conscience, you patiently endure unfair treatment. This suffering is all part of what God has called you to. Christ, who suffered for you, is your example. Follow in his steps.
—1 Peter 2:19, 21

It is one thing to submit to God, and that is hard enough. Submission enters a whole other league when you are called to submit to an incompetent boss, an unbelieving spouse, an immoral government, or an immature pastor. It is hard to believe that God expects this radical, even ridiculous, submission from us. But he does.

Peter spoke to this, telling Christian slaves how they should respond to an abusive, unbelieving master. The very image engenders feelings of resistance in us, doesn't it? We recoil at the idea of unreasonable and abusive people taking advantage of us or anyone else. Being mistreated without fighting back makes us appear weak, and we hate that. For us to submit to unfair treatment, God will have to be at work in us, because it doesn't come naturally.

Peter says we patiently endure unfair treatment so that our conscience is clear before God and because we want to please God (1 Peter 2:19). Why is he pleased? Submission to unfair treatment reflects utter reliance on the grace of God as well as unfettered obedience to his call. Suffering unjustly in this world is not a coincidence if you are a Christian. It is your calling. It is the way you make Christ real to people. This is what Jesus did—he showed us how to submit to unjust suffering.

Peter seemed to assume in these verses that it is God's plan for his people to suffer unjustly. In fact, he repeated himself later in his letter, writing, "It is better to suffer for doing good, if that is what God wants" (3:17). What God wants? God *wants* me to suffer injustice and unfair abuse? Why would he want that? Because he knows that as you and I graciously bear seemingly unbearable suffering by trusting God, we bring glory to God. We can be certain that God's glory will one day blaze from his seat of justice, but until then, he may choose to give the world glimpses of his glory through our patient, God-dependent endurance of unfair treatment. As we surrender our pride and seek to serve, the world is amazed and God is pleased.

My Example in suffering and submission, I want to follow in your steps, though I must admit I'm afraid of what it will cost me. Knowing my submission will please you gives me courage and increases my faith.

DIGGING DEEPER

To what people and positions are we to submit, according to 1 Peter 2:13–3:9?

WEEK 40

SUBMISSION

REFLECTION

To what or whom are you finding it difficult to submit? What can you learn from the examples of Mary, Hagar, and Jesus?

To what or whom have you been willing to submit in the past? How have you seen Jesus bless and use your sacrificial submission? What is he using to grow you in meekness?

MEDITATION

Your attitude should be the same that Christ Jesus had. Though he was God, he did not demand and cling to his rights as God. He made himself nothing; he took the humble position of a slave and appeared in human form. And in human form he obediently humbled himself even further by dying a criminal's death on a cross. Because of this, God raised him up to the heights of heaven and gave him a name that is above every other name, so that at the name of Jesus every knee will bow, in heaven and on earth and under the earth, and every tongue will confess that Jesus Christ is Lord, to the glory of God the Father.
—PHILIPPIANS 2:5-11

Read through this passage, stopping to take in the full meaning of each step Christ took as he descended to us and submitted to the Cross. Spend time exploring the full weight of every choice made by Jesus.

Then follow Christ each step upward to heaven, seeking to envision the glory of each honor God has bestowed upon him.

Ask God to show you how your attitude needs to change to more closely align with the attitude of Christ.

Praise God for his sovereignty and goodness that make him worthy of our complete submission.

Thank God for his example of submission that shows us what meekness looks like.

Confess your lingering anger toward God, and ask him for the grace to let it go.

Intercede for those who have run away from their problems but have not run to God.

Petition God to give you the inner resources of his Holy Spirit to enable you to patiently endure unfair criticism and unjust suffering.

WEEK 41

THE GLORY OF GOD

In the pages of Scripture, sometimes God's glory refers to the place where God dwells; sometimes it is what God does. Sometimes it is a gift God gives, and sometimes it is given to him. We see glory in the revelation of who God is and the reality of what God wants. We are called to give him glory and reflect his glory, and he has promised that one day we will share in his glory.

Ultimately, God's glory is the showing forth of all that God is. It is the manifestation of all his attributes. But this definition seems like mere words on the page in comparison to the radiant reality they represent.

In *It's Not About Me*, Max Lucado explains why we need to seek God's glory:

> *God's staff meetings, if he has them, revolve around one question, "How can we reveal my glory today?" God's to-do list consists of one item, "Reveal my glory." Heaven's framed and mounted purpose statement hangs in the angels' break room just above the angel food cake. It reads: "Declare God's glory."*
>
> *God exists to showcase God. Make no mistake. God has no ego problem. He does not reveal his glory for his good. We need to witness it for ours.*

THIS WEEK'S PASSAGE FOR MEDITATION

This message was kept secret for centuries and generations past, but now it has been revealed to his own holy people. For it has pleased God to tell his people that the riches and glory of Christ are for you Gentiles, too. For this is the secret: Christ lives in you, and this is your assurance that you will share in his glory. —Colossians 1:26-27

GIVEN A GLIMPSE OF GOD'S GLORY

An angel of the Lord appeared among them, and the radiance of the Lord's glory surrounded them. Suddenly, the angel was joined by a vast host of others—the armies of heaven—praising God: "Glory to God in the highest heaven, and peace on earth to all whom God favors." —Luke 2:9, 13-14

It is easy for us to believe that reality extends only as far as our senses can take us. But there is an ultimate reality in this universe far beyond what we can see. Only occasionally has God seen fit to give mortals a glimpse of what is beyond this world. God did this for a group of shepherds who were spending the night underneath the stars. After four hundred long years of silence, God broke into the darkness of our natural world with his radiant beauty, drawing back the curtain of heaven so the shepherds could see what had been there all along but hidden from human view.

It was as if heaven was bursting at the seams to let the glory of God loose on the earth, anxious to invade our existence with holy light and heavenly favor. Into a world deceived by lies, diminished by enslavement, and disillusioned by philosophy, a chorus of angels proclaimed, "Glory to God in the highest!" The phrase may fall flat on our dull modern ears, but in truth, the glory of God remains the most relevant message this hurting world has ever heard. It reinforces to us that God reigns supreme and will not allow evil to ultimately succeed in this world. It assures us that God is active in this world in ways we cannot see, and it reassures us that God is guiding history toward a God-glorifying conclusion. The angels started their message with "Glory to God" because they knew that God's glory is the context in which everything significant in this world is set. It is the foundation for finding meaning in what seems meaningless. This is the best news ever heard by human ears—that God is God and that his glory is supreme and sure, over and above everything, the righteous foundation for real and pervasive peace.

Will you open your ears to hear the message of the angels in the darkness of your difficulty? The glory of God may sound irrelevant at first, but the more you explore and experience it, the more you will discover it is the answer to your most perplexing questions, the object of your most profound longing.

Glorious Savior, would you break through the darkness in my world so I can see you at work behind the scenes, offering me your peace and your presence? Your glory is the supreme objective and sure foundation of my life.

DIGGING DEEPER

Just as Jesus came the first time in glory, he will come again in glory. But what will be different next time, according to Matthew 16:27; 24:30; and 25:31?

WE HAVE SEEN HIS GLORY

THE WORD BECAME FLESH AND MADE HIS DWELLING AMONG US. WE HAVE SEEN HIS GLORY, THE GLORY OF THE ONE AND ONLY, WHO CAME FROM THE FATHER, FULL OF GRACE AND TRUTH. —JOHN 1:14 (NIV)

The day Gabe was born, Sylvia, a reporter from *The Tennessean*, came to see us in the hospital to ask us if she could follow Gabe's life for a story that would run following his death. Knowing his life would be brief, we didn't want it to feel like an event for the cameras. But as we discussed the story possibility with Sylvia over lunch, she looked at me and said, "I don't understand this peace you have, but I want it." And that sealed the deal. I wanted her to see up close and personal the difference Jesus makes. So for six months Sylvia and Eric, the *Tennessean*'s photographer, were in and out of our home, at our special celebrations, and hanging out on ordinary days. Even in the heart-rending moments during which we said good-bye to Gabe's body, they were there, getting an up close view. We wanted them to see the difference Jesus makes even in the lowest moments of life.

Up close and personal. That is what God offered the world when Jesus became flesh and pitched his tent in our backyard. He came to show us what God looks like, the difference he makes. What did those who saw God up close and personal see? Rules? Rituals? No, most pronounced were truth and grace. Those with eyes to see saw that Jesus is true and real—ultimate reality and absolute truth. Jesus is grace, free and overflowing and lavished upon us. If you've seen God as harsh and stingy, if you've viewed his promises as untrustworthy or his claims as untrue, then you haven't really seen him. The most notable and noticeable aspects of God's character are grace and truth. Amazing grace and absolute truth.

Jesus came to show us the glory of God, but some of us simply can't see it because the eyes of our souls have been darkened by difficulty, constricted by bitterness, slanted by cynicism. If that is you, won't you ask God to restore your spiritual sight so you can not only see his glory but also receive it and experience it?

Word Made Flesh, thank you for choosing to make your home among us. You didn't have to show us what glory looks like. Allow me to see your unmistakable and unimaginable glory so I can receive your grace and believe your truth.

DIGGING DEEPER

Read John 1:1-18. What do you learn about the nature of God's glory shown in the Word? What was God's purpose in revealing his glory to us?

CONFIDENCE AND COURAGE

JESUS TOOK PETER AND THE TWO BROTHERS, JAMES AND JOHN, AND LED THEM UP A HIGH MOUNTAIN. AS THE MEN WATCHED, JESUS' APPEARANCE CHANGED SO THAT HIS FACE SHONE LIKE THE SUN, AND HIS CLOTHING BECAME DAZZLING WHITE.
—MATTHEW 17:1-2

It was supposed to be an adventuresome day of hiking in the Cascades. Our friends Dan and Sue had taken a rigorous route up to Lost Lake, which led them to a large fallen log that crossed over a deep ravine filled with rushing white water. Dan made it across the somewhat slippery log, but halfway across, Sue was struck with panic at the thought of slipping. She felt like the raging water below was going to suck her in, and she became frozen with fear. "Look at me," Dan said gently but firmly, coaxing Sue to continue moving forward. "Don't look down; just look at me." As she fixed her eyes on him and obeyed his instructions, Dan provided the confidence and courage Sue needed to move forward in spite of her fear.

Six days before taking Peter, James, and John up on a high mountain, Jesus told his disciples that he was going to Jerusalem where he would be killed, and he called them to give up their lives for him. It must have been overwhelming and disappointing to the disciples—not at all what they'd had in mind when they left everything to follow Christ. Perhaps Jesus knew they needed a confidence boost to embrace this difficult message. Perhaps Jesus knew they needed something to bolster their courage so they could endure the coming trauma of the Crucifixion. So Jesus gave them a glimpse of his glory. It was as if he said, "Look at me," knowing it was what they needed in order to face their fears. Far more than the inner glory of his character, Jesus showed them the intrinsic glory of his deity that had been veiled by human flesh. On this mountain, they not only saw the glory of God, they also heard the voice of God the Father proclaiming his love for his Son, his pleasure in and approval of Jesus' public ministry, and his command to obey. Humbled, awed, and no doubt somewhat shaken, they followed their Master down the mountain and toward the Cross.

Do you need a boost in your confidence to stake your life on the claims of Christ? Do you need a boost of courage to keep on following and trusting Christ? Fixing your gaze on the glory of God will give you confidence in the message of Jesus and courage to follow where he leads.

Glorious Son of God, following you sometimes seems overwhelming. Help me to see that only you can give me the confidence and courage I need to face my doubts and fears. Draw me closer to you by showing me your glory.

DIGGING DEEPER

Read 2 Peter 1:16-21 to find out how Peter remembered this experience with Jesus and the impact it had on him.

SUFFERING AND GLORY

In his kindness God called you to his eternal glory by means of Jesus Christ. After you have suffered a little while, he will restore, support, and strengthen you, and he will place you on a firm foundation. —1 Peter 5:10

Amy Carmichael wrote about the unmistakable connection between suffering and glory this way: "Hast thou no scar? No hidden scar on foot, or side or hand? As the master shall the servant be, and pierced are the feet that follow me; but thine are whole. Can he have followed far who has no wound? No scar?" Obviously she is suggesting that those who follow Jesus should be able to say with Paul, "I bear on my body the scars that show I belong to Jesus" (Galatians 6:17). We believe God has destined us for glory, but do we really have to suffer to experience it? Can't we enjoy the glory without enduring the suffering, and leave the wounds and scars to the super-saints?

Oh, how I wish I could assure you that you are the exception—that you will not have to hurt anymore on this earthly journey. But Paul wrote that "if we are to share his glory, we must also share his suffering" (Romans 8:17). To begin to grasp what this will mean for us, we must see that "suffering of Jesus" is an alternative term for the "glory of Jesus." Again and again in Scripture, Jesus' death by crucifixion is referred to as his glorification. For example, Jesus said, "The time has come for the Son of Man to enter into his glory" (John 12:23). He wasn't yet ascending to heaven; he was heading to the Cross. Unimaginable glory was put on display through the appalling suffering of the Cross. His greatest humiliation was also his ultimate exaltation. Suffering is glory in God's economy. They are not at opposite ends of the spectrum, but mysteriously intertwined.

"Wait a minute," we want to say. "This is not the kind of glory I had in mind!" But we must learn to see our suffering as glory.

I don't know what scars or wounds following Jesus will leave on your body, on your emotions, or on your soul. But the glory to come will be worth the wounds. Your scars will be cause for celebration. We'll be glad we followed the way of the Cross. One day we'll experience in reality what we now embrace by faith—that suffering is the pathway to glory.

My glorified Savior, I step out in faith and obedience to follow you. Give me eyes of faith to see beyond the struggle and focus on the glory.

DIGGING DEEPER

Look for the relationship between suffering and glory in these passages: Romans 8:17-23; 2 Corinthians 4:17; 1 Peter 1:11; 4:13; and 5:10.

WE CAN BE MIRRORS

All of us have had that veil removed so that we can be mirrors that brightly reflect the glory of the Lord. And as the Spirit of the Lord works within us, we become more and more like him and reflect his glory even more. —2 Corinthians 3:18

Does she or doesn't she? She does. I've started covering up the gray hairs sprouting all over my head by coloring my hair, but there's no denying I'm getting older. A glance in the mirror reminds me my body is aging. The truth is, while I don't mind getting older so much, I'm not content for my body to grow older while my spirit stays the same. As I grow older, I want to grow deeper. I want to become more and more like Jesus with every passing day. A year from now, if I am the same as I am today, if there has been no change in my character, no progress toward holiness, if I do not offer a brighter, clearer, more accurate reflection of Jesus in my attitudes and actions, then something has gone desperately wrong. If I'm not changing, reflecting more of his glory, the Spirit is not working on me or in me.

It was different for Moses. After he saw and experienced the glory of God on the mountain, the skin on his face literally glowed with the glory. Then, with each passing day, the glory began to fade away. But it doesn't have to be this way for us. We have something Moses didn't have. Moses didn't have the Holy Spirit living inside him. We do! The Spirit of God is at work within us, seeking to make us into mirrors so we can clearly reflect the radiance and beauty of God's glory in an ever-increasing way!

What is it going to take for you and me to brightly reflect the glory of the Lord? If we want to shine, we've got to let the Spirit get to work on us and in us, transforming us by taking away everything that doesn't look like Jesus in our lives and by nurturing in us the glorious attributes of Jesus. Can you see that the Spirit's work in us is our only hope for real and lasting change? Do you accept that until the Spirit of the Lord works within us, we can never break free of the personal habits we hate, the destructive tendencies that tyrannize us, and the worldly patterns that overpower us? The Spirit's work is what we want. We don't want to stay the same; we want to change.

Spirit of the Lord, keep working within me and making me more and more like Jesus. I'm not content to keep seeing the same old me in the mirror. I want to reflect the glory of the Lord by becoming more and more like Jesus.

DIGGING DEEPER

Read the story of Moses' fading glory in Exodus 34:27-35 and Paul's explanation of it in 2 Corinthians 3:12-18.

WEEK 41

THE GLORY OF GOD

REFLECTION

In what ways have you seen or experienced the glory of God? What difference has it made in your life?

How can a greater understanding of and appreciation for the supremacy of God's glory change your perspective about your suffering?

MEDITATION

This message was kept secret for centuries and generations past, but now it has been revealed to his own holy people. For it has pleased God to tell his people that the riches and glory of Christ are for you Gentiles, too. For this is the secret: Christ lives in you, and this is your assurance that you will share in his glory. —COLOSSIANS 1:26-27

Allow yourself to feel the privilege of learning this precious and powerful secret, and feel the pleasure of God in sharing it with you.

Ponder what it means to have Christ living in you now and to have him offer you the assurance of sharing his glory later.

PRAYER

Praise God for the radiant beauty of his character and attributes.

Thank God for allowing us to see that radiant beauty and to experience the richness and wonder of God's glory.

Intercede for those whose eyes have been veiled to the glory of God.

Confess the times you've considered the glory of God as unworthy of your earnest pursuit and costly sacrifice.

Petition the Holy Spirit to work in you, transforming you into a better reflection of the glory of Christ.

WEEK 42

BLESSING

For many, the word *blessing* sounds like religious jargon that doesn't really mean much. I used to think of blessings as good gifts from God—at the least the gifts that *I* categorized as good. But I'm beginning to see that blessings are God's way of showing us his favor, and sometimes his greatest favor comes to us in the form of hardship.

The Hebrew word for *blessed* is *ashr*, which means "to find the right path." If you are surrounded by many confusing ways and you find the right way to go, then you are happy. This Old Testament idea of happiness has to do with orientation, perspective, and the discovery of what is meaningful in the midst of shallow, superficial options.

And this is what we need, isn't it—to find the right way to go, to gain some perspective about what is meaningful? We're looking for a pathway lit by the radiance of God's face, a pathway that will lead us toward life, toward him. We want to be blessed.

THIS WEEK'S PASSAGE FOR MEDITATION

God blesses those who realize their need for him, for the Kingdom of Heaven is given to them.

God blesses those who mourn, for they will be comforted.

God blesses those who are gentle and lowly, for the whole earth will belong to them.

God blesses those who are hungry and thirsty for justice, for they will receive it in full.

God blesses those who are merciful, for they will be shown mercy.

God blesses those whose hearts are pure, for they will see God.

God blesses those who work for peace, for they will be called the children of God.

God blesses those who are persecuted because they live for God, for the Kingdom of Heaven is theirs.

God blesses you when you are mocked and persecuted and lied about because you are my followers. Be happy about it! Be very glad! For a great reward awaits you in heaven. And remember, the ancient prophets were persecuted, too. —Matthew 5:3-12

I WILL BLESS YOU

The Lord told Abram, "Leave your country, your relatives, and your father's house, and go to the land that I will show you. I will cause you to become the father of a great nation. I will bless you and make you famous, and I will make you a blessing to others. I will bless those who bless you and curse those who curse you. All the families of the earth will be blessed through you." —Genesis 12:1-3

A hidden agenda. As natural skeptics, and because we've encountered so many hidden agendas in the world around us, we can't help but wonder if God has one, especially when he doesn't do what we expect him to do. But God declared up front his agenda for this world. Nothing is hidden. His agenda is this: He plans to bless us. He wants to unleash his life-enriching goodness and mercy upon empty, dying, disillusioned people. He wants to flood our world with redeeming grace. Our problem with God's agenda is not that it is hidden, but that it simply seems too good to be true.

We don't deserve and can't earn God's blessing; it is a gift. In fact, when God chose to bless Abraham, he was no saint-in-training but was more likely an idol-worshiper-in-training since his father worshiped other gods (Joshua 24:2). But God chose to lavish his grace upon him. And in his promise to Abraham, God declared his whole purpose and agenda for redemptive history—to bless all people of the earth through Abraham and his descendants. The rest of Scripture is the story of God keeping his promise.

Don't let anyone convince you that you need to send in some money or jump through any spiritual hoops for God to bless you. He is not stingy or sour; he is ready and willing. But his blessing might not take the shape you were hoping for or expecting. God doesn't send his blessings like rain falling from the sky. He sent his truest blessing through a mediator, a messenger. The blessing promised to Abraham comes to all of us the same way: through Jesus. Jesus is the blessing of God sent to a hurting world. If you are disappointed that Jesus is the blessing of God in your life, if you were really hoping for more, perhaps God is not the one with the hidden agenda. Bring your agenda and all your hopes and dreams before him. He will meet you and he will bless you beyond what you can imagine.

Promise Keeper, I'm grateful for your many blessings, but I will not worship them by requiring them. You are the blessing I must have, the one I must worship. Jesus is mine! You have blessed me abundantly in Jesus!

DIGGING DEEPER

Read Galatians 3. Who was cursed so you could be blessed? How does a Gentile become a child of Abraham to inherit the promises of God?

A BRUISING BLESSING

When they walk through the Valley of Weeping, it will become a place of refreshing springs, where pools of blessing collect after the rains!
—Psalm 84:6

I saw Joni Eareckson Tada recently on *Larry King Live*. I could tell that Larry was completely perplexed by Joni's joy and that he was also inspired by her faith. Near the end of the program, he asked Joni if she longingly anticipates being able to walk in heaven. Here's what she said:

> *If I could, I would take this wheelchair to heaven with me. Standing next to my Savior, Jesus Christ, I would say, "Lord, do you see this wheelchair? Well, before you send it to hell, I want to tell you something about it. You were right when you said that in this world we would have trouble. There's a lot of trouble being a quadriplegic. But you know what? The weaker I was in that thing, the harder I leaned on you, and the harder I leaned on you, the stronger I discovered you to be. Thank you for the bruising blessing it was, this severe mercy. Thank you."*

How could Joni, who has spent most of her life bound to a wheelchair, thank God for this "bruising blessing"? Because in that chair is where she found rich fellowship with God, deep contentment in God. That is blessing.

To be blessed doesn't mean that you are untroubled, healthy, admired, or prosperous. It means that all is well between you and God, that you are deeply secure and profoundly content in God even though you may be weeping over the pain of a sick body, a deteriorating mind, a rebellious spirit, or a dysfunctional relationship. The blessing is not that he gives us what we want but that he gives us himself, especially in our painful places.

How has God shown his severe mercy in your life? Has he used a hospital bed, an antagonistic person, a foreclosure notification, or divorce papers to bring you to the place that you are willing to lean on him? Our places of pain become our richest blessings when we find God there. His very presence turns valleys of weeping into pools of blessing.

Blessed Refuge, thank you for even the painful places my journey has taken me, not because I've enjoyed them or wanted them, but because there I've drawn closer to you. Refresh me now with pools of blessing, more of you.

DIGGING DEEPER

Who will be blessed at the end of time, according to these verses in Revelation 14:13; 16:15; 19:9; 20:6; 22:7, 14?

UNLESS YOU BLESS ME

A MAN CAME AND WRESTLED WITH [JACOB] UNTIL DAWN. WHEN THE MAN SAW THAT HE COULDN'T WIN THE MATCH, HE STRUCK JACOB'S HIP AND KNOCKED IT OUT OF JOINT AT THE SOCKET. THEN THE MAN SAID, "LET ME GO, FOR IT IS DAWN." BUT JACOB PANTED, "I WILL NOT LET YOU GO UNLESS YOU BLESS ME." —GENESIS 32:24-26

"God wrenched his leg, and for the rest of his life Jacob walked with a limp. With every step he was reminded of the struggle and the surrender," my Bible study teacher, Sue, said in her lecture. She explained how the angel of God came to Jacob in the middle of the night and wrestled with him until dawn, knocking his hip out of its socket, leaving Jacob with a lifelong limp. After class I raced to my car, full of emotion. Life at that point was a day-to-day struggle to manage Hope's seizures. I knew that her life would soon be over and mine would never be the same. *I will walk with an emotional limp for the rest of my life,* I said to myself through tears. *But I don't want it to just remind me of the struggle and the pain; I want it to remind me of a place of surrender, a place where God met me and blessed me. Otherwise, it is just wasted pain.*

We often ask God to bless us, but perhaps it is a more dangerous prayer than we might imagine. Do you truly want all that God has for you? Don't think it will all be easy or comfortable, that it will come without a struggle. This is what God does with everyone he is going to use in a significant way. He comes to us at our pivotal point of surrender, and it is there we reveal how serious we are about him, how desperate we are for him, how much we truly want his blessing. The blessing is a changed life. And blessing comes through surrender.

Many people talk about wrestling with God when really I think they're talking about rebelling against God. We don't wrestle with God to force him to explain himself or to prove the power of our argument. Wrestling with God is not about pinning God down. It's about experiencing his power and enjoying his presence. Redemptive wrestling with God is when we can't bear to think about living without his blessing in our lives, when we value his blessing so much it is worth fighting for. Wrestling with God may leave us with a limp, but our limp becomes a beautiful reminder of God's blessing.

What a tragedy, God, if I walk away from this place of struggle unchanged and unusable. Lord, I will not let you go unless you bless me! Your blessing in my life is worth whatever mark you want to leave on my life.

DIGGING DEEPER

Read the story of Jacob's wrestling with the man in Genesis 32, noting Jacob's attitudes, emotions, and actions.

MAY THE LORD BLESS YOU

MAY THE LORD BLESS YOU AND PROTECT YOU. MAY THE LORD SMILE ON YOU AND BE GRACIOUS TO YOU. MAY THE LORD SHOW YOU HIS FAVOR AND GIVE YOU HIS PEACE.
—NUMBERS 6:24-26

On the card we sent out to let people know we were expecting Gabe, we wrote: "We are convinced this child is meant to be a blessing. But we have not known until now if this blessing will come in the form of a healthy child, like Matt, or a child with Zellweger, like Hope." The most amazing response we received to our card came from David Van Biema, the religion writer for *Time* magazine, whom I had worked with on a couple of stories. He was moved and mystified by our response to the news we received and, along with his personal remarks, asked if he could do a story on us for *Time*.

Over the four days he spent with us in Nashville, David listened to us and understood us. And even though he does not share our faith, he shared our sorrow. A couple of months later, on the day Gabriel was born, his story appeared in *Time*, entitled, "When God Hides His Face: Can Faith Survive When Hope Has Died? The Guthries Think So." We loved the story and were amazed and pleased with how David handled the complexity of the issues and conveyed our thoughts and feelings. The story was sensitive and intelligent and provocative.

But I must admit I never loved the title of the story. It's not that the notion of God hiding his face is unbiblical. In Job 34, Job's friend Elihu asks about God, "Yes, he hears the cries of the needy. But when he hides his face, who can find him?" (verses 28-29). The truth is, I have never felt that God has hidden his face from me in my suffering. In fact, the opposite is true. This is where I've seen him more clearly than ever. In the intensity of my questions and the desperation of my needs, God has revealed himself to me like never before. This is what it means to be blessed—not that God never allows anything hard to happen, but that he reveals himself in it, he shows you his favor, he gives you his peace.

Have you felt that God has hidden his face from you in the darkness of your suffering? He's not hiding. In fact, he wants to reveal aspects of his character and compassion to you in this dark place as he never has before. He wants to make his face to shine on you. Will you look up and see his face? He wants to bless you and be gracious to you.

Bless me, Lord, and protect me. Smile on me and give me your grace. Show me your favor and give me your peace.

DIGGING DEEPER

Read Genesis 32:30; Judges 6:13-24; Matthew 17:2; 1 Peter 3:12; 1 John 4:17; and Revelation 22:4. Note how God turned his face toward people in trouble in these passages.

COME BLESS THE LORD

Oh, bless the Lord, all you servants of the Lord, you who serve as night watchmen in the house of the Lord. Lift your hands in holiness, and bless the Lord. May the Lord, who made heaven and earth, bless you from Jerusalem.
—Psalm 134

I jumped at the chance to take author Richard Foster around the Dallas area for a day of book signings and interviews, because his writing had influenced me so significantly. When we stopped by my house for some breakfast, Matt, who was about fifteen months old at the time, was anxious to show his toys to our guest. And before I knew it, I turned around to find Richard Foster sitting on my kitchen floor playing with Matt and his race cars—and loving it.

This is a picture of the way God blesses us. You see, rather than staying far off and ruling by remote control, he bends down to our level, generously and graciously sharing himself with us. The blessing of God is that he enters into our need, gets under our skin, understands us better than we understand ourselves, and gives himself to us. The term *blessing* describes that which we most prize in God's dealings with us and what is best about living under his care.

And because God blesses us, we bless God. We can't help ourselves. We want to participate in what God is doing. In Psalm 134, the last in a series of ascent psalms (which Hebrew pilgrims sang as they went up to Jerusalem for worship festivals), the psalmist offers this invitational command: "Bless the Lord. . . . Lift your hands in holiness, and bless the Lord." He's inviting those of us who are weary and worn from the uphill journey of life to bless the Lord. He's reminding us why we made the trip in the first place. This is what we were created for and redeemed for, what we long for in eternity—to bless the Lord with our hearts full of joy and our hands lifted upward. On our journey we may feel like doing anything other than lifting up our hands to bless the Lord, and we hesitate to be hypocritical. But as we lift our arms in blessing, our hearts begin to get the message and are also lifted up.

Blessing on every step of our journey and blessing at the end of the road. What a pleasant path God leads us on as he brings us home to himself. Will you lift your hands and bless the Lord? Enjoying him is true blessing.

Lord, I lift up my hands and my heart to you, not to seek a blessing but seeking to bless you. You have blessed me abundantly with your very presence, and I can't help but seek to bless you in return.

DIGGING DEEPER

Read Psalm 16:7 and 96:2. What blessing from God prompts the psalmist to bless God in return?

WEEK 42

BLESSING

REFLECTION

What aspects or experiences of your life that you once saw as "bad" can you now see as blessings?

What blessings do you want to pursue from God more vigorously?

How can you bless God today in a way that is meaningful to you and to him?

MEDITATION

God blesses those who realize their need for him, for the Kingdom of Heaven is given to them.

God blesses those who mourn, for they will be comforted.

God blesses those who are gentle and lowly, for the whole earth will belong to them.

God blesses those who are hungry and thirsty for justice, for they will receive it in full.

God blesses those who are merciful, for they will be shown mercy.

God blesses those whose hearts are pure, for they will see God.

God blesses those who work for peace, for they will be called the children of God.

God blesses those who are persecuted because they live for God, for the Kingdom of Heaven is theirs.

God blesses you when you are mocked and persecuted and lied about because you are my followers. Be happy about it! Be very glad! For a great reward awaits you in heaven. And remember, the ancient prophets were persecuted, too. —MATTHEW 5:3-12

Listen to the words of Jesus; imagine yourself sitting on the hillside listening to him teach.

Read through this passage (often called the Beatitudes) slowly, looking for ways this wisdom of God turns the wisdom of the world upside down.

Read through these verses again with a willingness to examine yourself against these vital signs of spiritually healthy people.

Meditate on each of the promises Jesus makes, and enjoy the richness of each one.

PRAYER

Pray through the Beatitudes, asking God to shape you into this kind of child of the Kingdom. Open yourself to a radical readjustment of your value system.

WEEK 43

WORSHIP

Most of us think of worship as a Sunday morning series of events in which we gather in a church, sing some songs, and listen to a preacher. But if that is the only definition and dimension of our worship, our souls will wither away in the heat of difficulty.

We worship when we reflect God's glory—his character and likeness—to others in the way we live. We worship as we deem and declare him worthy of whatever loving him demands from us. Worship is a way of life, not a weekly event.

To worship God when we're hurting is a precious and powerful testimony to the world around us. Pain and loss equip us to worship in a way we never have before because when we hurt we are acutely aware of our desperate need for God and our own incapacitating weakness. Pain puts our helplessness and inadequacy in proper perspective to God's power and sufficiency.

Worship in the midst of difficulty saves us from a soul-numbing cycle of self-pity. It helps us to get our eyes off of ourselves and our sorrow and our problems. As we worship, we focus our hearts on God, which puts everything else into proper perspective.

THIS WEEK'S PASSAGE FOR MEDITATION

Shout with joy to the LORD, O earth! Worship the LORD with gladness. Come before him, singing with joy. Acknowledge that the LORD is God! He made us, and we are his. We are his people, the sheep of his pasture. Enter his gates with thanksgiving; go into his courts with praise. Give thanks to him and bless his name. For the LORD is good. His unfailing love continues forever, and his faithfulness continues to each generation. —PSALM 100

WORSHIPERS

The time is coming and is already here when true worshipers will worship the Father in spirit and in truth. The Father is looking for anyone who will worship him that way. For God is Spirit, so those who worship him must worship in spirit and in truth. —John 4:23-24

Ever since we got Hope's diagnosis, singing in corporate worship has never been the same for me. The music often moves me emotionally, and the exquisite beauty of the truth contained in lyrics often touches me at my core and leaves me unable to sing or speak. When we truly worship, our minds are engaged with the truth and beauty of God, and our emotions are open to being moved.

Sometimes the words have been difficult because they speak of a truth I want to believe, a faith I want to own, a commitment I want to make, but they seem beyond me in my questions or despair. While in the past I may have sung with mindless ease, I now feel ill-equipped at times to offer the passion and commitment expressed in these lyrics. To sing, "I sing for joy at the work of your hands, forever I'll love you, forever I'll stand," gets me. To declare my delight in everything God has done, to commit not to simply obey him, but also to *love* him forever, costs me something. And yet I don't want to just go through the motions without meaning what I am saying. I want to love him. I want to worship.

So what do we do when we simply don't have the want-to for worship? Do we just ignore our feelings and go through the motions? Our feelings matter to God, so we need to pray that God will restore our passion and reveal his truth. With every step we take in God's direction, he moves to meet us, and he begins to melt our hearts and bring meaning to the motions. Will you take that step toward him in worship, even when the cost seems great and your passion seems cold? When the pressure is on, when the pain is great, when you're pushed to the edge of your endurance, worship is the release you need, the relief you need, the rescue you need.

Father, as you seek true worshipers, how I want you to find one in me. I want to love you sincerely and passionately, even though my mind is sometimes confused and my heart is sometimes cold. Fill me with your Spirit; reveal to me your truth so I can be a true worshiper.

DIGGING DEEPER

What do these verses reveal about true worship versus insincere worship: Isaiah 1:11-20; Matthew 15:6-9; and Luke 18:11-13?

GRATITUDE

ALWAYS GIVE THANKS FOR EVERYTHING TO GOD THE FATHER IN THE NAME OF OUR LORD JESUS CHRIST. —EPHESIANS 5:20

We'd like to figure out how to water this verse down. We think to ourselves that Paul couldn't really mean *everything*. This seems like a tall order for anyone, but especially for those of us who have faced heartbreaking, soul-crushing loss.

And yet we see this kind of worship through gratitude lived out in the life and losses of Job. In the wake of losing nearly everything he owned and nearly everyone he loved, Job fell to the ground expressing gratitude, not just for all the blessings God had given him, but amazingly, for everything God had taken away. "I came naked from my mother's womb, and I will be stripped of everything when I die. The LORD gave me everything I had, and the LORD has taken it away. Praise the name of the LORD!"(Job 1:21).

God gives, and God takes away. But let's be honest. We just want him to give, don't we? And we certainly don't want him to take away the things or the people we love. We tend to think the possessions we have, the positions we hold, and the people we love are ours—that we've earned them, that we deserve them. But the truth is, everything we have is a gift. And it is only as we recognize that everything we have and everyone we love is a gift that we can enjoy those gifts with a heart of gratitude that honors God.

Genuine gratitude is a response not to the worth of the gift, but to the excellence of the Giver. If gratitude fluctuates with our estimation of the gifts, then it's not really gratitude. In reality, that kind of gratitude is disguised idolatry.

I know you can barely stand to think about being grateful in the midst of your loss. You may think I'm crazy to suggest that you could be grateful to God for who he is and all he has done for you as you face the empty chair, the empty bank account, the aching emptiness of what was once your life. But if you refuse to nurture gratitude, you will become bitter. So would you turn your eyes from your loss and disappointment to the great Giver, asking him to reveal more of himself to you so that you might grow in gratitude? Would you ask him for the peace and joy that only those who nurture gratitude are given?

Great Giver, have your way with my possessions, my position, my loved ones. Help me to loosen my grip on all I call my own and accept your promise that you are enough.

DIGGING DEEPER

Read 2 Corinthians 9:15; 1 Thessalonians 5:18; 1 Timothy 1:12; and Hebrews 12:28. For what and in what situations are we to be thankful?

PRAISE

With Jesus' help, let us continually offer our sacrifice of praise to God by proclaiming the glory of his name. —Hebrews 13:15

Remember Brylcreem? When I was a little girl, my dad used it on his hair every day. The red and white Brylcreem tube was dangerously similar to the red and white Colgate tube that was also often on the bathroom counter. I can still remember the awful flavor I tasted the day I mistakenly put Brylcreem on my toothbrush and began to brush my teeth.

When I squeezed the tube, what came out was what was inside: Brylcreem. And when our lives are squeezed by pressure and pain, what comes out is what's inside. As you've been pushed toward the breaking point, what has come spilling out of your life and off your tongue? Complaining or confidence in God? Panic or prayer?

The author of Hebrews instructs us to "continually offer our sacrifice of praise" (Hebrews 13:15). Continually? Even now? Does God really expect us to praise him when our hearts are broken, our spirits are crushed, and our song is silent? Why does God want us to praise him continually? Is he that needy? Is he like a vain woman with a new dress, waiting for a compliment? Or is there something else? Does our Creator know that praise is what ushers us into his presence, the only place we find the comfort we crave? Yes, God's desire for our praise reveals his love for us, because it puts us in the proper position to receive what we need from him. Praise fills our hearts with affection for God and floods our minds with remembrance of his attributes. In the process, our minds are emptied of God-diminishing thoughts, and our hearts are emptied of God-denying emotions.

Some days we praise God not with exuberance, but through tears. Some days we praise him not with complete clarity, but with many questions. Some days we praise him not with gratitude for what he's given to us, but with gratitude in spite of what we've lost. Our difficult circumstances do not call his character into question. We know that he is wise and powerful and good, and we praise him for it—continually. In fact, in the darkness of our lives he shines brighter. The death all around us makes his abundant, eternal life more precious. The disappointment we feel makes him more delightful.

Praiseworthy One, as I feel the squeeze of difficulty, may the fruit of my lips be continual praise, evidence of your Spirit inside me, making me new.

DIGGING DEEPER

Read Hebrews 13:10-16. How is this sacrifice of praise different from the Old Testament sacrifices God required?

GIVING

WHO AM I, AND WHO ARE MY PEOPLE, THAT WE COULD GIVE ANYTHING TO YOU? EVERYTHING WE HAVE HAS COME FROM YOU, AND WE GIVE YOU ONLY WHAT YOU HAVE ALREADY GIVEN US! —1 CHRONICLES 29:14

One Christmas, a member of our church gave one thousand dollars to Roy Carter, a pastor at our church, to be given to people who needed it in whatever way he saw fit. The man wasn't interested in getting a receipt to save on his taxes or accomplishing any particular agenda; he just wanted to experience the joy of giving. And he wasn't the only person to get a big kick out of it. Roy had a great time giving the money away! As staff members told him about various people's needs, he relished the fun of counting out the cash. "What made it so much fun," explained Roy, "was that it wasn't my money. I had no hesitancy to give it away because it wasn't mine to begin with."

It's easy to give away what belongs to somebody else. But it is much more painful to part with what we think belongs to us. And because we have a foundational misunderstanding about who really owns the things we think of as ours, we have a hard time giving to others and to God. We believe what we own is ours to do with as we please. But when we understand that everything we call our own has come from God and is, in fact, still God's, giving it away is not such a painful process. In fact, it becomes rich with joy. We're able to give with abandon because we realize that what we're giving away was never ours to begin with. We're just stewards of what really belongs to God, and he allows us the pleasure of enjoying what he owns as well as the joy of giving it back to him. We become people who love to give out of our love for God. Giving becomes a way we worship.

Do you have resources to meet the material needs of others, spiritual strength that could encourage others, experience or expertise that could benefit others? Can you see everything you have materially, emotionally, professionally, and personally as a gift from God? Giving it back to him to be used (or perhaps even misused, in our opinion) by others is an expression of genuine worship, showing the world that you choose to rest in God's provision for you.

Owner of everything, I want to experience the joy and freedom that come from worshiping you through giving. Show me how I can give myself and what is "mine" away in ways that bring you glory.

DIGGING DEEPER

Read Deuteronomy 8:17; 16:15; and Romans 11:35-36. How do these passages reinforce this truth that everything we have is really God's?

SPIRITUAL WORSHIP

I URGE YOU, BROTHERS, IN VIEW OF GOD'S MERCY, TO OFFER YOUR BODIES AS LIVING SACRIFICES, HOLY AND PLEASING TO GOD—THIS IS YOUR SPIRITUAL ACT OF WORSHIP. —ROMANS 12:1 (NIV)

Old Testament worshipers brought sheep, bulls, or pigeons to sacrifice on the altar as offerings to God. But God no longer requires the slaughter of animals as an expression of worship. The holy sacrifice that pleases God is a living person, a surrendered will upon his altar. God wants you to offer your body to him as a living sacrifice, as your way of worship.

To be a living sacrifice is to want the will of God to be done in your life more than you want life itself. Becoming a living sacrifice requires a willingness to go through the fire, to experience all the altar represents—purification and separation for the singular purpose of pleasing God. On this altar everything that is not useful or pleasing to God is burned away. But after you've gone through this fire, future flames will not have as much power to shake your joy or your confidence in God. The next time the fire heats up around you, you won't be so afraid, because you'll know by experience that the fire will not destroy you.

Are you willing to be poured out as an offering, to become a living sacrifice? Ask God for the faith and courage you need to crawl up onto the altar. Offer yourself to him, saying, "I'm yours. You can do whatever you want to do with me." This is pleasing sacrifice and holy surrender. This is spiritual worship.

But perhaps you feel you have sacrificed enough in this life, that God is asking too much here. If so, then you have not really seen or understood his great mercy. Perhaps your loss and disappointment have blinded you to his abundant kindness, because when we really see the mercy of God, we simply can't go on living for ourselves. Pleasing God becomes more valuable to us than our health, more meaningful than our career, more comfortable than our own ideas. The love of God shown to us in his mercy moves us and motivates us to lay it all down, to give it all up, to become a living sacrifice. "Love so amazing, so divine, demands my soul, my life, my all."

Holy Fire, I lay my body on your altar, giving you my secret thoughts, my sexual desires, my abilities, my energies, my emotions, my will.

DIGGING DEEPER

Read Romans 11, which draws a picture of God's mercy that motivates us to offer ourselves as living sacrifices. Note key phrases about God's mercy.

WEEK 43

WORSHIP

REFLECTION

What has been most difficult about private and public worship in the midst of your suffering, and how has worship been helpful and healing?

Are you content with your worship? If not, how would you like to develop your own worship to make it more pleasing to God and more meaningful for you?

MEDITATION

Shout with joy to the LORD, O earth! Worship the LORD with gladness. Come before him, singing with joy. Acknowledge that the LORD is God! He made us, and we are his. We are his people, the sheep of his pasture. Enter his gates with thanksgiving; go into his courts with praise. Give thanks to him and bless his name. For the LORD is good. His unfailing love continues forever, and his faithfulness continues to each generation. —PSALM 100

Read through this psalm several times, noting the elements and progression of worship.

Meditate on the attributes of God, as well as the attitude of his people.

Turn this psalm into a personal prayer, an experience of personal, private worship.

PRAYER

Praise God as worthy of all worship, praise, glory, and honor.

Thank God for everything he has given to you and even for what he has taken away.

Intercede for those who have settled for going through the motions and are missing out on the blessing of genuine worship.

Confess your reluctance and fear about offering yourself as a living sacrifice.

Petition the Father to make you into the kind of worshiper he seeks.

WEEK 44

PRAYER

"Would it even affect you if you were told you couldn't pray for thirty days?" This question, posed to me last summer by Bible teacher Paige Benton, pierced me to the core. Teaching on the book of Daniel, she explained that jealous administrators set Daniel up by encouraging King Darius to make a law that for thirty days "anyone who prays to anyone, divine or human—except to Your Majesty—will be thrown to the lions. . . . But when Daniel learned that the law had been signed, he went home and knelt down as usual in his upstairs room, with its windows open toward Jerusalem. He prayed three times a day, just as he had always done, giving thanks to his God" (Daniel 6:7, 10).

Paige pointed out that Daniel was not asked to deny God or give up his faith altogether—just to give up praying for thirty days. When she asked the audience if we would even be affected if we were told we couldn't pray for thirty days, the question seemed to slice me open, revealing the vacuousness of my prayer life. "We give up prayer so quickly and easily because we don't get any public credit for it," she added. Another ouch.

So as we consider what Scripture has to teach us about prayer this week, I find myself wanting to say along with the disciples, "Lord, teach us to pray" (Luke 11:1). Maybe you do too. Deep down, we want to pray in a way that makes a difference in ourselves, in those we love, and in our world. We want to deeply enjoy God's presence, receive his blessings, and be changed into his glorious likeness. *Lord, teach us to pray.*

THIS WEEK'S PASSAGE FOR MEDITATION

Pray like this: Our Father in heaven, may your name be honored. May your Kingdom come soon. May your will be done here on earth, just as it is in heaven. Give us our food for today, and forgive us our sins, just as we have forgiven those who have sinned against us. And don't let us yield to temptation, but deliver us from the evil one. —MATTHEW 6:9-13

KEEP ON ASKING

KEEP ON ASKING, AND YOU WILL BE GIVEN WHAT YOU ASK FOR. KEEP ON LOOKING, AND YOU WILL FIND. KEEP ON KNOCKING, AND THE DOOR WILL BE OPENED. —LUKE 11:9

Ever since Matt spent a week at my mother's house this summer, he has been asking me to buy a bucket of chocolate chip cookie dough at Sam's Club—not to make cookies with, but to eat by the spoonful! Because I know that it wouldn't be good for either one of us to have a bucket of yummy cookie dough easily available in the freezer, I have said no over and over . . . until last week. His repeated requests wore me down and I did it. (Come to think of it, I'll get a spoonful right now.)

But I think God is a better parent than I am. He doesn't give in by giving me everything I ask for when he knows it is not best for me. When we read Jesus' encouragement to keep on asking, we are tempted to think that the secret formula for getting what we want from God is to wear him down by repeating our request. Or sometimes we think the secret to getting what we want from God is to get as many people as possible to ask God for it. Is that what's really behind many massive prayer requests we email across the country? We think, *Surely if enough people are praying, God will grant our request.* Do sheer numbers or repetition really move the heart and hand of God?

I know as a parent I don't want Matt to take the approach of trying to wear me down by repeating his request or pounding on my door. I want to have a conversation. I want to hear his heart on the matter, and I want him to hear mine. And I have to believe that is how it is with our heavenly Parent. He loves us, and he cares about our needs. And while he values and invites our persistence in prayer, I think he would say to us, "Don't just pound on my door repeating your same request, refusing to listen or reason with me. Come in and talk to me. Share your heart with me and let me share mine with you." Prayer is about a conversation with God, not wearing him down to get what we want. Asking, seeking, and knocking have little to do with getting what we want from God but everything to do with getting God. And as we pursue God, he gives himself to us in fuller and newer ways.

My ever-patient Parent, you are more than anything I could ask for, you are the destination I am desperately seeking, and you are the door I'm knocking on that opens up the treasures of God. What more could I want or need?

DIGGING DEEPER

What is the progression implied in Luke 11:9-10?

WHAT IF GOD ALWAYS SAID YES?

He went on a little farther and fell face down on the ground, praying, "My Father! If it is possible, let this cup of suffering be taken away from me. Yet I want your will, not mine." —Matthew 26:39

While some people understandably took offense at what they deemed a lack of respect for God in the movie *Bruce Almighty*, I appreciated how it illustrated what might happen if God always said yes to our prayers. Jim Carrey's character in the movie is granted the power of omnipotence and assumes responsibility for answering prayer requests sent via email to God's computer. He takes the easy route and types "yes" over and over, which he later discovers has profound and harmful implications he never anticipated.

The fact that so many of us become indignant toward God when he does not answer our prayers as we would like him to reveals the superficiality and consumer mentality we have toward God. If he gives us what we want, we think he is good, and if he says no, we quickly assume he must not be good. But the reality is, often God's noes are the best gifts he can give us, because we pray as sinners, using prayer to advance our selfish interests. If we knew that God would grant our every request, certainly we would ask for those things *we* think are best for us—health and wealth and success and comfort—rather than what God has deemed to be best for us—our increasing holiness and humility, faithfulness in service, and awareness of our utter dependence on God. So in his mercy, God spares us from getting what we want. When God says no, he is protecting us, preparing us, and loving us.

And lest we think our Father doesn't love us when he says no, we need only consider the love for us that caused him to say no to his own Son. Kneeling in agony as he faced the Cross, the fully God, fully human Jesus asked God to take away the suffering that was ahead for him on the cross if there was any other way to accomplish our redemption. And God said no. Imagine if God had said yes to this prayer of Jesus. Jesus would have been spared the wrath of God pouring down on him, but we would not have been spared. In saying no to Jesus, God said yes to you and me and all those who will believe.

My eternal Yes, you have shown me how to submit my will and my desires to yours so that I want nothing more than for your will to be done. Teach me to hear the yes in every no I receive from you in prayer.

DIGGING DEEPER

How does Jesus' prayer progress in Matthew 26:36-46? What do John 18:11 and Hebrews 5:7-9 add to your understanding of how God answered Jesus' prayer?

MY WORDS IN YOU

IF YOU STAY JOINED TO ME AND MY WORDS REMAIN IN YOU, YOU MAY ASK ANY REQUEST YOU LIKE, AND IT WILL BE GRANTED! —JOHN 15:7

Ask any request I like and it will be granted? Gee, that sounds great! Like a genie in a bottle, it would seem that my wish becomes God's command. But there is an "if" there. *If* I have stayed joined to Christ, *if* the words of Christ are in me. How do I stay joined to Christ? How do his words come to be "in me"? And how does that affect what I ask for?

If we want his words to be in us, we have to listen, and we listen best when we meditate on Scripture. Once we have listened, we can then make our requests boldly because our requests are shaped by what God has said.

I must admit, sometimes I just don't know where to start with prayer. And even if I do start, I have such difficulty keeping my focus. I find myself saying the same phrases over and over and I'm embarrassed at how hollow they can sound. In these times, I find it helpful to "pray the Bible"—to use passages of Scripture to form my prayer. Here is an example of how it works: Do you have a child caught in the clutches of rebellion? Turn to 1 Peter 5:6-7 and pray, "I ask that my son will humble himself under your mighty power and in time come to honor you. I give my worries and fears about him to you, knowing that you care about what happens to him." Is your focus only on what you've lost and not on what God has given you? Turn to Isaiah 63:7 and pray, "Lord, your love never fails me. I praise you for all you have done. You have been good to me and made me your very own. You are even willing to suffer with me. At the lowest points of my life you lift me up and carry me." We can be confident we're praying in God's will if we use his words.

Ask any request I like and it will be granted? That sounds great! And it is. As praying the Bible shapes us and shapes our requests, our prayers align with God's will. The rough edges of our selfishness and the excesses of our appetites are conformed to the supreme purposes of God. What pleases him begins to please us, guiding and directing what we ask for. And he gladly says yes.

Eternal Word, you not only provide everything I need, you give me the words for my requests in the words of your Book. Show me the joy of being joined with you and being filled with your words and your will.

DIGGING DEEPER

Turn Colossians 3 into a personal prayer, fulfilling its instruction to "let the words of Christ, in all their richness, live in your hearts and make you wise" (verse 16).

SECRET PRAYER VS. SHOWY PRAYER

When you pray, don't be like the hypocrites who love to pray publicly on street corners and in the synagogues where everyone can see them. I assure you, that is all the reward they will ever get. But when you pray, go away by yourself, shut the door behind you, and pray to your Father secretly. Then your Father, who knows all secrets, will reward you. —Matthew 6:5-6

As I'm looking forward to my twenty-year college reunion next month, I'm reminded of one of my college friends who at one point described me as "a prayer warrior." I suppose I remember because it surprised me when she said it. I knew it wasn't true. I was all too aware of my meager efforts in the work of prayer. And although I'm sure I made a feeble effort to disclaim the mantle, the truth is, I enjoyed it.

As I read Jesus' warning about hypocrisy in prayer, I realize how well he understands people. He knows that we crave the admiration and applause of other people. He knows that we would much rather cultivate a reputation for being a person of prayer than to actually pray. This can work against our very real desire for authentic prayer, setting up the scene in which we put on a mask, step onto the stage, and play the role of "prayer warrior."

I step on the stage of hypocrisy when I tell someone that I will pray for her, knowing even as I say the words that most likely I will not. (But saying it makes me seem so spiritual and caring.) I put on the mask when I pray publicly using phrases or clichés or a tone of voice I've heard others use, making me seem practiced in prayer. But I am most hypocritical when I pray for the ears of my audience rather than to the heart of my Father. They might be fooled, but he isn't. He knows that my secret prayer place is too easily ignored, too rarely enjoyed.

Jesus says that when we pray to impress other people, we've already received our reward in full—their admiration—but what an empty and fleeting reward that is. And I simply don't want to settle for it anymore, do you? We can perform public prayers or make claims of private prayer and receive the applause of people, or we can go into our secret place, shut the door, and commune with God. There we find our most blessed reward, not in making an impression on others, but in finding intimacy with him.

My true Prayer Warrior, I don't want to settle for a reputation; I want the reality of an ongoing conversation with you that is something we share alone and intimately. Point out my pretense and performance so I can enjoy your approval.

DIGGING DEEPER

What do Genesis 5:21-24 and Hebrews 11:5-6 reveal about the nature of authentic fellowship with God and faith in God? What do they show about the reward of such fellowship?

BUT EVEN IF HE DOES NOT . . .

Shadrach, Meshach, and Abednego replied, "O Nebuchadnezzar, we do not need to defend ourselves before you. If we are thrown into the blazing furnace, the God whom we serve is able to save us. He will rescue us from your power, Your Majesty. But even if he doesn't, Your Majesty can be sure that we will never serve your gods or worship the gold statue you have set up."
—Daniel 3:16-18

Shadrach, Meshach, and Abednego are Sunday school felt-board heroes who were thrown into the fiery furnace because they refused to worship the gold statue of the Babylonian king. I suppose they gained Bible hero status because they refused to bow down to idols and because they survived the fire, but I don't think that is what made them heroic. What amazes me about these young men was their faith—not faith that God would certainly deliver them from the fire, but faith that wouldn't waver "even if he does not."

We heard a Bible college friend of David's, Barry Arnold, preach a sermon in which he admitted, "I used to think 'even if he does not' was an escape clause for a God who just might not come through. You wouldn't want your God to look bad. I remember hearing people pray, 'if it be thy will, Lord,' and thinking to myself, *Come on, don't give God a way out. How can you know if he ever answers prayer if you always say, 'thy will be done'?*"

Today Barry has a new perspective. He now says that prayers that leave no room for "even if he does not" are not truly prayers of faith. The prayer of faith is one of submission to God that does not presume to know what God will do or tell him what he should do. Shadrach, Meshach, and Abednego didn't pretend that they knew what God would do in their situation, and there is no evidence that they cried out to him, telling him what they thought he should do. Because they knew God and trusted God, they believed he would do what is right, even if it resulted in their death. Their commitment was not to read God's mind but to remain true to God no matter what.

Does it seem like weak faith for you to pray in your situation, "God, I know you have the power to deliver me from this fire of difficulty or pain, but I don't know if you will"? It isn't. That is a "but even if he does not" kind of prayer, and it makes you a faith hero in God's estimation.

God who is able to save, I want to place my faith in you alone rather than in what you will do for me. I entrust myself to you and refuse to bow down to the idol of any god of my own making who always saves in the way I want.

DIGGING DEEPER

What do you learn about those God saves and those he does not in Hebrews 11:29-39? What do you learn about what merits God's approval?

WEEK 44

PRAYER

REFLECTION

How authentic is the prayer in your secret place? And if you have no secret place of prayer, what is keeping you from it?

What are your greatest discoveries and delights in prayer, as well as your disappointments? Can you talk right now with God about them all?

MEDITATION

Pray like this: Our Father in heaven, may your name be honored. May your Kingdom come soon. May your will be done here on earth, just as it is in heaven. Give us our food for today, and forgive us our sins, just as we have forgiven those who have sinned against us. And don't let us yield to temptation, but deliver us from the evil one. —MATTHEW 6:9-13

Rather than simply repeating the familiar words of the Lord's Prayer, examine the model prayer Jesus offered to his disciples. Reflect on the ways this prayer is really a pattern in its simplicity and brevity, in its dependence and humility, in its worship and consecration, and in its specificity.

Meditate on the prayer phrase by phrase, seeking to enter the presence of God and to become one with Jesus in meaningful conversation with your Father.

PRAYER

Follow Jesus' direction in prayer:

Call out to God as his child.

Practice and appreciate his presence and purposes.

Welcome his will in your life.

Ask him to meet your physical and spiritual needs.

Ask him to protect you from your own desires that would lead you away from him and to protect you from the devil who would destroy you.

WEEK 45

WORD OF LIFE

Words are powerful. And no words are more powerful than words from God. With the power of his word, God created the world out of nothing, light out of darkness. With a word, he called Abram out of Haran, promising to bless him. He called to Moses from the burning bush, instructing him to deliver his people. He called to Job from the storm, challenging his embittered questioning.

And when the Word became flesh and lived among us, people saw not only the power of the Word, but his passion in the person of Jesus. The words he spoke were like none the people had ever heard because Jesus spoke with authority, with a consistency in his message and his person the people had never seen before or since.

But the power and the passion of the Word is not just biblical history; it is real-time reality. The Word of God is living and active, and it is the word we desperately need all the time—especially when we are hurting. The Word of God offers us power and perspective. Its truth brings comfort, not confusion. It is substantial, not merely sentimental. It is true, never trite.

Don't underestimate the power of God's Word in your life and in your situation. God's Word can create something good out of the chaos of your circumstances; his Word can still the storm that rages in your heart; his Word can bring healing to your deepest hurts.

THIS WEEK'S PASSAGE FOR MEDITATION

The law of the LORD is perfect, reviving the soul.
The decrees of the LORD are trustworthy, making wise the simple.
The commandments of the LORD are right, bringing joy to the heart.
The commands of the LORD are clear, giving insight to life.
Reverence for the LORD is pure, lasting forever.
The laws of the LORD are true; each one is fair.
They are more desirable than gold, even the finest gold.
They are sweeter than honey, even honey dripping from the comb.
They are a warning to those who hear them; there is great reward for those who obey them.

—PSALM 19:7-11

SWEETER THAN HONEY

The laws of the Lord . . . are more desirable than gold, even the finest gold. They are sweeter than honey, even honey dripping from the comb.
—Psalm 19:9-10

At the risk of boring you with our private banter, I will tell you that David and I often look at each other after a meal and say, "I just need that little taste of something sweet." Honestly, though I can remember when we first overheard a friend utter the phrase, I can't remember why we find it humorous. I suppose we repeat it now not because it is so funny, but because it is so often true. We often find ourselves unsatisfied, wanting a little "taste of something sweet."

In searching for metaphors to describe the sensory satisfaction of the Word of God, the psalmist reaches for the epitome of sweetness. And in the era before refined sugar, honey was the sweetest taste people ever enjoyed. So that is how he described what the Word of God tastes like for those whose taste buds have been trained to appreciate its flavor.

God wants to give you a taste of something sweet. That is why he has given you his Word. It is not meant to be drudgery you force-feed yourself because you know it is good for you. He intends for his Word to be a lavish and satisfying feast, an invigorating taste sensation, a treat. But we so easily turn what he has given as a delightful gift into a guilt-inducing demand.

If you find that the Word of God is often tasteless and unenjoyable, would you ask God to give you a spiritual sweet tooth? When he does, the sweetness of the Word of God will work its way into the blandness of your everyday life and the bitterness of your everyday pain.

Some days our experiences are far from sweet—they are as sour as our disposition, so overwhelmingly sad we think our hearts will burst. It is in these foul-tasting days, when our emotions are flat and our spirits are dry, that we come to the Word of God searching for a taste of something sweet. We've tasted before, and our taste memory tells us that the Lord is good. It is his goodness that draws us to him and his sweetness that satisfies as we feed on his Word.

Sweet Savior, how your words of life satisfy my hunger for truth and meaning and cleanse from my pallet the bitter taste of my sin and suffering. Keep satisfying my cravings with the sweetness of your words.

DIGGING DEEPER

See what the following verses say about the sweetness and delight of God's Word: Psalm 1:1-2; 19:8; 119:16, 97, 111; Jeremiah 15:16; and John 15:10-11.

FOOD FOR YOUR SOUL

Jesus told him, "No! The Scriptures say, 'People need more than bread for their life; they must feed on every word of God.'" —Matthew 4:4

When some people are going through intense grief, they lose their appetite. How often I have wished this would be my experience! It seems only fair that if I have to experience all the yucky stuff of grief, I should get the side benefit of weight loss without effort. My friend Angela, however, could barely get anything down for weeks after her husband, Wes, died suddenly. She simply had no appetite for food. Neither did she have an appetite for God's Word at first. "I didn't want to hear that God would be a Father to the fatherless," she told me. "I wanted Wes to father to my children. And I didn't want to hear that God would take care of me. I wanted Wes to take care of me." But after a while, acceptance of her loss and a growing awareness of her need awoke in her a voracious appetite for God's Word that she had never known after a lifetime spent in the church. Finding herself stripped of the security of a husband and struggling with the loneliness of loss, nothing less would satisfy.

For too much of my life, I haven't really believed that I *need* to feed on every word of God. Sure, it was a nice addition to my life if I was in the mood, but I didn't think I really *needed* it. Of course I would never have said this out loud, but the real test of what we believe is what we do. I might say that I believe I need to exercise, but if I don't exercise, I obviously don't believe it. I see it as beneficial but optional. But Jesus said, "These words I speak to you are not incidental additions to your life, homeowner improvements to your standard of living. They are foundational words, words to build a life on" (Matthew 7:24, *MSG*).

Have you come to the place where you truly believe that the survival of your soul is dependent on the extent to which you feed on the Word of God? Or have you so stuffed yourself with the junk food of entertainment, the sweetness of mere sentimentality, or the meaningless filling of busyness that you have dulled your appetite for the words of life? The Word of God satisfies your most profound hunger, your soul hunger for truth and meaning.

Food for my soul, why do I settle for snacking on this world's confections when you offer to nourish my soul with your very words of life? Satisfy me with your truth and sustain me with nothing less than yourself.

DIGGING DEEPER

What do Hebrews 5:12-14 and 1 Peter 2:2-3 reveal about how God's Word feeds us and about the type of spiritual food we should hunger for?

WORDS OF TRUTH

MAKE THEM PURE AND HOLY BY TEACHING THEM YOUR WORDS OF TRUTH. —JOHN 17:17

A big question these days seems to be whether our sources for news are truthful or bent by bias. We live in a world where "spin," half-truths, and even outright lies swirl around us, making us cynical and skeptical. We are tempted to think there is no one we can trust to tell us the truth, no place we can go where the air is free of deceit.

But when we open the Word of God, we breathe in a completely different atmosphere. There we discover truth, reality, sincerity, and an absence of ulterior motives and hidden agendas. We can believe everything God says because God is the personification of truth. And his words are not merely informational, they are powerful. Through the Holy Spirit, the truth of Scripture works on us and in us, renewing us and shaping us, healing us and cleansing us. Have you experienced the power of the Word of God to lift your burden, cleanse your conscience, and change your perspective?

We do not have to plod through the pages of Scripture to determine what is true and what is error, what we're willing to agree with and what we can't accept. There is never a disconnect between what Scripture teaches and the reality of the world we live in. Therefore, as my pastor Ray Ortlund says, we are invited to "swallow it whole." We come to the Word of God in humility, seeking to understand what it is saying so that we can allow its truth to permeate our intellect, intuitions, and interior life. God's truth has the power not only to withstand the skepticism and attacks of worldly wisdom, but also to transform worldly people, changing how we think and how we live, making us pure.

Many people set out on a journey toward truth under the assumption that it is inside themselves or that it can be whatever they determine it to be. But if we're going to discover the truth in this life, we need a word from outside ourselves, a word from God himself. And that is what he has given us. "The law of the LORD is perfect" (Psalm 19:7). Will you embrace his words as true?

Word of Truth, what a comfort to know I can rest in the reliability of your words and relish the ability of your Word to change how I think and how I live. Free me from the deception of the evil one and from deceiving myself so I can know the purity and holiness that your truth inspires.

DIGGING DEEPER

According to John 8:44 and Romans 3:9-18, what or who are the sources for lies? What does Ephesians 4:11-16 say about the responsibility of teachers?

EXTREME MAKEOVER

THE WORD OF GOD IS FULL OF LIVING POWER. IT IS SHARPER THAN THE SHARPEST KNIFE, CUTTING DEEP INTO OUR INNERMOST THOUGHTS AND DESIRES. IT EXPOSES US FOR WHAT WE REALLY ARE. —HEBREWS 4:12

Our culture is makeover crazy right now. I must admit it is interesting to see the dramatic changes in people who submit to the knife of a skilled plastic surgeon. When I watch these programs, I like to fast-forward to the end and see the before and after pictures and wonder at the transformation.

Did you know that God has chosen you for an "extreme makeover"? Most of us come to the Word of God looking for advice to help us fix ourselves up a little, only to discover that God wants to do something far more dramatic and intense. He wants to penetrate the dark corners of our inner lives and deal with the thoughts and attitudes of our hearts to transform us into a people who radiate his beauty and grace. This makeover is a painful, lifelong process, and the tool God often uses is his Word, which cuts deeply and lays bare the ugliness we might wish to keep hidden. Then he begins his work of cutting away what is keeping us from displaying the beauty of his presence in our lives. And the cutting away is painful.

It always surprises me that the people on these makeover shows are willing to have their photographs taken wearing only their underwear. These before and after photos are then displayed for the whole world to see. I would never want to be that exposed! And neither do I relish the idea of having my inner life exposed, my thought life and motives laid bare. But I am unable to hide anything from God's penetrating gaze. And I need not fear it. As he exposes my shallow beliefs and false intentions with the truth of his Word, he is able to cut away what displeases him, and I am better for the exposure.

Are you just looking for a little nip and tuck via a verse here and there, or are you willing to open yourself up to the whole Word of God for an extreme makeover? Would you allow the Great Physician to cut deep? He will transform your inner ugliness so that you radiate his glory, and he will clothe you with his own righteousness so that you display his holiness.

Great Physician, I open myself up for you to use the knife of your Word to judge, motivate, convict, instruct, and inspire me. Cut deep into my heart so that my life will be a beautiful testimony to your power and purity.

DIGGING DEEPER

What do you learn from Colossians 3:16; 2 Timothy 3:16-17; and James 1:22-25 about how God's Word exposes our sin and helps us to change?

WORDS OF LIFE IN THE FACE OF DEATH

THE VERY WORDS I HAVE SPOKEN TO YOU ARE SPIRIT AND LIFE. —JOHN 6:63

I remember seeing Robert Rogers on CNN shortly after they discovered the bodies of his wife and four children who all drowned when their van was washed off the interstate in a flash flood. I could see in his countenance and hear in his words that he was a man of faith. A couple of months later, he shared with me and David the tragic story of being with his family in the van as the water flooded in, of kicking out the window and being immediately sucked out and plunged into the water, of the agonizing experience of identifying the bodies of each member of his family. We shed tears together at the immensity of his loss. While we could barely fathom the horror of his experience and the emptiness of his world, we were once again struck by the peace of his countenance. No one could miss the fact that his words were consistently mingled with the words of Scripture, and it made me wish mine were as well.

Near the end of our breakfast I asked him, "How do you know so much Scripture?" He explained to me that he discovered Scripture memory as a Catholic high school student who was hungry to know God by knowing his Word. But his love affair with Scripture didn't end there. He lovingly remembered all the bedtimes spent with his children, memorizing Scripture together. "By the time she was five, our daughter Makenah could quote Psalm 121: 'I lift up my eyes to the hills—where does my help come from? My help comes from the LORD, the Maker of heaven and earth,' " he told us (verses 1-2, NIV).

So it was only natural that in the most fearful moment of their lives, as the water rose in and around their van, they began to speak Scripture from Psalm 46, "God is our refuge and strength, an ever-present help in trouble. Therefore we will not fear" (verses 1-2, NIV). Remembering those moments is bittersweet for Robert. "Had I not known God in that way and had his Word in my heart, I couldn't have found a Bible in that situation, much less a verse," he says. "His Word was life in that moment." God continues to be an ever-present help, rescuing Robert daily from despair as he clings to the promises of God and finds refuge in God. Wouldn't you love to plant words of life in your heart and mind so they will flow out of your life and off of your tongue?

Word of Life, give me a desire and a will to hide your words in my heart so they will be on my lips and in my life in my most desperate moments.

DIGGING DEEPER

Robert Rogers says that Psalm 112 has been the mainstay of his life. Read this Psalm and study its phrases, applying its instructions and promises to your life.

WEEK 45

WORD OF LIFE

REFLECTION

How has the Word of God been a source of strength, comfort, and conviction to you in your suffering?

Do you enjoy the sweetness of God's Word and do you embrace it as truth? Do you believe you *need* it for food, or does your neglect reveal that you believe it is beneficial but optional?

MEDITATION

The law of the LORD is perfect, reviving the soul.
The decrees of the LORD are trustworthy, making wise the simple.
The commandments of the LORD are right, bringing joy to the heart.
The commands of the LORD are clear, giving insight to life.
Reverence for the LORD is pure, lasting forever.
The laws of the LORD are true; each one is fair.
They are more desirable than gold, even the finest gold.
They are sweeter than honey, even honey dripping from the comb.
They are a warning to those who hear them; there is great reward for those who obey them.
—PSALM 19:7-11

Listen to the psalmist celebrate God's revelation of himself through his Word.

Read through the passage, circling the six words that describe God's Word in verses 7-9 and the six effects of the Word in a person's life. Meditate on each of these descriptions and their effects, and treasure them with the psalmist. Allow yourself to feel the desire, enjoy the sweetness, and anticipate the reward the psalmist describes.

PRAYER

Praise God for the power of his Word in the universe and in your life.

Thank God for sending his Word in the flesh in the person of Jesus.

Intercede for those who do not have ears to hear God's Word and have hardened their hearts toward it.

Confess your reluctance to open yourself completely to the transforming power of God's Word.

Ask God to give you a sweet tooth for his Word, a hunger for its nourishment, and a passion to hide it in your heart.

WEEK 46

FORGIVENESS

Do you want to skip this section because you don't think you have anyone you need to forgive? Or do you want to skip this section because you can hardly bear the thought of forgiving the people who have hurt you? You know they don't deserve it. They haven't even acknowledged what they did to hurt you. How could you even think about forgiving? I understand. I've been there, or I should say, I find myself there repeatedly, because no one goes through life without being hurt. Sin takes its toll on our lives and our relationships.

You can continue to play the waiting game with the person who has hurt you—waiting for him or her to apologize, to make things right. If so, you're allowing that person to hold you hostage. By saying, "If she apologizes . . ." "If he rehires me . . ." "If they invite me . . ." we play the game of waiting for others to make the first move. In the meantime, an unforgiving spirit weaves its way into the fabric of our entire lives.

The Greek word for forgive, *aphiemi*, means literally "to abandon" or "to leave behind." Aren't you ready to abandon this agonizing animosity? Don't you want to leave behind this burning sense of resentment, this burdensome weight of hurt feelings? Wouldn't you like to know the freedom of forgiveness?

THIS WEEK'S PASSAGE FOR MEDITATION

You have stripped off your old evil nature and all its wicked deeds. In its place you have clothed yourselves with a brand-new nature that is continually being renewed as you learn more and more about Christ, who created this new nature within you. Since God chose you to be the holy people whom he loves, you must clothe yourselves with tenderhearted mercy, kindness, humility, gentleness, and patience. You must make allowance for each other's faults and forgive the person who offends you. Remember, the Lord forgave you, so you must forgive others. And the most important piece of clothing you must wear is love. Love is what binds us all together in perfect harmony. And let the peace that comes from Christ rule in your hearts. For as members of one body you are all called to live in peace. And always be thankful. —Colossians 3:9-10,12-15

NAMING IT FOR WHAT IT IS—SIN

Get rid of all bitterness, rage, anger, harsh words, and slander, as well as all types of malicious behavior. Instead, be kind to each other, tenderhearted, forgiving one another, just as God through Christ has forgiven you. —Ephesians 4:31-32

I was by myself in a beautiful hotel, awake in the middle of the night—again. Once again I found myself too worked up by my mental rehearsal of the wrongs done against me to sleep, too intent on rehearsing my confrontation so that those who hurt me would know how much pain they had inflicted. But it was different this time. That night, the Holy Spirit inside me captured my attention and convicted me, revealing to me that my "issues" and "emotional baggage" were really unforgiveness. More pointedly, they were sin. That night I heard God calling me to repent. I realized I needed to stop tending my hurt and begin to get rid of the bitterness in my life if I ever wanted to move forward with God.

"I've tried to forgive," I said to God. "I can't do it on my own." But that night I asked God to meet me. I told him I would take steps of obedience toward him, away from my resentment, and I asked him to meet me at every step to change my feelings, which seemed impossible to me.

A few days later the phone rang. This was my first chance to live out my repentance. Instead of being cold, I was kind. Instead of being indifferent, I was interested. As I hung up the phone, tears stung my eyes, but it felt good—like a load was beginning to lift. God met me that day and in the days that followed as I started down the long path toward freedom, away from unforgiveness. No longer was I intent on making them pay, not because they didn't owe me but because I was canceling the debt. I even began to let go of my need for them to be sorry and my expectations that they would change. This meant reckoning with the fact that they might hurt me again, even repeatedly. But if they have, I've hardly noticed. I'm not so sensitive anymore.

Is it time that you name your unwillingness to forgive for what it really is—sin? Can you see that the longer you make it about someone else, the further your resentment takes you away from God? Turn away from your sin of unforgiveness, and turn toward God. He will empower you to forgive.

Holy Spirit, Freedom Giver, I can see that this is not about what someone else has done to me, but about my sin against you. I repent of my unforgiveness, and I want to walk in obedience. But I can't do this on my own. Will you meet me? Change my feelings, diffuse the tension, and set me free.

DIGGING DEEPER

What does Psalm 51 teach us about how to respond to conviction of sin?

TORTURED OR SET FREE?

THE KING CALLED IN THE MAN HE HAD FORGIVEN AND SAID, "YOU EVIL SERVANT! I FORGAVE YOU THAT TREMENDOUS DEBT BECAUSE YOU PLEADED WITH ME. SHOULDN'T YOU HAVE MERCY ON YOUR FELLOW SERVANT, JUST AS I HAD MERCY ON YOU?" —MATTHEW 18:32-33

I looked it up: bazillion is not really a number. But it is the best way to describe the debt the man owed the king in Jesus' parable of the debtor from Matthew 18. His debt was not just large, it was an incomprehensible amount of money, impossible for him to repay. But there are two debtors in this story, and the difference is in the amount they owe. The debt owed to the servant by another man was about three months' wages, not a negligible amount, but a pittance in comparison to the debt the servant had been forgiven.

In reality, however, this parable is not so much about the two debtors but about the character of the king. The generous forgiveness of the king illustrates the abundance of God's forgiveness, which sets prisoners free from an apparently hopeless situation, an unpayable debt. Have you truly understood how much God has forgiven you, that your debt was unpayable? Or is that an inconvenient subject that disrupts your self-assured anger?

What will it take for you to be willing to forgive what you see as an enormous wrong against you? You will have to see how big your wrong has been toward God, how much he's forgiven you. Forgiveness does not deem the offense against you as small or meaningless. But the debt becomes such when put into the perspective of your own offenses and debt to God. Until you see the enormity of your sin and the generosity of God's forgiveness, you'll forever feel justified in refusing to forgive someone else.

In this parable, the man who refused to forgive was handed over to torturers. Choosing not to forgive is like choosing to be tortured. It is relentless pain that serves no purpose. Aren't you tired of feeling tortured? Isn't it time you turned your focus from the wrongs done to you to the wrongs you've done toward others and, more important, toward God? Ask him to show you the magnitude of your forgiven sin, and be willing to take a long look. Allow God to change your perspective and change your heart. Allow him to empower you to forgive and set you free from the torturous prison of unforgiveness.

Generous Father, please help me to show my gratitude and recognition for the forgiveness you've extended to me by extending it to others.

DIGGING DEEPER

What does Matthew 18:21-35 reveal to you about the heart of God and the choices of the debtor?

HURT PEOPLE HURT PEOPLE

You must make allowance for each other's faults and forgive the person who offends you. Remember, the Lord forgave you, so you must forgive others. —Colossians 3:13

An email came from someone I hadn't seen in years, and it said, among other things, "What has occurred to me throughout Hope's life, from this distance, is that the focus was not necessarily on her, and I find that more saddening than her death. Her life and death seem to not be about Hope, the child, but more about the parents of Hope." I felt stunned that he would pick the lowest time of my life to reach out to hurt me. My first instinct was to defend myself and find others to defend me. I cried plenty as I weighed his words as well as his seeming desire to injure me. The next day I wrote to a friend:

> It has been a good exercise for me to consider his words carefully and examine myself in light of his criticism. As I look back at my communication with him, I can see how he got some of the impressions he did, and I want to learn from that. But he crossed the line in his accusation that this was about us and not about Hope. We can't talk about things she said, things she did, her character, or her personality. We didn't have the privilege of experiencing those things. So all we can talk about is how she impacted our lives in such positive ways without ever saying a word, and celebrate her life with beauty and excellence. He seems to see that as making it about us rather than about her. The best way I know to honor her is to tell how she revealed God and his ways more clearly to me and so many others. I've learned from it, and I'm letting it go.

The more I thought about it, the more I realized how much disappointment and hurt my old friend has had in his life. It was out of that aching pain that he reached out to hurt me. I began to wonder just how miserable he must be to want to add to my pain at such a low point in my life. The truth is, hurt people hurt other people. Can you see that in the lives of some of the people who have hurt you? Will you think about the person or people who have hurt you deeply and step into their shoes? Allow yourself to feel the hurts and disappointments they've experienced. Will you ask God to replace your criticism with compassion, your resentment with empathy?

Father, teach me to respond in compassion to hurting people who hurt me. Help me to let go of my need to defend myself and to learn to love others like you do.

DIGGING DEEPER

Read 1 Samuel 18–19 and 24:1-8. What hurts prompted Saul to want to hurt David? How did David respond?

THE FIRST STEP TOWARD FORGIVENESS

A stone is heavy and sand is weighty, but the resentment caused by a fool is heavier than both. —Proverbs 27:3

"I left while you were speaking because you really made me mad," the last woman in line said to me. I couldn't imagine what I'd said that made her so mad. "It was what you said about forgiveness," she said. An accumulation of offenses had left her so angry, she couldn't talk about it without tears.

"Forgiveness is not minimizing what someone has done or saying that it didn't matter," I had said. "Forgiveness says, 'You hurt me deeply, but I'm not going to make you pay. You don't owe me anymore—not even an apology.' " The suggestion that she didn't have to wait for the people who had hurt her to be sorry or even acknowledge what they had done before she forgave was too big a hurdle for her. And maybe it is for you, too. She saw the imagined confrontation she thought would feel so delicious slipping away, so she walked out.

But she was miserable inside and tired of carrying such a heavy load of resentment. And she knew she was making everyone around her miserable too, so she came back to talk. While she knew she needed to forgive, it felt to her like a mountain too tall to climb. "I know it feels like forgiving them is not only unfair, but impossible," I told her. "But you have a choice. You can decide it is too hard for you, and a year from now you will be more embittered, more miserable than you are now. Or you can begin to move forward, starting today, so that a year from now, your load will be at least a little bit lighter." Forgiveness doesn't usually happen overnight. The deeper the hurt, the longer the process. But that doesn't mean you can't start down that road today. You likely won't get rid of all your negative emotions immediately, but don't let that keep you where you are. Your first step toward finding freedom may be simply asking God to give you the want-to.

Aren't you tired of carrying around the heaviness in your heart that not only robs you of happiness, but also spreads its poison to everyone around you? Won't you take the first step toward forgiveness?

My Burden Bearer, this load is getting too heavy for me, and I know I must begin to let it go. Will you give me the want-to for forgiveness so I can take at least one step toward lightening my load?

DIGGING DEEPER

Read Psalm 55:22; 146:8; and Matthew 11:28. What does God promise to those who bear heavy burdens?

TASTE AND SEE

TASTE AND SEE THAT THE LORD IS GOOD. OH, THE JOYS OF THOSE WHO TRUST IN HIM!
—PSALM 34:8

Why is it that when someone in the family suspects the milk in the fridge has gone bad, he or she wants *you* to taste it, just to confirm the suspicion? *I'll take your word for it!* I want to say. *Why would I want to taste it if it is sour?*

Holding on to hurt and plotting your revenge is like choosing to chug a carton of sour milk. As the rotten stuff works its way through the facets of your personality, everything takes on that sour smell, taste, and temperament. The bitterness takes root inside you, coming out in the form of distrust, insecurity, criticism, guilt, anger, suspicion, and fear.

So if something has happened that left a bad taste in your mouth, how are you going to get rid of it? How are you going to keep the bitterness from taking root in your heart? Peter wrote, "So get rid of all malicious behavior and deceit. Don't just pretend to be good! Be done with hypocrisy and jealousy and backstabbing. You must crave pure spiritual milk so that you can grow into the fullness of your salvation. Cry out for this nourishment as a baby cries for milk, now that you have had a taste of the Lord's kindness" (1 Peter 2:1-3). His suggested antidote for the taste of bitterness is to crave the goodness of God.

You have tasted the Lord's kindness, haven't you? Can you remember how it tasted? Nurture that taste memory and spit the acid bitterness out. Fellowship with God tastes so much sweeter than the sourness of resentment and revenge. And the truth is, you can't have both. Either your bitterness will kill your appetite for his sweetness, or his sweetness will purify your bitterness. You simply can't nurture your grudge and also enjoy God. Deep down you know that is true. So does your desire for revenge and the anticipation of another person's humiliation or defeat taste so good that it is worth forfeiting a growing appetite for the goodness of God?

The cliché says that "time heals all wounds." But it isn't true. Only the goodness of God can get the taste of bitterness out of our mouths and the root of bitterness out of our hearts. Don't waste another day. Won't you taste and see how good God is and spit out the sourness in your spirit?

Sweet Savior, I thought revenge would be sweet, but it has turned so sour inside me. Increase my hunger for you, and take away the bitterness in me.

DIGGING DEEPER

Read Psalm 119:103; Proverbs 24:14; 2 Corinthians 2:14; and Ephesians 5:2. What sweetness does God offer in his goodness to replace our bitterness?

WEEK 46

FORGIVENESS

REFLECTION

Who immediately comes to your mind when you think about forgiveness? Are there some ways you are making that person pay? What steps do you need to take toward forgiveness?

Can you think of a situation or person the Holy Spirit has enabled you to forgive? How did that feel, and what did you learn from it to help you avoid bitterness in the future?

MEDITATION

Now is the time to get rid of anger, rage, malicious behavior, slander, and dirty language. Don't lie to each other, for you have stripped off your old evil nature and all its wicked deeds. In its place you have clothed yourselves with a brand-new nature that is continually being renewed as you learn more and more about Christ, who created this new nature within you. Since God chose you to be the holy people whom he loves, you must clothe yourselves with tenderhearted mercy, kindness, humility, gentleness, and patience. You must make allowance for each other's faults and forgive the person who offends you. Remember, the Lord forgave you, so you must forgive others. And the most important piece of clothing you must wear is love. Love is what binds us all together in perfect harmony. And let the peace that comes from Christ rule in your hearts. For as members of one body you are all called to live in peace. And always be thankful. —Colossians 3:8-10, 12-15

Read through these verses several times, marking words and phrases that are especially meaningful to you.

What do you learn about timing, motivation, and empowerment in these verses?

Listen to the Spirit of God and ask him to reveal to you any lingering bitterness that you need to get rid of and replace with love and peace.

PRAYER

Praise God as a generous forgiver, our pioneer and example in forgiving others.

Thank God for being willing to meet you at every step of obedience and to remove your heavy burden of bitterness.

Intercede for the people who have hurt you, asking God how he might use you to help them heal from the hurts in their lives.

Confess your unforgiveness as sin, and ask God to forgive and cleanse you.

Taste and see that the Lord is good.

WEEK 47

GOING DEEPER

Throughout our lives we come to thresholds at which we are asked to make important choices. Perhaps the difficulties in your life have brought you to one even now. Here you are faced with a choice: Will you resent this intrusion into your comfortable life, or will you view this intrusion as an invitation to go deeper with God than you've ever gone before?

Suffering calls us out of our shallowness into the dangerous and demanding but ultimately delightful depths of an intense life with God. We simply cannot confront the harsh realities of loss and pain without being stretched and deepened. Honestly, there have been times I have looked back longingly at my simpler, more shallow days before severe pain and intense questions forced me to dig more deeply into who God is and how he works. But the truth is, I would never go back. The taste of richer intimacy with God and the thrill of wading into deep waters with him draw me forward.

Aren't you ready to go deeper with God than you've ever gone before? Don't be afraid. He invites you to come, and he will walk with you.

THIS WEEK'S PASSAGE FOR MEDITATION

Just as you accepted Christ Jesus as your Lord, you must continue to live in obedience to him. Let your roots grow down into him and draw up nourishment from him, so you will grow in faith, strong and vigorous in the truth you were taught. Let your lives overflow with thanksgiving for all he has done. —Colossians 2:6-7

NEW SPIRITUAL ADVENTURES WITH GOD

SPEND YOUR TIME AND ENERGY IN TRAINING YOURSELF FOR SPIRITUAL FITNESS. PHYSICAL EXERCISE HAS SOME VALUE, BUT SPIRITUAL EXERCISE IS MUCH MORE IMPORTANT, FOR IT PROMISES A REWARD IN BOTH THIS LIFE AND THE NEXT. —1 TIMOTHY 4:7-8

Last year in science class, Matt studied the body and learned to name all the bones and major organs. One day he told me he had learned that muscles develop by being pushed beyond their capacity, which causes them to actually break down. It is in the recovery process they are rebuilt stronger, firmer, larger. What this means is that if I want to build up my physical muscles, I must repeatedly lift more weight than is really comfortable for me. I have to lift until it burns a little. This burn is a sign that the muscle is breaking down and will come back bigger and stronger.

It's that burn I don't really like in exercising my body. And it's the burn I avoid in exercising my spirit and soul. I have felt it, and I don't particularly like it. The truth is, I'd like to have the muscles without the burn, the spiritual strength without pain. Wouldn't you? But it doesn't work that way.

For years I have worked with authors who have made writing a book look easy. But for me, it hasn't been. For me, it has been a spiritual adventure, an opportunity to exercise and build my faith muscles, because it has required that I depend on God to supply the inspiration and understanding I need in ways I have never needed it before, in different ways than my experiences with Hope and Gabe required. I have felt the burn, and while it hasn't always been comfortable, it has been thrilling. Because the truth is, I don't want my greatest spiritual adventures to all be behind me! I want to keep going, keep growing. I want to know him better and love him more next year than I do today. I want to be more like him and do more for him. So I've got to keep building my spiritual muscles.

Do you want to settle for staying where you are, or do you long for more faith adventures with God? If you really want to go deeper and become stronger, it will require a willingness to feel the burn. But with the burn comes a promise not only for strength to live in this life, but a sure reward in the next.

Lord, I don't really want to hurt anymore, but I'm willing to feel the burn if that's what it takes to make me spiritually strong and fit for a great spiritual adventure. Keep stretching me and shaping me into someone you can use.

DIGGING DEEPER

What is needed to grow stronger, according to Colossians 2:7, 19 and 1 Peter 2:2? How do difficulties strengthen us, according to James 1:2-4 and 1 Peter 1:7?

BLESSED ARE THOSE WHO MOURN

GOD BLESSES THOSE WHO MOURN, FOR THEY WILL BE COMFORTED. —MATTHEW 5:4

One Sunday when I was in junior high, my Sunday school teacher drew a line on the board and numbered it from one to ten with one representing absolute coldness toward God and ten, burning hot for God. Then he asked each of us to put a dot on the line that represented where we were with God. I can't remember exactly where I put my dot, but it was way up there. In reality, this represented not my maturity in Christ but my immaturity. Because the deeper we go with God the clearer our vision becomes about our own coldheartedness toward him. As our understanding of his holiness increases, so does our accurate estimation of our own sinfulness. The mark of spiritual maturity is not an absence of sin but an ever-deepening awareness of it. This is why John wrote, "If we say we have no sin, we are only fooling ourselves and refusing to accept the truth" (1 John 1:8).

Feeling the pain of sin is good for us, though we'd much rather rush through the sorrow to find solace in the sure promise of forgiveness. But we mustn't be in too much of a hurry. Our mourning over sin has important work to do before we can go deeper with God. Deep sorrow over sin is a redemptive anguish. It breaks up the hardened ground in our hearts, making us more spiritually sensitive. Mourning means that instead of continuing to deny, blame, and compare, we've finally taken responsibility for who we are and what we've done. This is the starting place for growth and healing.

Are you so consumed with mourning over the losses in your life that you have no tears for your own sin and rebellion toward God? Mourning over sin is not as simple as a casual mention of our failings. It is a sincere expression of excruciating regret. It is looking squarely at what sin cost us and, more significantly, what it cost Christ, and saying, "I never want to do that again." It is seeing the offense we've caused God and being brokenhearted over how our sin has hurt him.

If you really want to go deeper with God, it is necessary that your sins hurt you a little, that you refuse to rush too quickly into peace. This is the sadness that will make you happy forever.

Holy One, I've taken such a casual approach to sin, taken your forgiveness for granted. But no more. I want to allow myself to mourn over the sin in my life along with the hurts in my life. Help me to see my sin for what it is and what it cost so I can repent, and in my repentance, go deeper with you.

DIGGING DEEPER

Read Romans 7:24; 1 Corinthians 5:2; and 2 Corinthians 7:8-13. What do these verses reveal about the appropriateness and benefit of mourning over sin?

I WILL NOT GIVE THAT WHICH COSTS ME NOTHING

I cannot present burnt offerings to the Lord my God that have cost me nothing. —2 Samuel 24:24

I started working in my dad's drugstore as soon as I could stand on a box and reach the cash register. The first big thing I bought with the money I earned was a bicycle. I took good care of that bicycle because I had worked so hard for it—probably better than I would have if it had been given to me. It's just human nature that we value what we sacrifice for.

Our willingness to sacrifice in pursuit of God reflects just how precious he is to us. And likewise, if he is not precious to us, perhaps it is because we have never sacrificed anything for him. While we may give lip service to our desire to go deeper with God, our willingness to sacrifice for it reveals whether or not our desire is genuine.

Perhaps the painful truth is that while we accept that we may have to sacrifice, we think we should be able to select what the sacrifice will be and the degree to which it will cost us. We want to stay in control of the cost. We simply don't want to become "a living sacrifice."

God doesn't require sacrifice because he is needy or demanding, but because he knows we need to sacrifice. Sacrifice sharpens our character, refines our faith, deepens our commitment. While it is not always a pleasant process, it is ultimately a glorious one. And as we go deeper, we discover that sacrifice becomes a sweet surrender—not because we're masochists and enjoy pain for its own sake, but because we learn by experience that the intimacy it gives us with him is more valuable than anything it may have cost.

Perhaps instead of remaining disillusioned by what God has withheld from you, you need to ask yourself what you have withheld from him. Going deeper will cost you something—maybe getting up early instead of lingering in bed, tithing on your gross income and not just your net, teaching a Sunday school class instead of sitting in one. Your sacrifice sends God the message that you are serious about seeking him, which he will reward with his very presence.

Precious Jesus, with every sacrifice I make for you, you become more valuable to me and I sense a growing nearness to you. Show me what you want me to let go of so I can come closer to you.

DIGGING DEEPER

Read 2 Samuel 24:18-25; Psalm 51:17; Luke 21:1-4; Romans 12:1; and Ephesians 5:2. What made these sacrifices acceptable to God?

TEAR DOWN YOUR IDOLS

Do not worship any other gods besides me. —Deuteronomy 5:7

They were one of the last couples I would expect to struggle in their marriage—friends who went to the mission field in Africa and then planted and pastored a church. So I was saddened and perplexed when she told me that he had moved out. Visiting her a few months later, I was expecting to hear that she was devastated and depressed. Instead what I saw in my friend was disappointment and grief mixed with acceptance, trust, and even joy. She told me the turning point for her was when her eyes were opened to the idols in her life, such as her identity as a stay-at-home mom, financial security through her husband's work, her desire for a complete family living the church life. By identifying these desires as idols and recognizing that even good things become idols if she worships and serves them more than God, she experienced a spiritual breakthrough. While she would love for her family to be whole again, she knows that if she holds on to these desires too strongly, she won't be able to grab hold of the new things God wants to do in her life.

While we may think of an idol as a statue of wood, stone, or metal worshiped by pagans, in reality an idol is anything apart from God that we depend on to be happy, fulfilled, or secure. It is anything other than God that motivates and masters us, anything we love and pursue in place of God. Idols begin with desires—often good and healthy desires. But when our desire becomes a demand, when we start believing that the object of desire is essential to our fulfillment and well-being, when it begins to control our thoughts and behavior, whatever it is we want has become an idol (1 Corinthians 6:12). What we want is not the problem; the problem is that we want it too much.

So if we want to go deeper with God, we must search our hearts for idols. This isn't easy because we tend to justify ourselves and disguise our real desires so we won't have to let go of what we love. Do you need to examine your life for idols, for desires that have become demands? Going deeper with God is a process of identifying and confessing our idols one by one and cooperating with God as he removes them, bit by bit, from our hearts.

My Idol Slayer, I repent of my idol worship and ask for your forgiveness and cleansing. Replace the idols in my life with a growing devotion to you, an increasing passion to worship and serve only you.

DIGGING DEEPER

Read Hosea 14:1-9. What precious promises does God make to those who are willing to get rid of the idols in their lives?

GOING PUBLIC

This precious treasure—this light and power that now shine within us—is held in perishable containers, that is, in our weak bodies. So everyone can see that our glorious power is from God and is not our own. —2 Corinthians 4:7

I had sat in on hundreds of media interviews with authors as they talked about matters of faith and conviction. But this time *I* was the one being interviewed. That night, after a long conversation during which the reporter took copious notes in preparation for quoting me in a national newspaper, I lay in bed feeling as if I had walked out on a plank and was getting ready to take a dive. This time it was *my* voice, *my* reputation, *me*. I realized that it is one thing for people around me to know that I go to church and work in Christian publishing, but another thing to proclaim publicly what I believe, to openly profess my devotion to Jesus in front of those who may ridicule or reject me.

Hardship often presents us with the opportunity to go public in big and small ways with what we really believe. Sometimes it is simple, such as telling those who ask how you're doing that you are determined to trust God with what is ahead. Going deeper with God means that we don't use religious-sounding language to discuss our lives with our church friends and a different set of vocabulary for our unbelieving neighbors and coworkers. We become authentic, no matter who we're talking to, expressing our very real fears and failures along with our desire to trust God, know God, and see him at work.

Perhaps we're hesitant to go public with our faith because we don't want to be held accountable for living a life that the world expects of those who claim to be Jesus' followers. But it is good for us to be held to a higher standard than those who make no claim of Christ, isn't it? Going public doesn't mean becoming perfect, but it does mean we never want to do anything that would bring shame to the name of Christ. When our desire to honor Christ overrides our desire to indulge in a little gossip, join the crowd in complaining, or compromise to get ahead, we know we've gone deeper with God. If you're really serious about going deeper with God, isn't it time you went public?

I'm ready to tell the world that you are mine and I am yours, Jesus. How I want you to shine beautifully in my life so that others see you in me.

DIGGING DEEPER

Read Matthew 10 to discover what Jesus had to say to the disciples as they prepared to go public with their faith in him.

WEEK 47

GOING DEEPER

REFLECTION

Looking back at the recent months in your life, have you been going deeper with God, or have you been resisting his invitation and keeping at a distance?

What would it mean for you to go deeper with God in the coming weeks? What would it take for you to make this decision? Are you willing?

MEDITATION

Just as you accepted Christ Jesus as your Lord, you must continue to live in obedience to him. Let your roots grow down into him and draw up nourishment from him, so you will grow in faith, strong and vigorous in the truth you were taught. Let your lives overflow with thanksgiving for all he has done. —Colossians 2:6-7

Read through the verses slowly several times, noting the words and phrases that are especially meaningful to you.

Notice the role we play and the role God plays in our growth.

Turn this passage into a prayer, telling God what you want to do and what you want him to do.

PRAYER

Praise God for being so big, so wise, and so loving that we can never plumb the depths of him.

Thank God for inviting you to go deeper with him, for wanting you to walk closely with him.

Ask God for the courage to go public with your faith.

Confess your love for the idols in your life, and ask God to remove them bit by bit.

Tell God you have counted the cost and you want to go deeper with him, knowing that the rewards will be worth the cost.

WEEK 48

WHO AM I?

Do you know who you are? Instinctively we define our identity by what we do, where we're from, how we look. I can easily believe the lies that my identity is defined by what I've accomplished, that my worth is determined by the number on my bathroom scale, and that my status is decided by who I know and who knows me. Likewise, I've often felt defined by my losses. Sometimes when I walk into a room I feel as if I'm wearing a badge that says, "Yes, I'm that woman who lost two children."

But is that really the sum of who I am? Is my identity merely an accumulation of my successes and sorrows? My identity is not about who I am, but *whose* I am. I belong to Christ. In him I find my true identity.

Rather than looking in the mirror or listening to others, we must look into God's Word and listen to the voice of God our maker to discover who we really are. It is only from him and in him that we can become who he has made us to be.

THIS WEEK'S PASSAGE FOR MEDITATION

Come to Christ, who is the living cornerstone of God's temple. He was rejected by the people, but he is precious to God who chose him. And now God is building you, as living stones, into his spiritual temple. What's more, you are God's holy priests, who offer the spiritual sacrifices that please him because of Jesus Christ. For you are a chosen people. You are a kingdom of priests, God's holy nation, his very own possession. This is so you can show others the goodness of God, for he called you out of the darkness into his wonderful light. Dear brothers and sisters, you are foreigners and aliens here. So I warn you to keep away from evil desires because they fight against your very souls. —1 Peter 2:4-5, 9, 11

BOND SERVANT

ACT AS FREE MEN, AND DO NOT USE YOUR FREEDOM AS A COVERING FOR EVIL, BUT USE IT AS BONDSLAVES OF GOD. —1 PETER 2:16 (NASB)

Occasionally I catch myself carefully preparing how I will introduce myself to someone I want to meet, carefully weighing what connection to mention that will give me credibility and status in that person's estimation, while also trying to appear unmistakably humble. Pretty pathetic, isn't it?

The first thing we say about ourselves or the way we identify ourselves when we meet someone new makes a strong statement about how we see ourselves and where we find our significance. This insight into ourselves adds meaning to the way Peter, Paul, John, and James introduced themselves at the beginning of their letters. Each of these writers introduced themselves the same way—as a bond servant or slave of Jesus Christ (see Romans 1:1; James 1:1; 2 Peter 1:1; and Revelation 1:1). It's as if they said, *The most important thing about me is that I've made Jesus Christ my master. Obeying him is the focus of my life. He is so precious to me, I've willingly bonded myself to him as his servant for life.* "Bond servant" didn't just describe them; it defined them. It reflected a recognition that they had been bought by and were owned by Christ and were utterly submitted to what pleased him.

What does it mean to be a bond servant? A bond servant is not just a slave, but a slave who has willingly committed himself to serve a master he loves and respects, even when given the opportunity to leave. This kind of slavery is chosen, not imposed—the result of freedom, not compulsion.

Do you see yourself as a bond servant, or do you see God as your servant, obligated to fulfill your desires and follow your instructions offered up as prayers? Becoming a bond servant is not solely for super-saints. It is the calling of every believer. Are you willing to define yourself by your yieldedness to Christ? When we see him for who he really is and for how well he loves us, becoming his bond servant is a sweet surrender—not because we're forced to, but because we *want* to.

Master Jesus, I realize that you are not forcing me into slavery. Becoming your bond servant is my choice. And my choice is made. I want to relinquish my independence, surrender my will, and declare my loyalty to you.

DIGGING DEEPER

Read Galatians 1:10; Philippians 2:7; 2 Timothy 2:24; and 1 Peter 2:16. What are the implications of being a bond servant?

LIVING STONES

Come to Christ, who is the living cornerstone of God's temple. He was rejected by the people, but he is precious to God who chose him. And now God is building you, as living stones, into his spiritual temple. What's more, you are God's holy priests, who offer the spiritual sacrifices that please him because of Jesus Christ. —1 Peter 2:4-5

On the front page of a newspaper from January 2005 is a photograph of hundreds of Buddhist monks in Thailand, surrounded by candles. The scene is a memorial service for victims of the tsunami that took the lives of thousands upon thousands of people. "The ceremony was primarily Buddhist, but included prayers from Christian and Muslim clerics," the story reads. "In the merit ceremony, people dedicate their own good deeds to those who have died suddenly to ensure them a good afterlife."

But if it is God they are offering their good deeds to, this kind of spiritual sacrifice is not what pleases him. What makes worship acceptable to God is not style or sincerity or sentimentality. The truth is, people all around the world worship God. But while God desires their worship, he rejects much of it, because it is not built on the foundation he chose for his spiritual house—the precious stone of Jesus. Jesus is the only mediator between God and man. For worship to be acceptable to God, it must come through Jesus.

But even while the world rejects Jesus, God is at work building his temple, not with rocks or mortar, religion or ritual, but with living stones—you and me and all those who love Jesus. We are being fit together with other believers into something that is more than a collection of individuals working toward God. As a living stone, you are part of something God is doing that is bigger than you are, more important than your petty concerns, more purposeful than your personal preferences. You are a living stone that God is using to build his spiritual house. So begin to see yourself that way. Willingly offer yourself to God so he can use you to build a place and a people in whom God would choose to dwell.

Master Builder, while the world may reject your Cornerstone, I will not. I become a living stone only as I am in Christ and united with Christ. He is the sure foundation of my life and the one who makes it possible for me to please you.

DIGGING DEEPER

Read Psalm 118:22; Isaiah 28:16; Acts 4:11-12; Ephesians 2:14-22; and 1 Peter 2:4-7. What do these verses reveal about the Cornerstone and the stones with which God is building his house?

GOD'S MASTERPIECE

We are God's masterpiece. He has created us anew in Christ Jesus, so that we can do the good things he planned for us long ago. —Ephesians 2:10

A masterpiece. Me? I don't think so. At least it's hard for me to see. All it takes is a glance in the mirror, a step on the scale, a few minutes of flipping through a magazine, for my self-image to nose-dive and my self-confidence to be shaken. Can you relate? Do you sometimes struggle with the way God has made you—the shape or size of your body, the personality you have, the abilities you were given? It's easy to allow the way we look to define who we are, but Paul says we are God's masterpiece. What does he mean?

When I think of a masterpiece, my first thought, and perhaps yours too, is great works of art by Da Vinci or Rembrandt or Van Gogh, great sculptors and painters who created the breathtaking works of art we gaze at in wonder. But I don't think this is the kind of masterpiece Paul had in mind, because God is not making us into his masterpiece simply so we can look good or even so we can be good. His purpose in making us a masterpiece is so that we can *do* good. Rather than Picasso or Monet, think instead of Stradivari. Antonio Stradivari made about 1,100 violins, harps, guitars, violas, and cellos during the seventeenth and eighteenth centuries. Each Stradivarius is a treasured masterpiece unsurpassed in sound. It is not made to sit on a shelf to be admired for its beauty, but to be played—to be put in the hands of a master musician to create beautiful music.

You are a masterpiece, not like the Mona Lisa, which hangs in a museum behind bulletproof glass, beyond the potentially damaging touch of dirty hands. You are like a Stradivarius violin, whose true beauty and value is seen and experienced in its usefulness—especially when it is used by a master. Being used by the master in this hurting world is thrilling. The reason it feels so good to offer food to those who are hungry, a coat to those who are cold, companionship to those who are lonely, a home to a child who is alone, is because this is what you were made for. This is the beauty of the Master Jesus using your life.

Master Designer, I've wasted too much time and energy looking in the mirror agonizing over my own reflection instead of feeling the pain of a hurting world around me and doing something about it. Make me a masterpiece that displays your beauty and demonstrates your love.

DIGGING DEEPER

Read Romans 8:28-30. How does this passage add to your understanding of God's plans and purposes?

ALIENS AND STRANGERS

DEAR BROTHERS AND SISTERS, YOU ARE FOREIGNERS AND ALIENS HERE. —1 PETER 2:11

Imagine God telling you that he has given you the country of Guatemala. You hop on the next plane and spend the rest of your life there, living not in a house, but in a camper. Your kids live in a camper by you, and their kids in the next camper over. You move from place to place with no citizenship and no rights—always an outsider, never fitting in.

This is what it was like for Abraham. God called him to leave his home and go to another land that he was promised as his inheritance. But Abraham never built a home there. In fact, the only land he ever owned was a cave in which he buried his wife, Sarah. But Abraham wasn't dissatisfied or disappointed. Hebrews says that when he reached the land God promised him, "he lived there by faith—for he was like a foreigner, living in a tent. And so did Isaac and Jacob, to whom God gave the same promise" (Hebrews 11:9). Evidently, Abraham's dreams for a homeland were not rooted in Canaan or anyplace else on this earth. Abraham's hopes were invested in his heavenly homeland. "He was confidently looking forward to a city with eternal foundations, a city designed and built by God" (verse 10). A city designed in God's mind and built with his hands. I imagine that as Abraham stepped into that heavenly homeland he had hoped for and dreamed of, he exclaimed, "Heaven was worth waiting for! Now I finally feel at home!"

When we see ourselves as aliens and strangers in this world, our losses in this life don't take such a toll, our disappointments don't cut so deep. In fact, we begin to see them as blessings, reminders that we're not yet home. We see through the illusions of security and success this world offers and remember that we are just visitors here. And our hope makes us homesick.

So if you feel like you never quite fit in, if you nurture a sense of restlessness, a sense of dissatisfaction with life as this earth defines it, congratulations! It's all part of embracing your identity as an alien and stranger, seeing yourself as you truly are: a citizen of heaven. Heaven is the place where you will finally feel at home. No need to put down deep roots here.

Lord of my heavenly home, sometimes I expect too much of this world, forgetting that my real home, my place of rest and belonging, is in heaven. Remind me that I'm an alien and stranger when I try to make my home here.

DIGGING DEEPER

Read Matthew 6:19, 25; 2 Corinthians 5:1-8; Philippians 2:15; and 1 Peter 2:11. What instructions are given to us as foreigners and aliens?

SALT AND LIGHT

You are the salt of the earth. But what good is salt if it has lost its flavor? Can you make it useful again? It will be thrown out and trampled underfoot as worthless. You are the light of the world—like a city on a mountain, glowing in the night for all to see. Don't hide your light under a basket! Instead, put it on a stand and let it shine for all. —Matthew 5:13-15

One might assume that if we are foreigners—exiles living here on earth and longing for our true home in heaven—we simply won't get involved in the affairs of the world around us. But the fact that we are exiles on the earth doesn't mean we're unconcerned, uncaring, or disconnected from this world. It means we exert our influence in the best of ways. We care because God cares, and we get involved because we want to be involved in what God is doing. We want our hearts to be broken by the things that break the heart of God.

When Jesus says that we are the salt of the earth and the light of the world, he is not only describing who we are but what we do. To those who heard Jesus speak these words, salt was not so much a flavor enhancer as it was an essential preservative prior to modern refrigeration. By calling us salt, Jesus invited us to become a part of his own preservation-and-health ministry in this decaying and sin-diseased world. Likewise, Jesus called us light, inviting us to join him in his work of penetrating the darkness, illuminating truth, and showing people how to find their way home to God.

Our ability to be preservation agents and illuminators is dependent on our connection to the Source of true light and true saltiness. On our own we cannot save or sustain anything, but Jesus has drawn us into the task he is about. His work has become our work. It begins to define not only what we do but who we are. Much more than a marginal note to an otherwise selfish existence, being salt and light is our part in God's plan for redeeming this broken world.

Salt and light don't simply serve themselves. Salt does its best work in decaying places, and light does its best in dark places. Has your salt lost its preservation power because you're too consumed with self-preservation? Have you hidden your light under a basket of self-protection or withdrawn to nurse your own wounds? If so, isn't it time you remembered who you are? You are salt, and you are light. Preserve. Shine.

Light of the World, don't let me become so preoccupied with my own pain that I am indifferent and uninvolved in people's lives and the world around me. Make me the preservation and illumination agent you've called me to be.

DIGGING DEEPER

Why does the world resist the light, according to John 3:18-21 and 2 Corinthians 4:4-7?

WEEK 48

WHO AM I?

REFLECTION

Think about how you usually introduce yourself or describe yourself to someone who does not know you. What does this reveal to you about what you value and what gives you significance?

What measurements of your worth or definers of your identity do you need to abandon so that you can embrace your true identity in Christ?

MEDITATION AND PRAYER

Meditate on what each of the following verses tells you about who you really are.

Turn each passage into a prayer, talking to God about who he has made you to be in Christ.

Come to Christ, who is the living cornerstone of God's temple. He was rejected by the people, but he is precious to God who chose him. And now God is building you, as living stones, into his spiritual temple. What's more, you are God's holy priests, who offer the spiritual sacrifices that please him because of Jesus Christ. For you are a chosen people. You are a kingdom of priests, God's holy nation, his very own possession. This is so you can show others the goodness of God, for he called you out of the darkness into his wonderful light. Dear brothers and sisters, you are foreigners and aliens here. So I warn you to keep away from evil desires because they fight against your very souls. —1 Peter 2:4-5, 9, 11

I no longer call you servants, because a master doesn't confide in his servants. Now you are my friends, since I have told you everything the Father told me. —John 15:15

You are among those who have been called to belong to Jesus Christ. —Romans 1:6

Once they were told, "You are not my people." But now he will say, "You are children of the living God." —Romans 9:26

You must display a new nature because you are a new person, created in God's likeness—righteous, holy, and true. —Ephesians 4:24

He has brought you back as his friends. He has done this through his death on the cross in his own human body. As a result, he has brought you into the very presence of God, and you are holy and blameless as you stand before him without a single fault. —Colossians 1:22

WEEK 49

WHAT DOES GOD WANT?

All kinds of voices presume to tell us what is important to God and how to live our lives. Some say what God wants is obedience, sacrifice, adherence to right doctrines or moral codes. Some say real religion is humanitarianism. Some say God just wants us to be happy and self-actualized. Others lead us to believe that sincerity is what matters, regardless of what we sincerely believe.

While all these voices may contain some degree of truth, we want to hear the full truth. We want to hear the true voice of God. We want God to reveal himself directly to us and show us what he wants. And in reality, he is not demanding or difficult. He has not set out a series of hurdles designed to trip us up or wear us down. He doesn't want to hurt us; he wants to love us. What does God want from you? He wants your heart.

THIS WEEK'S PASSAGE FOR MEDITATION

What can we bring to the LORD to make up for what we've done? Should we bow before God with offerings of yearling calves? Should we offer him thousands of rams and tens of thousands of rivers of olive oil? Would that please the LORD? Should we sacrifice our firstborn children to pay for the sins of our souls? Would that make him glad?

No, O people, the LORD has already told you what is good, and this is what he requires: to do what is right, to love mercy, and to walk humbly with your God.

—MICAH 6:6-8

DELIGHT IN THE LORD

TAKE DELIGHT IN THE LORD, AND HE WILL GIVE YOU YOUR HEART'S DESIRES.
—PSALM 37:4

For a long time I thought of Psalm 37:4 as the single person's verse of hope. How many times have we heard this verse quoted to or by a single person and interpreted as, "If I just get close to God, then he'll give me what I really want—a husband!" But if what we see in this verse is a formula for getting what we want from God, we're settling for much less than what God is offering. God wants to change what we want. He wants to free us from the tyranny of wanting what will never completely satisfy us.

You see, God is not after an external change in our behavior; he wants an internal change in our affections. He wants to transform and redirect our most personal and passionate longings and then satisfy them fully. The truth is, he wants us to become total pleasure seekers who recognize that *he* is our greatest pleasure. Our problem is that we don't always believe God is as good as he says he is. When we hear that he wants to give us himself, a part of us says to ourselves, *That's it? Just him? Honestly, I was hoping for more.* But Jesus is so much better than we think he is, and this world is simply not as good as we think it is. We discover these truths as we deliberately delight in him. And when we do, we find ourselves running in his direction rather than being dragged toward him.

The truth is, most of my Christian life has been about duty instead of delight. I'm only beginning to discover what it means to delight in the Lord and to understand that, as John Piper says, "God is most glorified when I am most satisfied in him." Understanding delight in the Lord is like a gift that has been given to me, and I hope to spend the rest of my life unwrapping and enjoying it. Because duty only gets us so far. Duty becomes a drain and leaves us dry. Duty is not enough to keep us clinging to God when the bottom falls out. But delighting in the Lord is like a refreshing spring in the desert. While duty will suck the life out of us, delight infuses us with life.

Can you see that God himself is the end of your search for what you want most, not the means to some further pleasure? Will you choose to delight in him even in your difficulty? Will you allow him to change what you want?

My greatest Delight, you are so much more pleasurable, so much more generous, than I have understood. Forgive my self-righteous sense of duty, and enjoy my ever-increasing delight in you.

DIGGING DEEPER

How do these psalms emphasize the delight God offers and wants us to find in him alone: Psalm 16:11; 73:25-26; 90:14; and 100:2?

FEAR GOD

WHAT DOES THE LORD YOUR GOD REQUIRE OF YOU? HE REQUIRES YOU TO FEAR HIM, TO LIVE ACCORDING TO HIS WILL, TO LOVE AND WORSHIP HIM WITH ALL YOUR HEART AND SOUL, AND TO OBEY THE LORD'S COMMANDS AND LAWS THAT I AM GIVING YOU TODAY FOR YOUR OWN GOOD. —DEUTERONOMY 10:12-13

To suggest in modern culture that one should fear God is to invite ridicule and perhaps even pity. It seems like an utterly outdated notion that was devised to control behavior and restrict freedom. Even to the biblically initiated, it sounds like an instruction meant for Old Testament times, not for New Testament Christians who breathe in the air of grace, in which "perfect love expels all fear" (1 John 4:18).

We know that anything God requires of us, even his command to fear him, flows from his love for us. The command to fear God is not outdated nor is it limited to Old Testament God followers. Peter wrote, "You must live in reverent fear of him" (1 Peter 1:17). So what does it mean to live in reverent fear of God?

To fear God is to live as if he is your only hope in this dark and dangerous world; and he is. To fear God is to live as if he is your only source of satisfaction; and he is. To fear God is to believe that he will supply all of your needs; and he will. To fear God is to live as if you have been loved supremely and bought at a tremendous price; and you have. To fear God is to "notice how God is both kind and severe . . . severe to those who disobeyed, but kind to you as you continue to trust in his kindness" (Romans 11:22). The more precious Jesus is to us, the less we have to fear from the world around us and the greater our fear of God becomes.

It is our fear of God that protects us from blaming God for the evil around us and especially the evil that has hurt us. The fear of God holds our tongue when we want to accuse God of wrongdoing; it halts our defiant finger-wagging; it humbles us in the midst of our self-righteous anger. Proverbs 9:10 says that "fear of the LORD is the beginning of wisdom." Do you really want to come to a better understanding of the big picture of what God is doing in the world and in your life? The starting place is to develop a healthy fear of God. Fear the heartbreak of dishonoring him, the tragedy of distrusting him, the consequences of disobeying him. See that he is on your side against any foe that would seek to harm you.

Perfect Love, I'm beginning to see that the more I grow in my fear of you, the less I will fear anything or anyone else.

DIGGING DEEPER

Read Isaiah 41:10. List five promises of God that reduce our fears of anything outside of God and increase our fear of God.

WITH ALL YOUR HEART

You must love the Lord your God with all your heart, all your soul, all your mind, and all your strength. —Mark 12:30

"I just want to be friends." Ugh. This is the phrase every hopeful lover dreads hearing from the object of his or her affection when stepping out onto the risky relational ledge of declaring feelings and desires. God, too, has taken this relational risk, declaring openly his love for you. "I have loved you, my people, with an everlasting love," he says (Jeremiah 31:3). He has made the first move, and what he wants is for you to love him in return. You see, God is not interested in being just a casual acquaintance. His desire is for a vibrant romance. Since the day God created Adam and Eve, placed them in the Garden, and walked with them there, he has been pursuing us to lavish his love on us and to be loved by us. God wants to fill your soul, capture your heart, and captivate your mind in a sacred romance.

Why does God want us to love him in such an all-consuming way? Is he desperate or needy? Of course not. Acts 17:25 tells us that "he has no needs. He himself gives life and breath to everything, and he satisfies every need there is." We are the ones who are desperate and needy. Loving God is what we were created for. He knows our hearts will never be satisfied until they are captured by him and committed to him.

God is looking for a love affair with you. He doesn't want you to exert all your energies following a moral code or figuring out doctrinal difficulties. He wants your heart. He wants you to invest every part of yourself not in serving him but in loving him. He wants to save you from becoming like the empty, unhappy people described in Isaiah 29: "These people say they are mine. They honor me with their lips, but their hearts are far away" (verse 13).

Extreme difficulties are like a jolt to our complacent hearts. They awaken our minds and emotions toward God. Can you see he is offering himself to you in the midst of your hurt, wanting an ever deeper intimacy with you? Will you let God love you? Will you love him in return with strong emotions, focused thoughts, a submissive will, and abundant energy?

My divine Lover, I no longer want to tolerate the distance between us or settle for a relationship devoid of passion and intensity. I want to love you with everything in me, with the essence of who I am.

DIGGING DEEPER

How do these psalms direct us to express our love for God: Psalm 18:1-3; 31:23; 63:1-8; 69:9; 97:10; and 119:97?

TAKE UP YOUR CROSS AND FOLLOW ME

JESUS BEGAN TO TELL HIS DISCIPLES PLAINLY THAT HE HAD TO GO TO JERUSALEM, AND HE TOLD THEM WHAT WOULD HAPPEN TO HIM THERE. HE WOULD BE KILLED, AND HE WOULD BE RAISED ON THE THIRD DAY. BUT PETER TOOK HIM ASIDE AND CORRECTED HIM. "HEAVEN FORBID, LORD," HE SAID. "THIS WILL NEVER HAPPEN TO YOU!"
—MATTHEW 16:21-22

"This baby will be fine. God wouldn't ask you to go through this *again*!" our friends said. We told only a handful of close friends that I was pregnant as we waited for the prenatal test results. These were godly people who loved us, and they just couldn't imagine that we might have to endure the heartbreak of loving and losing another child.

I think this was the same sentiment that caused Peter to respond to Jesus' words about his coming death by saying, in essence, "Don't even say it! Surely God's plan for you could not involve a cross!" Peter loved Jesus, and he didn't want him to suffer. But Jesus responded by telling Peter that he was seeing things merely from a human point of view and not from God's perspective. "If any of you wants to be my follower, you must put aside your selfish ambition, shoulder your cross, and follow me," Jesus said (Matthew 16:24).

The disciples knew well what taking up a cross meant. They had seen condemned criminals compelled to carry their instruments of suffering and death. We want to say to Jesus on their behalf and our own, "Surely God's plan for my life does not have to include a cross!"

What is Jesus saying here about what God wants? Does he want you to suffer? Lamentations says that "he does not enjoy hurting people or causing them sorrow" (Lamentations 3:33). It's not that he wants you to suffer, but Jesus knows that following him may require that you suffer for his sake. He is willing for you to suffer because he's seen the other side. He has the benefit of the complete picture, the long view. He's seen the glory ahead for those who are willing to carry their cross, and he wants to share it all with you. He wants you to experience the deep satisfaction that comes only from heeding his call to a crucified life. He wants you to experience the mysterious and amazing joy of taking up your cross and following him.

Crucified Jesus, I hear you calling me to the crucified life, telling me that the only way to find true life is to give up my life for you. Give me the mind of Christ so I will see my life and death to myself with your perspective.

DIGGING DEEPER

Read Matthew 16:21-28 and contemplate the differences between Peter's perspective and Jesus' perspective on suffering.

COME TO ME

Jesus said, "Come to me, all of you who are weary and carry heavy burdens, and I will give you rest. Take my yoke upon you. Let me teach you, because I am humble and gentle, and you will find rest for your souls."
—Matthew 11:28-29

You've been invited. This invitation is not to a party but to a person. Jesus wants to open his heart to you, so he has said, "Come to me." This invitation is addressed to all who are weary and carry heavy burdens. This invitation is for you. Jesus wants you to come to him so he can give you the gift of rest. He knows that what you need is real rest—not just for your body, but also for your soul. And only Jesus can give you soul rest. He wants you to rest from trying to be good enough and from doing too much. He wants you to fully rest in his finished work on the cross, his provision of salvation. This is rest that begins now and continues into eternity. Jesus knows that if we don't rest in him, we'll sacrifice the important for the urgent, the personal for the public. If we don't rest in him, we'll end up empty on the inside, moving through life in a fog of meaningless religious ritual.

So how do you RSVP to Christ's invitation? He said, "Take my yoke upon you. Let me teach you." At first this may sound like just another burden. But the yoke of Jesus is the burden that makes all other burdens bearable. This yoke is what connects us to Jesus so that he can share our load. He wants to bear the weight of your burdens with his strong shoulders.

So when you find yourself searching for something to soothe the pain in your life, will you listen for the voice of Jesus whispering his invitation into your ear, "Come to me"? When you feel your frustration building and your strength fading, hear Jesus saying, "Come to me, all of you who are weary and carry heavy burdens." When you find yourself weighed down by unrealistic expectations or unbearable emotions, Jesus says, "My yoke is easy and my burden is light" (Matthew 11:30, NIV).

Jesus stands with his arms outstretched saying, *Come away from what is insignificant and empty so you can enter into what is eternal, essential, restful. Come to me. Let me love you.* Who could resist such an invitation?

My Yoke Builder and Rest Provider, I come to you weary from life and bearing heavy burdens. I accept your yoke, allowing you to bear the weight of my burdens. I accept your rest that my soul is longing for.

DIGGING DEEPER

What do Isaiah 55:1-3; John 6:35-37; 7:37-38; and Revelation 22:17 add to your understanding of this invitation of Jesus to come to him?

WEEK 49

WHAT DOES GOD WANT?

REFLECTION

What beliefs about what God wants from you have determined how you spend most of your energy and emotion?

How do you want God to shape your life as you move forward with him?

MEDITATION

What can we bring to the LORD to make up for what we've done? Should we bow before God with offerings of yearling calves? Should we offer him thousands of rams and tens of thousands of rivers of olive oil? Would that please the LORD? Should we sacrifice our first-born children to pay for the sins of our souls? Would that make him glad?

No, O people, the LORD has already told you what is good, and this is what he requires: to do what is right, to love mercy, and to walk humbly with your God.

—MICAH 6:6-8

Meditate on the simplicity of what God requires.

Think through the implications of what it means to do what is right, to love mercy, and to walk humbly with God.

Apply these requirements to the specific circumstances of your life today.

PRAYER

Praise God for his humility and gentleness, for the wisdom of his ways, and for the lavishness of his love.

Thank God for the gift of soul rest.

Intercede for those bound up by misunderstandings about what God wants, for those unwilling to enter into the love of God.

Confess your hesitancy to take up your cross, and the fears you have about following.

Petition God to give you the desires of your heart as you delight yourself in him.

WEEK 50

WAITING

From my journal, February 21, 1999:

> *I got up early and took Mom to the airport to catch her 6 a.m. flight, came home and fell into bed for a while. David woke me up at 8 a.m. to tell me that the seizures we have been dreading have started for Hope. They weren't what I expected. I expected her to be out of control and in distress, but they were just gentle contractions of her arms and legs, and a blank stare. We spent about four hours in the emergency room, and I crawled onto the bed with her as the drug drained into her limp little body.*
>
> *I kept thinking about something I read last night in* Tracks of a Fellow Struggler *by John Claypool, a collection of sermons he preached when his daughter was diagnosed, treated, and then died of leukemia. I especially like what he had to say about the promise in Isaiah 40 to those who wait on the Lord: You shall "mount up with wings as eagles . . . run, and not be weary . . . walk, and not faint" [verse 31, KJV]. He wrote that while he was by his suffering daughter's side, the strength God supplied was not that of soaring like an eagle, and it wasn't as active as running, but that God had given him the strength to walk, and not faint. That's how I felt about our day. It wasn't fun, certainly not a day for soaring. It is another step in the process that will lead to death. But I'm grateful that God is giving us the strength to simply walk and not faint.*

It is natural to think of waiting as a time of inactivity, of stillness. But is that always what it means to wait on the Lord? What do we do while we wait?

THIS WEEK'S PASSAGE FOR MEDITATION

You must not forget, dear friends, that a day is like a thousand years to the Lord, and a thousand years is like a day. The Lord isn't really being slow about his promise to return, as some people think. No, he is being patient for your sake. We are looking forward to the new heavens and new earth he has promised, a world where everyone is right with God. And so, dear friends, while you are waiting for these things to happen, make every effort to live a pure and blameless life. And be at peace with God. —2 PETER 3:8-9, 11-14

WE NURTURE AN ETERNAL PERSPECTIVE

THOUGH OUR BODIES ARE DYING, OUR SPIRITS ARE BEING RENEWED EVERY DAY. FOR OUR PRESENT TROUBLES ARE QUITE SMALL AND WON'T LAST VERY LONG. YET THEY PRODUCE FOR US AN IMMEASURABLY GREAT GLORY THAT WILL LAST FOREVER!
—2 CORINTHIANS 4:16-17

Perspective. That's what our friend Bill Lee offered to me and to everyone else who attended the funeral service for his wife, Carol Ann. Bill told us how he had responded to his children's anguish over how long the future seemed before they would see their mom again. Holding up a small silver keepsake tube, he told his children, "This tube represents time." Then, pointing to progressive points on the tube, he explained, "Imagine here is where Mom was born, and here is where you were born. Right here is where Mom died, and somewhere out here is where you and I will die and go to heaven." Then, recalling a cross-country trip their family had taken two weeks before Carol Ann died, he said, "Now imagine a string extending from the tube out the door, down the street, and across the miles of Tennessee through the Midwest and across the Rocky Mountains and up into the stars. The time you will spend without your mom is shorter than the length of this tube, but the time you will spend with Mom in eternity is like the string that goes on and on and never ends." Putting the years of life *without her* in perspective of eternity *with her* made the time of waiting seem bearable and even brief.

When we read Paul's description of his troubles as "small" and "momentary," we wonder if he really knew what it is like to suffer. But the truth is that Paul's suffering included being imprisoned, beaten, stoned, shipwrecked, robbed, hungry, thirsty, cold, and naked—none of which I would describe as insignificant or brief. It is hard for us to understand how he could view these things as inconsequential, isn't it? But he saw them through the perspective of eternity, in light of the glory to come. Our problem is not so much in seeing our current affliction as light or our suffering as long, but that we think so little of eternity. The truth is, if we were to live for a hundred years and suffer significantly every day of our lives, by the measure of eternity, it would be just a moment. So while we wait, we nurture an eternal perspective, a view in which our struggles look small and brief in comparison to the vast joys and eternal satisfaction of forever-life with God.

My Perspective Giver, as I wait for your deliverance, help me to see my troubles as small and brief in light of the glory of eternity so I won't give up.

DIGGING DEEPER

Read 2 Corinthians 5:1-10, looking for what we can anticipate in eternity in regard to our future body, future home, future purpose, and future reward.

WE FIX OUR EYES OF FAITH ON WHAT WE CANNOT SEE

WE FIX OUR EYES NOT ON WHAT IS SEEN, BUT ON WHAT IS UNSEEN. FOR WHAT IS SEEN IS TEMPORARY, BUT WHAT IS UNSEEN IS ETERNAL. —2 CORINTHIANS 4:18 (NIV)

As Hope was born the week of Thanksgiving, our plan had been to create a combination Christmas card/birth announcement to send out in December. I suppose that is what it was, but in a sense it was also a death pronouncement. We sent out hundreds of cards, telling everyone we knew about the diagnosis Hope had been given. We wrote:

> *So what does this mean for Hope and for our family? It means we may have only a short time to love and enjoy Hope this side of heaven, and that is what we intend to do. She is a beautiful, peaceful child and is already bringing us so much joy. We know that God has a purpose for her life that will be completely accomplished during her days on this earth.*

We knew people would look at our circumstances and see only sorrow and tragedy. Some who read our card said we were in serious denial. But it wasn't denial. We were experiencing an inner reality of God's presence and purpose that can't be seen with the eye but is nevertheless very real. Perhaps you know exactly what I mean because you've experienced it too. Each day we were given grace and courage that defied explanation, and eyes to see that there is much more that is as real as what we see and touch today.

Choosing to see God working in and through your circumstances for your good and for his glory is not merely "positive thinking," nor is it denial of reality. It is the ultimate embracing of reality—the reality that can't be seen with the human eye or processed by human understanding.

What does it mean to fix our eyes on what is unseen? It means that though we have never seen Christ with our physical eyes, we fix our eyes of faith on him and believe. Though we have never seen bodies raised up out of graves, we fix our eyes of faith on Scripture and anticipate that day. Though we have never seen a place called heaven, cannot find it on the map, and can't imagine what it will be like, we fix our eyes of faith on God's promises and long to be there.

My unseen Reality, how I need the lens of faith to see who you are, what you are doing, and where you will take me, even as I struggle with the difficult realities of my circumstances.

DIGGING DEEPER

Read John 20:29 and Hebrews 11:1. What do these passages reveal about what it means to fix your eyes on what is unseen? How did Moses do this, according to Hebrews 11:24-28?

WE GROAN INWARDLY WHILE WE WAIT EAGERLY

WE KNOW THAT THE WHOLE CREATION HAS BEEN GROANING AS IN THE PAINS OF CHILDBIRTH RIGHT UP TO THE PRESENT TIME. NOT ONLY SO, BUT WE OURSELVES, WHO HAVE THE FIRSTFRUITS OF THE SPIRIT, GROAN INWARDLY AS WE WAIT EAGERLY FOR OUR ADOPTION AS SONS, THE REDEMPTION OF OUR BODIES. —ROMANS 8:22-23 (NIV)

Do you know what it is like to *groan* inwardly or audibly with sorrow or pain? There are days when I can't bear to watch the news or get an update on someone in crisis because I am overwhelmed with the suffering and sadness in the world. Sometimes I wonder, *When will this hurting end? God, why don't you just come now and take us out of this world that is so full of pain?*

Romans 8:22 says that "the whole creation has been groaning as in the pains of childbirth." Now, I remember the pains of childbirth. I also remember saying to myself at the time, *Do* not *allow yourself to get into this situation again!* The groans of childbirth, however, are quickly forgotten when we hold that beautiful child in our arms, aren't they? The joy and fulfillment the child brings is worth the nine months of waiting, worth the pain of delivery.

And that's how it will be when we are "delivered" into the presence of God. The groaning and anticipation will be over and we will say, "Heaven was worth the wait. Jesus, you are worth all the waiting!"

Perhaps you have sometimes wondered if something is wrong with you or if you are deficient in your faith because you just can't share in the happy-all-the-time religion some people seem to have. When you find yourself groaning because of the death and destruction and disease and depression and deprivation in this world, and you find deep inside an intense longing for it all to be erased and made right, take heart. That is a sacred longing, placed deep within you by the Holy Spirit. The Holy Spirit has given us a longing for the day described in Romans 8, when "creation itself will be liberated from its bondage to decay and brought into the glorious freedom of the children of God" (verse 21, NIV). Until then, we groan inwardly while we wait eagerly.

Savior, as I see the cruel effects of sin on this world, on those whom I love, and even on myself, I long for you to make things right. This sacred longing assures me I am yours and will be yours forever. Lord Jesus, come quickly!

DIGGING DEEPER

Compare Romans 8:18-25 and 2 Corinthians 5:1-5. What do both passages affirm about waiting, groaning, our bodies, and the role of the Holy Spirit?

WE AIM TO PLEASE HIM ALWAYS

OUR AIM IS TO PLEASE HIM ALWAYS, WHETHER WE ARE HERE IN THIS BODY OR AWAY FROM THIS BODY. —2 CORINTHIANS 5:9

I hadn't seen my childhood friend for years and was happy to catch up with her while on a trip to her city. But her pained expression told me that something significant was going on. Her husband had discovered her emotional affair with another man. She was afraid for her family, ashamed, and grieving over the necessary break with the other man, now her closest friend. About her husband, she told me, "I don't think I've ever really loved him."

I hardly knew what to say, and I didn't want to offer the expected lines. I knew she knew the Scriptures, but I also knew she was miserable in her marriage and that the prospect of spending the rest of her life that way was unbearable. I tried to be a good listener and share her sorrow about the state of her heart and her marriage. But before we left, I shared this verse that God had been using in my own life: "So we make it our goal to please him" (2 Corinthians 5:9, NIV).

While we can't control what happens to us, this verse shows us what we *can* do as we wait for him to take us away from this world of pain. We can throw everything we are into this singular aim: to please God. Pleasing God is more important than if we survive or if we die. When hard things come (and they will) and we wonder what we will do, we make it our goal to please him in how we respond. When we feel the sting of undeserved criticism, the fearfulness of being alone, the weight of overwhelming responsibility, we make it our aim to please him. And it will be worth it. Jesus will be worth everything your sacrificial obedience has cost you and will cost you.

There is a deep and sustaining joy in simply seeking to please God. "I don't know what you should do," I told my friend. "But I do know that regardless of the choices you have made to this point, from now on, you can make choices that are guided by a desire to please God. And I am completely confident that a year from now, many years from now, no matter what happens, if you make choices out of a desire to please God more than to please yourself, you will have peace and joy rather than regret and shame."

Ever-watching One, I want to experience the joy of bringing a smile to your face as you look on my life. Free me from lesser pursuits so that pleasing you becomes my sole aim.

DIGGING DEEPER

According to Hebrews 13:1-21, what is pleasing to God and where do we get the power to do what is pleasing to God?

WE WORK HARD TO PERSUADE OTHERS

WE MUST ALL STAND BEFORE CHRIST TO BE JUDGED. WE WILL EACH RECEIVE WHATEVER WE DESERVE FOR THE GOOD OR EVIL WE HAVE DONE IN OUR BODIES. IT IS BECAUSE WE KNOW THIS SOLEMN FEAR OF THE LORD THAT WE WORK SO HARD TO PERSUADE OTHERS.
—2 CORINTHIANS 5:10-11

I spent a year working closely with Gracia Burnham, a missionary to the Philippines who was held hostage by terrorists for a year before being rescued. Sadly, her husband, Martin, was shot and killed in the rescue. One of the stories Gracia told me was about Musab, one of her captors, who made himself out to be a spiritual leader even though he was really, in her words, "a rat." So she was especially disgusted when Musab forced Martin to carry his heavy load of supplies on top of what Martin was already carrying. "Someday that man is going to burn in hell, and I hope I'm there to see him judged!" Gracia hissed to her husband. At her outburst, Martin said sadly, "Oh Gracia, don't say that. Someday God *is* going to judge that man, but you don't want to be there to see it. Can you imagine how horrible it will be?"

Picture for a moment what judgment will be like for those who reject Christ. Our self-centered satisfaction of knowing that our sin has been covered and that we are free from condemnation has made us apathetic about the destiny ahead for those who reject Christ. Those who are not covered by the righteousness of Christ will receive the punishment they deserve for their sin. If we really believe this, shouldn't it compel us to work hard to persuade others to receive the gift of salvation offered lovingly by God?

This time of waiting is a time of grace, when God's offer of forgiveness and restoration is available to all. But this time will soon come to a close. So we don't want to waste these days of waiting by amusing ourselves, satisfying ourselves, or closing our eyes to the coming reality of eternal judgment. What could make this time of waiting more meaningful than to use every means at your disposal to convince those outside of Christ of their need for him? Who do you know who is not prepared to stand before the judgment seat of Christ? What are you waiting for?

Righteous Judge, though it may be unpopular to talk about and I don't like to even think about it, judgment is certain and will be terrifying for those who are not saved from it. Give me a vivid vision of the judgment to come so I will be willing to work hard to persuade others of their need for you.

DIGGING DEEPER

Read Hebrews 10:21-39 and 1 John 4:17. What do you learn about how judgment will be different for believers and unbelievers?

WEEK 50

WAITING

REFLECTION

What are you waiting for from God? What is the basis for your expectation?

What do you believe God is calling you to do and to become while you wait? Do you sense his pleasure in your progress?

MEDITATION

You must not forget, dear friends, that a day is like a thousand years to the Lord, and a thousand years is like a day. The Lord isn't really being slow about his promise to return, as some people think. No, he is being patient for your sake. He does not want anyone to perish, so he is giving more time for everyone to repent. Since everything around us is going to melt away, what holy, godly lives you should be living! You should look forward to that day and hurry it along—the day when God will set the heavens on fire and the elements will melt away in the flames. But we are looking forward to the new heavens and new earth he has promised, a world where everyone is right with God. And so, dear friends, while you are waiting for these things to happen, make every effort to live a pure and blameless life. And be at peace with God. —2 PETER 3:9, 11-14

Read through this passage several times, noting the words or phrases that especially speak to you. As you read, envision the future we wait for and appreciate the compassion of God that keeps us waiting.

Speak the passage back to God in the form of a prayer, praising him for who he is, what he has done, and what he will do. Personalize his promises to you and affirm your desire to wait on the Lord.

PRAYER

Praise God for his eternal nature and the eternal nature of his salvation.

Thank God for clearly revealing what is pleasing to him and for the joy and freedom that a life bent toward pleasing him provides.

Intercede for those who groan over the pain in the world and in their own world as they wait for God.

Confess your apathy about the harsh judgment that awaits those around you who continue to reject Christ, and resolve to work hard to persuade others.

Petition God to give you the lenses of faith that will allow you to fix your eyes on what is unseen.

WEEK 51

PERSEVERANCE

In the Goldie Hawn movie *Private Benjamin*, Judy Benjamin is a pampered socialite who has been lured into the army by a cunning recruiter who showed her pictures of yachts and condos and talked about paid vacations in exotic locales. But when Judy gets to basic training, she decides there has been a huge mistake, that she has joined the "wrong army." "I mean look at this place," she complains, "the army couldn't afford curtains? I'll be up at the crack of dawn!"

Has your experience in the Christian life made you wonder if you have joined the "wrong army"? Were you convinced that once you became a Christian, things would get easier in your life? Have you been disappointed by difficulty? disillusioned by people? Have you doubted the truth of what you've said you believe? Maybe in your disappointment you decided to keep going to church and to keep going through the motions, but you've settled into a comfortable place of doubt and disillusionment, unwilling to keep on moving forward in pursuing more of God in your life. Or maybe your pain makes you want to quit the walk of faith completely.

The early Christians knew what it was like to suffer for their faith, and they knew the temptation to turn back when things became difficult. So in his letter to the Hebrews, the writer comes alongside these struggling believers to encourage them, saying: Don't give up. Don't stop. Don't waver. Keep going. Keep moving forward in faith, confident that your perseverance will be rewarded. And the message is the same for us in our struggles: Don't give up.

THIS WEEK'S PASSAGE FOR MEDITATION

Dear brothers and sisters, whenever trouble comes your way, let it be an opportunity for joy. For when your faith is tested, your endurance has a chance to grow. So let it grow, for when your endurance is fully developed, you will be strong in character and ready for anything. —James 1:2-4

FINISHING THE RACE OF FAITH

LET US RUN WITH ENDURANCE THE RACE THAT GOD HAS SET BEFORE US. —HEBREWS 12:1

As we watched the summer Olympics on television, I could almost feel the anguish of the marathon runner who was overcome with exhaustion and emotion after another runner overtook her for the third place position. She slowed down and became disoriented and finally sat down by the side of the road, unable to make it across the finish line. My heart broke for her as I thought about all of her preparation and her inability to persevere to the end.

What a disappointment if that is what happens to us as we run the race of faith God has set before us! We don't want to be disqualified; we want to finish the race. But if you want to run the race, first you have to choose to enter the race. You can't sit on the sidelines and watch others run. You can't just listen to the radio or sit in the pew and hear about other people who are running. You have to decide that you don't want to stay where you are, just as you are, doing what you're doing, but that you want to enter the race.

Running the race will require energy. God himself supplies the energy as you run your race of faith toward him. As you feed on the fuel of his Word and as the Holy Spirit blows the wind at your back and fills your lungs with his very breath, you are empowered to run and keep running.

Completing the race requires perseverance, a steady determination to keep going. Many people start the Christian life with great vigor and then give up when it becomes difficult. But if you want to complete your race well, you have to keep going, even when you're tired, even when you're not sure what the road ahead will take you through.

Sometimes this race will be very lonely. Sometimes you will wonder why more people are not running with you. Don't think that something is wrong. Jesus said, "The gateway to life is small, and the road is narrow, and only a few ever find it" (Matthew 7:14). Many people around us are running races of good works or religiosity, but they aren't running the race of faith.

We each have to run the race that is set before us. I may not be able to run the course your race takes you on, and you may not be able to run mine, but we can both finish the course God has marked out for us. Some of us might sprint and some of us might plod; we all must persevere.

My enduring Energy, some days I just want to sit down and give up. Fill me with your energy and endurance, and keep me moving toward you.

DIGGING DEEPER

What does 1 Corinthians 9:24-27 teach about how and why to run the race?

KEEPING OUR EYES ON JESUS

LET US RUN WITH ENDURANCE THE RACE THAT GOD HAS SET BEFORE US. WE DO THIS BY KEEPING OUR EYES ON JESUS, ON WHOM OUR FAITH DEPENDS FROM START TO FINISH.
—HEBREWS 12:1-2

Remember the mistake Harold Abrahams made in the movie *Chariots of Fire*? Leading in the race, he took his eyes off of the finish line and looked around to see where the other runners were—and it cost him the race. All great racers know that if you look around at others and evaluate or compare the race they are running, you will be distracted from your own race and it will slow you down.

It is the same for us who are running the race of faith. Don't look around at others—they will distract you. But that is our natural tendency, isn't it? *His race is easier. She's not applying herself, and yet she seems to be doing so well. He is so far ahead of me; I will never be able to catch up.* Don't get distracted by the race others are running. It will only hinder your progress.

Likewise, don't look inward—it will discourage you. If you spend all your time and energy focused on your own resources or lack thereof, distracted by your own "issues" or your own limitations, you will become completely discouraged—perhaps to the point of simply quitting the race.

Some of the runners this writer to the Hebrews was addressing had begun to look back—at the old ways of Judaism, the old system of the law, and it only delayed their progress. Don't look back—it will delay you. If you look back longingly at the way things used to be, you will not be prepared for the future God has for you. It can be hard for us to leave behind the comfortable and the familiar. Most of us don't like change. But do you really want to keep wasting time where you are, or do you want to move forward with God? Determine to persevere, and don't look back.

If we don't look around or inside or behind us, where do we look? We look up—to Jesus. Putting our focus on Jesus puts everything and everyone else in proper perspective. When you keep your eyes on Jesus, you won't stumble or become distracted. You will find the energy and example you need to run this race of faith. He will become your sole aim and sole source.

Jesus, my eyes are on you as I run this race of faith. I see in your example what it looks like to persevere and stay faithful even in hardship. You are who I'm aiming for and my source of strength for getting there.

DIGGING DEEPER

What do you see when you look at Jesus in Hebrews 2:9-13? What confidence does this give us for persevering?

TRAMPLING THE SON OF GOD

If we deliberately continue sinning after we have received a full knowledge of the truth, there is no other sacrifice that will cover these sins. Think how much more terrible the punishment will be for those who have trampled on the Son of God and have treated the blood of the covenant as if it were common and unholy. —Hebrews 10:26, 29

When you walk along a sidewalk and you look down and spot a quarter, you pick it up because you see it as something of value. But when you see a discarded gum wrapper or a used ticket stub, you don't pick it up; you just walk over it or step on it, because it is worthless to you. This is the picture the writer of Hebrews draws as he calls us to persevere in living out what we've already learned. He explains what we are doing when there is a sin in our lives that we refuse to relinquish. When we keep on deliberately sinning, it is as if we look and see Christ on the cross and then just walk right over the cross, trampling it, because we see it as worthless to us.

It's a painful picture, isn't it? Perhaps most painful because we know we've done it. We've held on to destructive habits, we've justified our resentment, we've indulged our sexual curiosity, and we've convinced ourselves that our actions harm no one. We've excused ourselves as a work in progress rather than exposing ourselves to Christ's cleansing blood.

Does this mean that if we are believers we will never sin? Of course not! But it does mean that if we say, "I know it is sin but I am going to do it anyway," we're basically rejecting the sacrifice of Christ, saying, "I don't need you or your holiness. I want to live my way, not your way." If we do this, we are, in effect, rejecting Christ. We can't fool ourselves into thinking that after knowing and experiencing the truth we can keep walking toward sin, trampling underfoot the Son of God. We can't act as if God owes us and will save us from judgment because we prayed a prayer or walked down an aisle one day. As a believer you *will* sin, but if you find that you sin repeatedly and deliberately with no sense of conviction or sadness over your sin, then you need to question if you have really placed your faith in Christ. He welcomes even those who have trampled on him, and he gives the grace and power we need to persevere in our battle with sin.

Son of God, now I see my deliberate sin as a personal offense toward you and a rejection of your sacrifice. Forgive me for belittling the gift you bought with your blood, and give me your grace and power to relinquish sin.

DIGGING DEEPER

What does Romans 6:1-18 teach about deliberate sin in the believer's life?

PERSEVERANCE RESULTS IN REWARD

You suffered along with those who were thrown into jail. When all you owned was taken from you, you accepted it with joy. You knew you had better things waiting for you in eternity. Do not throw away this confident trust in the Lord, no matter what happens. Remember the great reward it brings you! —Hebrews 10:34-35

Near the top of the list of hard things I've had to do was telling Matt that I was pregnant but that this child would also die. It broke our hearts to tell him that he would have the brother he'd hoped for, but for only a short time. David told him, "You remember what it was like with Hope. It was hard, but it was also rich. It will be hard again, but it will be good again."

In a sense, this is what the writer of Hebrews was saying to prepare believers to persevere in the hardships ahead as he reminded them of their suffering and perseverance in the past. "Remember how you remained faithful even though it meant terrible suffering" (verse 32). He reminded them of public ridicule and beatings they endured because of their faith, of having everything they owned taken from them. All of it, he reminded them, "you accepted it with joy."

Hello? Accepted it with joy? How could they accept such significant suffering and persecution with joy? How could they stand with others at great cost and risk to themselves and to their families? Their secret to letting go of things here was that they knew they had "better and lasting" possessions somewhere else. They were confident their perseverance would be rewarded. They knew that what they let go of here would be returned to them with interest later. No skimping. No disappointment. They would receive what God promised, and it would be more than they could ever have dreamed. The reward God promised them—and the reward God promises you for your patient perseverance in suffering and persecution—is really coming. It is not pie-in-the-sky hopes. It is a reality not yet realized.

What have you given up out of love for Christ? Have you traded leisure or acceptance or comfort for working for Christ? Have you been rejected for your stand for the gospel? Have you been treated with disrespect because of your choice to be obedient to God? It will be worth it! Jesus will be worth everything that your commitment to him has cost you and will cost you as you continue to persevere.

My Reward Keeper, I choose to remember your faithfulness to me in the suffering in my past. And I choose to believe in your promise of eternal reward for those who are faithful in suffering. Jesus, I believe you are worth everything my love for you costs me in this life.

DIGGING DEEPER

How did the Hebrew believers show that they believed the truth expressed in Matthew 6:19-21?

PERSEVERANCE REFLECTS WHOSE WE ARE

WE ARE NOT LIKE THOSE WHO TURN THEIR BACKS ON GOD AND SEAL THEIR FATE. WE HAVE FAITH THAT ASSURES OUR SALVATION. —HEBREWS 10:39

My parents love to put me next to my mother and say something like, "Can you tell whose daughter she is? Doesn't she look like her mother?" And they are right. I look more and more like her all the time. Some days I look in the mirror and I realize, *I'm becoming my mother!* If you look at me and then you look at my mother, you know instantly whose child I am. And while we're on the topic, you might as well know what I inherited from my father. My maiden name is Jinks. Jinkses are often loud and opinionated. But Jinkses are also generous and look for ways to help people in practical ways in times of need. Jinkses love the church and love God's people. Jinkses live life to the fullest. So I suppose when I walk into a room, looking every bit like my mother, my voice carrying above the crowd to offer my opinion, or when I offer you a bed to sleep in or come to see you when you are in the hospital, it is a reflection of whose I am.

In this verse, the writer to the Hebrews was appealing to the "family traits" of the people of faith. Living by faith is who we are; it is what we do. Our perseverance is a reflection of whose we are. We are not people who shrink back in the face of persecution. We are people who believe and keep on believing. We are people who live by faith. It is just who we are.

When you choose to live by faith and keep on believing, we can see the family resemblance. We recognize whose you are. We also see what you believe. And it is the power of what you believe that will enable you to persevere when the going gets tough in your life. What you know to be true—because it is what God has said—will become the foundation for the decisions you make and the actions you take. Your perseverance will reflect what you believe—which is what God has said is trustworthy and true—that his promise to you of salvation is reliable.

When people look at you, is it obvious whose you are and what you believe? As you persevere through difficulty in your life, you will "grow up" looking and sounding and acting more and more like your Father every day.

My Father, how I want to carry the family resemblance by persevering through faith in the suffering I am facing. I place my confidence in your salvation and refuse to turn my back on you as I face the future.

DIGGING DEEPER

Read the book of 1 John looking for "family traits" seen in God's children.

WEEK 51

PERSEVERANCE

REFLECTION

What aspects of the Christian life and your life have left you disillusioned or disappointed, wanting (at least at times) to give up?

Are you determined to persevere? What will a determination to persevere look like in your life?

MEDITATION

Dear brothers and sisters, whenever trouble comes your way, let it be an opportunity for joy. For when your faith is tested, your endurance has a chance to grow. So let it grow, for when your endurance is fully developed, you will be strong in character and ready for anything. —James 1:2-4

Read through the passage several times, circling words or phrases that are especially meaningful to you.

Allow these phrases to challenge your presuppositions about what brings joy and what brings pain.

Offer the verse back to God in the form of a determined prayer to persevere.

PRAYER

Praise God for his grace, mercy, and forgiveness, which are freely offered to people who have little endurance, little energy, and little faith.

Thank Jesus for running the perfect race of faith, offering us an example to look to and encouragement to run with.

Intercede for those who are tempted to throw away their confident trust in the Lord because of suffering in their lives.

Confess any ongoing, deliberate sin that you have excused until now, and see your failure to relinquish that sin as trampling on the cross of Christ.

Petition God for the energy and endurance you need to keep moving forward in him and to him.

WEEK 52

LETTING GO

You might not like what I have to say to you this week. But it is what I would say to you if we were sitting at Starbucks, tearfully talking about what it is going to take for you to feel better, to have joy again. It is what I would say to you if you told me your pain makes you feel like a misfit. I'm going to invite you to begin letting go, and I know it won't be easy. This excerpt from a letter I wrote to Hope in a journal entry on January 1, 2000, reminds me how hard it has been for me:

> *Hope,*
>
> *We've just entered a new millennium. Everyone is relieved that Y2K was not a disaster and excited about what the future holds, but I don't want it to be another year; it just takes me further away from you. I want so desperately to feel close to you, to be able to hear you in my mind even if all I ever got to hear from you was a cry. I want to feel your skin and stroke your cheek. I want to wake up and find you here. But you are so far away and becoming even more distant in my memory, and it is so painful. I don't know how to let you go and hold on to you at the same time. How can I stay close to you if I don't stay sad? Sometimes I want to scream because I feel so torn.*
>
> *Forgive me for going on with life without you. Forgive me for forgetting what you sound like and what you looked like and what it felt like to spend the morning in bed with you on my chest. It just keeps moving farther and farther away.*

THIS WEEK'S PASSAGE FOR MEDITATION

I once thought all these things were so very important, but now I consider them worthless because of what Christ has done. Yes, everything else is worthless when compared with the priceless gain of knowing Christ Jesus my Lord. I have discarded everything else, counting it all as garbage, so that I may have Christ and become one with him. I am focusing all my energies on this one thing: Forgetting the past and looking forward to what lies ahead, I strain to reach the end of the race and receive the prize for which God, through Christ Jesus, is calling us up to heaven. —PHILIPPIANS 3:7-9, 13-14

LETTING GO OF IT ALL

I AM TRUSTING YOU, O LORD, SAYING, "YOU ARE MY GOD!" MY FUTURE IS IN YOUR HANDS. —PSALM 31:14-15

David stayed home with Hope on Wednesdays so I could go to Bible study. One morning in January, I got into the car after class and called him from my mobile phone. He didn't answer, which I thought was strange. So I tried his mobile. He answered. "Where are you?" I asked.

"We're all fine," he said. (Now you know when someone starts with that, we're not all fine, right?) "We're at Dr. Ladd's office, but not for Hope," he continued. "Matt fell in PE this morning and broke off his front tooth." I took a deep breath and just couldn't say anything for a minute. I guess it hit me in the area of my greatest fear—that Hope might not be our only loss. That night, as David and I talked about the day, we realized that we'd both had an unspoken agreement with God that went something like this: *Fine. We will accept losing Hope and all that that brings. But we don't lose Matt. We don't lose each other. No car accidents. No cancer. No financial collapse. This is it!* But as we voiced our deepest feelings and fears out loud, we realized that we had to let go of those things too. We have to trust God with everything we have. We have to open ourselves up to God and say, "God, it is all yours to do with as you will!"

Some days I wonder if the letting go will ever stop. After Hope's death, I had to let go of her physical body, my dreams for her, and so many of her things. I let go of her room and turned it back into a guest room. Then came Gabe, and I had to let go of him along with my hopes for Matt to have a sibling.

The truth is, eventually, we will let go of everything in this life. Life is a constant barrage of having things and people we love ripped away from us. Every ripping away takes a piece of us with it, leaving us raw and stinging with pain. But when we recognize that everything we have and everyone we love is on loan to us from God, when we learn to hold loosely to the things and people we love, we can then embrace the freedom that comes with entrusting everything to his care.

Father, thank you for everything you have given me and for the grace to let go of everything that has been taken away. I know I can trust you with everything and everyone I love, and one day I will know complete fulfillment with you, with no more letting go.

DIGGING DEEPER

Read Genesis 22:1-18; 1 Samuel 1; and Job 1. How did these biblical characters show a willingness to release what they loved to God?

LETTING GO OF YOUR EXPECTATIONS OF OTHERS

MEANWHILE, ALL HIS DISCIPLES DESERTED HIM AND RAN AWAY. —MARK 14:50

What a lonely place it must have been for Jesus in the garden of Gethsemane. As he prayed, his soul crushed with grief to the point of death, he repeatedly found the ones who had pledged their lives to him sleeping instead of praying. A short time later, as a mob arrived with swords and clubs to arrest him, all of his beloved disciples ran for their lives.

They say you find out who your friends are when the chips are down. I suppose that's true. Some I had expected to walk with us in our time of crisis seemed to disappear instead. And then there were those I had barely known before who felt called to serve us in some of our difficult days. What a gift.

I'm embarrassed to tell you that I kept very close tabs in our walk with Hope. Not an actual list, mind you, but I knew who had spoken to us and who hadn't, who had called and who hadn't, who reached out and who withdrew. My expectations of those around us were high, and I was often disappointed.

By the time Gabe came, I had learned that some people are called by God to minister grace in the hard places. Some people aren't. This time around, I was free from the tyranny of expectations, free from keeping a scorecard on everyone around me and taking note of who had made an effort in our direction. What a relief! But don't think I'm naive. I know that some people are just too self-centered to share your pain. But I've come to realize that so much we label as uncaring is simply an inability to overcome the awkwardness and fear of doing or saying the wrong thing. The reason some people have never said anything to you about your divorce or your job loss or the death of one you love is that they simply don't know how to overcome the awkwardness.

Would you be willing to take another look at those around you with that perspective of grace? What a relief it is to let go of your heavy expectations of others and instead appreciate every gentle touch, every shared tear, and every knowing smile as sheer gifts of grace. What a relief to follow the example of Jesus and instead of placing blame, offer forgiveness.

Forsaken Jesus, you understand what it feels like to be deserted by those you thought would be there for you in your darkest hour. Give me your spirit of forgiveness and your spirit of grace to help me let go of my disappointment in people who've failed or forgotten me.

DIGGING DEEPER

How did Paul appreciate those who were called to serve him in 1 Corinthians 16:13-18? What do you pick up about Paul's expectations and attitude in Philippians 4:10-20? How did he exhibit both gratitude and contentment?

LETTING GO OF THE SPOTLIGHT

Don't be selfish; don't live to make a good impression on others. Be humble, thinking of others as better than yourself. Don't think only about your own affairs, but be interested in others, too, and what they are doing.
—Philippians 2:3-4

How we love to be in the spotlight. Can we be honest enough to admit it feels good to be the center of attention? And nothing puts you in the spotlight quite like a significant loss or a dreaded diagnosis. Those of us connected to the body of Christ experience the tangible love of Jesus through the care and concern of others. Our needs become their concerns, and our issues become the constant topic of conversation.

The problem with the spotlight suffering puts us in is that it can be as addictive as a drug. Many of us who have been through a public struggle find ourselves hooked on the attention, endlessly hungry for the sympathy and significance we've come to crave. We seek it in subtle ways. We look for an opportunity in the conversation to drop something others cannot ignore, drawing the focus to us and bringing out some sympathy. I was talking about this with my editor Jan, who had a bout with breast cancer a few years ago, and she knew just what I meant. She said a friend had confronted her on the issue, saying to her one day, "When are you going to quit playing the cancer card?" Youch! You got me.

Do you find yourself resentful that people no longer ask about your loss or struggle? Are you frustrated that they seem to have moved on and forgotten? Perhaps rather than pointing your finger at them, it is time you shine the spotlight on the needs of those around you rather than demanding it stay fixed on you and your needs. Don't be afraid they'll forget. Don't be afraid they'll think you're fine when you are still hurting deeply. Just let it go, and determine to find your satisfaction in focusing on others, resisting the easy attention grab.

Perhaps this hits home with you and makes you feel uncomfortable. Are you willing to hold the mirror up to your behavior to see if it's time to let go of the spotlight your suffering has put on you? I've found that it isn't easy. It takes a conscious choice to turn conversations away from my pain, to stop trying to make sure everyone understands my hurt and has considered my feelings. But it is a step toward normalization, and a step closer to Christ.

Jesus, I must admit I love the spotlight, but I know it is not pleasing to you. You love it when I put the needs, concerns, and experiences of others before my own. Help me to let go of the spotlight and turn it on the people around me.

DIGGING DEEPER

Read about Paul's hardships in 2 Corinthians 6:3-13. What was more important to Paul than the spotlight or relief from his suffering?

LETTING GO OF YOUR RIGHTS

HUMBLE YOURSELVES UNDER THE MIGHTY POWER OF GOD, AND IN HIS GOOD TIME HE WILL HONOR YOU. —1 PETER 5:6

I felt misunderstood and maligned. Confusion over my role and responsibilities on a project, and offense taken by abrupt emails I'd written in my busyness, had made me the target of harsh criticism. The whole thing hurt my pride, and I feared the relationship was damaged beyond repair. Honestly, I wanted to walk away and nurse my wounds. But God spoke to me through his Word, though it wasn't necessarily what I wanted to hear. "Humble yourself in the sight of the Lord, and he will lift you up," I heard him say (see 1 Peter 5:6). But he wasn't done. "So far as it depends on you, be at peace with all men" (Romans 12:18, NASB). God gave me clear instructions to let go of my prideful expectations that others should treat me and think of me as I thought they ought to. Rather than cut and run, I had to pick up the phone, apologize, and ask for forgiveness. I explained but tried not to defend. I humbled myself, and it cost me. But it had become a matter between God and me, and it didn't matter how they responded; I knew I needed to obey. And honestly, that felt good.

There was more criticism and coldness to come before things turned around. And by the time apology and appreciation came back around to me, it didn't matter that much anymore because I had experienced more pleasure in pleasing God than I ever could have in impressing people. Even if they had never recognized my contribution, the inner confidence that I had pleased God through costly obedience—by letting go of my rights, by entrusting my justification and reputation to him—was more than enough.

Have you been demanding your right to be treated as you "deserve"? Demanding your right to fairness, happiness, respect, or retaliation? Would you lay down your rights and let them go? Would you recognize that the matter is more between you and God than you and anyone else? Would you be willing to humble yourself under him, trusting he has the power to lift you up and honor you in his timing, in his way? Isn't the load of demanding your rights becoming much too heavy to bear?

My Defender, it goes against everything in me to let go of my rights. My culture tells me I'm a fool to do so—that it will make me a victim. But because I want to go deeper with you, I will entrust my rights to you.

DIGGING DEEPER

What does Philippians 2:1-11 tell us about Jesus' example in laying down his rights?

LETTING GO OF YOUR GRIEF

There is a time for everything, a season for every activity under heaven. A time to cry and a time to laugh. A time to grieve and a time to dance.
—Ecclesiastes 3:1, 4

There is a tyranny in grief. We realize at some point that we have to figure out how to keep on living, how to incorporate the loss into our lives. We want to feel normal again, to feel joy again. But the energy and emotion of grief keep us feeling close to the one we love or connected to what we've lost. Letting go of our grief feels like letting go of the one we love, leaving him or her behind and moving on. The very idea of it is unbearable.

I suppose we have a choice. We can hold on to the pain, accepting the misery it brings if it means we won't have to move forward with the emptiness. Or we can release it, process it, talk about it, cry over it, let it wash over us, and then let it wash away with our tears. We can make the painful choice to let it go—not all at once, but a little every day. We begin to find that we have the choice of whether or not we will let ourselves sink to that place of unbearable pain when the flashes of memories and reminders of loss pierce our hearts. And we can begin to make that hard choice. We can begin to let go of our grief so we can grab hold of life and those who are living. But I think the only way we can do that is by telling ourselves the truth—that if we choose to let go of the pain, or at least let it become manageable, it does not mean we love the one we've lost any less. And it doesn't mean that person's life was any less significant or meaningful, or that we will forget.

A couple of Sundays ago, a friend who had recently lost her husband stopped me after church to talk. "I cry at the office, cry all the way home, and then cry all evening," she told me . . . while crying. And I cried with her.

"Wasn't your husband worthy of a great sorrow?" I asked her. When you love something or someone, the process of letting go is a painful one that takes some time, and it need not be rushed. Nor should it be avoided altogether. We feel the pain, mourn the loss, shed our tears, and with time we can begin to let go of the grief that has had such a hold on us. Perhaps it's not so much that we let go of our grief, but more that we give our grief permission to lessen its grip on us.

Jesus, I know you don't want to rush me through my grief, but neither do you want me to be burdened and limited by it any longer than is needed for my healing. Will you meet me and walk with me as I begin to let go?

DIGGING DEEPER

Take comfort in the honesty of the psalmist in Psalm 13, and take instruction from his determination.

WEEK 52

LETTING GO

REFLECTION

Is it time to begin to lessen your grip on your sorrow so that you can embrace joy? What are your fears about staying in your grief or about letting it go? What truths from God's Word address those fears?

In what way do you need to let go of the spotlight as well as your expectations of others?

What does your ability or inability to trust God with your life reveal about your understanding of God and his ways?

MEDITATION

I once thought all these things were so very important, but now I consider them worthless because of what Christ has done. Yes, everything else is worthless when compared with the priceless gain of knowing Christ Jesus my Lord. I have discarded everything else, counting it all as garbage, so that I may have Christ and become one with him. I am focusing all my energies on this one thing: Forgetting the past and looking forward to what lies ahead, I strain to reach the end of the race and receive the prize for which God, through Christ Jesus, is calling us up to heaven. —PHILIPPIANS 3:7-9, 13-14

Read through these verses several times, marking the words or phrases that are especially meaningful to you.

Listen for the passion in Paul's words and the purpose in his actions, seeking to embrace that passion and purpose personally.

Turn the passage into a prayer, asking God to help you let go of anything and everything that keeps you from embracing this passion and purpose.

PRAYER

Praise God for his trustworthiness. We can place our lives in his hands with confidence!

Thank God for showing us through the person and work of Christ what it looks like to give up our rights and expectations of others.

Intercede for those who have disappointed you, asking God to equip them for greater service to others in the future.

Confess your love for attention and your unhealthy addiction to the spotlight.

Ask God to reveal to you what you need to let go of and to give you the strength and grace you need to let go.

NOTES AND SOURCES

General Reference
John MacArthur, *The MacArthur Study Bible*, (Nashville: Word Publishing, 1997).

NIV Quest Study Bible (Grand Rapids, Mich.: Zondervan, 1994).

Jesus, Man of Sorrows
Anne Graham Lotz, *Why?: Trusting God When You Don't Understand* (Nashville: W Publishing Group, 2004). Anne first drew for me the picture of tears on God's face at the tomb of Lazarus.

Harold S. Kushner, *When Bad Things Happen to Good People* (New York: Random House, 1981).

Holy Spirit, Comforter
Calvin Miller, *Loving God Up Close: Rekindling Your Relationship with the Holy Spirit* (New York: Warner Faith, 2004).

Death
Various versions of the Barnhouse story have been related by different writers. This version was related to me by Dr. James Walters, who sat under Dr. Barnhouse's teaching.

The Love of God
Max Lucado, *A Love Worth Giving* (Nashville: W Publishing Group, 2002).

David Kopp and Heather Kopp, *Praying the Bible for Your Marriage* (Colorado Springs: WaterBrook Press, 1998). I adapted the Kopps' prayer based on 1 Corinthians 13.

Raymond Ortlund Jr., "The Love of God (John 3:16)," Christ Presbyterian Church, Nashville, Tennessee, June 6, 2004. Dr. Ortlund asked the question, "Is a human kiss our final experience, the most we can hope for or is a human kiss only a kind of living metaphor for the ultimate kiss?"

Anne Graham Lotz, *Why?: Trusting God When You Don't Understand* (Nashville: W Publishing Group, 2004). Writing about the story of Lazarus, Anne points out that we tend to interpret God's love by looking at our circumstances instead of interpreting our circumstances through the lens of his love.

Sovereignty of God
Michael D. McMullen, ed., *The Blessing of God: Previously Unpublished Sermons of Jonathan Edwards* (Nashville: Broadman & Holman Publishers, 2003). Edwards's sermon "The Day of a Godly Man's Death Is Better than the Day of His Birth" was instructive to me on Ecclesiastes 7:1.

John Piper, "To Be a Mother Is a Call to Suffer," Bethlehem Baptist Church, Minneapolis, Minnesota, May 13, 2001. In this sermon Piper discussed Psalm 105 and its radical representation of God's sovereignty. He also quoted Jim Bowers at the funeral for his wife, Veronica, and daughter, Charity, calling the bullet that killed them a "sovereign bullet."

Joni Eareckson Tada, "Suffering and the Sovereignty of God," *World Evangelization Magazine*, March/April 1996. Joni told her story of accepting her injury as God's "Plan A" for her life.

Miracles

Kelly Minter, *Water into Wine* (Colorado Springs: WaterBrook Press, 2004). Thank you, Kelly, for the insight of how God revealed his secrets to the servants.

BSF Notes, John (San Antonio, Tex.: Bible Study Fellowship International, 1960, 1994, 2002).

BSF Notes, Matthew (San Antonio, Tex.: Bible Study Fellowship International, 1963, 1992, 1999).

Adrian Rogers, *Believe in Miracles but Trust in Jesus* (Wheaton, Ill.: Crossway Books, 1997). The list of applications from the miracles of Jesus is adapted from a list in this book.

Healer of My Soul

BSF Notes, John (San Antonio, Tex.: Bible Study Fellowship International, 1960, 1994, 2002).

BSF Notes, Matthew (San Antonio, Tex.: Bible Study Fellowship International, 1963, 1992, 1999). The list of spiritual sicknesses represented by physical sicknesses is adapted from a list in the BSF notes on Matthew.

Adrian Rogers, *Believe in Miracles but Trust in Jesus* (Wheaton, Ill.: Crossway Books, 1997).

The Presence of God

The Practice of the Presence of God: Conversations and Letters of Brother Lawrence (Lightheart, 2004).

Knowing God

J. I. Packer, *Knowing God* (Downers Grove, Ill.: InterVarsity Press, 1973).

Paige Benton, "Singled Out for Good by God," *PCPC Witness*, February 1998. Paige wrote: "Can God be any less good to me on the average Tuesday morning than he was on that monumental Friday afternoon when he hung on a cross in my place? The answer is a resounding NO. God will not be less good to me tomorrow either, because God cannot be less good to me. His goodness is not the effect of his disposition but the essence of his person—not an attitude but an attribute."

John Piper, "A Generation Passionate for God's Holiness, OneDay03," Sherman, Texas, May 26, 2003. Piper points out that we are not the center of the universe but that God created us to make him the center of our universe.

God's Name

Herbert Lockyer, *All the Divine Names and Titles in the Bible* (Grand Rapids, Mich.: Zondervan, 1976).

Gifts of God

Charles Colson, "Making the World Safe for Religion," *Christianity Today*, November 8, 1993. Here Colson tells the story of Humaita prison.

Paige Benton, "Fruit of the Spirit" teaching series, Covenant Presbyterian Church, Nashville, Tennessee, fall 1998–spring 1999. Paige helped me to understand the difference between grace and mere generosity.

Gerald L. Sittser, *A Grace Disguised: How the Soul Grows through Loss* (Grand Rapids, Mich.: Zondervan, 1995). Sittser introduced me to the arrogance of believing that we don't deserve to suffer.

My former pastor, Roy Carter, told the story of his esteemed professor at Master's Seminary, Dr. James Rosscup. He also graciously pointed out to me that credit is due to Jack Miller and Tim Keller for the statement that Jesus "lived the life we could not live and died the death we should have died."

John Piper, "He Trusted to Him Who Judges Justly," Bethlehem Baptist Church, Minneapolis, Minnesota, August 25, 1991. Piper calls us to entrust ourselves to God rather than seek revenge. He said, "This is not merely a rule to be kept, but a miracle to be experienced, and grace to be received."

Looking to the Cross

Raymond Ortlund Jr. "All Things for Good? (Romans 8:28)," First Presbyterian Church, Augusta, Georgia, May 7, 2000. Ortlund points out that either *everything* works for good or we have no assurance that anything works for good in the life of the believer.

Steven Curtis Chapman quotes taken from www.stevencurtischapman.com.

Meaning in the Cross

Charles H. Spurgeon, "Bought with a Price," August 6, 1871.

John Piper, *The Passion of Jesus Christ* (Wheaton, Ill.: Crossway Books, 2004).

Hope

Dan B. Allender, *The Healing Path* (Colorado Springs: WaterBrook Press, 1999).

The Mysteries of Heaven

Gregory Floyd, *A Grief Unveiled: One Father's Journey through the Death of a Child* (Brewster, Mass.: Paraclete Press, 1999).

Joni Eareckson Tada, *Heaven: Your Real Home* (Grand Rapids, Mich.: Zondervan, 1996).

Heaven: Longing for Home

Anne Graham Lotz, *Heaven: My Father's House* (Nashville: W Publishing Group, 2001). No, I am not quick enough to come up with the response I did for my friend outside the athletic club. This is something I have heard Anne explain and have read about in her book. The book also contains the essence of the message she gave at Hope's memorial service, including the idea that in heaven there will be no more separation.

C. S. Lewis, *The Last Battle* (New York: HarperCollins, 1956).

C. S. Lewis, *Mere Christianity* (New York: HarperCollins, 1952).

Resurrection

Raymond Ortlund Jr., "We Are Not 'the Hollow Men' (Romans 8:9-11)," First Presbyterian Church, Augusta, Georgia, February 27, 2000. Ortlund said, "The world tells us, 'If you're not in shape, if you're not thin, if you're not beautiful, if you're not sexually active, if you're not young, you're not alive.' But is it true? If it were true, then all the fit, thin, beautiful, sexually active, young people in this world would be on cloud nine. But they're not. Why? Because life does not flow into our experience through the body but through the spirit."

John Piper, "Irrevocable Joy," Bethlehem Baptist Church, Minneapolis, Minnesota, March 26, 1989. Piper helped me understand why "no one can rob you of this joy."

Rewards

Bruce Wilkinson with David Kopp, *A Life God Rewards* (Sisters, Ore.: Multnomah Publishers, 2002). This book helped me see that eternal rewards are an honorable motive for pleasing God.

Raymond Ortlund Jr., *Supernatural Living for Natural People* (Ross-shire, Great Britain, Christian Focus Publications, 2001). Dr. Ortlund helped me see how undervaluing our eternal inheritance causes us to hold on to things here too tightly.

Angels

David Jeremiah, *What the Bible Says about Angels* (Sisters, Ore.: Multnomah Books, 1996). Jeremiah relates the quote from the *Life* magazine story by a writer who attended an angels conference. He also added to my understanding of how angels worship.

Robert Paul Lightner, *Angels, Satan, and Demons* (Nashville: Word Publishing, 1998). Lightner was especially helpful in understanding the angel of the Lord as the preincarnate Christ.

The Enemy

Robert Paul Lightner, *Angels, Satan, and Demons* (Nashville: Word Publishing, 1998).

Max Lucado, *The Great House of God* (Dallas: Word Publishing, 1997). In chapter 13, Max states that Satan has no power that God does not permit and that God gave Satan the permission and set the parameters for Satan to harm Job.

John Piper, "The Sifting of Simon Peter (Luke 22:31-34)," Bethlehem Baptist Church, Minneapolis, Minnesota, April 26, 1981. Dr. Piper helped me answer the question of why God would continue to allow Satan to inflict so much pain in this world.

The School of Suffering

Kay Arthur, *As Silver Refined* (Colorado Springs: WaterBrook Press, 1997). Kay Arthur provided the understanding of the work of a silversmith and the refining process.

My Soul Source

Raymond Ortlund Jr., "The Joy of Christ's Majesty in our Contentment (Philippians 4:10-23)," First Presbyterian Church, Augusta, Georgia, October 18, 1998. This is when I saw that real contentment is accepting less than what we want because we are so satisfied in Jesus.

Storms

Anne Graham Lotz, *God's Story* (Nashville: W Publishing Group, 1998). I first understood Jesus as our "ark of safety" from this book.

Parables

James Montgomery Boice, *The Parables of Jesus* (Chicago: Moody Press, 1983).

Earl F. Palmer, *Laughter in Heaven and Other Surprising Truths in the Parables of Jesus* (Nashville: W Publishing Group, 1987).

Raymond Ortlund Jr., "All Things for the Sake of the Gospel—Our Repentance (Luke 18:9-14)," Christ Presbyterian Church, Nashville, Tennessee, March 28, 2004. Not being a huge fan of *Rocky & Bullwinkle* myself, I must give Dr. Ortlund credit for the description of Pharisees as a cross between Snidely Whiplash and a member of the Taliban, as well as depicting them as the middle-class pillars of society in their day. He has also helped me to see the insidiousness of self-righteousness.

BSF Notes, Matthew (San Antonio, Tex.: Bible Study Fellowship International, 1963, 1992, 1999). Jews did not consider the pearl to be precious. Invariably they preferred other stones. For instance, no pearl is included in the breastplate of precious stones worn by the priest (Exodus 39:10-14). However, the Jews knew that Gentiles considered the pearl precious.

Paradox

A. W. Tozer, *The Root of the Righteous* (Christian Publications, 1986).

John Piper, "How Much Do You Own?" Bethlehem Baptist Church, Minneapolis, Minnesota, March 13, 1988. Piper describes how we are a paradoxical blend of self-sufficiency and insecurity.

Nancy Leigh DeMoss, *Brokenness* (Chicago: Moody Press, 2003). DeMoss offers a clear description and definition of brokenness, which I adapted.

Anne Graham Lotz, *My Heart's Cry* (Nashville: W Publishing Group, 2002). Anne introduced to me the principle of serving others when we want to be served in her chapter "More of His Dirt on My Hands."

Raymond Ortlund Jr., "Prizing Christ (Philippians 3:7-15)," First Presbyterian Church, Augusta, Georgia, November 14, 1999. Dr. Ortlund said, "The measure of your prizing is in your losing."

The Good Shepherd

Phillip Keller, *A Shepherd Looks at Psalm 23* (Grand Rapids, Mich.: Zondervan, 1970).

Phillip Keller, *A Shepherd Looks at the Good Shepherd and His Sheep* (Grand Rapids, Mich.: Zondervan, 1978).

Joy

Raymond Ortlund Jr., "Luke 2:14 and Reasons for Joy at Christmas," First Presbyterian Church, Augusta, Georgia, December 24, 1998. Ortlund said, "God is good, and his goodness is of a spreading nature, spilling out of heaven down into this world, spreading out widely, to all the people, without rank or distinction. . . . You and I are the problem. Our good intentions are not strong enough to control our evil impulses. We need a Savior to rescue us from ourselves."

Paige Benton, "Fruit of the Spirit" teaching series, Covenant Presbyterian Church, Nashville, Tennessee, fall 1998–spring 1999. Paige pointed out that the reason we don't have more joy is because we're just not that sorry over our sin.

Joy Robbers

John Piper, "It Is Never Right to Be Angry with God," Bethlehem Baptist Church, Minneapolis, Minnesota, November 13, 2000. Piper says, "First, many assume that feelings are not right or wrong, they are neutral. So to say that anger (whether at God or anybody else) is 'not right' is like saying sneezing is not right. You just don't apply the labels right and wrong to sneezing. It just happens to you. That is the way many people think about feelings: they just happen to you."

Finding Purpose in Pain

Philip Yancey, *Where Is God When It Hurts?* (Grand Rapids, Mich.: Zondervan, 1990).

"Rare Disease Makes Girl Unable to Feel Pain: Genetic Disorder Deprives Kindergartner of Natural Alarms," *Associated Press*, November 1, 2004.

Fruitfulness

Bruce Wilkinson, *Secrets of the Vine* (Sisters, Ore.: Multnomah Publishers, 2001).

Evelyn Christenson, *Gaining through Losing* (Wheaton, Ill.: Scripture Press Publications, 1980).

Anne Graham Lotz, *My Heart's Cry* (Nashville: W Publishing Group, 2002).

Raymond Ortlund Jr., "Psalm 1: Planted in the Right Place," First Presbyterian Church, Augusta, Georgia, August 9, 1998.

Self

Oswald Chambers, *My Utmost for His Highest.* In the devotional for November 1, "You Are Not Your Own," Chambers writes, "Most of us collapse at the first grip of pain. We sit down at the door of God's purpose and enter a slow death through self-pity. And all the so-called Christian sympathy of others helps us to our deathbed."

Raymond Ortlund Jr., "Our Mission: Delighting Ourselves in the Lord of the Church," Christ Presbyterian Church, Nashville, Tennessee, October 24, 2004. Ortlund introduced me to the concept of self-ministry in place of self-medication.

Submission

Anne Graham Lotz, *The Vision of His Glory* (Nashville: W Publishing Group, 1997).

Raymond Ortlund Jr., "Matthew 5:5 and the Gospel Mentality," Christ Presbyterian Church, Nashville, Tennessee, August 22, 2004. Ortlund pointed out that Jesus described himself as meek and said that "the only people who will get anything that lasts out of this life are people who learn to be meek."

Kay Arthur, *As Silver Refined* (Colorado Springs: WaterBrook Press, 1997). Arthur describes what it means to respond to disappointment in meekness.

John Piper, "How to Suffer for Doing What Is Right (1 Peter 2:18-23)," Bethlehem Baptist Church, Minneapolis, Minnesota, June 5, 1994.

The Glory of God

Max Lucado, *It's Not about Me* (Nashville: Integrity Publishers, 2004).

Raymond Ortlund Jr., "Luke 2:14 and Reasons for Joy at Christmas," First Presbyterian Church, Augusta, Georgia, December 24, 1998. Ortlund said that "the most relevant message to this sin-ruined world was, is, and always will be 'Glory to God in the highest.' "

Blessing

Raymond Ortlund Jr., "Our Three Primary Emphases: The Mission of the Church (Genesis 12:1-3)," First Presbyterian Church, Augusta, Georgia, August 18, 2002. Ortlund describes God's agenda of blessing.

David Van Biema, "When God Hides His Face: Can Faith Survive When Hope Has Died? The Guthries Think So," *Time* magazine, July 16, 2001.

Eugene Peterson, *A Long Obedience in the Same Direction* (Downers Grove, Ill.: InterVarsity Press, 1980). Peterson helped me understand the significance of Psalm 134 as an ascent psalm and what it means to bless God.

Worship

John Piper, *Desiring God* (Sisters, Ore.: Multnomah Press, 2003). Reading this book prompted a real paradigm shift in my thinking and relationship with God, including what God wants in worship and what we do when we don't feel like worshiping.

Raymond Ortlund Jr., "The Great Disturbance (Romans 12:1-2)," First Presbyterian Church, Augusta, Georgia, September 17, 2000.

Prayer

Paige Benton, teaching series on Daniel, Covenant Presbyterian Church, Nashville, Tennessee, summer 2004.

Hank Hanegraaff, *The Prayer of Jesus* (Nashville: W Publishing Group, 2001).

Jerry Sittser, *When God Doesn't Answer Your Prayer* (Grand Rapids, Mich.: Zondervan, 2003).

David Kopp and Heather Kopp, *Praying the Bible for Your Marriage* (Colorado Springs: WaterBrook Press, 1998). The Kopps offer insightful directions in how to "pray the Bible," which I adapted.

Barry Arnold, "Even If He Does Not (Daniel 3:1-18)," Highland Park Baptist Church, Dearborn, Michigan, October 7, 2001.

Word of Life

Raymond Ortlund Jr., "Our Mission: Delighting Ourselves in the Lord of Truth," Christ Presbyterian Church, Nashville, Tennessee, October 3, 2004. Ortlund talks about having a "spiritual sweet tooth" that makes us hungry for God's Word.

Forgiveness

Raymond Ortlund Jr., "Learning to Lose with God: The Expulsive Power of a New Affection (1 Peter 1:22–2:3)," First Presbyterian Church, Augusta, Georgia, September 2, 2001. Ortlund said, "Either your bitterness will kill your appetite for his sweetness, or his sweetness will purify your bitterness. But you can't have both."

Going Deeper

Raymond Ortlund Jr., "Matthew 5:4 and the Gospel Mentality," Christ Presbyterian Church, Nashville, Tennessee, August 8, 2004. Ortlund called mourning over sin a "redemptive anguish."

Gary Thomas, *Authentic Faith: The Power of a Fire-Tested Life* (Grand Rapids, Mich.: Zondervan, 2003). Among other meaningful and instructive insights, Gary Thomas writes, "It's human nature to value most that which has cost us something. If you don't highly value your faith, perhaps you've never sacrificed for it." He also writes, "If spiritual growth is truly a goal in your life, it's okay to make your sins hurt a little. Don't rush so quickly into peace."

Ken Sande, *Peacemaking for Families* (Carol Stream, Ill.: Tyndale House Publishers, 2002). An article based on this book provided this definition of idols.

Who Am I?

Raymond Ortlund Jr., "Learning to Lose with God: What Really Builds Up the Church?" First Presbyterian Church, Augusta, Georgia, September 9, 2001. Ortlund explained what makes worship acceptable to God and what it means to be living stones.

Raymond Ortlund Jr., "Do You Know Who You Are? (1 Peter 2:9-10)," First Presbyterian Church, Augusta, Georgia, August 15, 1999.

Earl F. Palmer, *The Enormous Exception: Meeting Christ in the Sermon on the Mount* (Waco, Tex.: Word Books 1985). Palmer explained the nature and purposes of salt and light.

What Does God Want?

Brent Curtis and John Eldredge, *The Sacred Romance* (Nashville: Nelson Books, 1997).

Waiting

John Claypool, *Tracks of a Fellow Struggler* (New Orleans: Insight Press, 1995).

You can read more about Gracia Burnham's experiences in her books, *In the Presence of My Enemies* (Tyndale House, 2003) and *To Fly Again* (Tyndale House, 2005).

BY NANCY GUTHRIE

Holding On to Hope

The One Year® Book of Hope Devotional

Hearing Jesus Speak into Your Sorrow

When Your Family's Lost a Loved One (with David Guthrie)

What Grieving People Wish You Knew about What Really Helps (and What Really Hurts)

One Year® of Dinner Table Devotions and Discussion Starters

The One Year® Book of Discovering Jesus in the Old Testament

Abundant Life in Jesus

The One Year® Praying through the Bible for Your Kids

God Does His Best Work with Empty

Seeing Jesus

What Every Child Should Know about Prayer

All Is Bright

Hoping for Something Better

Let Every Heart Prepare Him Room

CP1149